CROSSWORD DICTIONARY

from

Ian

CROSSWORD DICTIONARY

A Guide to Successful Puzzle Solving

This edition published 1993 by
Diamond Books
77-85 Fulham Palace Road
Hammersmith
London W6 8JB

Printed and bound in Great Britain

CONTENTS

Abbreviations 1
Agriculture 7
Animals 10
Architecture 20
Artists 31
Astronomy 33
Biblical Names 36
Biological Sciences 39
Birds 43
Capacity 51
Cereals 51
Character Types 52
Chemical Sciences 62
Cinema and Television 69
Cities 72
Clothes 75
Colours 88
Composers 91
Computing 93
Deadly Sins 94
Drink 95
Education 98
First Names 106
Fish 113
Flowers 117
Food 122
Foreign Words and Phrases 131
French Revolutionary Calendar 137
Fruit 138
Furniture 141
Geography 144
Government 154
Heraldry 167
Household Items 171
Insects 179
Islands 185
Jewellery 187
Lakes 189
Law 190
Length, Area, Volume, Speed 202
Literary Characters 203
Literature 208
Machinery 224
Marine 232
Mathematics 234
Measurement 239
Medicine 241
cont.

CONTENTS, *cont.*

Meteorology 261
Military Leaders 265
Minerals 266
Money 270
Mountains 273
Muses 275
Music 275
Mythology 290
Occupations 301
Oceans and Seas 325
Physical Sciences 326
Plants 334
Political Leaders 340
Presidents of the USA 342
Relations 343
Religions 345
Rivers 356
Shakespearean Characters 358
Sports, Games and Pastimes 363
Theatre 383
Time 390
Tools 401
Trade 403
Transport and Communications 423
Trees 446
Vegetables 451
Virtues 453
Visual Arts 454
Warfare 462
Weight 478
Wonders of the World 478
Works of Literature and Music
Writers 485
Zodiac, Signs of the 489
Notes 490

Index 501

FOREWORD

This new version of the popular GEM DICTIONARY FOR CROSSWORD PUZZLES has been completely revised and reorganized. The content has been expanded by increasing the word length to include words of up to 15 letters, thus making the coverage more relevant to the standard cryptic crossword grid. The word count now totals over 55,000 items.

This increased content has been arranged in a larger number of separate fields – 81 in all – alphabetically arranged, from Abbreviations to Writers. This greater degree of subdivision should significantly reduce the search time required. Additional help in this respect is provided by a short Index which relates some possible alternative categories to their relevant fields.

The fact that the author is a practising crossword compiler has meant that he has been able to draw on his experience in this area to tailor the content to items that crossword solvers actually meet. Irrelevant items have been excluded and the coverage has been generally updated to include the kind of material today's compilers make use of.

These improvements make this new *Gem*

Crossword Dictionary the ideal aid for all crossword fans.

NOTE: In order to facilitate scrutiny for letter placement within words a special typeface has been used that keeps the letters of each word vertically in line with those of the words above and below it.

To preserve this helpful columnar arrangement the following symbols have been used:

| = word space, as in speed|the|plough
ˌ = hyphen, as in dairyˌfarm
' = apostrophe, as in lady's|finger

Abbreviations

3D
AA
AB
AC
ac
AD
ad
AG
AI
am
AV
av
BA
BB
BC
BD
bf
bk
BL
BM
bn
BP
Bp
BR
Br
br
Bt
CA
ca
CB
CC
cc
CD
CF
cf
CH
Ch
ch
CI
cl
cm
c/o
CO
Co
CP
cp
CR
cr
CS
ct
Cu
cu
cv
DA
DC
DD
DF
DG
DJ
DM
do
DP
Dr
DS
DV
EC
Ed
ed
eg
EP
ER
Ex
Ez
FA
FD
ff
fl
FM
FO
FP
fp
Fr
fr
FT
ft
GB
GC
GI
Gk
GM
gm
GP
GR
gr
GS
gs
GT
gu
HC
HE
hf
HM
ho
HP
HQ
hr
HT
ib
i/c
id
ie
in
IQ
Ir
Is
It
JP
Jr
KB
KC
KG
km
KO
kr
KT
Kt
LA
lb
lc
Ld
lh
LM
LP
LT
Lt
LV
MA
mb
MB
MC
MD
mf
MG
mg
MI
mk
ml
mm
MM
MN
MO
MP
MR
Mr
MS
Ms
Mt
mv
MW
NB
nd
NE
NI
nl
no
nr
NS
NT
NW
NY
NZ
OB
ob
OC

ABBREVIATIONS

OE	qr	SU	yr	Aug	CBI
OK	qt	SW	AAA	AVM	CCF
OM	qv	TA	ABC	bar	Cdr
OP	RA	TB	Abp	BBC	CET
op	RB	TD	acc	BCC	cfi
OR	RC	Th	act	BEd	CGS
OS	RD	tp	ADC	BEF	ChB
OT	Rd	tr	adj	BEM	Chr
OU	rd	TT	adv	bhp	CIA
oz	RE	Tu	AEC	BHS	Cia
pa	RF	TV	aet	BIM	CID
PA	rh	UK	AEU	BMA	Cie
PC	RI	UN	AFC	BMJ	cif
pc	RN	UP	AFM	BMW	CMG
pd	ro	US	agm	BOC	CMS
PE	RS	UU	agr	bor	CND
PG	RT	ux	AID	BOT	COD
pH	RU	vb	aka	Bro	cod
pl	RV	VC	Ald	BRS	COI
pm	ry	VD	alt	BSA	Col
PM	s/c	VE	amp	BSc	col
PO	sc	VJ	amt	BSM	con
po	sd	vo	ans	BST	Cor
pp	SE	VP	aob	BTA	cos
PR	SF	vs	aor	BTU	cot
Pr	SI	vt	APR	Btu	Cpl
pr	SJ	VW	Apr	BVM	CPR
PS	SM	wc	APT	BWV	CRE
Ps	SO	WD	ARP	CAB	CSE
PT	SP	WI	arr	cal	CST
pt	sp	wk	ASA	Cal	CSV
PU	sq	WO	ASH	CAP	CTC
pw	Sr	wp	ATC	cap	CUP
QC	SS	WS	ATS	car	CVO
ql	St	wt	ATV	CAT	cwo
QM	st	yd	AUC	CBE	CWS

3 LETTERS

cwt
Dan
dau
DBE
dbl
DCL
DCM
DDR
DDT
DEA
Dec
dec
def
deg
del
DEP
Dep
dep
DES
DFC
DFM
Dip
Dir
div
DIY
DNA
DNB
dob
DOE
dom
doz
DPP
DSC
DSO
dsp
DTI
DTs
EBU
ECG
ECO
EDC
EEC
EEG
EFL
EIS
EMI
ENE
Eng
eng
ENT
Eph
ESE
ESN
ESP
esp
Esq
est
ESU
ETA
etc
ETD
ETU
Exc
fam
FAO
fas
FBA
FBI
FCA
FCO
fcp
FDR
Feb
fec
fem
fig
FIS
fob
foc
for
FPA
Fri
FRS
fur
fut
fwd
Gal
GBA
gbh
GBS
GCB
GCE
GDP
GDR
GEC
Gen
gen
Geo
ger
GHQ
Gib
GLC
GMC
GMT
GNP
GOC
GOM
Gov
GPI
GTC
GUS
Hab
HAC
Hag
HCF
Heb
her
HGV
HLI
HMC
HMG
HMI
HMS
HMV
HNC
HND
Hon
hor
Hos
HRH
HSE
HTV
IBA
IBM
ICI
ICS
ill
ILO
ILP
IMF
imp
inc
ind
inf
int
IOM
IOU
IOW
IPC
IRA
ITN
ITV
Jan
Jas
JCR
jct
Jer
Jno
Jnr
Jud
Jul
KBE
KCB
KGB
KKK
KLM
km/h
ktl
Lab
lab
Lat
lat
lbw
LCC
LCJ
lcm
LDS
LDV
LEA
Lev
lit
LLB
log
loq
LPO
LSA
LSD
LSE
LSO
LTA
Ltd
LWT
mag
Maj
Mal
Mar
max
MBE
MCC
Mc/s
MEP
met
mfd
MFH
Mgr
Mic
mil
Min
min
mis
MIT
MLR
Mme
MOD
mod
MOH

ABBREVIATIONS

Mon	NSW	PLA	rep	SDP	TSB
MOT	NUJ	PLC	rev	Sec	TUC
mph	NUM	PLO	RFA	SEN	Tue
MPS	Num	PLP	RFC	Sen	TVA
MRA	NUR	PLR	RFU	seq	UAE
MRC	NUS	PMG	RGS	ser	UAR
Mrs	NUT	PMO	RHA	SET	UDC
MSC	NYO	pop	RHS	SFA	UDI
msl	OAP	pos	RIC	sfz	UDR
mss	OAS	POW	RIP	sin	UFO
MTB	OBE	ppc	Rly	SMO	UHF
mus	obj	PPE	RMA	SMP	UHT
MVO	Oct	PPS	RMO	SNP	ult
Nat	oct	PRO	RMP	sob	UNO
nat	OED	psc	RMS	Soc	USA
nav	ONC	PTA	ROC	sol	USN
NBC	OND	Pte	Rom	sop	USS
nbg	ono	PTO	RPI	SOS	usu
NCB	opp	PVC	RPM	sqn	usw
NCO	Ops	QED	rpm	SRN	VAD
NEB	opt	QEF	RPO	SSE	val
NEC	ord	QEH	RRE	SSW	var
neg	OSB	QMG	RSA	STD	VAT
Neh	OTC	QPR	RSM	std	VDU
NFS	OUP	qty	RTE	str	veg
NFT	Oxf	RAC	RTZ	TV	vel
NFU	pap	rad	RUC	sub	Ven
NGA	par	RAF	RYS	Sun	VHF
NHI	pat	RAM	sae	tan	vid
NHS	PBI	RBA	SAM	TCD	VIP
NNE	PCC	RCM	Sam	tel	viz
NNW	PEN	RCO	SAS	ten	voc
nom	PEP	RCT	Sat	Thu	vol
NOP	PGA	RDC	SCE	Tim	VSO
Nov	PhD	rec	SCM	Tit	WEA
NPL	phr	ref	SCR	TNT	Wed

wef
WHO
WNW
wpb
wpm
WSW
WVS
YOP
abbr
ABTA
ACAS
ACGB
AERE
AIDS
AMDG
ammo
anat
anon
arch
asap
Asst
at|no
at|wt
AUEW
AWOL
AWRE
BAOR
Bart
B|Cal
B|Com
Beds
Belg
B|ès|L
B|ès|S
BFPO
Bibl
biog
biol
bldg
BMus
BNOC
BOAC
Brig
Brit
Bros
BThU
BUPA
caps
Capt
CARD
Card
Cath
cath
CCPR
CEGB
cent
cert
chap
Chas
Chem
choc
CIGS
C|in|C
circ
co|ed
C|of|E
C|of|I
C|of|S
comp
conj
co|op
Corp
cosh
coth
CPRE
CRMP
CSYS
DAAG
D|day
decl
dept
derv
Deut
DHSS
dial
diam
dict
diff
dist
DMus
DUKW
Ebor
Eccl
Edin
EFTA
El|Al
ELDO
elec
ENSA
EOKA
EPNS
Esth
et|al
exec
Exon
Ezek
FIAT
FIDO
FIFA
floz
FRCP
FRCS
GATT
GCMG
GCVO
Gdns
gent
geog
geol
geom
Glam
Glos
guin
HIDB
hist
hi|fi
HMSO
Hons
IATA
ibid
ICBM
ILEA
incl
INRI
Inst
IOUS
Irel
ital
Josh
Judg
junc
KCMG
KCVO
KGCB
kilo
lang
L|of|C
Lond
long
LRAM
LRCP
LRCS
mach
marg
masc
math
Matt
mech
memo
MIRV
Mlle
Mods
MORI
morn
MRCP
NADA
NATO
naut
Nazi
NCCL
NEDC
neut
NFER
non|U
Obad
obdt
OCTU
OEEC
OHMS
OPEC
orig
ORTF
OUDS
Oxon
pass
PAYE
PDSA
perf
perh
pers
Phil
phon
phot
phys
pinx
plup
plur
Preb
prep
Pres
Prin
prob
Prof
prop
Prot
Prov
prox
PSBR
RADA
RADC
RAEC
RAMC
RAOC
RAPC
RAVC
RCMP

ABBREVIATIONS

recd
regt
REME
rhet
RIBA
RNAS
RNIB
RNLI
RNVR
ro,ro
RSPB
RSVP
SALT
SATB
Scot
SDLP
sect
Sept
Serg
sing
sinh
SNCF
Solr
SPCK
SPQR
STOL
subj
Supt
syst
tanh
TASS
TCCB
tech
temp
TGWU
Thos

Thur
TocH
trig
Trin
Tues
UCCA
UEFA
Univ
USAF
USSR
VSOP
VTOL
vulg
WAAC
WAAF
WACS
WAVE
W/Cdr
WFTU
WRAC
WRAF
WRNS
WRVS
Xmas
YMCA
AAQMG
ad|lib
admin
ad|val
ALGOL
Anzac
ANZUS
appro
arith
Asdic
ASLEF

Assoc
ASTMS
BALPA
B|and|B
b|and|s
Bart's
BASIC
Berks
BLitt
Bucks
Cambs
CAMRA
CENTO
Chron
circs
COBOL
COHSE
Comdr
contd
cosec
cresc
cusec
D|and|C
Dip|Ed
DLitt
DPhil
ERNIE
et|seq
ex|lib
G|and|S
h|and|c
Hants
Herts
Hunts
indef
indiv

in|loc
intro
Lancs
LASER
Leics
Lieut
Lincs
Lt,Col
Lt,Gen
maths
meths
Middx
NAAFI
Notts
NSPCC
op|cit
OXFAM
P|and|O
PLUTO
pro,am
pseud
R|and|A
R|and|D
ROSLA
RoSPA
RSPCA
Rt|Hon
Rt|Rev
Salop
Sarum
sci|fi
SCUBA
SEATO
SHAEF
SHAPE
SLADE

SOGAT
SSAFA
STOPP
subst
SWALK
SWAPO
theol
Thess
trans
treas
UMIST
UNRRA
UWIST
V|and|A
vocab
WAACS
WAAFS
Wilts
Worcs
WRACS
Xtian
Yorks
ab|init
approx
attrib
Cantab
cet|par
cosech
Dunelm
E|and|OE
Fid|Def
Hon|Sec
incorp
indecl
Lit|Hum
loc|cit

6/9 LETTERS

Londin	SABENA	Nat|West
Lonrho	sculpt	non|obst
Man|Dir	Staffs	per|cent
Messrs	transf	Pol|Econ
mod|con	UNESCO	prox|acc
Mus|Bac	UNICEF	Reg|Prof
Mus|Doc	Winton	var|lect
Nat|Sci	Benelux	verb|sap
nem|con	Cantuar	infra|dig
NIBMAR	COMECON	Interpol
non|com	Consols	Northumb
Noncon	Dip|Tech	Oxbridge
non|seq	Euratom	Cominform
Norvic	FORTRAN	Comintern
pro|tem	intrans	Northants
QARANC	nat|hist	
quango	NATSOPA	

Agriculture

ear	corn	mare	silo	ditch	mower
hay	crop	milk	skep	drill	mulch
lea	dung	neat	soil	fruit	ovine
mow	farm	neep	till	grain	plant
rye	herd	oats	vega	grass	ranch
bale	husk	peat	weed	graze	rumen
barn	jess	pest	baler	guano	sheep
bull	kine	rake	bothy	haulm	shoat
byre	lamb	rape	calve	hedge	stock
calf	lime	root	churn	horse	straw
cart	loam	seed	crops	humus	tilth
clay	lush	shaw	dairy	maize	tuber

AGRICULTURE

veldt
wagon
wheat
yield
animal
arable
barley
binder
butter
cattle
cereal
clover
colter
cowman
cutter
digger
fallow
farmer
fodder
forage
furrow
gimmer
grains
grange
harrow
heifer
hopper
manger
manure
meadow
merino
millet
piglet
pigsty
plough
porker

potato
reaper
roller
sheave
silage
sowing
stable
trough
turnip
warble
weevil
anthrax
bullock
cabbage
calving
combine
compost
cowherd
cowshed
digging
drought
erosion
farming
fertile
harvest
haycart
hayrick
lambing
lucerne
milkcan
milking
newmown
paddock
pasture
piggery
poultry

prairie
rancher
reaping
rearing
rustler
savanna
stubble
subsoil
tillage
tilling
tractor
wagoner
agronomy
breeding
clippers
cropping
drainage
elevator
ensilage
farmyard
forestry
gleaning
hayfield
haymaker
haystack
landgirl
loosebox
pedigree
pigswill
rootcrop
rotation
rotavate
rotovate
shearing
sheepdip
vineyard

9/15 LETTERS

allotment
cornfield
dairy farm
dairymaid
fertility
grassland
harvester
haymaking
husbandry
implement
incubator
livestock
pasturage
phosphate
pig trough
ploughing
root house
rotavator
rotovator
shorthorn
sugar beet
swineherd
threshing
wasteland
winnowing
agronomist
battery hen
cattle cake
cultivator
fertilizer
harvesting
husbandman
irrigation
weed killer
agriculture
chicken farm
cultivation
farm produce
germination
insecticide
pasture land
poultry farm
agricultural
horticulture
insemination
market garden
smallholding
agriculturist
agrobiologist
cattle breeder
cattle farming
chicken farmer
electric fence
horticultural
kitchen garden
sheep shearing
stock breeding
tea plantation
viticulturist
collective farm
market gardener
milking machine
milking parlour
speed the plough
agriculturalist
market gardening
rotation of crops

Animals

ai	moo	byre	hoof	paca	toad
ox	nag	cage	horn	pack	tusk
ape	pad	calf	howl	pard	tyke
ass	paw	cavy	hump	peba	unau
bat	pet	chow	ibex	pelt	ursa
bay	pig	claw	jill	pest	urus
cat	pod	colt	kine	pika	urva
cob	pom	cony	kudu	poll	vole
cow	pug	coon	lair	pony	wolf
cry	pup	deer	lamb	prad	yelp
cub	ram	dray	ling	prey	yoke
cur	rat	drey	lion	puma	yowl
dam	run	fang	lynx	puss	zebu
den	set	fawn	mane	rein	addax
doe	sow	Fido	mare	roan	apery
dog	sty	foal	meow	roar	beast
elk	teg	form	mews	rout	billy
ewe	tod	frog	mink	runt	biped
fox	tom	gaur	moke	saki	bison
fur	tup	goat	mole	seal	bitch
gam	yak	hack	mona	sett	bleat
gnu	zoo	hare	mule	stag	bongo
hob	Arab	hart	musk	stot	borer
hog	beak	herd	mutt	stud	boxer
kid	bear	hern	myna	tail	brock
kit	boar	hide	neat	teal	brood
kob	bray	hind	oont	team	Bruin
low	buck	hock	oryx	tike	brush
mew	bull	hole	oxen	titi	brute

5/6 LETTERS

bunny
burro
camel
caple
capul
catch
civet
coati
coney
coypu
crawl
cuddy
daman
dhole
dingo
dogie
drill
drove
earth
eland
fauna
feral
field
filly
fitch
flock
fossa
gayal
genet
genus
girth
grice
growl
grunt
hinny
hippo
horse
hound
husky
hutch
hutia
hyena
hyrax
izard
jenny
Jumbo
kaama
kiang
kitty
koala
kulan
lapin
leash
lemur
liger
llama
loris
manis
manul
miaow
moose
morse
mount
mouse
nanny
Neddy
neigh
okapi
orang
otary
otter
ounce
panda
pi-dog
piggy
pinto
pongo
pooch
potto
pouch
pound
pride
puppy
pussy
rache
rasse
ratel
reins
rhino
sable
saiga
sasin
satyr
sheep
shire
shoat
shrew
skunk
slink
sloth
snarl
snort
snout
spitz
stall
steed
steer
stoat
stray
swine
tabby
takin
talon
tapir
tatou
tiger
tigon
troop
trunk
udder
urial
vixen
waler
whale
whelp
zebra
zibet
zoril
zorro
agouta
agouti
albino
alpaca
angora
antler
aoudad
argali
aye-aye
baboon
badger
baleen
bandog
barren
barton
basset
bayard
beagle
beaver
bellow
beluga
bharal
bident
bobcat
borzoi
bovine
bow-wow
Briard
bridle
bronco
burrow
cackle
canine
castor
cat-nap
cattle
cayman
chacma
circus
coaita
cocker
collie
colugo
corral
cougar
coyote
coypou
cruive
curtal
cus-cus
dassie

ANIMALS

desman
dewlap
dikdik
dobbin
donkey
dragon
dugong
embryo
entire
equine
ermine
farrow
feline
fennec
ferine
ferret
fossil
fox|bat
garron
gee|gee
genera
gennet
gerbil
gibbon
gnawer
gobble
gopher
grison
grivet
guenon
gun|dog
hackee
hackle
he|goat
heifer
hogget
hog|rat
hooves
houdah
howdah
humble
hummel
hunter
hyaena
hybrid
impala
instar
jackal
jaeger
jaguar
jennet
jerboa
jumart
jungle
kennel
killer
kindle
kit|fox
kitten
koodoo
langur
lap|dog
lionet
litter
lowing
lowrie
lupine
mad|dog
mammal
manati
manege
manger
margay
marmot
marten
merino
merlin
monkey
mouser
moussè
mulish
musk|ox
muster
muzzle
nilgai
nilgau
ocelot
onager
pallah
pariah
pastor
phylum
piglet
pig|rat
pig|sty
poodle
porker
possum
pug|dog
pye|dog
quagga
rabbit
racoon
ranger
red|fox
reebok
rhesus
rodent
saddle
saluki
sambar
school
sea|ape
sea|cow
sea|dog
serval
setter
shelty
simian
sleuth
sorrel
sphinx
stable
string
summer
tarpan
taurus
teetee
teledu
tenrec
tomcat
toy|dog
tracer
tusker
ursine
vermin
vervet
vicuna
walrus
wapiti
warren
weasel
wether
whinny

wild|ox
wombat
wyvern
ant|bear
asinine
aurochs
barking
basenji
bear|cat
beavery
bestial
big|game
bighorn
bird|dog
blesbok
blue|fox
brocket
buffalo
bull|bat
bulldog
bullock
bush|cat
caracal
carcase
carcass
caribou
catling
cattalo
centaur
cervine
cetacea
chamois
charger
cheetah
Cheviot
chikara
chimera
colobus
coon|cat
courser
cowshed
croaker
dasyure
deerdog
deer|hog
deerlet
denizen
dew|claw
dolphin
echinus
epizoon
ewe|lamb
extinct
fetlock
finback
fitchet
fitchew
foreleg
forepaw
foumart
fur|seal
gambrel
gazelle
gelding
gemsbok
giraffe
gizzard
glutton
gnu|goat
gorilla
grampus
grey|fox
griffin
griffon
gryphon
grysbok
guanaco
guereza
habitat
hackney
half|ape
hamster
hanuman
harness
harrier
hexapod
hindleg
hindpaw
hircine
hog|deer
hogwash
ice|bear
jacchus
jackass
karakul
keitloa
lambkin
land|rat
lemming
leonine
leopard
leveret
linsang
lioness
lurcher
macaque
madoqua
mammoth
manatee
Manx|cat
markhor
marmose
mastiff
meerkat
metazoa
milk|cow
mole|rat
mongrel
monster
mouflon
muridae
musimon
musk|hog
musk|rat
mustang
nandine
narwhal
nosebag
opossum
pack|rat
paddock
painter
palfrey
palmcat
panther
pastern
peccary
Pegasus
piebald
pig|deer
pit|pony
pointer
pole|cat
polypod

porcine
pricket
primate
raccoon
rathole
rattler
red|deer
redpoll
Reynard
roebuck
roe|deer
rorqual
rotifer
saimiri
Samoyed
sapajou
sea|lion
she|goat
shippon
siamang
sirenia
sondeli
sounder
sounder
spaniel
spouter
sumpter
sun|bear
tadpole
tamarin
tanager
tarsier
terrier
tigress
tree|fox
trotter
twinter
unicorn
urodele
vaccine
vampire
vulpine
wallaby
warthog
water|ox
web|toed
whippet
whisker
wild|ass
wild|cat
wistiti
withers
wolf|dog
wood|rat
aardvark
aardwolf
abattoir
Airedale
animalia
anteater
antelope
Antilope
argonaut
bactrian
black|cat
black|fox
black|rat
blauwbok
blinkers
blow|hole
blue|buck
blue|hare
brancard
brown|rat
bull|calf
bull|frog
bush|baby
bush|buck
cachalot
cachelot
cannibal
capuchin
capybara
carapace
carcajou
cariacou
castrate
cave|bear
cavicorn
ceratops
Cerberus
cetacean
chestnut
chimaera
chipmuck
chipmunk
chowchow
civet|cat
coach|dog
cowhouse
creature
dairy|cow
deer|park
demi|wolf
Derby|dog
dinosaur
Doberman
dog|house
dog|pound
dog's|life
dormouse
duckbill
earth|hog
edentate
elephant
elkhound
entellus
entrails
fin|whale
foxhound
frogling
fruit|bat
Galloway
grey|mare
grey|wolf
hair|seal
hair|tail
hedgehog
hedgepig
hoggerel
horse|box
hound|dog
house|dog
humpback
hydrozoa
Irish|elk
jenny|ass
kangaroo
keeshond
kinkajou
kitty|cat
kolinsky
labrador
lancelet

leporine
lion's|den
long|horn
loosebox
mandrill
man|eater
mangabey
marmoset
mastodon
maverick
Minotaur
mongoose
monk|seal
mule|deer
musquash
nautilus
neat|herd
night|ape
nose|band
oliphant
omnivore
ouistiti
pack|mule
palomino
pangolin
Pekinese
penny|dog
pinniped
pinscher
platanna
platypus
polar|fox
polliwog
polo|pony
porkling
porpoise
predator
protozoa
pussy|cat
rabbitry
reindeer
rhizopod
river|hog
ruminant
sand|mole
sapi|utan
sauropod
sea|horse
sealyham
sea|otter
sea|swine
serotine
sheep|dog
shepherd
Shetland
skewbald
spitz|dog
squirrel
stallion
stegodon
steinbok
stray|cat
stray|dog
suborder
suricate
tabby|cat
terrapin
theropod
tiger|cat
tortoise
tree|frog
troutlet
turnspit
turn|tail
ungulate
viscacha
vivarium
wanderoo
war|horse
warragal
watchdog
water|cow
water|dog
water|rat
wharf|rat
whistler
white|fox
wild|boar
wild|goat
wild|life
wolf|pack
woof|woof
yeanling
yearling
amphibian
Angora|cat
Arctic|fox
armadillo
arthropod
babirussa
babyrussa
badger|dog
bandicoot
bangsring
beaver|rat
billy|goat
binturong
black|bear

ANIMALS

Black Bess
blackbuck
blue sheep
blue whale
boarhound
brood mare
brown bear
brush deer
brush wolf
buck hound
burro deer
caballine
Caffre cat
camass rat
caparison
carnivore
cart horse
catamount
cat and dog
caterwaul
ceratodus
chickaree
chihuahua
coleopter
cotton rat
crocodile
curry comb
dachshund
dairy herd
Dalmatian
dark horse
deerhound
deer mouse
deer tiger
desert rat
dinothere
dog collar
dog kennel
dray horse
dromedary
dziggetai
earth wolf
Eskimo dog
feralized
fill horse
flying fox
frog spawn
gazehound
gift horse
ginger tom
Great Dane
greyhound
grimalkin
ground hog
guinea pig
herbivore
herpestes
high horse
honey bear
hoofprint
horse shoe
horse whip
Houyhnhnm
ichneumon
iguanodon
Incitatus
infusoria
Jersey cow
Judas goat
jungle law
Kerry blue
koala bear
lamp shell
latration
lion heart
livestock
Lowrie Tod
mammalian
manticora
manticore
March hare
mare's nest
marsupial
marsupium
megathere
menagerie
monoceros
monotreme
mouldwarp
mouse deer
mousehole
mule train
musk shrew
Nandi bear
nanny goat
native cat
neat house
neat stall
on the hoof
orangutan
oviparous
pachyderm
pademelon
palm civet
pariah dog
Pekingese
percheron
phalanger

pinnipede
pipistrel
pocket rat
polar bear
police dog
poodle dog
porcupine
prayer dog
predatory
proboscis
pronghorn
protozoan
quadruped
racehorse
razor back
red setter
rescue dog
retriever
ridgeback
Rosinante
sarcodina
scavenger
schnauzer
sea canary
sea squirt
shorthorn
shrew mole
silver fox
skunk bear
sloth bear
springbok
staghound
St Bernard
stegosaur
studhorse
tarantula
tiffen bat
tiger wolf
Tod Lowrie
toy poodle
tree shrew
trilobite
ululation
waterbuck
water bull
water deer
water mole
water vole
Welsh pony
whalebone
white bear
wild sheep
wolfhound
wolverine
woodchuck
wood mouse
woodshock
yellow dog
youngling
zeuglodon
Angora goat
angwantibo
animalcule
animal life
arthropoda
babiroussa
Barbary ape
bear garden
Bedlington
bell the cat
bellwether
bezoar goat
black sheep
blood horse
bloodhound
bottle nose
Bucephalus
bull roarer
Burmese cat
camelopard
camel train
cannon bone
cattle grid
cephalopod
chevrotain
chimpanzee
chinchilla
Clydesdale
coach horse
cottontail
crio sphinx
dachshound
dapple grey
dermoptera
dog's chance
dumb animal
dumb friend
equestrian
Evangeline
fallow deer
fatted calf
field mouse
flagellata
fox terrier
freemartin
giant panda
golden mole
ground game

ANIMALS

hammerhead
hartebeest
heterocera
hippogriff
hippogryph
honey mouse
horned toad
horn footed
horseflesh
horse sense
hunting dog
Iceland dog
Indian pony
jack rabbit
jaguarundi
Kodiak bear
kookaburra
leopardess
lion's share
loggerhead
Maltese cat
Maltese dog
martingale
megalosaur
molluscoid
neat cattle
omnivorous
ornithopod
otterhound
otter shrew
pack animal
pack of dogs
pantheress
paradoxure
Persian cat
phyllopoda
pig in a poke
pine marten
Pomeranian
pouched rat
prairie dog
prairie fox
raccoon dog
radiolaria
rat terrier
rhinoceros
right whale
river horse
rock badger
Russian cat
sabre tooth
saddleback
sand hopper
sausage dog
schipperke
sea blubber
sea leopard
sea monster
sea unicorn
sheep's eyes
Shire horse
short sheep
shrew mouse
Siamese cat
snaffle bit
sperm whale
springbuck
spring hare
springtail
stock horse
stone horse
sub species
sucking pig
Syrian bear
tailwagger
tantony pig
tardigrade
thill horse
Tiergarten
timber wolf
toy spaniel
toy terrier
trace horse
tracker dog
Turkish cat
vampire bat
vertebrate
water mouse
Weimaraner
white whale
wild animal
wildebeest
woolly bear
xiphopagus
Afghan hound
basset hound
beast of prey
Belgian hare
black cattle
bloodsucker
buffalo wolf
bull mastiff
bull terrier
bunny rabbit
Buridan's ass
Cape buffalo
cardophagus
carriage dog

cat's pyjamas
cat squirrel
Cheshire cat
church mouse
crown antler
dairy cattle
daisy-cutter
Diana monkey
eager beaver
Egyptian cat
elephantine
entire horse
fishing-frog
flickertail
flying lemur
globigerina
green-turtle
grizzly bear
ground-sloth
hibernation
Highland cow
hircocervus
honey-badger
horned horse
insectivore
Irish setter
kangaroo rat
Kilkenny cat
killer-whale
land spaniel
lion-hearted
Malayan bear
orang-outang
ornithosaur
paper-sailor
Pavlov's dogs
plantigrade
pocket mouse
prairie wolf
rabbit hutch
red squirrel
reservation
rhynchodont
saddle-girth
saddle-horse
sand-skipper
sea-elephant
shepherd dog
sleuth-hound
snaffle-rein
snow-leopard
social whale
sorrel-horse
sporting dog
stone-marten
sumpter mule
swamp rabbit
titanothere
wheel-animal
white ermine
wishtonwish
wolf whistle
American lion
Archangel cat
baby elephant
bay at the moon
beard the lion
bonnet monkey
bottom animal
brontosaurus
Cairn terrier
Cashmere goat
catamountain
cat's whiskers
cattle market
cinnamon bear
dog in a manger
draught-horse
dumb creature
field spaniel
French poodle
gazelle hound
goat antelope
grey squirrel
Guinea baboon
hare and hound
harvest-mouse
hippopotamus
hoofed animal
horse-blanket
Irish terrier
jumping mouse
jumping shrew
king of beasts
marmalade cat
mating season
mountain goat
mountain hare
mountain lion
national park
Newfoundland
pantophagous
platanna frog
pocket gopher
quarter horse
rhesus monkey
rock squirrel
Saint Bernard

ANIMALS

Shetland pony
Spanish horse
Spanish sheep
spider monkey
Suffolk punch
sumpter horse
thoroughbred
tree squirrel
ursine monkey
Virginia deer
water buffalo
water spaniel
Welsh terrier
Aberdeen Angus
affenpinscher
ailourophilia
ailourophobia
animalisation
animal kingdom
animal worship
baggage animal
beast of burden
Boston terrier
cocker spaniel
Dandie Dinmont
draught animal
echinodermata
gadarene swine
mountain sheep
nature reserve
rogue elephant
Scotch terrier
sheep and goats
tortoiseshell
Clumber spaniel
domestic animal
Highland cattle
horse of the year
Indian elephant
man's best friend
pedigree cattle
Aberdeen terrier
animal magnetism
golden retriever
miniature poodle
Newfoundland dog
Scottish terrier
Sealyham terrier
springer spaniel

Architecture

3D	bay	inn	rib	arch	barn
RA	cot	kip	tie	area	base
wc	den	nef	adit	aula	bead
bar	hut	pub	apse	balk	beam

bell
bema
berm
boss
byre
cell
coin
cote
cove
cusp
cyma
dado
dais
digs
dome
door
drip
drum
eave
exit
face
farm
flag
flat
flue
fort
foss
fret
gate
haha
hall
head
home
jamb
keep
lift
list
loft
mews
mill
moat
mole
naos
nave
nook
ogee
pale
pane
park
path
pier
pile
plan
post
quad
rail
ramp
raze
reed
rima
rind
rise
road
roof
roof
room
sash
seat
shed
shop
sill
silo
site
slab
slum
span
step
stoa
tent
tige
tile
toft
tope
vane
wall
weir
well
wing
yard
zeta
abbey
abode
adobe
adyta
agora
aisle
alley
ancon
arena
arris
attic
berth
booth
bothy
bower
brick
broch
brogh
cabin
cella
cheek
close
coign
court
croft
crown
crypt
decor
ditch
domus
Doric
dowel
drain
drive
eaves
entry
facia
fanal
fence
flats
floor
flush
flute
folly
forum
fosse
foyer
gable
glass
glebe
glyph
grate
groin
hatch
helix
hinge
hoist
hotel
hotel
house
hovel
hutch
igloo
ingle
inlay
Ionic
jetty
joint
joist
jutty
kiosk
ledge
level
lobby
lodge
lotus
mains
manor
manse
mitre
motel
newel
niche
ogive
order
oriel
ovolo
panel
patio
pitch
plaza
porch
pylon
quoin
ranch
range
revet
ridge
riser
rooms
salle
salon
scale
sewer
shack
shaft
shore
slate
slums
socie
sough
speos
spire
splay
stage
stair
stall
stele
stile
stoep
stone
stria
strut
study
stupa
suite

ARCHITECTURE

talon	castle	fillet	listel	rafter
tepee	cellar	finial	loggia	recess
torus	cement	fleche	lounge	refuge
tower	centre	fluted	louvre	reglet
trave	chalet	founds	lyceum	regula
tread	chapel	fresco	maison	relief
trunk	church	frieze	mantel	rococo
tupek	circus	garage	marble	rubble
tupik	closet	garden	metope	saloon
usine	coffer	garret	milieu	school
vault	column	gazebo	module	sconce
villa	concha	ghetto	mortar	scotia
adytum	convex	girder	mosaic	screen
alcove	coping	godown	mosque	scroll
annexe	corbel	gopura	mud|hut	shanty
arbour	corner	Gothic	muntin	sluice
arcade	corona	gradin	museum	soffit
aspect	course	grange	mutule	spence
atrium	cranny	granny	oculus	spiral
avenue	crenel	gravel	office	spring
awning	cupola	griffe	pagoda	square
bagnio	damper	grille	palace	stable
barrow	dentil	ground	palais	storey
barton	donjon	gutter	paling	street
batten	dormer	hangar	parget	stucco
bedsit	dorsal	hawhaw	parvis	studio
belfry	dosser	header	pharos	suburb
billet	dry|rot	hearth	piazza	summer
bistro	duplex	hostel	picket	tablet
bridge	durbar	hostel	pillar	taenia
brough	estate	impost	plinth	tavern
by|room	exedra	insula	podium	temple
camber	fabric	kennel	portal	thatch
camera	facade	lancet	posada	tholos
canopy	facing	lean|to	prefab	tholus
canopy	fascia	lintel	purlin	timber

toilet	capital	estrade	low|rise
torsel	caracol	eustyle	lunette
trench	carving	factory	mansard
tunnel	cavetto	fencing	mansion
turret	ceiling	festoon	marquee
vallum	chamber	fitment	masonry
volute	chambre	fixture	megaron
wicket	chancel	fluting	minaret
wigwam	chapter	Fossway	mirador
window	charnel	free|end	moellon
zoning	chateau	fusarol	mudsill
academy	chez|moi	galilee	mullion
address	chimney	gallery	munting
air|duct	choltry	garland	mutular
archlet	cipolin	gateway	narthex
archway	cistern	godroon	necking
areaway	citadel	gradine	new|town
armoury	cloison	granary	nursery
arsenal	cob wall	granite	obelisk
asphalt	concave	grating	offices
astylar	conduit	grounds	ossuary
balcony	console	hallway	outlook
barmkin	contour	hip|roof	outwork
baroque	cornice	hospice	palazzo
barrack	cottage	housing	pannier
beading	crocket	hydrant	pantile
bearing	cubicle	keyhole	parapet
bedroom	culvert	kitchen	parlour
boudoir	cushion	klinker	parquet
box room	derrick	lagging	passage
bracing	dinette	landing	pendant
bracket	doorway	lantern	pension
bulwark	dungeon	larmier	pergola
cabaret	echinus	lattice	plafond
canteen	edifice	library	plaster
cantina	entasis	lodging	ponceau

ARCHITECTURE

portico	terrace	banister	curb roof
postern	theatre	bannerol	cymatium
purlieu	tie-beam	barbican	dark-room
pyramid	tracery	bartisan	dead wall
railing	transom	base line	detached
rampart	trefoil	basement	diggings
Rathaus	trellis	basilica	domicile
reredos	tribune	bathroom	doorhead
roofage	tumulus	bell tent	doorjamb
roofing	upright	best room	doorpost
rooftop	veranda	blinding	doorsill
roomlet	viaduct	brattice	downpipe
rosette	vitrail	building	driveway
rostrum	abamurus	bulkhead	dwelling
rotunda	abatjour	bull's-eye	ebenezer
sanctum	abatvoix	bungalow	entrance
Schloss	abbatoir	buttress	entresol
sea wall	abutment	canephor	epistyle
shebeen	acanthus	cantoned	erection
shelter	acrolith	capstone	espalier
shelter	air-drain	caracole	estancia
shingle	anteroom	caryatid	exterior
shore up	aperture	casement	extrados
shoring	apophyge	catacomb	fanlight
shutter	aqueduct	chapiter	farmyard
sinkage	arcature	chaptrel	fastness
skew-put	archives	chez nous	faubourg
skid row	artefact	cincture	fire plug
slating	astragal	clithral	fireside
station	Atlantes	cloister	fire stop
steeple	aularian	colossus	flat arch
storied	back door	concrete	flat roof
subbase	baguette	corridor	flooring
sundial	baluster	cross-tie	fortress
surbase	bandelet	cul-de-sac	fossette
Telamon	banderol	cupboard	fountain

funk hole
fusarole
gable end
game room
gargoyle
gatepost
hacienda
handrail
headpost
headsill
high rise
hospital
hothouse
housetop
interior
intrados
isodomon
keystone
kingpost
lavatory
lich gate
lodgings
lodgment
log cabin
lotus bud
love nest
magazine
martello
mess hall
messuage
monolith
mon repos
monument
ogee arch
open plan
ornament

outhouse
palisade
palmette
Pantheon
parabema
parclose
parterre
pavilion
peak arch
pedestal
pediment
pilaster
pinnacle
platform
playroom
pointing
property
prospect
quarters
rocaille
sacristy
scaffold
scullery
semi dome
shoulder
shutters
side door
skewback
skylight
slum area
snack bar
solarium
spandril
stairway
stockade
storeyed

subtopia
suburbia
sun porch
tectonic
tenement
teocalli
terraced
thalamus
tile roof
tolbooth
top floor
town hall
transept
trap door
traverse
triglyph
triptych
tympanum
underpin
upstairs
verandah
voussoir
wainscot
wall tent
windmill
woodworm
ziggurat
acoustics
acropolis
alignment
almshouse
angle iron
anthemion
apartment
architect
archivolt

Attic|base
banderole
banquette
bas|relief
bay|window
bead|house
bell|tower
belvedere
blueprint
bolection
bottoming
bow|window
box|girder
breezeway
brickwork
bunkhouse
butt|joint
cafeteria
campanile
cartouche
cartulary
cathedral
cauliculi
chophouse
clapboard
classical
cleithral
cloakroom
clubhouse
coal|house
coffer|dam
coffering
colonnade
Colosseum
columella
composite
converted
courtyard
cross|beam
crossette
crown|post
cubby|hole
cubiculum
curtilage
curvature
cyma|recta
decastyle
door|frame
door|panel
doorstone
dormitory
doss|house
drainpipe
dripstone
dry|fresco
earthwork
edificial
elevation
esplanade
estaminet
extension
fan|window
farmhouse
fastigium
fireplace
fixed|arch
flagstone
flathouse
floor|plan
flophouse
footstone
forecourt
framework
front|door
front|room
fundament
gable|roof
garderobe
glory|hole
green|belt
guildhall
guttering
gymnasium
headboard
headmould
headpiece
hexastyle
homecroft
homestall
homestead
hoodmould
houseboat
house|plan
impromptu
inglenook
ingleside
inner|city
landscape
low|relief
marquetry
masonwork
mausoleum
mezzanine
mock|Tudor
modillion
mouldings
neo|Gothic
Nissen|hut

octastyle
open floor
outskirts
paintwork
panelling
Parthenon
partition
pedentive
penthouse
peridrome
peristyle
pontlevis
proseuche
prothesis
reception
refectory
reservoir
residence
revetment
ridgepole
rigid arch
ring fence
roadhouse
rough arch
roughcast
round arch
rus in urbe
sally port
scagliola
scantling
shopfront
skew table
slate roof
staircase
stairhead
stanchion
stateroom
still room
stone wall
storm door
structure
stylobate
sunk fence
sun lounge
swing door
synagogue
telamones
threshold
tierceron
tollbooth
tollhouse
town house
tree house
triforium
truss beam
Tudor arch
vallation
vestibule
wallboard
warehouse
whitewash
window bay
window box
acroterion
arched door
arched roof
architrave
art gallery
auditorium
balustrade
barge board
base course
battlement
bedchamber
bidonville
blind alley
breakwater
bressummer
canephorus
cantilever
cauliculus
cellar door
chimney pot
cinquefoil
clearstory
clerestory
clock tower
coffee shop
common room
compluvium
conversion
Corinthian
covered way
crosswalls
damp course
denticular
diaconicon
dining hall
dining room
doll's house
Doric order
downstairs
drawbridge
earthworks
excavation
family seat
fan tracery
fire escape

ARCHITECTURE

first floor
first story
footbridge
French roof
garden wall
glass house
glebe house
Greek Ionic
greenhouse
ground plan
groundsill
groundwork
habitation
hammer beam
hipped roof
Ionic order
ivory tower
jerry-built
lancet arch
Lebensraum
lighthouse
living room
luxury flat
maisonette
manor house
manteltree
masonry pin
mitre-joint
monolithic
opera house
orthograph
orthostyle
passageway
paving flag
pebble-dash
pentastyle
pied-à-terre
pigeonhole
pile bridge
portcullis
priest hole
projection
proportion
propylaeum
proscenium
quadrangle
quatrefoil
Quonset hut
ranch house
real estate
repository
restaurant
retrochoir
ribbed arch
ridge strut
rising arch
rising damp
road bridge
Roman Doric
Romanesque
rose window
rumpus room
Saxon tower
screenings
scrollhead
sewing room
skew-bridge
skew-corbel
skyscraper
split level
storehouse
stronghold
structural
sun parlour
terra cotta
trust house
tumbledown
turret room
undercroft
university
ventilator
watch-tower
wicket door
wicket gate
antechamber
atmospheric
barge-couple
barge-stones
barrel vault
buttressing
campaniform
caravansary
chimney tops
coffee-house
common stair
compartment
concert hall
coping stone
cornerstone
country seat
crazy paving
crenellated
cyma reversa
drawing room
duplex house
eating house
entablature
fan vaulting

foundations
gambrel|roof
ground|floor
ground|table
hanging|post
hearthstone
ichnography
inhabitancy
kitchenette
lancet|style
latticework
laundry|room
leaded|glass
lecture|hall
linen|closet
little|boxes
mansard|roof
mantelpiece
mantelshelf
masonry|arch
mews|cottage
morning|room
Norman|tower
oeil|de|boeuf
oriel|window
outbuilding
pantile|roof
paving|stone
pendant|post
picket|fence
pitched|roof
plasterwork
pointed|arch
public|house
rampant|arch
restoration
roofing|tile
room|divider
scaffolding
service|lane
service|lift
shingle|roof
sitting|room
smoking|room
stately|home
step|terrace
street|floor
summerhouse
sunken|fence
trefoil|arch
Tuscan|order
urban|sprawl
utility|room
ventilation
wainscoting
waiting|room
water|closet
weathercock
willow|cabin
window|frame
window|glass
wrought|iron
amphitheatre
architecture
assembly|hall
audience|hall
Bailey|bridge
balustrading
bead|moulding
billiard|room
breastsummer
building|line
buttress|pier
caravanserai
chapter|house
charnel|house
chimney|shaft
chimney|stack
city|planning
common|bricks
conservatory
construction
country|house
dividing|wall
Dormer|window
double|glazed
double|scroll
entrance|hall
espagnolette
false|ceiling
fluted|column
French|Gothic
french|window
frontispiece
galilee|porch
garden|suburb
head|moulding
hitching|post
hotel|de|ville
hunting|lodge
inner|sanctum
lake|dwelling
lancet|window
lodging|place
machicolated
Maiden|Castle
main|entrance
mansion|house

meeting|house
Nelson|column
phrontistery
pier|buttress
plaster|board
porte|cochere
prefabricate
privy|chamber
rooming|house
salle|à|manger
semi|detached
shutting|post
smallholding
snubbing|post
stained|glass
string|course
substructure
swinging|post
thatched|roof
town|planning
underpinning
urban|renewal
weatherboard
accommodation
architectonic
architectural
assembly|rooms
boarding|house
building|block
building|board
butler's|pantry
chimney|corner
community|home
council|estate
county|council
cross|vaulting
dormitory|town
double|glazing
dwelling|house
dwelling|place
emergency|exit
ferroconcrete
fire|resisting
floodlighting
furnished|flat
Gothic|revival
housing|estate
jerry|building
lattice|girder
master|builder
open|plan|house
owner|occupied
palais|de|danse
partition|wall
picture|window
prefabricated
public|gallery
public|library
retaining|wall
revolving|door
shooting|lodge
sound|proofing
triumphal|arch
wattle|and|daub
apartment|house
apartment|to|let
banqueting|hall
bed|sitting|room
consulting|room
country|cottage
funeral|parlour
housing|problem

housing project
interior design
listed building
office building
picture gallery
pleasure ground
prefabrication
slaughterhouse
superstructure
system building
air conditioning
architectonical
banqueting house
clustered column
community centre
discharging arch
dormitory suburb
foundation stone
married quarters
owner occupation
reception centre
spiral staircase
state apartments
unfurnished flat

Artists

Arp
Low
Adam
Cuyp
Dali
Etty
Eyck
Gill
Gogh
Goya
Hals
Hunt
John
Klee
Lely
Nash
Opie
Wren
Bacon
Berry
Blake
Bosch
Clark
Corot
Crome
David
Degas
Dürer
Frith
Giles
Kelly
Lippi
Lowry
Manet
Monet
Orpen
Piper
Pugin
Rodin
Scott
Smith
Soane
Steer
Watts
Wyatt
Bewick
Braque
Casson
Claude
Corbet
Cotman
Duccio
Giotto
Ingres
Knight
Laszlo
Lavery
Ledoux
Mabuse
Millet
Morris
Panini
Pisano
Renoir
Romney
Rubens
Ruskin
Seurat

ARTISTS

Sisley
Spence
Stubbs
Tadema
Titian
Turner
Van Ryn
Warhol
Bassano
Bellini
Bernini
Boucher
Cellini
Cézanne
Chagall
Chardin
Cimabue
Courbet
Daumier
Da Vinci
De Hooch
El Greco
Epstein
Gauguin
Gibbons
Gillray
Gropius
Hobbema
Hockney
Hogarth
Holbein
Matisse
Memlinc
Millais
Murillo
Pasmore

Phidias
Picasso
Poussin
Raeburn
Raphael
Sargent
Sickert
Spencer
Tenniel
Tiepolo
Uccello
Utrillo
Van Dyck
Van Eyck
Van Gogh
Vermeer
Watteau
Zoffany
Angelico
Brancusi
Brangwyn
Brueghel
Hepworth
Landseer
Leonardo
Mantegna
Montegna
Munnings
Perugino
Pissarro
Rossetti
Rousseau
Vanbrugh
Veronese
Vlaminck
Whistler

9/15 LETTERS

Beardsley
Canaletto
Constable
Correggio
Delacroix
Donatello
Fragonard
Giorgione
Hawksmoor
Rembrandt
Velásquez
Botticelli
Caravaggio
Mackintosh
Praxiteles
Rowlandson
Sutherland
Tintoretto
Fra|Angelico
Ghirlandaio
Le|Corbusier
Gainsborough
Michelangelo
Winterhalter
Leonardo|da|Vinci
Toulouse-Lautrec

Astronomy

sky
sun
Argo
Bora
Hebe
Juno
Lynx
lyra
Mars
moon
nova
Pavo
Rhea
star
Vega
Algol
apsis
Ariel
Cetus
comet
Dione
Draco
Hydra
Indus
Lepus
lunar
Lupus
Mensa
Musca
nadir
Norma
orbit
Orion
phase
Pluto
Rigel
saros
solar
Spica
stars
Titan
umbra
Venus
albedo
Antlia
apogee
Aquila
astral
Auriga
bolide
Boötes
Caelum
Castor
Caurus
corona
Corvus
cosmic
cosmos
Cygnus
dipper
Dorado
galaxy
gnomon
heaven
Hyades
Hydrus
meteor
Nereid
Oberon
Octans
Pictor
planet
Pollux
quasar
Saturn
Selene
Sirius
starry
syzygy
Tethys

ASTRONOMY

Triton
Tucana
Uranus
Vulcan
zodiac
Antares
appulse
apsides
azimuth
Canopus
Cepheus
Columba
day|star
dog|star
eclipse
equinox
faculae
gibbous
heavens
Jupiter
Lacerta
Neptune
new|moon
Pegasus
perigee
Perseus
Phoenix
Polaris
Procyon
Regulus
Sagitta
Serpens
sextile
stellar
sunspot
Titania

transit
Achernar
aerolite
Almagest
aphelion
Arcturus
asteroid
Canicula
Cepheids
Circinus
Cynosure
ecliptic
empyrean
Erodanus
evection
fenestra
flocculi
full|moon
galactic
ganymede
half|moon
heavenly
Hercules
hyperion
isochasm
luminary
Milky|Way
mock|moon
moonbeam
night|sky
nutation
parallax
penumbra
Pleiades
Pointers
pole|star

red|dwarf
red|giant
Sculptor
sidereal
solarium
sunspots
universe
upper|air
Aldebaran
Andromeda
anthelion
astrolabe
astrology
astronomy
celestial
Centaurus
coelostat
corposant
cosmogony
cosmology
Delphinus
ephemeris
fenestral
firmament
fixed|star
flocculus
giant|star
Great|Bear
heliostat
light|year
lunar|halo
lunar|rays
meteorite
meteoroid
Monoceros
moonlight

9/11 LETTERS

moonshine
Ophiuchus
parhelion
planetary
planetoid
polar star
quasi star
radio star
refractor
satellite
scintilla
solar wind
starlight
supernova
telescope
uranology
Ursa Major
Ursa Minor
Vulpecula
almacantar
Canis major
Canis minor
Cassiopeia
Chamaeleon
collimator
double star
geocentric
green flash
Horologium
ionosphere
Lesser Bear
light curve
luminosity
Orion's belt
outer space
paraselene
perihelion
phenomenon
precession
quadrature
selenology
solar cycle
solar flare
star stream
terminator
tropopause
waning moon
waxing moon
Andromedids
Baily's beads
coronagraph
cosmography
cosmosphere
evening star
falling star
Gegenschein
Kelper's laws
league table
lunar crater
major planet
midnight sun
minor planet
morning star
observatory
occultation
Orion's sword
photosphere
planetarium
planisphere
polar aurora
polar lights
radio source

solar corona
solar energy
solar system
star cluster
stella maris
stratopause
tail of comet
Telescopium
translunary
astronomical
astrophysics
Canis majoris
Charles's wain
chromosphere
crescent moon
Halley's comet
heavenly body
man in the moon
meteor crater
meteorograph
selenography
shooting star
space station
spectrograph
spectroscope
spectroscopy
star-spangled
stratosphere
variable star
vertical rays
constellation
extra-galactic
printed matter
Southern Cross
annular eclipse
astrogeologist
heavenly bodies
northern lights
partial eclipse
radioastronomy
radio-telescope
southern lights
St Anthony's fire
Astronomer Royal
Hubble's constant
Nautical Almanac
sun, moon and stars

Biblical Names

Ur	Ham	Abel	Amon	Cana	Gath
Dan	Job	Adam	Amos	Eden	Gaza
Eli	Lot	Agag	Baal	Edom	Jael
Eve	Nod	Ahab	Boaz	Esau	Jehu
Gad	Abba	Ahaz	Cain	Ezra	Joel

4/7 LETTERS

John
Jude
Leah
Levi
Luke
Magi
Mark
Mary
Moab
Noah
Omri
Paul
Ruth
Saul
Seth
Shem
Aaron
Abihu
Abner
Abram
Annas
Asher
Babel
Barak
Caleb
Cyrus
Dagon
David
Dinah
Elias
Elihu
Endor
Enoch
Haman
Herod
Hiram
Hosea
Isaac
Jonah
Jacob
James
Jesse
Joppa
Jubal
Judah
Judas
Laban
Micah
Moses
Nahum
Naomi
Peter
Sarah
Sheba
Silas
Simon
Sinai
Sodom
Titus
Uriah
Zadok
Zimri
Amalek
Andrew
Ararat
Balaam
Belial
Bethel
Canaan
Carmel
Daniel
Darius
Dorcas
Elijah
Elisha
Emmaus
Esther
Eunice
Exodus
Festus
Gehazi
Gibeon
Gideon
Gilboa
Gilead
Gilgal
Goshen
Haggai
Hannah
Hebron
Isaiah
Israel
Jairus
Jethro
Jordan
Joseph
Joshua
Josiah
Judaea
Kishon
Martha
Miriam
Mizpah
Naaman
Naboth
Nathan
Nimrod
Patmos
Pilate
Rachel
Reuben
Romans
Salome
Samson
Samuel
Simeon
Sisera
Thomas
Abaddon
Abigail
Abilene
Abraham
Absalom
Adullam
Ananias
Antioch
Antipas
Azariah
Babylon
Calvary
Cherith
Cleopas
Corinth
Deborah
Delilah
Didymus
Eleazar
Elkanah
Ephesus
Ephraim
Ezekiel
Gabriel
Galilee
Genesis

BIBLICAL NAMES

Gentile
Goliath
Hebrews
Ichabod
Ishmael
Japheth
Jericho
Jezebel
Jezreel
Lazarus
Malachi
Matthew
Meshach
Messiah
Michael
Nineveh
Obadiah
Pharaoh
Rebekah
Solomon
Stephen
Timothy
Zebedee
Abednego
Abinadab
Adonijah
Akeldama
Amorites
Appelles
Ashkelon
Barabbas
Barnabas
Behemoth
Benjamin
Bethesda
Caesarea
Caiaphas
Chorazin
Damascus
Ebenezer
Gadarene
Gamaliel
Gehennah
Golgotha
Gomorrah
Habakkuk
Herodias
Hezekiah
Immanuel
Iscariot
Issachar
Jephthah
Jeremiah
Jeroboam
Jonathan
Manasseh
Matthias
Naphtali
Nazareth
Nehemiah
Potiphar
Abimelech
Ahasuerus
Arimathea
Bathsheba
Beelzebub
Beersheba
Bethlehem
Bethphage
Bethsaida
Boanerges
Capernaum

9/14 LETTERS

Elimelech
Elisabeth
Esdraelon
Galatians
Jerusalem
Magdalene
Nicodemus
Pharisees
Sadducees
Samaritan
Zacchaeus
Zachariah
Zechariah
Zephaniah
Armageddon
Bartimaeus
Belshazzar
Colossians
Gethsemane
Methuselah
Shibboleth
Bartholomew
Jehoshaphat
Philippians
Philistines
Sennacherib
Thessalonians
Nebuchadnezzar

Biological Sciences

lab
ova
sac
alar
axil
cell
cone
cyte
gene
germ
ovum
talc
tank
algae
bifid
bursa
class
clone
cyton
fauna
fibre
flora
gemma
genes
genus
group
hypha
linin
lymph
lysin
order
ovate
ovoid
ovule
petri
slide
spore
still
taxis
virus
zooid
aerobe
agamic
amoeba
biogen
bionic
biotin
botany
coccus
cohort
colony
cytode
embryo
enzyme
fibrin
foetus
foment
gamete
gas|jar
hybrid

BIOLOGICAL SCIENCES

lacuna
lamina
lanate
lipase
nekton
ovisac
phylum
plasma
staple
system
theory
tissue
zymase
acyclic
aerobic
albumen
albumin
amylase
anatomy
anomaly
aquaria
atavism
benthos
biology
blubber
booster
breeder
calorie
cell|sap
congeal
cordate
culture
deltoid
dentine
diploid
dissect
ecology
egg|cell
enation
fertile
fistula
flaccid
forceps
gametes
genesis
gliadin
habitat
haploid
histoid
lactase
lamella
lateral
microbe
mitosis
monitor
myology
nascent
network
obovate
obovoid
oxidase
paracme
pedicel
pigment
plastid
primary
primate
protein
radicle
saltant
scanner
science
section
shellac
stimuli
synapse
synergy
syringe
trypsin
vaccine
vascula
vitamin
yolk|sac
zoology
zootomy
adhesion
adhesive
amitosis
aquarium
autology
basidium
bioblast
biometer
biophore
blastema
body|cell
cell|wall
co|enzyme
cohesion
conchate
cyclosis
cytology
demersal
diastase
diatomic
ectogeny
effluent
entozoon
epiblast
eugenics
feedback
fistular
follicle
genetics
geotaxis
homogamy
inositol
involute
isotropy
lenticel
meniscus
mutation
mycology
nucleole
organism
plankton
prophase
rudiment
sex|ratio
sitology
specimen
sphenoid
stimulus
sub|order
synapsis
syndesis
taxonomy
thiamine
transect
trencher
unciform
vascular
virology

8/10 LETTERS

vitamin A
vitamin B
vitamin C
vitamin D
vitamin E
vitellus
xenogamy
zoospore
ambergris
anabolism
anaerobic
archetype
atavistic
attenuate
bifarious
bigeneric
bilateral
bionomics
bisulcate
body clock
chromatin
coenobium
conjugate
convolute
cytoplasm
dichotomy
dimorphic
duplicate
ectoplasm
effluvium
endoplasm
endosperm
endospore
evolution
folic acid
geobiotic
gestation
halophily
herbarium
heterosis
histology
incubator
initiator
injection
isotropic
klinostat
lactation
life-cycle
limnology
luciferin
metaplasm
microsome
microtome
morphosis
myography
nutrition
occlusion
ovulation
paralyser
petri dish
phenology
phenotype
phycology
phytotron
potometer
processed
protogyny
prototype
pyrogenic
scientist
subdivide
symbiosis
telophase
threshold
toast-rack
vitelline
yolk stalk
zoobiotic
zoogamete
achromatin
albuminoid
anisotropy
antecedent
antibodies
antitoxins
biochemics
biochemist
biogenesis
biometrics
biophysics
biorhythms
blastoderm
blastomere
cacogenics
carcinogen
catabolism
cell tissue
centrosome
chromosome
consequent
culture jar
deep freeze
depilatory
dissection
egg-albumen
embryology
entomology
enzymology

BIOLOGICAL SCIENCES

ephemerist
etiolation
exobiology
formic acid
generation
growth ring
homochromy
incubation
involution
katabolism
laboratory
maturation
metabolism
microscope
microscopy
morphology
mother cell
odontogeny
organology
osteoblast
pasteurise
petri plate
physiology
primordial
protogenic
protoplasm
riboflavin
scientific
sensitizer
somatology
spirometer
sterilizer
vital stain
viviparous
zoophysics
accelerator

agglutinate
attenuation
auxanometer
benthoscope
bioengineer
bipartition
cellulation
chlorophyll
chloroplast
chromoplast
coagulation
cod liver oil
culture tube
eccrinology
elimination
environment
generic name
heterotopes
homogenizer
hygroscopic
insecticide
lactalbumin
lactoflavin
lipoprotein
microscopic
monomorphic
pure culture
sensitivity
somatic cell
stimulation
synoecology
systematics
thermolysis
thermolytic
unicellular
X chromosome

Y chromosome
zoochemical
zooplankton
acceleration
anthropogeny
anthropology
anthropotomy
antithrombin
astrobiology
bacteriology
biochemistry
biosatellite
biosynthesis
carbohydrate
cell division
cross section
cryoplankton
culture flask
dietotherapy
disinfectant
essential oil
eurythermous
experimental
fermentation
formaldehyde
immune bodies
keratogenous
microspecies
mitotic index
monomorphous
palaeobotany
pyridoxamine
radiobiology
reflex action
regeneration
serum albumin

12/15 LETTERS

simple|tissue
specific|name
trace|element
ultramicrobe
vitaminology
water|culture
zoochemistry
zoogeography
acotyledonous
biodegradable
biogeographer
blastogenesis
crossbreeding
fertilisation
hermaphrodite
heterogenesis
heterogenetic
micro|organism
sterilisation
aerobiological
anthropologist
bacteriologist
biodegradation
bioengineering
breeding|ground
electrobiology
microbiologist
natural|history
natural|science
photosynthesis
plant|formation
anthropological
bacteriological
biological|clock
dissecting|table

Birds

auk	owl	chat	eyry	kiwi	rail
caw	pen	claw	fowl	kora	rhea
coo	pet	coop	game	lark	rook
cry	pie	coot	guan	loon	ruff
daw	roc	crow	gull	lory	skua
emu	tit	dodo	hawk	mina	smew
fly	tui	dove	honk	mute	sord
hen	zoo	down	hoot	nest	swan
jay	bevy	duck	ibis	nide	tail
kea	bill	erne	kaka	pavo	tern
moa	bird	eyas	kite	pern	weka

BIRDS

wing
wisp
wren
aerie
agami
argus
avian
booby
brace
brant
capon
cavie
charm
cheep
chick
chirp
cluck
covey
crake
crane
crest
diver
drake
eagle
egret
eider
eyrie
finch
geese
genus
glede
goose
grebe
harpy
hatch
heron

hobby
homer
jenny
junco
larus
macaw
madge
mavis
merle
moray
moult
murre
nandu
nidus
ornis
ousel
ouzel
owlet
oxeye
peggy
pekan
pewit
picus
pipit
pitta
poker
Polly
poult
quack
quail
raven
reeve
robin
roost
rotch
saker

serin
skart
skein
snipe
solan
squab
stilt
stork
torsk
trill
tweet
veery
vireo
wader
aquila
argala
auklet
aviary
avocet
bantam
barbet
blenny
bonito
bulbul
canary
chough
clutch
condor
corbie
coucal
covert
cuckoo
culver
curlew
cushat
cygnet

darter
dipper
drongo
dunlin
eaglet
elanet
falcon
flight
fulmar
gaggle
gambet
gander
gannet
garrot
garuda
godwit
gooney
grouse
henrun
herald
honker
hooper
hoopoe
howlet
jabiru
jacana
kakapo
lanner
linnet
magpie
martin
mopoke
motmot
nandoo
oriole
oscine

6/7 LETTERS

osprey
oxbird
palama
parrot
passer
pavone
peahen
peewee
peewit
petrel
phoebe
pigeon
plover
pouter
puffin
pullet
rallus
redcap
roller
scoter
seacob
seamew
seaowl
shrike
simurg
siskin
thrush
toucan
towhee
trogon
turdus
turkey
volary
warble
weaver
wigeon

willet
ynambu
antbird
barnowl
bittern
blueeye
bluejay
bluetit
brooder
bunting
bushtit
bustard
buzzard
cariama
catbird
chewink
chicken
chirrup
coaltit
colibri
cotinga
cowbird
creeper
dopping
dorhawk
dovecot
dunnock
eggbird
emuwren
fantail
feather
fernowl
flapper
flicker
gadwall
gobbler

goldeye
gorcock
gorcrow
goshawk
gosling
grackle
greyhen
greylag
greyowl
haggard
halcyon
hawkowl
hencoop
hennery
hoatzin
hootowl
hornowl
icebird
jacamar
jackdaw
kestrel
killdee
lapwing
lichowl
mallard
manakin
marabou
martlet
migrant
moorhen
mudlark
oilbird
ortolan
ostrich
Partlet
peacock

peafowl
pelican
penguin
phoenix
pinguin
pinnock
pintado
pintail
plumage
pochard
pollack
poulard
poultry
puttock
quetzal
redbird
redwing
rookery
rooster
rosella
ruddock
sagehen
seabird
seadove
seaduck
seagull
seahawk
sealark
seriema
simurgh
sirgang
skimmer
skylark
sparrow
staniel
striges

BIRDS

sturnus
sunbird
swallow
tattler
tiercel
tinamou
titlark
titling
tumbler
twitter
vulture
wagtail
warbler
waxwing
webfoot
widgeon
woodowl
wrentit
wryneck
aasvogel
accentor
adjutant
aigrette
albacore
alcatras
amadavat
anserine
anserous
antpipit
apterous
aquiline
arapunga
avifauna
baldpate
barnacle
beeeater
bellbird
berghaan
birdbath
birdcage
birdcall
bird'segg
blackcap
bluebill
bluebird
bluewing
boatbill
boattail
bobolink
bobwhite
brownowl
bushwren
caracara
cardinal
cargoose
cockatoo
cockerel
curassow
dabchick
deadduck
didapper
dobchick
dotterel
dovecote
duckhawk
duckling
duckmole
duckpond
eagleowl
fauvette
feathers
fishhawk
flamingo
forewing
gamecock
garefowl
garganey
greatauk
grosbeak
guacharo
hangbird
hawfinch
henhouse
hernshaw
hindwing
hornbill
killdeer
kingbird
kingcrow
kiwikiwi
lameduck
landrail
lanneret
laverock
lovebird
megapode
moorcock
moorfowl
muskduck
muteswan
nightjar
nightowl
nuthatch
ovenbird
oxpecker
parakeet
pavonian
pheasant
philomel
podargus
poorwill
popinjay
puffbird
raraavis
rarebird
redshank
redstart
reedbird
ricebird
ringdove
ringtail
rockbird
rockdove
rocklark
sagecock
sandlark
sandpeep
screamer
seasnipe
shelduck
shoebill
skuagull
snowbird
songbird
starling
sungrebe
surfbird
swiftlet
tapaculo
tawnyowl
tealduck
thrasher
throstle
titmouse

tragopan
trembler
troupial
waterhen
wheatear
whimbrel
whinchat
white cap
wild duck
wildfowl
wingspan
woodchat
woodcock
wood duck
wood ibis
woodlark
wood wren
yoke toed
yoldring
aepyornis
albatross
ant thrush
bald eagle
beaf eater
bean goose
beccafico
birdhouse
bird's nest
bird table
blackbird
blackcock
blackgame
blackhead
black swan
black tern
blue heron
bottle tit
bower bird
brambling
bull finch
campanero
cedarbird
chaffinch
chickadee
cockatiel
cock robin
cocks comb
columbary
columbine
crossbill
currawong
dicky bird
eagle eyed
eider duck
fieldfare
fieldlark
firecrest
flute bird
frogmouth
gallinazo
gallinule
gerfalcon
gier eagle
goldcrest
goldeneye
goldfinch
goldspink
goosander
grey goose
guillemot
guinea hen
gyrfalcon
heath cock
heronshaw
horned owl
jacksnipe
Jenny wren
king eider
kittiwake
little auk
merganser
migration
migratory
mound bird
nightbird
night crow
night fowl
nighthawk
nocturnal
on the wing
ossifrage
owl parrot
parrakeet
partridge
passerine
peregrine
phalarope
pine finch
ptarmigan
quail dove
razorbill
redbreast
redbreast
red grouse
rifle bird
ringouzel
rock pipit
salangane

sanctuary
sandpiper
sapsucker
scamp duck
scrubbird
sea dragon
sea parrot
sedge bird
sedge wren
seed snipe
sheldrake
shore bird
snake bird
snow fleck
snow goose
solitaire
sooty tern
spoonbill
stilt bird
stock dove
stonechat
stone hawk
talegalla
tom turkey
trumpeter
turnstone
water bird
water cock
water fowl
water rail
web footed
wheatbird
whitehead
whitewing
wild goose
windhover
aberdevine
aviculture
battery hen
bird of prey
bluebreast
blue pigeon
bluethroat
brent goose
budgerigar
burrow duck
bush shrike
butter bird
canvas back
Cape pigeon
cheep cheep
chiff chaff
chittagong
cow bunting
crab plover
crested jay
deep litter
demoiselle
dickeybird
didunculus
ember goose
fallow chat
flying fish
get the bird
goatsucker
greenfinch
green goose
greenshank
grey parrot
guinea cock
guinea fowl
harpy eagle
hen harrier
herald duck
honey eater
honey guide
hooded crow
hoodie crow
house finch
Indian kite
indigo bird
jungle fowl
kingfisher
meadow lark
missel bird
mutton bird
night churr
night heron
night raven
nutcracker
parrotbill
parson bird
pigeon hawk
pigeon loft
poll parrot
pratincole
quack quack
Quaker bird
ring plover
road runner
rock hopper
rock pigeon
sage grouse
sailorbird
sanderling
sand grouse
sand martin
screech owl

sea swallow
sea vampire
setting hen
shearwater
sheathbill
sickle bill
solan goose
song thrush
stone snipe
summer duck
summer teal
sun bittern
tailor bird
talk turkey
tawny eagle
thick knees
tropic bird
turkey cock
turtle dove
wading bird
water ousel
weaver bird
willow wren
wood grouse
woodpecker
wood pigeon
wood shrike
wood thrush
wren thrush
yellow bird
zebra finch
accipitrine
bastard wing
black grouse
black martin
brush turkey

butcher bird
Canada goose
carrion crow
Chanticleer
Cochin china
cock a doodle
cock sparrow
columbarium
dead as a dodo
fallow finch
fan tail dove
gnatcatcher
golden eagle
green linnet
ground robin
honey sucker
king penguin
king vulture
lammergeier
man o war bird
meadow pipit
muscovy duck
nightingale
pied wagtail
pigeon house
pigeon's milk
Pretty Polly
pterodactyl
purple finch
reed bunting
reed sparrow
reed warbler
rock sparrow
rooster fish
scissorbill
sea dotterel

singing bird
sitting duck
snow bunting
song sparrow
Spanish fowl
sparrowhawk
stilt plover
stone curlew
stone falcon
stone plover
swallowtail
tree swallow
Vanga shrike
wattled crow
weaver finch
whitethroat
wood swallow
wood warbler
adjutant bird
barndoor fowl
barnyard fowl
bird's eye view
bramble finch
brown pelican
burrowing owl
bustard quail
capercaillie
capercailzie
cardinal bird
chicken house
chimney swift
cliff swallow
crested swift
crowned eagle
cuckoo roller
cuckoo shrike

BIRDS

diving|petrel
domestic|fowl
elephant|bird
falcon,gentil
fighting|cock
flowerpecker
fully|fledged
gallinaceous
golden|oriole
golden|plover
ground,cuckoo
hedge,sparrow
hedge,warbler
hermit|thrush
homing|pigeon
honey,buzzard
mandarin|duck
marsh,harrier
merrythought
missel,thrush
mistle,thrush
mourning|dove
painted|snipe
rifleman,bird
ring,dotterel
sedge,warbler
serpent,eater
stonechatter
stormy|petrel
stubble,goose
tropical|bird
ugly|duckling
umbrella|bird
velvet|scoter
water,wagtail
whip,poor,will
wingless|bird
wood|pheasant
yellow,hammer
barnacle|goose
bird|of|passage
carrier|pigeon
ornithologist
oyster,catcher
spring|chicken
trumpeter|swan
turkey|buzzard
willow,warbler
yellow,bunting
bird|of|paradise
bird,of,paradise
ornithological
Rhode|Island|Red
robin,redbreast
wild|goose|chase
birds|of|a|feather
peregrine|falcon

Capacity

cran
gill
peck
pint
homer
litre
pinta
quart
barrel
bushel
chopin
cupful
gallon
magnum
dry|pint
dry|quart
hogshead
spoonful
teaspoon
decalitre
decilitre
fluid|dram
kilolitre
centilitre
millilitre
tablespoon
thimbleful
teaspoonful
imperial|pint
cubic|capacity

Cereals

awn
ear
lea
oat
rye
sow
soy
corn
crop
husk
oats
reap
rice
soya
durra
field
flour
glean
grain
maize
paddy
pulse
spear
spike
straw
wheat
barley
cereal

CEREALS

farina	soy|flour	ground|rice
groats	wild|oats	Indian|corn
hominy	broomcorn	kaffir|corn
lentil	buckwheat	paddy|field
mealie	corn|bread	rolled|oats
millet	corn|field	wheat|field
corncob	cornflour	whole|wheat
harvest	corn|salad	corn|in|Egypt
oatmeal	ear|of|corn	corn|in|Israel
tapioca	rice|paddy	corn|on|the|cob
wild|oat	sweetcorn	decorticated
ripe|corn	barley|corn	
semolina	brome|grass	

Character Types

ass	doll	rake	puppy	Amazon
cad	dolt	scab	rogue	apache
fop	drip	snob	saint	beauty
hag	dude	thug	scamp	bibber
ham	dupe	toff	scold	cadger
hex	fool	twit	shrew	canter
oaf	gull	wimp	siren	carper
pal	guru	joker	sneak	codger
rat	heel	Judas	spark	con|man
rip	hick	knave	sport	coward
sot	hype	macho	stoic	dodger
wit	liar	miser	toady	dotard
bore	lout	moron	toper	duffer
brat	minx	mouse	trier	egoist
chum	ogre	nomad	vixen	faggot
cove	prig	prude	wally	fantod

fawner
fellow
fibber
gasbag
gay dog
genius
gossip
grouch
hassle
hep-cat
hippie
humbug
jet-set
junkie
layman
leader
loafer
madman
martyr
nobody
nutter
ogress
old boy
pariah
pedant
pundit
puppet
purist
rabbit
rascal
roamer
Romany
rotter
rustic
sadist
sexist
sinner
square
stooge
vandal
virago
voyeur
Watson
worthy
wretch
zealot
zombie
a bad egg
also-ran
ancient
ascetic
avenger
babbler
beatnik
bonkers
bounder
bucolic
buffoon
bumpkin
charmer
chauvin
cheater
copy-cat
coxcomb
cry baby
cuckold
culprit
dabbler
dallier
darling
devotee
diehard
dilutee
doubter
dreamer
drifter
drop-out
dullard
egghead
egotist
epicure
eremite
faddist
fall guy
fanatic
fathead
flaneur
gabbler
gallant
glutton
gourmet
groupie
haggler
half-wit
hangdog
hard man
has-been
hellcat
hellier
heretic
hoodlum
hothead
hotspur
hustler
hyped up
infidel
Jezebel
Joe Soap
king pin
know-all
liberal
lie-abed
lounger
low brow
Luddite
lunatic
man's man
marxist
meddler
Mr Right
niggard
nut case
oddball
old fogy
old maid
outcast
paragon
parvenu
patriot
Paul Pry
peasant
playboy
prodigy
puritan
radical
recluse
ruffian
runaway
sad sack
saviour
sceptic
Scrooge
showman
show-off

CHARACTER TYPES

shyster
slacker
sponger
suspect
swinger
thinker
tippler
tosspot
traitor
trueman
twister
upstart
villain
vulture
wastrel
welcher
welsher
whipcat
windbag
wise guy
workshy
wrecker
absentee
aesthete
agitator
agnostic
alarmist
alter ego
altruist
anti-hero
antipope
apostate
banterer
beginner
betrayer
big noise
blighter
bluenose
Bohemian
braggart
busybody
carouser
cenobite
crackpot
criminal
deceiver
defector
derelict
dirty dog
do-gooder
drunkard
everyman
evildoer
feminist
fine lady
folk-hero
follower
front-man
funnyman
gadabout
gamester
gaolbird
gourmand
great man
groupnik
hanger-on
hectorer
hedonist
highbrow
hooligan
humorist
idolater
imbecile
impostor
innocent
intruder
jabberer
jailbird
jawsmith
John Bull
laid-back
lame duck
layabout
live wire
lone wolf
low lifer
machismo
man hater
martinet
Napoleon
nepotist
nihilist
nuisance
numskull
objector
offender
optimist
outsider
pacifist
paleface
paramour
parasite
partisan
penitent
perjurer
plebeian
poltroon
poor soul

popinjay
prattler
quackery
quisling
rakehell
renegade
romancer
romantic
saucebox
scalawag
skinhead
slattern
somebody
sorehead
spitfire
stranger
swindler
sybarite
tell|tale
theorist
tightwad
truckler
turncoat
two|timer
underdog
vagabond
whizz|kid
wiseacre
wise|fool
accessory
adulterer
adversary
alcoholic
aunt|sally
bacchanal
barbarian
battle|axe
Bluebeard
blusterer
boy|wonder
careerist
career|man
character
charlatan
chatterer
chiseller
churchman
comforter
consenter
coughdrop
dark|horse
defeatist
defrauder
demagogue
desperado
dignitary
dissenter
dogmatist
dolly|bird
early|bird
eccentric
Edwardian
exploiter
extravert
extrovert
family|man
favourite
fire|eater
flag|waver
fossicker
free|agent
gentleman
good|mixer
gradgrind
greenhorn
harebrain
Hellenist
honest|man
honour|man
hypocrite
ignoramus
inamorata
inebriate
introvert
jet|setter
ladies|man
late|riser
lazybones
libertine
log|roller
lost|sheep
loudmouth
man|of|mark
man|of|note
masochist
nonentity
non|smoker
odd|man|out
pacemaker
patrician
Pecksniff
peculator
persuader
pessimist
plutocrat
poetaster
poison|pen
pothunter

pretender
queer|fish
racketeer
reprobate
roisterer
roughneck
Samaritan
sassenach
scapegoat
scoundrel
screwball
simpleton
skylarker
slowcoach
sob-sister
socialist
socialite
star|pupil
strongman
sundowner
suppliant
swaggerer
swellhead
sycophant
tactician
termagant
terrorist
underling
visionary
warmonger
womanizer
womenfolk
wrongdoer
xenophobe
young|fogy
adventurer
aficionado
anglophile
anglophobe
antagonist
aristocrat
benefactor
best|friend
Big|Brother
blackguard
black|sheep
bobbysoxer
bootlicker
career|girl
chatterbox
chauvinist
church-goer
Cinderella
confidante
daydreamer
delinquent
Don|Quixote
drug|addict
Dutch|uncle
enthusiast
fly-by-night
fuddy-duddy
gastronome
gentlefolk
girl|Friday
girl|friend
gold-digger
goody-goody
human|wreck
jackanapes
Jesus|freak
lady-killer
lawbreaker
left-winger
lotus-eater
malefactor
malingerer
man|of|straw
mastermind
matchmaker
merrymaker
Methuselah
middlebrow
militarist
misogynist
mountebank
ne'er-do-well
non-starter
old|soldier
past|master
peeping|Tom
philistine
pragmatist
prima|donna
psychopath
recidivist
ringleader
secularist
shoplifter
smart|aleck
sneak|thief
social|lion
spoilsport
squanderer
street|arab
sugar-daddy
taskmaster
time-server

troglodyte
tub-thumper
upper crust
utopianist
vacillator
vegetarian
wallflower
well-wisher
wine-bibber
woman-hater
young blood
Young Fogey
adventuress
animal lover
beachcomber
Bible reader
blackmailer
blue-eyed boy
braggadocio
cattle thief
centenarian
chain smoker
cheese-parer
Cinemascope
close friend
common scold
connoisseur
country girl
deadly enemy
dipsomaniac
eager beaver
femme fatale
francophile
francophobe
freethinker
gallows bird
gate-crasher
grave robber
guttersnipe
hard drinker
helping hand
homo sapiens
human nature
imperialist
lickspittle
lifemanship
line-shooter
living image
man of genius
materialist
mental giant
merry-andrew
misanthrope
name-dropper
nationalist
nosey-parker
opportunist
personality
pettifogger
philanderer
prodigal son
quacksalver
rapscallion
rationalist
reactionary
reparteeist
right-winger
Sabbatarian
scaremonger
self-made man
simple Simon
sleep-walker
soliloquist
spendthrift
stool pigeon
suffragette
sympathiser
teacher's pet
teeny-bopper
town-dweller
Walter Mitty
artful dodger
awkward squad
babysnatcher
backwoodsman
bible-thumper
blue stocking
bobby-dazzler
carpet-knight
collaborator
Colonel Blimp
conservative
cosmopolitan
doppelganger
eavesdropper
featherbrain
flittermouse
flower people
grey eminence
hair-splitter
headshrinker
humanitarian
kleptomaniac
lounge-lizard
mad as a hatter
man-about-town
modest violet
moneygrubber

one upmanship
poor relation
prevaricator
right hand man
rolling stone
rough diamond
salvationist
scatterbrain
single person
somnambulist
street urchin
stuffed shirt
swashbuckler
transgressor
transvestite
troublemaker
truce breaker
ugly customer
ugly duckling
woolgatherer
absence of mind
accident prone
Anglo American
angry young man
anthropomorph
anthropophagi
antichristian
anythingarian
apple pie order
barbarousness
bare faced liar
bargain hunter
best of friends
clapperclawer
clishmaclaver
companionship
compassionate
conceitedness
condescending
condescension
conscientious
consternation
controversial
country cousin
courteousness
deserving poor
determination
dishonourable
dispassionate
distinguished
double crosser
double dealing
dyed in the wool
egocentricity
egotistically
excitableness
exhibitionism
exhibitionist
foolhardiness
fool's paradise
forgetfulness
fortune hunter
fresh air fiend
frivolousness
gentle hearted
gentlemanlike
gentlewomanly
go as you please
good influence
good Samaritan
go the whole hog
grandiloquent

13 LETTERS

hair-splitting
half-heartedly
heartlessness
hole-and-corner
hunger marcher
hypercritical
hypochondriac
idiosyncratic
impassiveness
imperturbable
impetuousness
impulsiveness
inconsiderate
inconsistency
incorruptible
indefatigable
individualist
infant prodigy
in honour bound
insignificant
insubordinate
intransigence
introspective
irrepressible
irresponsible
lackadaisical
Lady Bountiful
latchkey child
laughing stock
long suffering
lunatic fringe
misadventurer
misanthropist
mischief maker
over-confident
overcredulous
overexcitable
overindulgent
pain in the neck
panic-stricken
penny-pinching
perspicacious
plain-speaking
procrastinate
prophet of doom
pusillanimous
quiet as a mouse
ray of sunshine
remittance man
riotous living
rough-and-ready
rough customer
round the twist
sanctimonious
scandalmonger
self-appointed
self-approving
self-assertive
self-conceited
self-conscious
self-deceitful
self-important
self-indulgent
self-satisfied
sense of humour
sense of values
sharp practice
short-tempered
sign the pledge
sit on the fence
smooth-tongued
soap-box orator

CHARACTER TYPES

sober as a judge
social climber
social outcast
sophisticated
soul-searching
stick-in-the-mud
stiff upper lip
supercritical
superstitious
sweet-tempered
swelled-headed
swollen-headed
sycophantical
temperamental
tender-hearted
tongue in cheek
unadventurous
uncomplaining
uncooperative
undisciplined
unenlightened
ungentlemanly
unimaginative
unintelligent
unsympathetic
untrustworthy
unworkmanlike
well-respected
well-thought-of
wheeler dealer
willing helper
willing worker
auto-suggestion
back-scratching
back-seat driver
beat generation
changeableness
characteristic
class-conscious
claustrophobia
common or garden
credibility gap
crocodile tears
culture vulture
disciplinarian
dog in the manger
doubting Thomas
easy come, easy go
factitiousness
fastidiousness
fish out of water
flower children
formidableness
free-spokenness
frolicsomeness
full of mischief
glutton for work
good-for-nothing
gracious living
hell for leather
high-handedness
high-mindedness
high-principled
holier-than-thou
hot-air merchant
hypersensitive
impressionable
inveterate liar
jealous husband
larger than life
Macchiavellian
male chauvinist

man in the street
man-in-the-street
man of many parts
man of substance
man of the moment
mods and rockers
nasty bit of work
nimble-fingered
obstructionist
overscrupulous
petit bourgeois
philanthropist
pleased as Punch
pleasure-seeker
pluck up courage
practical joker
presence of mind
public nuisance
public-spirited
rich as a Croesus
salt of the earth
scatter-brained
self-advertiser
self-controlled
self-interested
self-sufficient
sensationalist
sentimentalist
someone or other
straight as a die
supersensitive
tail-end Charlie
terror-stricken
three bottle man
total abstainer
traditionalist
troubleshooter
unconventional
unenterprising
universal aunts
unostentatious
unprofessional
ambulance-chaser
ancestor-worship
antivivisection
awkward customer
bats in the belfry
birds of a feather
connoisseurship
conservationist
conventionalist
conversationist
cool as a cucumber
cryptocommunist
cuckoo in the nest
dual personality
eternal triangle
flibbertigibbet
good-naturedness
half-heartedness
hope against hope
humanitarianism
little Englander
middle-of-the-raod
model of industry
non-professional
paragon of virtue
philanthropical
pillar of society
platitudinarian
quite a character
ready and willing

CHARACTER TYPES

second|childhood
self-considering
self-destructive
self-opinionated
sensation-monger
snake|in|the|grass
stable|companion
stage-door|Johnny
stand|on|ceremony
stark,|staring|mad
strong,|silent|man
thorn|in|the|flesh
too|clever|by|half
to|the|manner|born
tower|of|strength
unaccommodating
uncommunicative
undemonstrative
under-privileged
undistinguished
unprepossessing
unsportsmanlike
unstatesmanlike
well-intentioned
whited|sepulchre
with|bated|breath
yours|faithfully

Chemical Sciences

pH	muon	borax	oxide	action
dye	neon	boron	ozone	air|gas
gas	norm	dregs	poise	alkali
gel	otto	ester	radon	amylum
ion	rust	ether	resin	anneal
lab	soda	ethyl	rosin	atomic
sol	zein	flask	salts	barite
acid	agene	fluid	toxin	barium
alum	agent	hexad	uredo	baryta
amyl	alkyl	inert	U-tube	beaker
atom	amide	latex	vinyl	boffin
buna	amine	leach	xenon	borate
calx	argon	monad	xylem	bunsen
dyad	assay	nitre	yeast	calcar
etna	basic	nylon	acetic	calxes

carbon
carboy
casein
cerate
cerium
citric
cobalt
curium
decane
dilute
diplon
dry|ice
erbium
ethane
filter
funnel
fusion
galena
gas|jar
gluten
halide
helium
indium
inulin
iodide
iodine
isomer
ketone
labile
litmus
lutein
lysine
matter
methyl
natron
niacin
octane
osmium
oxygen
pectin
pepsin
petrol
phenol
poison
potash
radium
reflux
retort
ribose
saline
silica
sinter
sodium
spirit
stable
starch
symbol
theory
thoron
toxoid
tripod
vapour
xylose
acetate
acetone
acetose
acid|dye
acidity
acyclic
aerosol
alchemy
alcohol
alembic
amalgam
ammonia
ampoule
aniline
antacid
arsenic
atrazin
balance
bell|jar
benzene
bismuth
bitumen
boiling
bromide
bromine
burette
cadmium
caesium
calomel
capsule
carbide
chemism
chemist
citrate
coal|tar
colloid
corrode
crystal
cuprite
cyanide
deposit
dextrin
dialyse
dibasic
diluent
dioxide
element
essence
eutropy
exhaust
ferment
formula
gallium
geogony
geology
glucose
hafnium
halogen
holmium
hydrate
hydride
hyperon
iridium
isotope
isotopy
isotron
keratin
krypton
lacquer
lactate
lactose
lanolin
leucine
lipoids
lithium
matrass
melanin
mercury
metamer
methane
micelle

CHEMICAL SCIENCES

mixture
muonium
niobium
nitrate
nitride
nitrite
nonacid
nuclide
osmosis
oxalate
oxidant
oxidase
oxonium
oxyacid
pentose
peptide
reagent
rhenium
rhodium
science
sebacic
silicon
solvent
spatula
spireme
spirits
subacid
sucrose
sulphur
tarnish
terbium
terpene
thermal
thorium
thulium
tinfoil
titrate
toluene
tritium
uranide
uranium
valence
valency
vinegar
vitriol
yttrium
zymurgy
acid bath
acid salt
acid test
actinism
actinium
actinoid
activate
activity
additive
agar agar
alcahest
aldehyde
alkahest
alkaline
amandine
ammonium
analogue
analyser
analysis
analytic
antimony
arsenate
arsenide
asbestos
astatine
Bakelite
basicity
benzoate
biochemy
bivalent
carbonyl
catalyst
catalyse
charcoal
chemical
chemurgy
chlorate
chloride
chlorine
chlorite
chromate
chromium
cleveite
cobalite
cohesion
collagen
compound
copperas
crucible
cucurbit
cyanogen
dendrite
dextrose
dialysis
dialytic
dilution
diplogen
divalent
docimasy
dye stuff
emulsion
equation
ethylene
europium
exhalant
filtrate
fluoride
fluorine
formulae
francium
gasoline
gelatine
globulin
glutelin
glutenin
glycogen
honey dew
hydrogen
isomeric
isoteric
isotopic
kerosene
leaching
lecithin
levulose
litharge
lutetium
magnesia
marsh gas
melamine
mercuric
miscible
molecule
monoxide
nicotine
nitrogen
nobelium

non|metal
oxidizer
pedology
pentosan
peroxide
phenolic
phosgene
plastics
platinum
polonium
polyacid
quantity
reactant
reaction
reactive
research
resinoid
rheology
rubidium
samarium
scandium
sediment
selenium
silicate
silicone
solation
solution
spagyric
sulphate
sulphide
sulphite
tantalum
tartrate
test|tube
thallium
tincture
titanium
tribasic
trioxide
tungsten
unstable
uric|acid
vanadium
volatile
absorbent
actinides
alchemist
allotropy
americium
amino|acid
anglesite
anhydride
apparatus
aqua|regia
aspirator
atmolysis
atmometer
autoclave
barricade
basic|salt
berkelium
beryllium
bivalence
bivariant
boric|acid
carbonate
carbonize
catalysis
catalytic
celluloid
cellulose
chemiatry
chemurgic
colloidal
co|polymer
cork|borer
corrosion
covalence
covalency
desiccant
detergent
detonator
deuterium
developer
dimorphic
dispenser
distiller
elastomer
elemental
emanation
erythrite
erythrose
fulminate
fungicide
galactose
germanium
glucoside
glutinous
glycerine
histidine
homocycle
hydrazine
hydrolist
hydrolyte
hydroxide
inhibitor
isinglass
isocyclic

isomerism
lanthanum
magnesium
malic|acid
manganese
metalloid
metameric
neodymium
neptunium
nitration
oxidation
palladium
petroleum
phosphate
phosphide
phosphite
photogene
plutonium
polybasic
polyester
polythene
potassium
prolamine
protamine
pyrolysis
pyrometer
raffinose
reservoir
ruthenium
saccharin
saltpetre
scientist
still|room
strontium
sulphacid
synthesis

synthetic
teleology
tellurite
tellurium
tetroxide
titration
univalent
verdigris
virginium
viscosity
ytterbium
zirconium
alkalinity
alpha|helix
amylaceous
antifreeze
antimatter
aqua|fortis
ballistite
biochemics
biochemist
bisulphate
bisulphide
calcareous
calciferol
cellophane
chloroform
chrome-alum
citric|acid
coalescent
cyanic|acid
decinormal
decompound
denaturant
dichromate
disulphate

disulphide
dysprosium
elementary
emulsifier
equivalent
estimation
eudiometer
experiment
fibrinogen
fluorotype
formic|acid
gadolinium
gallic|acid
heavy|water
high-octane
homocyclic
hydrolysis
hydrolytic
hypothesis
immiscible
ion|counter
ionization
laboratory
lactic|acid
lead|glance
metamerism
molybdenum
monovalent
neutralize
nitric|acid
nucleonium
octavalent
oxalic|acid
phlogiston
phosphorus
photolysis

picric acid
promethium
rare earths
reactivity
resolution
saccharate
saccharose
scientific
sodium lamp
solubility
sorbic acid
sulphation
suspension
technetium
technology
trivalence
tryptophan
univalence
viscometer
wash bottle
water still
Winchester
yield point
zero valent
accelerator
acidulation
acrylic acid
agglomerate
arsenic acid
atomic table
atomologist
beaker flask
benzene ring
benzoic acid
bicarbonate
brittleness
butyric acid
calcination
calibration
californium
calorimeter
calorimetry
carbonation
chloric acid
chromic acid
closed chain
cobalt bloom
constituent
contaminate
dehydration
dissolution
double helix
endothermal
evaporation
filter paper
fume cabinet
gas detector
haloid acids
heptavalent
heterocycle
hydrocarbon
hydrogen ion
hydrogenoid
impermeable
interaction
lanthanides
lipoprotein
litmus paper
mendelevium
mensuration
monovalence
neutralizer
niacinamide
opalescence
oxidization
oxygen meter
pectization
pentavalent
peptization
phosphorous
pitchblende
plasmolysis
polymorphic
polyvalence
proteolysis
prussic acid
quantometer
quicksilver
radiocarbon
retort stand
rule of thumb
sal ammoniac
sal volatile
sub critical
technocracy
tetravalent
transuranic
tripod stand
volatile oil
xanthophyll
acceleration
acid solution
aspartic acid
atomic theory
atomic weight
Avogadro's law
barrier cream
bicarbonates

biochemistry
breathalyzer
bunsen|burner
burette|stand
carbolic|acid
carbonic|acid
chemical|bond
chemical|pump
chlorination
chlorous|acid
cobalt|glance
constituents
deactivation
deionization
deliquescent
dissociation
distillation
effervescent
experimental
ferrous|oxide
flocculation
fluorocarbon
fluorography
fume|cupboard
geochemistry
glutamic|acid
glycoprotein
gram|molecule
heterocyclic
hydrocarbons
hydrogen|atom
hydrostatics
iatrochemist
inactivation
ion|exchanger
liquefaction
liquid|oxygen
lysergic|acid
melting|point
mesomorphous
microbalance
microburette
microelement
minor|element
multivalence
muriatic|acid
nicotinamide
nitromethane
oil|of|vitriol
oxycellulose
oxychromatin
pangamic|acid
permanganate
permeability
photochemist
praseodymium
quadrivalent
radiochemist
radioelement
radioisotope
radionuclide
reactivation
spark|chamber
thermocouple
transuranian
zoochemistry
carbon|dioxide
carbonisation
chain|reaction
compatibility
corrosiveness
decomposition

13/15 LETTERS

demonstration
diffusion tube
dissolubility
hydrochloride
hydrosulphide
hydrosulphite
hydroxylamine
nitro compound
nitrogen cycle
periodic table
petrochemical
precipitation
radioactivity
reducing agent
sulphuric acid
carbon monoxide
distilled water
electrochemist
microchemistry
nitroglycerine
petroleum jelly
phosphorescent
photochemistry
photosynthesis
surgical spirit
biogeochemistry
decarbonisation
electrochemical
molecular weight
nitro derivative
phosphorescence
trinitrotoluene

Cinema and Television

TV
act
BBC
cue
fan
ITV
set
cast
crew
film
hero
mike
part
play
plot
role
shot
show
star
unit
actor
cable
drama
enact
extra
flick
movie
odeon
oscar
radio
scene
telly
video
camera
Ceefax
cinema
comedy
critic
make up
movies
rushes
screen
script
serial
series
sit com
studio
talkie
TV show
actress
cartoon
compere

CINEMA AND TELEVISION

feature
film|set
flicker
heroine
musical
network
perform
phone|in
pop|star
portray
present
produce
sponsor
tragedy
trailer
audience
bioscope
chat|show
Cinerama
comedian
director
festival
film|club
film|crew
film|star
fruit|pie
newsreel
pictures
premiere
producer
quiz|show
tape|deck
telecast
telefilm
blue|movie
broadcast

cameraman
character
direction
entertain
exhibitor
film|actor
film|extra
film|strip
flash|back
goggle|box
guest|star
interview
movie|goer
movie|show
movie|star
performer
photoplay
programme
projector
recording
rehearsal
soap|opera
spectacle
title|role
voice|over
commercial
crowd|scene
home|movies
horror|film
horse|opera
microphone
movie|actor
needle|time
newscaster
newsreader
on|location

performing
production
screenplay
silent film
television
the critics
broadcaster
credit title
documentary
echo chamber
entertainer
feature film
performance
picture show
radio caster
sound effect
talking film
academy award
cinéma vérité
clapperboard
film festival
picture house
scriptwriter
show business
silver screen
sound effects
technicolour
Chinese puzzle
cinematograph
cine projector
clapperboards
closed circuit
continuity man
entertainment
global village
motion picture
motion picture
Nouvelle Vague
picture palace
tape recording
telerecording
television set
videocassette
video recorder
book at bedtime, a
cinematography
continuity girl
feature picture
features editor
moving pictures
question master
supporting cast
supporting film
supporting part
supporting role
television play
Third Programme
animated cartoon
cable television
cinematographer
cinematographic
documentary film
French subtitles
peak viewing time
situation comedy
slapstick comedy
spot advertising

Cities

Baku
Bari
Bonn
Brno
Cork
Gifu
Giza
Graz
Homs
Hull
Ipoh
Kano
Kiel
Kiev
Kobe
Lima
Lodz
Nice
Omsk
Oran
Oslo
Riga
Rome
Accra
Adana
Amman
Basle
Basra
Belem

Berne
Bursa
Cairo
Chiba
Dacca
Davao
Delhi
Essen
Genoa
Gorky
Haifa
Halle
Hanoi
Izmir
Kabul
Kazan
Kyoto
Lagos
La|Paz
Leeds
Lyons
Malmo
Mecca
Miami
Milan
Mosul
Omaha
Osaka
Padua

Paris
Patna
Perth
Poona
Quito
Rabat
Sakai
Seoul
Sofia
Surat
Tampa
Tokyo
Tomsk
Tunis
Turin
Aachen
Abadan
Aleppo
Ankara
Asmara
Athens
Austin
Baroda
Beirut
Berlin
Bilbao
Bochum
Bogota
Bombay

Boston
Bremen
Cracow
Dallas
Dayton
Denver
Dublin
Dundee
Durban
El|Paso
Frunze
Fukoka
Fushun
Gdansk
Geneva
Harbin
Havana
Ibadan
Indore
Jaipur
Kanpur
Khulna
Kumasi
Lahore
Lisbon
London
Luanda
Lübeck
Lusaka

Madras
Madrid
Málaga
Małang
Manila
Moscow
Multan
Munich
Mysore
Nagpur
Nantes
Naples
Newark
Odessa
Oporto
Ottawa
Oxford
Peking
Penang
Poznan
Prague
Puebla
Quebec
Santos
Shiraz
St|Paul
Sydney
Tabriz
Taipei

6/8 LETTERS

Talinn
Toledo
Venice
Verona
Vienna
Warsaw
Zagreb
Zürich
Abidjan
Algiers
Antwerp
Atlanta
Baghdad
Bangkok
Barnaul
Belfast
Bologna
Brescia
Bristol
Buffalo
Caracas
Cardiff
Chengtu
Chicago
Cologne
Colombo
Córdoba
Corunna
Detroit
Donetsk
Dresden
Firenze
Foochow
Glasgow
Gwalior
Hamburg
Hanover
Houston
Irkutsk
Isfahan
Jakarta
Kalinin
Karachi
Kharkov
Kowloon
Kwangju
La Plata
Leipzig
Lucknow
Managua
Memphis
Messina
Mombasa
Nairobi
Nanking
Oakland
Palermo
Phoenix
Rangoon
Rosario
San Jose
San Juan
Santa Fe
Sapporo
Saratov
Seattle
Seville
Soochow
Stettin
St Louis
Taranto
Tbilisi
Teheran
Tel Aviv
Toronto
Trieste
Tripoli
Utrecht
Aberdeen
Adelaide
Amritsar
Auckland
Augsburg
Belgrade
Bordeaux
Bradford
Brasilia
Brisbane
Brussels
Budapest
Bulawayo
Cagliari
Calcutta
Campinas
Canberra
Capetown
Columbus
Coventry
Curitiba
Damascus
Dortmund
Duisburg
Edmonton
Florence
Gorlovka
Hague, The
Haiphong
Hamilton

CITIES

Hangchow
Helsinki
Honolulu
Istanbul
Katmandu
Katowice
Khartoum
Kingston
Kinshasa
Kumamoto
Kweiyang
Mandalay
Mannheim
Montreal
Murmansk
Nagasaki
Peshawar
Plymouth
Portland
Port|Said
Pretoria
Pyongang
Richmond
Salonika
San|Diego
Santiago
Sao|Paulo
Sarajevo
Shanghai
Sholapur
Srinagar
Tashkent
Tientsin
Toulouse
Winnipeg
Yokohama
Ahmedabad
Allahabad
Amagasaki
Amsterdam
Archangel
Asahikawa
Astrakhan
Baltimore
Bangalore
Barcelona
Brunswick
Bucharest
Cambridge
Cartagena
Chengchow
Chihuahua
Cleveland
Des|Moines
Edinburgh
Fort|Worth
Frankfurt
Guayaquil
Hamamatsu
Hiroshima
Hyderabad
Jerusalem
Karlsruhe
Krasnodar
Kuibyshev
Kwangchow
Las|Palmas
Leicester
Leningrad
Liverpool
Magdeburg
Maracaibo
Marrakesh
Melbourne
Milwaukee
Nuremberg
Reykjavik
Rotterdam
Salisbury
Samarkand
Saragossa
Sheffield
Singapore
Stockholm
Stuttgart
Vancouver
Volgograd
Wuppertal
Addis|Ababa
Alexandria
Baton|Rouge
Birmingham
Bratislava
Canterbury
Casablanca
Chittagong
Cincinnati
Coimbatore
Copenhagen
Düsseldorf
Gothenburg
Jamshedpur
Kansas|City
Krivoi|Roig
Los|Angeles
Louisville
Manchester
Marseilles

10/14 LETTERS

Mexico City
Montevideo
New Orleans
Nottingham
Panama City
Pittsburgh
Portsmouth
Rawalpindi
Sacramento
San Antonio
Strasbourg
Sunderland
Sverdlovsk
Tananarive
Valparaiso
Washington
Wellington
Baranquilla
Buenos Aires
Chelyabinsk
Dar-es-Salaam
Guadalajara
Kuala Lumpur
Mar del Plata
New York City
Novosibirsk
Pondicherry
Rostov-on-Don
San Salvador
Southampton
Vladivostok
Barquisimeto
Bloemfontein
Braunschweig
Indianapolis
Jacksonville
Johannesburg
Magnitogorsk
Oklahoma City
Philadelphia
Port-au-Prince
Rio de Janeiro
Salt Lake City
San Francisco
Santo Domingo
Stoke-on-Trent
Gelsenkirchen
Guatemala City
Karl-Marx-Stadt
Port Elizabeth
Shihkiachwang
Wolverhampton
Dnepropetrovsk

Clothes

alb
bag
bib
boa
bob
bra
bun
cap
fez
fob
fop
fur

CLOTHES

hat	drag	muff	warp	cymar	moire
hem	duck	mule	wear	dandy	motif
kid	elan	peak	weft	denim	mufti
mac	felt	poke	welt	derby	mules
nap	fold	pump	woof	dhoti	nappy
net	frog	rags	wool	drape	ninon
pin	gamp	ring	wrap	dress	nylon
rag	garb	robe	yarn	drill	Orlon
rig	gear	ruff	yoke	ducks	paint
sox	gilt	sack	A-line	ephod	pants
tab	gore	saga	amice	fanon	parka
tag	gown	sari	ao dai	fichu	patch
tie	haik	sark	apron	flare	patte
wig	heel	sash	array	flash	pique
zip	hood	seal	badge	frill	pixie
Afro	hoop	seam	baize	frock	plaid
alba	hose	shoe	bands	gauze	plait
bags	hyke	silk	bangs	get-up	pleat
band	hype	skip	batik	glove	plume
bang	jean	slip	beard	grego	plush
bead	jupe	sock	beret	guimp	point
belt	kepi	sole	blond	guise	print
bias	kilt	stud	blues	gunny	pumps
boot	knot	suit	boots	habit	purse
brim	lace	talc	braid	jabot	queue
cape	lame	tick	busby	jeans	rayon
clog	lawn	tile	chain	jupon	robes
coat	list	toga	chaps	lapel	romal
coif	lock	togs	check	Levis	rumal
comb	mask	torc	cloak	linen	sable
cope	maud	tuck	clogs	lisle	sabot
cord	maxi	tutu	cotta	lungi	sagum
cowl	mini	vamp	crape	lurex	satin
cuff	mink	veil	crash	manta	scarf
curl	mitt	vent	crepe	manto	scrim
dart	mode	vest	crown	model	serge

shako	V-neck	brogan	denier	infula
shawl	voile	brogue	diaper	insole
sheer	waist	brolly	dickey	jacket
shift	wamus	buckle	dimity	jemima
shirt	watch	burlap	dirndl	jerkin
shoes	weave	buskin	dittos	jersey
simar	wigan	bustle	dolman	jumper
skein	woven	button	duffel	kaftan
skirt	achkan	byssus	ermine	kagool
smock	afghan	caftan	fabric	kimono
snood	alnage	calash	facial	kirtle
spats	alpaca	calico	facing	lappet
specs	angora	camise	faille	lining
stays	anklet	canvas	fallal	livery
stock	anorak	capote	fannel	locket
stole	armlet	casque	fascia	madras
stuff	attire	castor	fedora	magyar
style	basque	cestus	feeder	make-up
suede	bauble	chimer	fillet	mantle
tabby	beaver	chintz	finery	mantua
tails	bertha	chiton	fox-fur	marcel
talma	biggin	choker	frills	melton
tammy	bikini	chopin	fringe	minium
terry	blazer	cilice	gaiter	mitten
thrum	blouse	cloche	galosh	mob-cap
tiara	boater	coatee	gamash	mohair
topee	bodice	collar	garter	moreen
toque	bodkin	collet	girdle	muslin
train	bolero	corset	goatee	nankin
tress	bonnet	cotton	greave	needle
trews	bootee	cravat	gusset	nylons
tulle	bouclé	crewel	hairdo	outfit
tunic	bowler	curler	hankie	panama
tweed	bow-tie	Dacron	hat-box	parure
twill	braces	damask	hatpin	patent
upper	briefs	dapper	helmet	peplos

CLOTHES

peplum
peruke
pocket
pomade
pompom
poncho
pongee
poplin
powder
raglan
rebato
reefer
revers
ribbon
rigout
rochet
roller
ruffle
sacque
samite
sandal
sarong
sateen
scarab
semmit
serape
sheath
shoddy
shorts
shroud
ski|cap
slacks
sleeve
slip-on
sun|hat
switch

tabard
talcum
tartan
tassle
tettix
thread
tiepin
tights
tin|hat
tippet
tissue
toecap
tongue
top|hat
topper
torque
toupee
tricot
trilby
trunks
T-shirt
tucker
turban
tussah
tusser
tuxedo
tweeds
ulster
unisex
uppers
velure
velvet
waders
wallet
wampus
whites

wimple
woolly
zoster
Acrilan
à|la|mode
alamode
apparel
armband
armhole
baboosh
baldric
bandana
bandbox
bandeau
bath|oil
batiste
beading
belcher
biretta
bombast
brocade
buckram
bunting
burdash
burnous
bycoket
cagoule
calotte
cambric
capuche
cassock
casuals
cat's|eye
cat|suit
chamois
chapeau

chaplet
chechia
chemise
cheviot
chevron
chiffon
chignon
chimere
chlamys
chopine
civvies
clobber
clothes
cockade
compact
corsage
costume
couture
coxcomb
crewcut
crochet
cuculla
culotte
doeskin
doublet
drawers
dress|up
droguet
drugget
elastic
falsies
fashion
feather
felt|hat
ferrule
fig|leaf

filibeg
fitting
flannel
flounce
foulard
freckle
frocked
frogged
fur coat
fustian
gaiters
garment
gingham
girasol
glasses
grogram
G-string
guipure
gumboot
gym slip
haircut
hairnet
hairpin
handbag
hatband
hemline
hessian
high hat
hip boot
homburg
hosiery
jaconet
jaegers
kilt pin
layette
leather
leghorn
leotard
loafers
long bob
Mae West
malines
maniple
manteau
manteel
mascara
Mechlin
modesty
modiste
monocle
mozetta
mudpack
muffler
nankeen
necktie
New Look
nightie
oil silk
oilskin
organdy
organza
orphrey
outsize
overall
Oxfords
padding
paenula
page-boy
paisley
pajamas
paletot
pallium
panache
pannier
panties
parasol
partlet
pattern
pegtops
pelisse
pendant
percale
perfume
peridot
periwig
petasus
pigskin
pigtail
pillbox
pin curl
pith hat
porkpie
puttees
pyjamas
raiment
ringlet
rompers
rosette
rubbers
rug gown
sacking
sagathy
sandals
sarafan
selvage
shampoo
shingle
silk hat
singlet
skimmer
slicker
soft hat
soutane
spencer
sporran
stammel
stetson
sun suit
surcoat
surtout
swaddle
sweater
tabaret
taffeta
taffety
tarbush
tatters
tatting
tea gown
textile
texture
ticking
tiffany
tile hat
tonsure
top boot
topcoat
top hose
topknot
torchon
tricorn
trinket
tunicle
turn-ups

CLOTHES

twinset
undress
uniform
veiling
velours
webbing
wellies
worsted
yashmak
aigrette
appliqué
Ascot|tie
babouche
Balmoral
barathea
basquine
bath|cube
bathrobe
bearskin
bedsocks
birretta
black|tie
bloomers
boat|neck
bobbinet
body|suit
bongrace
boot-lace
bouffant
braiding
brass-hat
breeches
brocatel
buckskin
burberry
bustline
calyptra
camisole
capeline
capuchin
cardigan
cashmere
Celanese
chaperon
chasuble
chenille
cheverel
ciclaton
cincture
cingulum
cloth|cap
clothing
coiffure
cold|wave
corduroy
corselet
cosmetic
creepers
cretonne
crew|neck
crush|hat
culottes
dalmatic
day|dress
disguise
dress-tie
drilling
drop|curl
dunce|cap
dust|coat
Dutch|cap
ear-muffs
elflocks
ensemble
Eton|crop
Eton|suit
eyeshade
face-lift
face-pack
fair|isle
fastener
fatigues
fillibeg
fish-tail
flannels
fob|watch
fontange
fool's|cap
footwear
frippery
froufrou
furbelow
fur|stole
galoshes
gamashes
gambados
gambeson
gauntlet
glad|rags
gold|lamé
gossamer
grey|hair
gridelin
guernsey
gym|pants
gym|shoes
gym|tunic
hair|band
hairline
half-boot
half-hose
hand-knit
hat-guard
headband
headgear
headwear
high|heel
himation
hipsters
homespun
hot|pants
inch|tape
jackboot
Jacquard
jodhpurs
kerchief
kiss|curl
knickers
knitwear
leggings
leotards
lingerie
lip|brush
lip|rouge
lip|salve
lipstick
mackinaw
manicure
mantelet
mantilla
material
moccasin
moleskin
mourning

muscadin
mustache
nail|file
nainsook
near|silk
neckband
neckline
negligee
nightcap
nose|ring
oilcloth
oilskins
opera|hat
overalls
overcoat
pabouche
paduasoy
pedicure
peignoir
pelerine
perruque
philabeg
pinafore
play|suit
plimsoll
pochette
polka|dot
polo|neck
pomander
ponyskin
pony|tail
postiche
pullover
pure|silk
quilting
rag|trade
raincoat
red|sable
reticule
sandshoe
scanties
scapular
sealskin
seamless
Shantung
shirring
shirting
shirt|pin
shoehorn
shoelace
shoe|tree
short|bob
shot|silk
sideburn
side|vent
siege|cap
ski|boots
ski|pants
skullcap
slipover
slippers
smocking
snap|brim
sneakers
snub|nose
sombrero
spit|curl
stickpin
stocking
straw|hat
streamer
subucula
surplice
swaddled
swim|suit
taglioni
tail|coat
tapestry
tarboosh
tarlatan
Terylene
Thai|silk
toilette
top|boots
trimming
trot|cozy
trousers
tweezers
two|piece
umbrella
vestment
wardrobe
war|paint
whiskers
white|tie
wig|block
woollens
wristlet
zoot|suit
Alice|band
astrakhan
baby|linen
balaclava
baldachin
ball|dress
bath|salts
bed|jacket
billycock

CLOTHES

blue|jeans
bobbin|net
bombasine
bowler|hat
brassiere
breast|pin
Breton|hat
broadloom
bush|shirt
calamanco
camel|coat
camel|hair
caparison
cap|in|hand
cap|sleeve
cassimere
chantilly
chevelure
China|silk
chinstrap
coat-frock
coat-tails
cocked|hat
cold|cream
comforter
corduroys
cosmetics
crinoline
Cuban|heel
cuff-links
décolleté
demob|suit
deodorant
djellabah
dog-collar
drainpipe
drape|suit
dress|coat
dress|ring
dress|suit
duffel|bag
dungarees
epaulette
eye|shadow
face|cream
false-face
farandine
filoselle
fingering
floss|silk
forage|cap
frock|coat
full|dress
full|skirt
gabardine
gaberdine
georgette
girandole
gold|watch
great|coat
Greek|lace
grenadine
grosgrain
hairbrush
hair|cloth
hairpiece
hair|shirt
hand|cream
headdress
headpiece
high|stock
hip|pocket
hoop|skirt
horsehair
housecoat
huckaback
in|fashion
Inverness
jockey|cap
Juliet|cap
kick|pleat
kid|gloves
kirby|grip
knee-socks
lambswool
linenette
loincloth
longcloth
longcoats
lorgnette
millinery
miniskirt
model|gown
moustache
muckender
mustachio
nauticals
neckcloth
neckpiece
nightgown
nightwear
nun's|habit
off|the|peg
overdress
overshoes
overskirt
Panama|hat
pantalets

9/10 LETTERS

Paris doll
pea jacket
peaked cap
percaline
petersham
petticoat
phillibeg
pinstripe
pixie hood
plus-fours
point lace
polo shirt
pompadour
pourpoint
press stud
ready-made
redingote
Roman lace
round neck
sack dress
safety pin
sailcloth
sailor hat
school cap
school hat
scoop neck
separates
sharkskin
sheepskin
shirt-band
shirt-stud
shirt-tail
shovel hat
shower cap
sideburns
siren suit
ski-jacket
ski-jumper
skin-tight
sloppy Joe
slouch hat
snowshoes
solitaire
sou'wester
sphendone
spun rayon
steenkirk
stitching
stockinet
stomacher
strapless
sun bonnet
sun helmet
swansdown
sweatband
swing curl
tarpaulin
toilet bag
towelling
track suit
trousseau
tube dress
undervest
underwear
urchin cut
velveteen
victor'ine
waistband
waistcoat
waistline
war bonnet
wedge heel
whalebone
wrap-round
wristband
zucchetto
after-shave
all the rage
ankle socks
astringent
Balbriggan
ballet shoe
bathing cap
beauty spot
Berlin wool
black dress
bobbed hair
bobbin lace
bobbysocks
boiler suit
boudoir cap
bovver boot
broadcloth
bubble-bath
bush jacket
buttonhole
button-hook
camel's hair
cap and gown
chaparajos
chatelaine
chevesaile
chinchilla
claw-hammer
coat hanger
coat of mail
collarette
collar-stud

CLOTHES

college cap
cossack hat
cotton wool
court dress
court shoes
covert coat
cummerbund
curling pin
dentifrice
deshabille
dinner gown
dishabille
double chin
drainpipes
dressing up
dressmaker
dress shirt
duster coat
embroidery
emery board
empire line
Eton collar
Eton jacket
evening bag
eyeglasses
face powder
false teeth
fancy dress
fascinator
fearnought
feather boa
fitted coat
flak jacket
foundation
fourchette
fustanella

Geneva gown
grass skirt
habit cloth
hair ribbon
half kirtle
halter neck
hand lotion
headsquare
hook and eye
hop sacking
hugmetight
jersey silk
jersey wool
lappet head
life jacket
lounge suit
lover's knot
mackintosh
maquillage
marcel wave
masquerade
mess jacket
monk's cloth
monk's habit
mousseline
nail polish
needlecord
nightdress
nightshirt
old clothes
overblouse
Oxford bags
Oxford ties
pantaloons
Paris model
party dress

persiennes
picture hat
pillow lace
pin cushion
pith helmet
plastic mac
poke bonnet
powder puff
print dress
puff sleeve
rabbitskin
riding hood
romper suit
roquelaure
rubber sole
sailor suit
scalloping
scatter pin
scratch wig
seersucker
shaving kit
shirtdress
shirt frill
shirtfront
shoe buckle
silhouette
silver lamé
ski sweater
sleeveless
smock frock
smoking cap
solar topee
spectacles
sports coat
sport shirt
sports suit

sportswear
square-neck
suede shoes
Sunday best
sunglasses
suspenders
sweat shirt
tailor-made
terry cloth
the cap fits
threadbare
tight skirt
toiletries
toilet soap
toothbrush
toothpaste
trench coat
turtle neck
underlinen
underpants
undershirt
underskirt
upper-stock
vanity case
virgin knot
wampum belt
watch-chain
watchstrap
waterproof
Wellington
widow's peak
Windsor tie
wing collar
wrap-around
wraprascal
wrist watch
aiguillette
alexandrite
barrel dress
bathing suit
beauty sleep
bellbottoms
best clothes
black patent
black velvet
Blucher boot
blue clothes
boiled shirt
boutonniere
boxer shorts
button shoes
campaign hat
candy stripe
canvas shoes
cap and bells
casual shoes
cheesecloth
Chinese silk
clodhoppers
cloth of gold
contact lens
crash helmet
cutaway coat
dark glasses
décolletage
deerstalker
dinner dress
dreadnought
dress length
dressmaking
dress-shield
evening gown
farthingale
fine feather
flannelette
flared skirt
flying panel
formal dress
granny dress
grease paint
guipure lace
hand-me-downs
Harris tweed
herringbone
high fashion
hobble skirt
Indian shawl
kilted skirt
lacing shoes
lawn sleeves
leatherette
leg-of-mutton
leopardskin
marquisette
matinee coat
Mechlin lace
middy blouse
morning coat
morning gown
mortarboard
mutton chops
nail varnish
neckerchief
needle point
orangestick
overgarment
Oxford shoes
panty girdle

CLOTHES

Persian|lamb
Phrygian|cap
pilot|jacket
ready|to|wear
regimentals
riding|habit
school|dress
set-in|sleeve
shaving|soap
shawl|collar
shell|jacket
shirt-button
shock-headed
shoe|leather
shoulder|bag
Spanish|comb
spatterdash
stiff|collar
subcingulum
suede|gloves
Sunday|black
swagger|coat
swallowtail
tailor|tacks
tam-o'shanter
tennis|dress
tennis|shoes
toilet|water
tooth|powder
torchon|lace
trencher|cap
trouser|suit
walking|shoe
wash|leather
watch-pocket
watered|silk
white|collar
widow's|weeds
windbreaker
windcheater
Windsor|knot
wooden|shoes
work|clothes
woven|fabric
antigropelos
apron|strings
bathing|dress
bespectacled
bib|and|tucker
bicycle|clips
birthday|suit
bluestocking
body|stocking
brass|buttons
breast|pocket
brilliantine
business|suit
cap|of|liberty
cardinal's|hat
cavalry|twill
chastity|belt
chesterfield
chin|whiskers
clothes|brush
clothes-horse
collar|and|tie
college-scarf
combinations
crepe-de-Chine
crewel|needle
curling|tongs
dinner|jacket
divided|skirt
donkey|jacket
double|jersey
dressing|case
dressing|gown
dressing|room
dress|uniform
dropped|waist
duchesse|lace
duffel|jacket
Easter|bonnet
eau-de-Cologne
evening|cloak
evening|dress
evening|shoes
fashion|house
fashion|plate
fatigue|dress
flaxen|haired
football|boot
full|mourning
galligaskins
glass|slipper
golden-haired
haberdashery
hair|dressing
hair|restorer
half|mourning
handkerchief
haute|couture
Hessian|boots
hummel-bonnet
if|the|cap|fits
knee|breeches
knitting|wool
lightning|zip

lumberjacket
magyar sleeve
monkey jacket
morning dress
mousquetaire
nail clippers
nail scissors
night clothes
old-fashioned
out of fashion
Paisley shawl
Paris fashion
pedal-pushers
Penang lawyer
plain clothes
pressure-suit
Prince Albert
Princess line
raglan sleeve
set one's cap at
beauty parlour
camel-hair coat
carpet-slipper
casual clothes
cocktail dress
fashion parade
hacking-jacket
Highland dress
Inverness cape
lavender water
leather-jacket
made to measure
matinee jacket
patent leather
period costume
quizzing glass
shoulder strap
smoking jacket
sock-suspender
suspender-belt
underclothing
unfashionable
anti-perspirant
artificial silk
chest protector
cleansing cream
clerical collar
collar attached
double-breasted
evening clothes
fireman's helmet
fully fashioned
hobnailed boots
mandarin collar
off the shoulder
ostrich feather
pair of slippers
pair of trousers
pyjama trousers
riding-breeches
shooting-jacket
single-breasted
stocking stitch
tartan trousers
top-hat and tails
vanishing cream
wedding garment
winter woollies
working clothes
Balaclava helmet
civilian clothes
crease-resistant

CLOTHES

foundation|cream
fullˌbottomed|wig
highland|costume
outdoor|clothing
pair|of|stockings
regulation|dress
sheepskin|jacket
shrinkˌresistant
swallowˌtail|coat
swimming|costume
wellington|boots

Colours

dun	flame	cerise	emerald
red	green	cobalt	filemot
tan	helio	copper	gamboge
blue	henna	indigo	iron|red
buff	ivory	lustre	magenta
fawn	khaki	madder	new|blue
flam	lemon	maroon	old|blue
gold	lilac	modena	old|gold
grey	mauve	murrey	ruby|red
lake	ochre	orange	saffron
navy	peach	pastel	scarlet
pink	perse	purple	sea|blue
puce	rouge	reseda	sky|blue
rose	sepia	russet	tile|red
rust	taupe	sienna	ashˌblond
sage	tawny	silver	baby|blue
saxe	umber	titian	blood|red
wine	white	violet	brunette
azure	albert	yellow	Burgundy
beige	annato	apricot	chestnut
black	auburn	carmine	dark|blue
brown	blonde	citrine	dove|grey
cream	bronze	crimson	dyestuff

eau-de-nil
iron grey
lavender
mulberry
navy blue
off-white
pea green
poppy red
primrose
raw umber
red ochre
sanguine
sap green
sapphire
saxe blue
sea green
tincture
viridian
xanthein
azure blue
blue black
burnt lake
burnt rose
cameo pink
champagne
cherry red
chrome red
claret red
duck green
Dutch pink
Indian red
jade green
leaf green
light blue
lime green
livid pink
madder red
moss green
mouse grey
Naples red
Nile green
olive drab
opera pink
pearl grey
raw sienna
royal blue
smoke grey
solferino
soot black
steel blue
steel grey
tangerine
Turkey red
turquoise
vermilion
acid yellow
apple green
aquamarine
Berlin blue
beryl green
brown ochre
burnt umber
Chinese red
cobalt blue
direct blue
fast yellow
flake white
French blue
French grey
grass green
green ochre
heliotrope
Irish green
madder blue
madder lake
madder pink
marine blue
olive brown
olive green
Oxford grey
Paris green
Persian red
powder blue
raven black
rose madder
salmon pink
silver grey
terra cotta
trypan blue
bottle green
brown madder
burnt orange
burnt sienna
cardinal red
carmine lake
chrome green
chrome lemon
cobalt green
crimson lake
cyanine blue
Dresden blue
English pink
flesh-colour
hunting pink
incarnadine
Italian blue
Italian pink
Japanese red

king's yellow
lemon yellow
Paris yellow
Persian blue
Persian blue
Prussian red
Russian jade
terra sienna
ultramarine
Venetian red
Vienna green
yellow ochre
air force blue
burnt carmine
canary yellow
cerulean blue
Chinese white
chrome orange
chrome yellow
electric blue
emerald green
golden yellow
gun-metal grey
hyacinth blue
lavender blue
Lincoln green
madder orange
madder violet
madder yellow
midnight blue
orange madder
pastel colour
pillar-box red
Prussian blue
quince yellow
sapphire blue
scarlet ochre
black-and-white
Cambridge blue
flame-coloured
kaleidoscopic
lemon-coloured
monochromatic
multicoloured
particoloured
peach-coloured
pepper-and-salt
slate-coloured
stone-coloured
straw-coloured
sulphur-yellow
tortoise-shell
cornflower blue
glowing colours
heather mixture
imperial purple
livery-coloured
orange-coloured
platinum blonde
primary colours
salmon-coloured
strawberry roan
swaddling-cloth
turquoise green
colour blindness
colouring matter
greenery-yallery
rainbow-coloured
secondary colour

Composers

Bax
Gay
Suk
Adam
Arne
Bach
Berg
Blow
Byrd
Cage
Ives
Lalo
Nono
Orff
Wolf
Alwyn
Auber
Auric
Balfe
Berio
Bizet
Bliss
Bloch
Boito
Boyce
Brian
Bruch
Cilea
d'Indy

Dukas
Elgar
Fauré
Field
Finzi
Gluck
Grieg
Haydn
Henze
Holst
Ibert
Lehár
Liszt
Locke
Lully
Parry
Ravel
Reger
Satie
Sousa
Spohr
Suppé
Verdi
Weber
Weill
Widor
Alfven
Arnold
Barber

Bartók
Brahms
Bridge
Busoni
Coates
Czerny
Daquin
Delius
Duparc
Dvořák
Flotow
Franck
Gliere
Glinka
Gounod
Gretry
Handel
Herold
Hummel
Joplin
Kodaly
Lassus
Ligeti
Mahler
Moeran
Morley
Mozart
Piston
Rameau

Rubbra
Schutz
Searle
Tallis
Varese
Wagner
Walton
Webern
Wilbye
Albeniz
Allegri
Bellini
Bennett
Berlioz
Borodin
Britten
Copland
Corelli
Creston
Debussy
Delibes
Dowland
Duruflé
Falla, de
Gibbons
Howells
Ireland
Janáček
Lambert

COMPOSERS

Litolff
MacCunn
Martinu
Mathias
Medtner
Menotti
Milhaud
Nielsen
Poulenc
Puccini
Purcell
Quilter
Rodrigo
Rossini
Roussel
Salieri
Schuman
Shankar
Smetana
Stainer
Stamitz
Strauss
Tartini
Thomson
Tippett
Vivaldi
Warlock
Weelkes
Albinoni
Benedict
Benjamin
Berkeley
Boughton
Bruckner
Chabrier
Chausson
Cimarosa
Clementi
Couperin
Gabrieli
Gershwin
Giordano
Grainger
Granados
Honegger
Ketelbey
Korngold
Kriesler
Mascagni
Massenet
Messiaen
Paganini
Panufnik
Respighi
Sarasate
Schubert
Schumann
Scriabin
Sibelius
Stanford
Sullivan
Taverner
Telemann
Beethoven
Bernstein
Boellmann
Buxtehude
Cherubini
Donizetti
Glazounov
Hindemith
Hoddinott
MacDowell
Meyerbeer
Offenbach
Pachelbel
Pergolesi
Prokoviev
Scarlatti
Birtwistle
Boccherini
Kabalevsky
Monteverdi
Mussorgsky
Palestrina
Penderecki
Ponchielli
Praetorius
Rawsthorne
Rubinstein
Saint Saens
Schoenberg
Stravinsky
Villa Lobos
Waldteufel
Wieniawski
Williamson
Butterworth
Charpentier
Dittersdorf
Humperdinck
Leoncavallo
Lloyd Webber
Lutoslawski
Mendelssohn
Rachmaninov
Stockhausen
Szymanowski

11/15 LETTERS

Tchaikovsky
Khachaturian
Shostakovich
Maxwell Davies
Rimsky-Korsakov
Coleridge-Taylor
Vaughan Williams

Computing

baud
byte
chip
read
Algol
Basic
Cobol
input
micro
adding
binary
hacker
on line
Fortran
gigabit
off-line
program
bistable
computer
data bank
database
hardware
print-out
software
terminal
deprogram
mainframe
programme
slide rule
alphameric
memory bank
peripheral
throughput
binary digit
binary scale
multi-access
punched card
punched tape
programmable
random access
adding machine
microcomputer
shift register
word processor
analog computer
data processing
microprocessor
systems analyst
computerisation
computer science

COMPUTING

digital|computer
electronic|brain
storage|capacity
systems|analysis

Deadly Sins

envy
lust
anger
pride
sloth
wrath
accidie
gluttony
covetousness

Drink

ale
bin
gin
jug
nip
pop
rum
tea
tot
tyg
urn
vat
beer
brew
cafe
cask
coke
dram
flip
grog
hock
kola
lees
mead
milk
must
ouzo
port
sack
sake
soup
Toby
wine
wino
booze
broth
cider
cocoa
cream
drain
dregs
drink
gumbo
jorum
julep
lager
Médoc
mocha
punch
quaff
stock
stout
syrup
toddy
treat
vodka
water
bibber
bisque
borsch
bottle
brandy
carafe
cassis
cellar
claret
coffee
cognac
egg nog
goblet
imbibe
kirsch
kumiss
kummel
liquid
liquor
magnum
muscat
nectar
noggin
oxtail
Pernod
porter
posset
potage
rummer
Scotch
shandy
sherry
spirit
squash
tea bag
teacup
tipple
whisky
absinth
alcohol
aniseed
Bacardi
beef tea
beer mug
bitters
borscht
bouquet
bourbon
carouse
chianti
cobbler
cordial
curacao
custard
draught
dry wine
egg flip
gin fizz
iced tea

DRINK

limeade
liqueur
Madeira
malmsey
martini
Moselle
new wine
philtre
potable
red wine
sherbet
shoe-box
sloe gin
spirits
spritza
tea-leaf
tequila
vintage
wassail
whiskey
absinthe
Adam's ale
anisette
aperitif
armagnac
audit ale
beverage
Bordeaux
bouillon
Burgundy
China tea
cocktail
consommé
daiquiri
demijohn
Drambuie
Dubonnet
fruit cup
gin and it
gin sling
green tea
hangover
highball
hot drink
hot toddy
hydromel
ice water
infusion
julienne
lemonade
libation
muscatel
nightcap
pink lady
port wine
potation
rice-beer
rice soup
Riesling
root beer
ruby port
rum punch
Sauterne
schnapps
schooner
tantalus
tea-caddy
verjuice
vermouth
Adam's wine
appetiser
aqua vitae
black drop
cappucino
champagne
clear soup
Cointreau
cold drink
dishwater
doorframe
dry sherry
firewater
ginger ale
ginger pop
heavy wine
light wine
metheglin
milk shake
mint julep
muscadine
neat drink
onion soup
orangeade
Rhine wine
rye whisky
small beer
soda water
soft drink
still wine
sweet wine
tawny port
tea leaves
tiger milk
white wine
yard of ale
Beaujolais
Bloody Mary
buttermilk

café au lait
cappuccino
Chambertin
Chartreuse
fruit juice
ginger beer
grape juice
half-bottle
Holland gin
iced coffee
intoxicant
Jamaica rum
lemon juice
liquid diet
love-potion
malt whisky
malted milk
manzanilla
maraschino
minestrone
mixed drink
mock turtle
Mulled wine
Munich beer
on the rocks
Russian tea
slivowitza
soda syphon
stiff drink
stirrup cup
Tom Collins
tomato soup
tonic water
turtle soup
usquebaugh
Vichy water
whisky sour
amontillado
apple brandy
barley broth
barley water
beef extract
Benedictine
black coffee
brandy smash
chicken soup
coffee-break
cooking wine
cowslip wine
draught beer
French wines
ginger punch
Irish coffee
orange juice
peach brandy
Scotch broth
strong drink
sweet sherry
tomato juice
vintage wine
white coffee
breathalyser
café espresso
Danzig brandy
hot chocolate
ice-cream soda
Irish whiskey
mineral water
non-alcoholic
Pilsener beer
sarsaparilla
spirit of wine

supernaculum
apricot|brandy
brandy|and|soda
coffee|grounds
condensed|milk
cooking|sherry
creme|de|menthe
dandelion|wine
deoch,an,doruis
estate|bottled
gin|and|bitters
instant|coffee
liqueur|brandy
liquid|measure
mild|and|bitter
morning|coffee
prairie|oyster
round|of|drinks
Scotch|and|soda
sparkling|wine
whisky|and|soda
as|drunk|as|a|lord
bottle|of|brandy
bottle|of|claret
bottle|of|Scotch
bottle|of|whisky
champagne|lunch
cocktail|shaker
coffee|strainer
elderberry|wine
espresso|coffee
evaporated|milk
French|vermouth
John|barleycorn
lemonade|shandy
little|brown|jug
Napoleon|brandy
pineapple|juice
Scotch|and|water
beer|and|skittles
drop|of|good|stuff
gin|and|angostura
grapefruit|juice
green|Chartreuse
Italian|vermouth
one|over|the|eight
wines|and|spirits

Education

BA	ABC	ink	book	dean	fail
Dr	con	jot	co,ed	demy	form
go	den	pen	copy	desk	gown
IQ	dux	ambo	cram	exam	grad
MA	fag	blot	crib	fact	guru

4/7 LETTERS

head
lore
mark
mode
mods
note
nous
oral
pass
prep
prof
quad
quiz
read
roll
sage
seat
soph
swat
swot
talk
tech
term
test
tyro
atlas
board
chair
chalk
class
coach
dunce
ecole
edify
essay
final
flunk
forum
fresh
gaudy
gloss
grade
grind
guide
hadji
house
imbue
khoja
kudos
learn
lines
loach
lycee
major
merit
minor
paper
poser
prime
prize
quill
sizar
slate
spell
staff
study
teach
tutor
usher
alumna
brains
brainy
browse
bursar
campus
course
creche
debate
degree
docent
doctor
duenna
eraser
examen
fellow
finals
genius
grader
grades
gradus
greats
ground
homily
infant
infuse
inkpot
jotter
junior
lector
lesson
lyceum
manual
master
matron
mentor
mullah
munshi
novice
old|boy
optime
pandit
pedant
pencil
period
peruse
preach
primer
pundit
reader
recite
rector
regius
remove
report
rubber
savant
school
scroll
senior
sermon
smalls
syndic
taught
teaser
theory
tripos
truant
vellum
academy
alumnus
amateur
boarder
bookish
bookman

EDUCATION

Braille
brush up
bursary
coacher
college
crammer
culture
dabbler
degrees
diploma
dominie
Dunciad
egghead
entrant
erudite
examine
explain
expound
faculty
failure
fresher
grammar
great go
grinder
hearing
honours
inkhorn
inkwell
instill
learned
learner
lectern
lecture
letters
lexicon
lowbrow
maestro
major in
minor in
monitor
nursery
old girl
oppidan
pandect
papyrus
passman
pointer
precept
prefect
primary
problem
proctor
qualify
read for
reading
satchel
scholar
schools
seminar
student
studier
studies
teacher
teach-in
the arts
theatre
thinker
three R's
trainee
tuition
varsity
writing
written
academic
aegrotat
agitprop
aularian
beginner
book lore
bookworm
classman
coaching
commoner
copybook
cramming
cultural
cultured
didactic
disciple
division
dry nurse
educable
educated
educator
elective
emeritus
examiner
exercise
foolscap
freshman
Gamaliel
glossary
gownsman
graduand
graduate
guidance
half-term
harangue
highbrow
homework
humanism
inceptor
informed
inkstand
instruct
Latinist
learning
lecturer
lettered
liripipe
liripoop
literacy
literate
little go
memorize
mistress
moralize
neophyte
note book
Oxbridge
pansophy
pass mark
pedagogy
pedantic
pedantry
playtime
polemics
polyglot
pore over
postgrad
preacher
punditry
question
read up on

redbrick
research
revision
roll-cast
sciolist
semester
seminary
servitor
spelling
studious
studying
teaching
textbook
training
treatise
tutoring
tutelate
tutorage
tutoress
tutorial
vacation
versed in
well-read
wordbook
wrangler
absey book
alma mater
art school
assistant
associate
Athenaeum
booklover
brainwave
brainwork
catechism
catechize
chalkdust
chalk talk
champaign
classmate
classroom
collegian
cosmogony
day school
dean of men
desk-bound
didactics
diligence
direction
discourse
doctorate
dunce's cap
education
enlighten
erudition
extempore
fifth form
final year
first form
first year
formalist
gaudeamus
gazetteer
governess
greenhorn
Gymnasium
homiletic
honourman
hortatory
ignoramus
ingestion
inspector
institute
knowledge
law school
lucubrate
masterate
notepaper
novitiate
orography
palaestra
parchment
pedagogic
pedagogue
pensioner
playgroup
portioner
precentor
preceptor
prelector
pre-school
principal
professor
proselyte
qualified
receptive
refresher
rough note
scholarch
scholarly
schoolboy
schooling
schoolish
school kid
school lad
schoolman
sermonize
sixth form

smatterer
sophister
sophomore
staffroom
star|pupil
streaming
supplicat
syndicate
take|notes
teachable
thesaurus
third|form
third|year
timetable
tuitional
tutorhood
tutorship
undergrad
abiturient
academical
arithmetic
bibliology
bibliomane
bibliosoph
blackboard
brainchild
brain|storm
cap|and|gown
catechumen
chautauqua
classicism
classicist
college|boy
collegiate
common|room
coryphaeus

curricular
curriculum
dame|school
dictionary
dilettante
discipline
dual|school
educatress
eleven-plus
escritoire
exposition
extramural
fellowship
form|master
fourth|form
fraternity
free|period
free|school
graduation
hard|lesson
headmaster
high|school
humanities
illiterate
illuminate
illuminati
imposition
inquisitor
instructed
instructor
intramural
junior|high
lead|pencil
lower|fifth
lower|sixth
lower|third

memorandum
middle-brow
Nobel|prize
past|master
pedagogics
pedagogist
pensionnat
Philistine
playground
playschool
postmaster
preceptive
prep|school
prize|idiot
prolocutor
propaganda
quadrangle
quadrivium
quiz|master
readership
report|card
Sabbatical
scholastic
schoolbook
school|chum
schooldame
schoolgirl
schoolma'am
schoolmaid
schoolmarm
schoolmate
school|meal
school|miss
schoolroom
scrutinize
second|form

second|head
second|year
self-taught
senior|high
shibboleth
smattering
specialist
specialize
sub-culture
supervisor
tenderfoot
university
upper|fifth
upper|sixth
upper|third
vocabulary
well-versed
widely|read
abecedarian
abecedarium
academician
arts|college
attainments
Bible|school
bibliolatry
bibliomania
bibliophile
board|school
bookishness
brain|teaser
bright|pupil
certificate
charm|school
class|fellow
coeducation
college-bred
college|girl
collegianer
crash|course
enlightened
examination
fellow|pupil
former|pupil
give|a|lesson
grade|school
head|teacher
house|master
inculcation
information
informative
institution
instruction
instructive
intelligent
invigilator
lecture|hall
lecture|room
lectureship
liberal|arts
literary|man
litterateur
moral|lesson
mortarboard
music|lesson
music|school
naval|school
night|school
omniscience
point|a|moral
polytechnic
preceptress
preparation
preparation
prizegiving
prizewinner
probationer
questionist
read|a|lesson
reading|desk
re-education
researchist
responsions
scholarship
School|Board
sharp|lesson
spelling|bee
student|body
teachership
teacher's|pet
teaching|aid
trade|school
upper|fourth
wide|reading
writing|desk
amphitheatre
aptitude|test
assimilation
baccalaureus
battle|of|wits
bibliomaniac
blue|stocking
book|learning
brain|twister
church|school
classicalist
College|Board
conservatory
disciplinary

disquisition
encyclopedia
exercise book
exhibitioner
form mistress
French lesson
ground school
headmistress
indoctrinate
infant school
instructress
intellectual
intelligence
junior school
kindergarten
learn by heart
make the grade
man of letters
master of arts
matter of fact
memorization
mental labour
middle school
naval academy
normal school
painting book
parish school
perscrutator
phrontistery
postgraduate
preselection
professorate
professorial
psychometric
pupil teacher
riding school
roll of honour
school dinner
schoolfellow
schoolkeeper
schoolmaster
self-educated
senior school
spelling book
summer school
Sunday school
teach a lesson
training slip
underteacher
writing table
academic dress
advanced level
baccalaureate
Berkeleianism
careers master
charity school
coeducational
comprehension
comprehensive
concentration
conceptualism
conceptualist
contemplation
contemplative
contradiction
educationally
encyclopaedia
enlightenment
faculty of arts
grammar school
home economics
honours degree

infant|prodigy
learning|curve
matriculation
metaphysician
misunderstand
moment|of|truth
non,collegiate
nursery|school
ordinary|level
parrot|fashion
philosophical
primary|school
private|school
professorship
psychoanalyst
Rhodes|scholar
scholasticism
school,leaving
school|prefect
schoolteacher
social|science
speech|therapy
undergraduate
understanding
vice,president
vice,principal
vicious|circle
word|blindness
approved|school
beg|the|question
boarding|school
Cuisenaire|rods
educationalist
encyclopaedist
epistemologist
existentialism
existentialist
high|technology
honorary|degree
honorary|fellow
intelligentsia
lending|library
loaded|question
metempsychosis
misinstruction
moral|certainty
multiple,choice
multiracialism
Open|University
parapsychology
postmastership
predestination
psychoanalysis
sandwich|course
schoolmistress
senior|wrangler
speech|training
vice,chancellor
a|little|learning
analytical|logic
Aristotelianism
audio,visual|aids
careers|mistress
combination|room
domestic|economy
domestic|science
epistemological
extra,curricular
finishing|school
first|principles
higher|education
horns|of|a|dilemma

EDUCATION

lateral|thinking
logical|analysis
moral|philosophy
open|scholarship
oral|examination
pathetic|fallacy
psychometrician
refresher|course
regius|professor
schoolboy|howler
school|inspector
secondary|modern
secondary|school
tertiary|college
training|college

First Names

Abe
Ada
Alf
Amy
Ann
Bab
Bea
Bel
Ben
Bob
Dan
Don
Dot
Ena
Eva
Eve
Fay
Flo
Gay
Ger
Gus
Guy
Ian
Ina
Isa
Jan
Jim
Joe
Joy
Kay
Kim
Kit
Len
Leo
Liz
Lyn
Max
May
Meg
Nan
Nat
Ned
Net
Nye
Pam
Pat
Peg
Pen
Pip
Pru
Rab
Rae
Ray
Reg
Rex
Roy
Sal
Sam
Sid
Sis
Sue
Tam
Ted
Tim
Tom
Una
Val
Vic
Viv
Wal
Zoe
Abel
Abie
Adam
Alan
Aldo
Ally
Alma
Amos
Andy
Anna
Anne
Avis
Babs
Bart
Bert
Bess
Beth
Bill
Cara
Carl
Chad
Ciss
Clem
Cleo
Dave
Dawn
Dick
Dirk
Dora
Drew
Duke
Earl
Edna
Ella
Elma
Elsa
Emma
Enid
Eric
Evan
Ewan
Fred
Gail
Gene
Gill
Gina
Gwen
Gwyn
Hope
Hugh
Hugo
Iain
Iona
Iris
Ivan

4/5 LETTERS

Ivor	Nell	Aaron	Cecil	Effie	Hetty
Jack	Nick	Abbie	Celia	Elias	Hilda
Jake	Nina	Adele	Chloe	Eliot	Hiram
Jane	Nita	Aggie	Chris	Elise	Honor
Jean	Noel	Agnes	Clara	Eliza	Inigo
Jeff	Olaf	Aidan	Clare	Ellen	Irene
Jess	Olga	Ailie	Cliff	Ellis	Isaac
Jill	Oona	Ailsa	Clive	Elmer	Jacky
Joan	Owen	Alfie	Colin	Elsie	Jacob
Jock	Paul	Algie	Coral	Emily	James
John	Pete	Alice	Corin	Enoch	Jamie
Josh	Phil	Aline	Cyril	Ernie	Janet
Judy	Rene	Alvin	Cyrus	Errol	Janey
June	Rhys	Angus	Daisy	Ethel	Jason
Karl	Rick	Anita	Danny	Faith	Jayne
Kate	Rita	Annie	Darby	Fanny	Jenny
Leah	Rolf	April	D'Arcy	Felix	Jerry
Lena	Rory	Avril	David	Fiona	Jesse
Leon	Rosa	Barry	Davie	Fleur	Jimmy
Lily	Rose	Basil	Delia	Flora	Josie
Lisa	Ross	Becca	Denis	Frank	Joyce
Lois	Ruby	Bella	Derek	Freda	Julie
Lola	Ruth	Benny	Diana	Garry	Karen
Lucy	Ryan	Berry	Diane	Garth	Keith
Luke	Sara	Beryl	Dilys	Gavin	Kevin
Lynn	Saul	Betsy	Dinah	Geoff	Kitty
Mark	Sean	Betty	Dodie	Gerda	Lance
Mary	Stan	Biddy	Dolly	Giles	Laura
Matt	Tess	Boris	Donna	Ginny	Leila
Maud	Theo	Brian	Doris	Grace	Lenny
Mick	Toby	Bruce	Dylan	Greta	Leona
Mike	Tony	Bruno	Eamon	Harry	Lewis
Muir	Vera	Caleb	Eddie	Hazel	Libby
Myra	Walt	Carla	Edgar	Helen	Linda
Neal	Will	Carol	Edith	Helga	Lindy
Neil	Yves	Cathy	Edwin	Henry	Lloyd

FIRST NAMES

Lorna
Louis
Lucia
Lydia
Lynne
Mabel
Madge
Maeve
Magda
Mamie
Manny
Marge
Margo
Maria
Marie
Mario
Marty
Maude
Mavis
Merle
Miles
Milly
Mitzi
Moira
Molly
Morag
Moray
Morna
Moses
Myles
Myrna
Nancy
Nanny
Naomi
Nelly
Netty

Niall
Nicky
Nicol
Nigel
Norma
Orson
Oscar
Paddy
Patty
Paula
Pearl
Peggy
Penny
Perce
Percy
Perry
Peter
Polly
Ralph
Rhoda
Rhona
Robin
Rodge
Roger
Rufus
Sadie
Sally
Sandy
Sarah
Sarah
Simon
Sonia
Steve
Susan
Susie
Sybil

Tania
Tanya
Tatum
Terry
Tilly
Tracy
Vicky
Vince
Viola
Wanda
Wayne
Wendy
Adrian
Agatha
Aileen
Albert
Aldous
Alexis
Alfred
Alicia
Alison
Althea
Amanda
Amelia
Andrea
Andrew
Angela
Antony
Arabel
Archie
Arline
Arnold
Arthur
Astrid
Athene
Aubrey

Audrey
Aurora
Austin
Aylwin
Barney
Bertha
Billie
Blaise
Bobbie
Brenda
Bryony
Calvin
Carmen
Carole
Carrie
Caspar
Cedric
Cherry
Cheryl
Claire
Claude
Connor
Conrad
Damian
Daniel
Daphne
Darsey
Davina
Debbie
Denise
Dermot
Dianne
Donald
Doreen
Dougal
Dudley

Dugald
Dulcie
Duncan
Dustin
Dwight
Easter
Edmund
Edward
Edwina
Egbert
Eileen
Eilidh
Elaine
Elinor
Elisha
Elvira
Emilia
Ernest
Esmond
Esther
Eugene
Eunice
Evadne
Evelyn
Fergus
Gareth
Gaston
George
Gerald
Gerard
Gertie
Gideon
Gladys
Gloria
Gordon
Graham

6 LETTERS

Gregor
Gretel
Gwenda
Hamish
Hannah
Harold
Harvey
Hattie
Hector
Hester
Hilary
Horace
Howard
Hubert
Hunter
Imogen
Ingram
Ingrid
Irving
Isabel
Isaiah
Isobel
Isolde
Israel
Jackie
Janice
Jasper
Jemima
Jeremy
Jerome
Jessie
Joanna
Joanne
Joseph
Joshua
Josiah
Judith
Julian
Juliet
Julius
Justin
Kenelm
Kirsty
Larrie
Laurie
Lesley
Leslie
Lester
Lilian
Lionel
Lolita
Lottie
Louisa
Louise
Lucius
Luther
Maggie
Magnus
Maisie
Manuel
Marcia
Marcus
Margie
Marian
Marion
Marius
Martha
Martin
Maxine
Melvin
Melvyn
Merlin
Mervyn
Michel
Mickey
Minnie
Miriam
Monica
Morgan
Morrie
Morris
Morven
Muriel
Murray
Myrtle
Nadine
Nathan
Nessie
Nettie
Nicola
Nicole
Noelle
Norman
Norris
Odette
Oliver
Oonagh
Oriana
Osbert
Oswald
Pamela
Petrus
Petula
Philip
Phoebe
Rachel
Regina
Reuben
Robert
Robina
Rodney
Roland
Ronald
Rowena
Roxana
Rupert
Sabina
Salome
Samuel
Sandra
Selina
Selwyn
Serena
Sharon
Sheena
Sheila
Sidney
Silvia
Sophia
Sophie
Stella
Steven
Stuart
Sydney
Sylvia
Tamsin
Thelma
Thomas
Trevor
Tricia
Trixie
Trudie
Ursula
Verity

FIRST NAMES

Victor
Violet
Vivian
Vivien
Wallis
Walter
Warner
Warren
Wesley
Wilbur
Willie
Willis
Winnie
Yehudi
Yvette
Yvonne
Abigail
Abraham
Adriana
Alfreda
Alister
Ambrose
Annabel
Annette
Anthony
Antonia
Ariadne
Aurelia
Baldwin
Barbara
Barnaby
Belinda
Bernard
Bernice
Bertram
Blanche
Brendan
Bridget
Bronwen
Cameron
Camilla
Candida
Carlton
Carolyn
Cecilia
Celeste
Charity
Charles
Charlie
Chrissy
Christy
Clarice
Claudia
Clement
Clemmie
Corinna
Cynthia
Deborah
Deirdre
Desmond
Diarmid
Dolores
Dominic
Dorothy
Douglas
Eleanor
Elspeth
Emanuel
Erasmus
Estella
Eugenia
Ezekiel
Fenella
Florrie
Flossie
Frances
Francis
Gabriel
Geordie
Geraint
Gilbert
Gillian
Giselle
Godfrey
Gregory
Gwyneth
Harriet
Heather
Herbert
Horatio
Jeffrey
Jessica
Jocelyn
Juliana
Justine
Katrina
Kenneth
Kirstie
Lachlan
Lavinia
Leonard
Leonora
Leopold
Letitia
Lillian
Lindsey
Linette
Lucille
Lucinda
Malcolm
Margery
Marilyn
Martina
Martine
Matilda
Matthew
Maureen
Maurice
Maxwell
Melanie
Melissa
Michael
Mildred
Mirabel
Miranda
Modesty
Montagu
Murdoch
Myfanwy
Natalie
Natasha
Neville
Nicolas
Obadiah
Ophelia
Ottilie
Patrick
Pauline
Perdita
Petrina
Phyllis
Queenie
Quentin
Raphael

7/8 LETTERS

Raymond
Rebecca
Richard
Roberta
Rosalie
Rudolph
Rudyard
Russell
Sabrina
Shelagh
Shelley
Shirley
Siobhan
Solomon
Spencer
Stanley
Stephen
Stewart
Susanna
Suzanne
Terence
Theresa
Timothy
Valerie
Vanessa
Vaughan
Vincent
Wallace
Wilfred
William
Windsor
Winston
Wyndham
Yolande
Adrienne
Alasdair

Alastair
Aloysius
Angeline
Arabella
Augustus
Barnabas
Beatrice
Benedict
Benjamin
Bertrand
Beverley
Carlotta
Carolina
Caroline
Cathleen
Catriona
Charlton
Charmian
Clarence
Claribel
Clarissa
Claudius
Clemence
Clifford
Collette
Cordelia
Cressida
Cuthbert
Danielle
Dominica
Dorothea
Drusilla
Ebenezer
Euphemia
Farquhar
Felicity

Florence
Francine
Geoffrey
Georgina
Gertrude
Hercules
Hermione
Humphrey
Iseabail
Jeanette
Jennifer
Jonathan
Kathleen
Lancelot
Laurence
Lawrence
Llewelyn
Lorraine
Madeline
Magdalen
Margaret
Marianne
Marigold
Marjorie
Matthias
Meredith
Michelle
Montague
Morrison
Mortimer
Nicholas
Octavius
Odysseus
Patience
Patricia
Penelope

FIRST NAMES

Percival
Perpetua
Philippa
Primrose
Prudence
Prunella
Reginald
Roderick
Rosalind
Rosamund
Rosemary
Samantha
Scarlett
Sherlock
Silvanus
Sinclair
Somerset
Theodora
Theodore
Veronica
Victoria
Violette
Virginia
Winifred
Alexander
Alexandra
Alphonsus
Anastasia
Annabella
Archibald
Augustine
Cassandra
Catherine
Charlotte
Christian
Christina
Christine
Constance
Cornelius
Elizabeth
Esmeralda
Ethelbert
Ferdinand
Francesca
Frederica
Frederick
Genevieve
Geraldine
Gwendolyn
Henrietta
Jacquetta
Josephine
Katharine
Madeleine
Magdalene
Marmaduke
Millicent
Mirabelle
Nathaniel
Nicolette
Peregrine
Priscilla
Rosabella
Sebastian
Sempronia
Seraphina
Siegfried
Stephanie
Sylvester
Veronique
Antoinette
Bernadette

10/11 LETTERS

Christabel	Marguerite	Wilhelmina
Christiana	Maximilian	Bartholomew
Clementine	Montgomery	Christopher
Jacqueline	Petronella	Constantine

Fish

bib	goby	cohog	skate	cockle
cod	hake	dorse	smelt	comber
dab	huso	fluke	smolt	conger
eel	kelt	gaper	snook	cottus
fin	keta	gaper	spawn	cuttle
gar	luce	genus	sprat	darter
hag	opah	guppy	squid	dorado
ide	parr	hydra	sting	ellops
ray	pike	lance	tench	fogash
roe	pout	murex	trout	garvie
barb	rudd	murry	tunny	grilse
bass	scad	ormer	umber	groper
blay	scup	perch	whelk	gurnet
carp	shad	pinna	alevin	kipper
char	sole	pogge	angler	launce
chub	tail	polyp	barbel	limpet
chum	tope	porgy	beluga	maigre
clam	tuna	prawn	bester	marlin
claw	basse	roach	bowfin	meagre
coho	blain	roker	burbot	medusa
crab	bleak	saury	Cancer	megrim
dace	bream	scale	caplin	merman
dory	brill	shark	caribe	milter
fish	cobia	shell	cheven	minnow
gill	cohoe	shoal	chevin	mud-eel

FISH

mullet
murena
murine
murray
murrey
mussel
nekton
ostrea
oyster
partan
pholas
pirana
pisces
plaice
pollan
puffer
quahog
redeye
redfin
remora
robalo
salmon
sea bat
sea cat
sea ear
sea eel
sea fox
sea hog
sea pen
sea pig
serran
shiner
shrimp
sponge
squama
sucker
tarpon
tautog
triton
turbot
twaite
urchin
weever
wrasse
abalone
abalone
acaleph
alewife
anchovy
aquatic
benthos
bergylt
bivalve
bluecap
bummalo
capelin
catfish
cichlid
codfish
codling
cyclops
dogfish
eel pout
finnock
flipper
garfish
gar pike
grouper
gudgeon
gurnard
haddock
halibut
herring
hogfish
homelyn
jawfish
jewfish
lamprey
lobster
mahseer
merling
mermaid
mollusc
mollusk
mudfish
muraena
mytilus
oarfish
octopod
octopus
osseter
pellock
piddock
piranha
piscine
pomfret
pompano
redfish
rock cod
sand eel
sardine
sawfish
scallop
scomber
sculpin
sea bass
sea bear
sea calf
sea cock
sea dace
sea hare
sea pike
sea slug
sea star
sea wife
sea wolf
sea worm
sockeye
spawner
sun fish
tiddler
titling
toheroa
torpedo
trepang
whiting
anguilla
band fish
blue back
bluefish
bonefish
brisling
bullhead
calamary
carapace
coalfish
congo eel
crawfish
crayfish
deal fish
dragonet
eagle ray
earshell
filefish

firebird
fishpond
fish tank
flatfish
flounder
fox shark
frog fish
game fish
goatfish
goldfish
grayling
hornbeak
John Dory
king crab
kingfish
land crab
lemon dab
lion fish
lump fish
lungfish
mackerel
man eater
man of war
menhaden
monkfish
nauplius
physalia
pickerel
pilchard
pipefish
plankton
red belly
rock cook
rock fish
rockling
rose fish

sailfish
salmonid
sandling
sand sole
sea acorn
sea adder
sea beast
sea bream
sea devil
sea eagle
sea hound
sea lemon
sea lungs
sea perch
sea robin
sea snail
sea trout
sparling
spawning
starfish
sting ray
sturgeon
tentacle
tuna fish
univalve
wallfish
weakfish
wolf fish
angel fish
barracuda
black bass
blackfish
blindfish
blue shark
brandling
bull trout

conger eel
crossfish
devil fish
dog salmon
dorsal fin
Dover sole
fish garth
fish louse
gaspereau
gastropod
ghost crab
globe fish
goldfinny
goldsinny
green bone
horny head
ichthyoid
jellyfish
lake trout
langouste
lemon sole
pike perch
pilot fish
porbeagle
razorfish
red mullet
rock perch
round clam
royal fish
sandpride
scaldfish
schnapper
sea nettle
sea salmon
sea sleeve
sea urchin

FISH

selachian
shellfish
solenette
stonefish
surmullet
swordfish
sword tail
thornback
trachinus
troutling
trunkfish
water flea
whitebait
white bass
whitefish
widow bird
acorn shell
archer fish
bêche de mer
bitterling
Bombay duck
bottle fish
brook trout
brown trout
butterfish
candlefish
coelacanth
crustacean
cuttle fish
demoiselle
fish ladder
hammer fish
hellbender
hermit crab
kabeljauer
lancet fish

lumpsucker
mossbunker
mud skipper
paddlefish
parrot fish
periwinkle
purple fish
rabbit fish
red herring
ribbon fish
rock salmon
rock turbot
salamander
sand dollar
sand launce
sand sucker
sea poacher
sea surgeon
shovelhead
silverfish
spider crab
spotted ray
squeteague
tiger shark
vinegar eel
whale shark
bellows fish
brine shrimp
calling crab
channel bass
Dolly Varden
electric eel
flying squid
golden trout
heart urchin
hippocampus

lantern fish
laterigrade
lophobranch
muskellunge
pearl oyster
pelican fish
piranha fish
piscatorial
salmon trout
sea cucumber
sea hedgehog
sea scorpion
soldier crab
spawning bed
stickleback
striped bass
sucking fish
trumpet fish
whiting pout
basking shark
branchiopoda
fighting fish
golden salmon
goldfish bowl
ground feeder
ichthyopsida
kettle of fish
man of war fish
mantis shrimp
miller's thumb
paradise fish
rainbow trout
scorpion fish
sea butterfly
sea porcupine
sentinel crab

12/15 LETTERS

sergeant fish
silver salmon
spring keeper
swimming crab
trachypterus
tropical fish
trout nursery
white herring
findon haddock
finnan haddock
horse mackerel
ichthyologist
spermaceti whale

Flowers

bed
bud
lei
sow
arum
bulb
corm
cyme
flag
geum
irid
iris
lily
pink
poke
posy
rosa
seed
spur
stem
wort
agave
aster
bloom
calyx
clump
daisy
dwale
flora
graft
hardy
lotus
malva
mould
ocrea
oxlip
pansy
peony
petal
phlox
poppy
sepal
shoot
spray
sprig
stalk
stock
style
thorn
tulip
viola
yulan
althea
annual
anther
azalea
border
carpel
cistus
corona
corymb
cosmos
crocus
dahlia
exotic
floret
florid
flower
garden
growth
hen bit
hybrid
lupine
maguey
mallow
mimosa
nectar
orchid
orchis
pistil
pollen
raceme
rosery
runner
salvia
scilla
silene
smilax

FLOWERS

spadix
spathe
stamen
stigma
sucker
violet
wreath
yarrow
zinnia
aconite
althaea
alyssum
anemone
begonia
blawort
blossom
bouquet
burgeon
campion
chaplet
clarkia
climber
corolla
corsage
cowslip
cutting
day|lily
dogˌrose
erodium
figwort
fuchsia
garland
gentian
godetia
jasmine
jonquil
kingcup
leafage
leaflet
lily|pad
lobelia
mayˌlily
mimulus
mullein
nemesia
nigella
nosegay
panicle
papaver
pedicel
petiole
petunia
primula
pruning
ragweed
ragwort
rambler
rampion
red|rose
rockery
rosebay
rosebud
roselle
saffron
seaˌpink
seed|pod
setwall
spiraea
sub|rosa
tagetes
tea|rose
thyrsus
verbena
verdant
verdure
weed|out
amaranth
anthesis
arum|lily
auricula
bear's|ear
biennial
bird'sˌeye
bluebell
buddleia
camellia
camomile
catchfly
chinampa
clematis
cornˌflag
cyclamen
daffodil
dianthus
dogˌdaisy
epicalyx
feverfew
floweret
foxglove
gardenia
geranium
gladioli
gloxinia
goat'sˌrue
greenery
harebell
hawkweed
henequen

8/9 LETTERS

hot house
hyacinth
japonica
larkspur
lily pond
marigold
maybloom
moss rose
musk rose
myosotis
offshoot
peduncle
perianth
petalody
pond lily
primrose
red poppy
rock rose
rose bush
roseroot
scabiosa
scabious
sea heath
seedcase
seedling
seminary
snowdrop
stapelia
sun drops
sweetpea
trillium
veronica
wild rose
wistaria
woodbind
woodbine

wood sage
Aaron's rod
amarantus
amaryllis
aquilegia
bear's foot
bedded out
bulb field
buttercup
calendula
campanula
candytuft
capitulum
carnation
celandine
China rose
cineraria
clove pink
colchicum
coltsfoot
columbine
composite
coreopsis
cotyledon
culver key
dandelion
digitalis
dog violet
dry garden
duck's foot
edelweiss
eglantine
flowerage
flower bed
flowering
flower pot

full bloom
gelsemium
gladiolus
golden rod
gynophore
half hardy
hellebore
herb Paris
hollyhock
home grown
lady smock
mayflower
moon daisy
naked lady
narcissus
nelumbium
perennial
perpetual
pimpernel
pollen sac
pollinate
poppy head
pyrethrum
remontant
richardia
root prune
rootstock
rose elder
saxifrage
seed plant
snowflake
speedwell
sunflower
tiger lily
wake robin
water flag

FLOWERS

water lily
wax flower
white wood
window box
wolf's bane
amaranthus
anthophore
belladonna
bellflower
bluebottle
burnet rose
buttonhole
carpophore
China aster
cinquefoil
compositae
corncockle
cornflower
crane's bill
cuckoo pint
cut flowers
daisy chain
damask rose
delphinium
Dutch tulip
field poppy
fleur de lis
floral leaf
floribunda
flower head
flower show
frangipani
fritillary
garden city
gelder rose
German iris
goldilocks
gypsophila
heart's ease
helianthus
heliotrope
herbaceous
Indian pink
Indian poke
Indian shot
king's spear
lady's smock
maiden pink
marguerite
marshlocks
mayblossom
mignonette
mock orange
nasturtium
nightshade
opium poppy
orange lily
ox eye daisy
passiflora
periwinkle
pillar rose
poinsettia
polyanthus
ranunculus
red jasmine
rock garden
rock violet
roof garden
rose mallow
sarracenia
Scotch rose
snapdragon
stavesacre
stork's bill
sweet briar
sweet brier
wallflower
water elder
water lemon
wild flower
willow herb
wood sorrel
yellow root
yellow weed
yellow wort
Aaron's beard
antirrhinum
bear's breech
boutonniere
cabbage rose
calceolaria
convallaria
convolvulus
dusty miller
everlasting
forget me not
garden glass
gillyflower
guelder rose
hardy annual
honeysuckle
Indian cress
lady's mantle
London pride
loosestrife
love in a mist
Madonna lily
meadow sweet

Nancy pretty
night flower
orange grass
Parma violet
phyllomania
plum blossom
pollen grain
pollination
propagation
ragged robin
rambler rose
red hot poker
rose campion
stephanotis
St John's wort
tiger flower
water garden
white bottle
wild flowers
wood anemone
Adam's flannel
alpine flower
apple blossom
autumn crocus
bog pimpernel
bridal wreath
Carolina pink
century plant
corn marigold
cuckoo flower
fennel flower
flower border
flower de lice
flower de luce
flower garden
flower of Jove
fresh flowers
Iceland poppy
lady's slipper
monkey flower
morning glory
old man's beard
orange flower
pasque flower
peach blossom
rambling rose
rhododendron
rose of Sharon
Shirley poppy
snow in summer
Solomon's seal
St Peter's wort
sunken garden
sweet alyssum
sweet William
virgin's bower
waterflowers
wild hyacinth
bougainvillea
cherry blossom
Christmas rose
chrysanthemum
eschscholtzia
Flanders poppy
floricultural
marsh marigold
meadow saffron
orange blossom
passion flower
traveller's joy
bladder campion
bunch of flowers

FLOWERS

Canterbury bell
floriculturist
lords and ladies
love-in-idleness
love-in-idleness
night-flowering
shepherd's glass
shepherd's purse
butterfly-orchis
evening-primrose
lily-of-the-valley
Michaelmas-daisy
woody nightshade

Food

bin	cafe	lamb	stew	crust	lunch
bun	cake	lard	suet	curds	manna
can	chop	loaf	tart	curry	mince
egg	chow	loin	tuck	dicer	offal
fry	curd	malt	tuna	dough	pasta
ham	deli	mash	veal	feast	pasty
ice	diet	meal	whet	flank	patty
jam	dine	meat	whey	fudge	pecan
leg	dish	menu	wing	gigot	pilaf
nut	duck	nosh	yolk	goody	pilaw
oil	duff	olio	zest	goose	pizza
ort	eats	olla	à demi	gorge	poach
pie	Edam	pate	aspic	Gouda	purée
poi	fare	peel	bacon	gravy	quail
roe	feed	pork	bread	grill	roast
sup	flan	puff	bully	gruel	round
wok	food	rare	candy	honey	salmi
beef	fool	rock	capon	icing	sauce
bite	fowl	roll	cheer	jelly	sauté
boil	game	rump	chips	joint	scone
bolt	grub	rusk	chuck	kebab	scrag
bran	hash	salt	crumb	liver	shank

slops
snack
spice
steak
sugar
sweet
swill
table
T|bone
toast
torte
treat
tripe
vegan
wafer
addled
almond
banger
batter
blintz
bonbon
breast
brunch
buffet
butter
cachou
canape
cashew
catsup
caviar
cheese
cockle
collop
comfit
cookie
cornet

course
croute
cutlet
dainty
dining
dinner
dragee
eat|out
eclair
edible
egg|box
entree
flitch
fodder
fondue
forage
frappe
fridge
gammon
gateau
giblet
grouse
hot|dog
hot|pot
humbug
jam|jar
jam|pot
jujube
junket
kernel
kidney
kipper
leaven
morsel
mousse
muffin

mutton
noodle
nougat
nutmeg
omelet
oxtail
paella
panada
parkin
pastry
peanut
pepper
pickle
picnic
pilaff
quiche
ragout
rasher
ration
recipe
relish
repast
saddle
salami
salmon
sponge
spread
sundae
supper
sweets
tamale
tamara
tiffin
titbit
toffee
tongue

trifle
tucker
tuck|in
turbot
turkey
umbles
viande
viands
waffle
walnut
albumen
aliment
anchovy
bannock
banquet
banting
Bath|bun
biscuit
boiling
brisket
brittle
broiler
cake|mix
calorie
candies
caramel
catchup
caviare
cayenne
charqui
chicken
chowder
chutney
commons
compote
cookery

cooking
cracker
crumpet
cuisine
cupcake
deep|fry
dine|out
edibles
egg-yolk
epicure
essence
fig|roll
fondant
fritter
game|pie
gelatin
giblets
glucose
glutton
gnocchi
goulash
gourmet
granish
grocery
Gruyère
gumdrop
helping
hot|cake
ice|cube
ingesta
jam|roll
jam|tart
ketchup
knuckle
lardoon
lozenge
matzoth
meat|pie
mustard
nurture
oatcake
pabulum
pancake
paprika
parfait
pikelet
pimento
poisson
popcorn
popover
pork|pie
pottage
poultry
praline
pretzel
protein
pudding
ratafia
rations
ravioli
risotto
rissole
rum|baba
sardine
sausage
saveloy
savoury
seafood
seltzer
sirloin
soufflé
soupçon
strudel
tabasco
teacake
treacle
truffle
vanilla
venison
vinegar
vitamin
wine|gum
yoghurt
acid|drop
a|la|carte
allspice
ambrosia
angelica
antepast
ante-room
appetite
apple|pie
baked|egg
barbecue
betel|nut
bull's|eye
caneloni
chapatty
chop|suey
chow|mein
cinnamon
clambake
cold|meat
conserve
coq|au|vin
cross|bun
croutons
crudités
date|roll
déjeuner
delicacy
doggy|bag
doughnut
dressing
dried|egg
dripping
duckling
dumpling
egg-shell
egg-white
Emmental
escalope
escargot
flan|case
flapjack
flesh|pot
fried|egg
frosting
fruit|gum
gelatine
grilling
hard|tack
hazelnut
ice|cream
kedgeree
licorice
loin|chop
lollipop
luncheon
macaroni
macaroon
main|dish
marinade
marinate

marzipan
meat|ball
meat|loaf
meat|roll
meat|stew
meringue
mince|pie
molasses
moussaka
mushroom
olive|oil
omelette
pastille
pastrami
pemmican
pheasant
pigs|feet
pig|swill
plum|cake
pope's|eye
pork|chop
porridge
pot|roast
preserve
quenelle
rock|cake
rock|salt
roly,poly
rye|bread
salt|beef
salt|pork
sandwich
scrag|end
scramble
shoulder
side,dish
soy|sauce
stockpot
stuffing
supplies
syllabub
take,away
tamarind
tarragon
teabread
tea|break
tortilla
trotters
turnover
viaticum
victuals
water|ice
wishbone
yoghourt
zwieback
acid|drops
addled|egg
aitchbone
angel|cake
antipasto
arrowroot
banquette
barmbrack
bean|feast
beefsteak
beer|glass
bite|to|eat
boiled|egg
Brazil|nut
breakfast
bubble|gum
bully|beef
butter|pat
calf's|head
Camembert
cashew|nut
charlotte
club|steak
cochineal
colcannon
collation
condiment
confiture
cough|drop
crackling
cream|cake
cream|horn
cream|puff
croissant
croquette
croustade
dark|bread
dried|eggs
drop|scone
drumstick
egg,powder
elevenses
entremets
epicurean
epulation
foodstuff
forcemeat
foretaste
fricassee
fried|rice
fried|sole
fruit|cake
galantine

gravy soup
groceries
groundnut
guest room
half a loaf
hamburger
humble-pie
Irish stew
jelly baby
lamb chops
lamb fries
layer cake
left-overs
leg of lamb
liquorice
loaf sugar
lump sugar
macedoine
marchpane
margarine
marmalade
meat paste
mincemeat
mint sauce
monkey nut
nutriment
patty-cake
peanut bar
petit four
phosphate
picnic ham
piping hot
pistachio
pot-pourri
pound cake
preserves
provender
provision
rabbit pie
red pepper
rice paper
roast beef
rock candy
Roquefort
rump steak
Scotch egg
seasoning
shortcake
short ribs
soda bread
soda scone
spaghetti
spareribs
spearmint
spun sugar
sugar lump
sweet corn
sweetmeat
Swiss roll
tasty dish
tipsy cake
vol-au-vent
wheat germ
white meat
wild honey
apple-cover
apple sauce
aristology
baked beans
Bath oliver
bill of fare
blancmange
blue cheese
boiled fish
boiled meat
Bombay duck
bon appetit
brandy snap
breadcrumb
bread sauce
bread stick
Brie cheese
brown sugar
calf's brain
candy floss
caper sauce
cooking fat
cooking oil
corned beef
corned meat
cornflakes
custard pie
daily bread
Danish blue
devil's food
dill pickle
dinner roll
dog biscuit
double loin
dropped egg
Edam cheese
fatted calf
flank steak
food supply
fork supper
frangipane
French cake
fresh cream

fricandeau
frozen food
garlic salt
ginger snap
Gorgonzola
ham and eggs
hearty meal
hickory nut
honey crisp
hot and cold
icing sugar
ingredient
jardinière
jugged hare
lamb cutlet
light lunch
liverwurst
maple syrup
marble cake
marrow bone
mayonnaise
meal ticket
Melba toast
mint humbug
mortadella
mozzarella
mutton chop
pastry case
pâtisserie
peach melba
peppermint
piccalilli
pickled egg
plat du jour
poached egg
potted meat
provisions
puff pastry
regalement
rolled lamb
rolled pork
round steak
royal icing
saccharine
salmagundi
sea biscuit
shallow fry
sheep's head
shirred egg
shish-kebab
shortbread
shortcrust
silverside
Simnel cake
sour pickle
spatchcock
sponge cake
spotted dog
square meal
staple diet
stroganoff
stuffed egg
sucking pig
sugar candy
sugar mouse
sweetbread
sweet stuff
table d'hôte
tea biscuit
tenderloin
veal cutlet
vermicelli
Vienna loaf
Vienna roll
water icing
white bread
white sauce
zabaglione
almond icing
almond paste
banana split
barley sugar
beef sausage
black butter
black pepper
bonne bouche
brandy sauce
breadcrumbs
burnt almond
caster sugar
Castile soap
chicken feed
chilli sauce
clam chowder
clove pepper
comestibles
cottage loaf
cover charge
cream cheese
curry powder
custard tart
devilled egg
devilled ham
dinner party
double cream
dressed crab
Dutch cheese
Eve's pudding

festal|board
fillet|steak
flank|mutton
frankfurter
French|bread
French|toast
fresh|butter
gammon|steak
gingerbread
Gouda|cheese
green|pepper
griddlecake
ground|spice
health|foods
Hollandaise
hors|d'oeuvre
hot|cross|bun
hot|luncheon
ice|lollipop
invalid|fare
iron|rations
jam|turnover
jellied|eels
leg|of|mutton
light|repast
link|sausage
loaf|of|bread
Madeira|cake
marshmallow
milk|pudding
morning|roll
olla|podrida
parson's|nose
petits|fours
pig's|trotter
plum|pudding
poached|fish
pork|sausage
potato|crisp
potato|salad
preparation
pressed|beef
refreshment
rice|pudding
roast|grouse
roast|potato
room|service
sausage|roll
self|service
ship|biscuit
side|of|bacon
single|cream
sliced|bread
smörgasbord
spotted|Dick
staff|of|life
suet|pudding
sweet|almond
sweet|pepper
sweet|pickle
Swiss|cheese
tagliatelle
toffee|apple
tomato|sauce
tossed|salad
treacle|tart
Vienna|steak
wedding|cake
Welsh|rabbit
wheaten|loaf
white|pepper
white|potato
afternoon|tea
apple|fritter
apple|strudel
bacon|and|eggs
bakewell|tart
birthday|cake
bitter|almond
black|pudding
blood|pudding
bouquet|garni
breast|of|lamb
breast|of|veal
brewer's|yeast
butcher's|meat
butterscotch
caraway|seeds
cheeseburger
chilli|pepper
chitterlings
chocolate|box
choice|morsel
cinnamon|ball
clotted|cream
club|sandwich
Cornish|pasty
coupe|Jacques
crust|of|bread
curds|and|whey
custard|sauce
Danish|pastry
delicatessen
fillet|of|sole
finnan|haddie
fish|and|chips
fish|dressing
Forfar|bridie

French pastry
grated cheese
grilled steak
ground almond
ground ginger
ground pepper
Hamburg steak
hasty pudding
haute cuisine
ice cream cone
Leyden cheese
luncheon meat
mulligan stew
peanut butter
pease pudding
pickled onion
pig's knuckles
pistachio nut
planked steak
pork and beans
potato crisps
pumpernickel
Russian salad
sage and onion
salted peanut
scrambled egg
sherry trifle
short commons
sirloin steak
smoked salmon
sponge finger
streaky bacon
sweet and sour
tabasco sauce
tartare sauce
vegetable oil

Waldorf salad
water biscuit
Welsh rarebit
whipped cream
apple crumble
apple dumpling
apple fritters
apple turnover
barbecue sauce
bouillabaisse
bread and water
breakfast food
burnt offering
buttered toast
cayenne pepper
chateaubriand
cheddar cheese
cheese biscuit
Christmas cake
confectionery
contamination
cottage cheese
custard powder
Edinburgh rock
finnan haddock
food poisoning
French mustard
fruit cocktail
lemon meringue
meals on wheels
meat and two veg
mess of pottage
milk chocolate
minced collops
Neapolitan ice
pease porridge

pickled walnut
rasher of bacon
roll and butter
salad dressing
scrambled eggs
smoked sausage
soused herring
starch reduced
stilton cheese
strawberry ice
strawberry jam
sugar and spice
summer pudding
toad in the hole
transport cafe
veal and ham pie
vegetable dish
apple charlotte
banana fritters
bangers and mash
bar of chocolate
bread and butter
bread and cheese
bread and scrape
cabinet pudding
Canterbury lamb
charlotte russe
cheese sandwich
Cheshire cheese
college pudding
curried chicken
French dressing
gooseberry fool
hearty appetite
ice cream sundae
macaroni cheese
mock turtle soup
nutritiousness
Parmesan cheese
pate de fois gras
peppermint drop
pickled herring
plaice and chips
plain chocolate
polyunsaturate
pontefract cake
saddle of mutton
sausage and mash
Scotch woodcock
steak and kidney
tapioca pudding
tea and biscuits
treacle pudding
tripe and onions
Turkish delight
vegetable curry
vegetable salad
vegetarian dish
Worcester sauce
box of chocolates
breakfast cereal
bubble and squeak
Camembert cheese
chicken Maryland
chocolate eclair
chocolate sundae
convenience food
cooked breakfast
Devonshire cream
French breakfast
fricassee of veal
grilled sausages

15 LETTERS

grilled|tomatoes
orange|marmalade
peaches|and|cream
peppermint|cream
ploughman's|lunch
redcurrant|jelly
roly|poly|pudding
sausage|and|chips
sausages|and|mash
Wiener|schnitzel

Foreign Words and Phrases

ami
jeu
mot
à|bas
abbé
doge
gene
in|re
lied
vivo
ab|ovo
addio
à|deux
ad|hoc
adios
ad|lib
ad|rem
adsum
à|gogo
aidos
apage
arras
assai
buffo

ca|ira
canto
corno
desto
dolce
domus
école
étude
grave
largo
lento
lycée
mores
obiit
per|se
plaza
pleno
Reich
salle
segno
segue
sordo
tacet
torte

tutti
usine
abattu
abrege
agrege
allons
aperçu
à|terre
aubade
au|fait
au|fond
avanti
avenir
bel|air
bêtise
bon|mot
bon|ton
Cortes
crible
da|capo
dégagé
déja|vu
de|jure
der|Tag

emptor
en|fête
fi|donc
flèche
giusto
grazia
ibidem
in|vivo
legato
Lieder
maison
mañana
nobile
ottava
palais
posada
presto
rubato
sempre
subito
tenuto
torero
troppo
vivace

acharne	chanson	peccavi	au|revoir
ad|astra	château	pension	autobahn
ad|finem	chez|moi	pesante	aux|armes
ad|litem	clavier	piacere	à|volonté
à|droite	codetta	plafond	banlieue
ad|vivum	comedia	pomposo	bel|canto
affaire	con|brio	pro|rata	bienˌêtre
affiche	con|moto	qui|vive	bona|fide
agaçant	couloir	ragazza	boutˌrime
à|gauche	cui|bono	Rathaus	chez|nous
agitato	d'accord	Rigsdag	col|legno
à|jamais	danseur	Riksdag	con|amore
à|la|mode	ébauche	ripieno	con|fuoco
alcaide	en|prise	rondeau	coryphée
alcalde	en|route	rondino	cum|laude
al|conto	ex|aequo	rosalia	dal|segno
altesse	fagotto	roulade	danseuse
animato	farceur	Schloss	déjeuner
a|priori	fermata	sine|die	démarche
à|quatre	friture	sordino	Deus|vult
attacca	furioso	sub|rosa	dies|irae
au|mieux	Gestalt	tant|pis	distrait
Auslese	giocoso	vibrato	doloroso
bas|bleu	gouache	abatˌjour	duettino
battuta	haut|ton	abatvoix	enceinte
berceau	ich|dien	abatˌvoix	entresol
bonjour	in|utero	ad|summum	estancia
bonsoir	in|vacuo	agaçerie	et|cetera
bourrée	in|vitro	agrément	excerpta
bravura	Ländler	à|la|carte	ex|gratia
calando	laus|Deo	alta|moda	faubourg
cantina	Märchen	apéritif	Fine|Gael
canzona	morceau	a|piacere	gendarme
canzone	morendo	aprèsˌski	grand|mal
caramba	palazzo	à|quoi|bon	hacienda
chambre	pas|seul	au|gratin	hic|jacet

idée|fixe
leggiero
maestoso
maggiore
mala|fide
mal|de|mer
mandamus
mea|culpa
moderato
mon|repos
mot|juste
ostinato
par|avion
parlando
parlante
pro|forma
raisonné
rara|avis
ritenuto
sayonara
scordato
semplice
serenata
Sobranje
spianato
staccato
sub|poena
trouvère
una|corda
Vorspiel
à|bon|droit
ab|origine
a|cappella
ad|hominem
ad|libitum
ad|nauseam
ad|valorem
a|fortiori
alla|breve
alma|mater
âme|perdue
Anschluss
antipasto
à|outrance
arc-en-ciel
aria|buffa
assez|bien
au|courant
au|naturel
au|secours
Ausgleich
autopista
autoroute
bal|masque
beaux|arts
beaux|yeux
bel|esprit
belle|amie
ben|venuto
bête|noire
bon|marché
bon|vivant
bon|viveur
bon|voyage
Bundesrat
Bundestag
buona|sera
cantabile
carpe|diem
cauchemar
cave|canem
centumvir
coup|d'état
das|heisst
dei|gratia
de|rigueur
dolce|vita
en|famille
en|passant
et|tu,|Brute
flute-a-bec
Folketing
gemütlich
glissando
grandioso
grand|prix
haut|monde
inter|alia
ipse|dixit
ipso|facto
Landsting
Leitmotiv
Mardi|Gras
meden|agan
mezza|voce
nisi|prius
obbligato
objet|d'art
pari|passu
pas|de|deux
passepied
per|capita
per|contra
petit|four
piacevole
piangendo
Politburo
pro|patria

pro re nata
ricercare
rus in urbe
scherzoso
sforzando
siciliana
sine prole
smerzando
solfeggio
sostenuto
sotto voce
spiritoso
sub judice
sub specie
succès fou
tant mieux
taoiseach
tête-à-tête
tout à fait
tout court
vers libre
Volkslied
vox humana
à bon marché
absente reo
ad absurdum
affettuoso
aficionado
alla Franca
allargando
anno Domini
art nouveau
au pis aller
autostrada
avant-garde
bar mitzvah
bêche-de-mer
ben trovato
billet doux
bon appetit
buon giorno
café au lait
camino real
canto fermo
canzonetta
certiorari
cinquepace
confiserie
con sordini
con spirito
cordon bleu
danke schön
Deo gratias
Deo volente
dernier cri
Eisteddfod
feuilleton
Fianna Fáil
fortepiano
Gesundheit
in excelsis
in extremis
jardinière
jus commune
jus gentium
Lebensraum
magnum opus
mezzo forte
mezzo piano
nom de plume
opera buffa
ottava rima
perdendosi
pied-à-terre
plat du jour
ponticello
prima facie
Prix unique
pro hac vice
quid pro quo
recitativo
ritardando
ritornelle
ritornello
scherzando
scordatura
seguidilla
semper idem
sens unique
sine qua non
stringendo
sui generis
table d'hôte
terra firma
thé dansant
Tiergarten
tout de même
tremolando
ultra vires
urbi et orbi
villanella
accelerando
ad avizandum
ad infinitum
aetatis suae
aide-mémoire
alla tedesca
allez-vous-en

alto-relievo	hors d'oeuvre	ante meridiem
amor patriae	in medias res	appassionata
amour-propre	in principio	appoggiatura
à nos moutons	lèse majesté	à quatre mains
a posteriori	lignum vitae	arrière-garde
Arcades ambo	litterateur	ave atque vale
arrivederci	mise en scène	ballon d'essai
au contraire	motu proprio	basso-relievo
avec plaisir	musica ficta	basso-rilievo
à votre santé	ne plus ultra	buenas noches
belle époque	nihil obstat	carte blanche
bien entendu	nom de guerre	cause célèbre
bonne bouche	nous verrons	caveat emptor
boutonnière	obiter dicta	compos mentis
capriccioso	objet trouvé	Concertstück
carte du jour	opera bouffe	conseil d'état
cavo-relievo	papier-mâché	contra mundum
che sera sera	pas de quatre	crème caramel
comme il faut	pax vobiscum	degringolade
concertante	politbureau	Donnerwetter
contrapunto	raison d'être	doppelganger
contredanse	rallentando	eppur si muove
coram populo	savoir-faire	experto crede
crème brûlée	Schottische	fait accompli
Dail Eireann	smörgasbord	ferae naturae
decrescendo	summum bonum	feu d'artifice
degringoler	tempo giusto	force majeure
de haut en bas	tempus fugit	Gesellschaft
de profundis	tempus fugit	glockenspiel
ex hypothesi	tertium quid	Habeas corpus
ex post facto	tout le monde	hasta la vista
femme fatale	und so weiter	haute couture
fieri facias	vivacissimo	haute cuisine
fin de siècle	acciaccatura	homme du monde
fritto misto	amicus curiae	honoris causa
hasta mañana	ancien régime	hors concours

hors de combat
hotel de ville
laissez-faire
lapsus calami
lite pendente
mezzo-relievo
modus vivendi
nolens volens
obiter dictum
opéra comique
piobaireachd
pollice verso
pons asinorum
porte-cochère
porte-monnaie
quelque chose
rien ne va plus
salle à manger
sauve qui peut
s'il vous plait
terminus a quo
Zigeunerlied
ab urbe condita
aggiornamento
à la bonne heure
à propos de rien
ariston metron
arrière-pensée
avant-gardiste
avis au lecteur
basso profondo
Champs Élysées
cogito ergo sum
corps de ballet
corpus delicti
couleur de rose
crème de menthe
croix de guerre
cum grano salis
deux ex machina
éminence grise
exempli gratia
ex proprio motu
faites vos jeux
fête champêtre
force de frappe
in vino veritas
laissez-passer
lapsus linguae
magna cum laude
mirabile dictu
modus operandi
multum in parvo
noli-me-tangere
nolle prosequi
Nouvelle Vague
nulli secundus
palais de danse
poisson d'avril
quartier latin
Schadenfreude
succès d'estime
summa cum laude
très au sérieux
a minori ad majus
annus mirabilis
auf Wiedersehen
bureau de change
ceteris paribus
crème de la crème
Deuxième Bureau
dis aliter visum

14/15 LETTERS

divide|et|impera
dolce|far|niente
double|entendre
ejusdem|generis
enfant|terrible
et|in|Arcadia|ego
facile|princeps
hapax|legomenon
homme|d'affaires
in|loco|parentis
ipsissima|verba
maxima|cum|laude
ne|obliviscaris
obiit|sine|prole
petit|bourgeois
terminus|ad|quem
terra|incognita
tertius|gaudens
valet|de|chambre
ad|misericordiam
amende|honorable
à|propos|de|bottes
argumentum|ad|rem
cherchez|la|femme
cordon|sanitaire
crime|passionnel
gaudeamus|igitur
mutatis|mutandis
persona|non|grata
rem|acu|tetigisti

French Revolutionary Calendar

Nivose
Cavalli
Floreal
Ventose
Brumaire
Dohnanyi
Fervidor
Frimaire
Germinal
Messidor
Pluviose
Prairial
Fructidor
Thermidor
Vendemière

Fruit

cob
fig
fir
haw
hip
hop
nut
pip
uva
yam
aloe
core
crab
date
gean
hull
lime
okra
pear
peel
pepo
pina
pith
plum
pome
rind
ripe
seed
sloe

anise
apple
areca
berry
cacao
cocoa
drupe
fruit
gourd
graft
grape
guava
gumbo
hazel
lemon
mango
melon
olive
orris
papaw
peach
pecan
pinon
prune
shell
shoot
stalk
stipe
stone

achene
acinus
almond
ananas
banana
cashew
cherry
citron
citrus
cobnut
damson
dog hip
durian
kernel
litchi
locust
lovage
lychee
mammee
medlar
muscat
nutmeg
orange
papaya
pawpaw
peanut
pippin
pollen
pomato

pomelo
punica
quince
raisin
rennet
rocket
russet
savory
squash
tomato
unripe
vinery
apricot
avocado
blossom
bramble
brinjal
buckeye
capsule
catawba
coconut
cola nut
cumquat
currant
dessert
dika nut
egg plum
filbert
grapery

harvest
kola nut
kumquat
lettuce
malmsey
morello
orchard
palm nut
pimento
plumcot
putamen
rhubarb
rose-hip
ruddock
ruellia
salsify
sea-kale
seed pod
sorosis
soursop
succory
sultana
tangelo
vintage
aesculus
apple pip
autocarp
beechnut
beetroot
bergamot
betel nut
bilberry
bromelia
calabash
capparis
caprifig
chestnut
citrange
cocoanut
coco-palm
cow-berry
date-plum
dewberry
dogberry
earthnut
endocarp
follicle
fructose
hagberry
hazelnut
hot-house
locoweed
mad-apple
mandarin
May apple
mulberry
muscatel
musk-pear
musk-plum
nutshell
oak-apple
oleaster
orangery
peachery
pericarp
pimiento
prunello
sainfoin
self-heal
shaddock
sloebush
tiger nut
vine leaf
vineyard
alligator
apple tree
baneberry
blaeberry
blueberry
Brazil nut
candle nut
cashew nut
cherimoya
coco-de-mer
corozo nut
crab apple
cranberry
fruit tree
grapevine
greengage
groundnut
grugru nut
home grown
in blossom
Indian fig
jackfruit
jenneting
jequirity
Juneberry
king-apple
kiwi fruit
lemon peel
love-apple
manzanita
melocoton
monkey-nut
muscadine
muskmelon

nectarine
nux vomica
orange pip
persimmon
physic nut
pineapple
pistachio
poison nut
raspberry
salad herb
sapodilla
succulent
sugar plum
tangerine
wild-grape
wild-olive
banana skin
bird-cherry
blackberry
blackheart
breadfruit
cantaloupe
chokeberry
conference
dried fruit
elderberry
French plum
fruit salad
gooseberry
granadilla
grapefruit
hickory nut
holly berry
Idaean vine
loganberry
mangosteen
orange peel
peach-bloom
peppercorn
prayer-bead
Punic apple
red currant
rowan berry
sand-cherry
strawberry
sugar apple
watermelon
wild-cherry
an apple a day
anchovy pear
avocado pear
bittersweet
boysenberry
bramble bush
candleberry
chokecherry
citrus fruit
eating apple
goldenberry
hesperidium
huckleberry
Indian berry
Jaffa orange
mammee apple
navel-orange
phyllomania
pomegranate
pompelmoose
prickly pear
quince jelly
suwarrow nut
sweet cherry

tutti-frutti
American aloe
apple of Sodom
blackcurrant
bottled fruit
cherry-laurel
cooking apple
custard apple
Dead Sea apple
Dead Sea fruit
ground-cherry
mulberry-bush
passion fruit
Persian berry
Persian melon
pistachio nut
sassafras nut
seaside grape
service-berry
Victoria plum
white currant
whortleberry
alligator pear
bunch of grapes
honeydew melon
raspberry cane
Ribston pippin
Seville orange
conference pear
gooseberry-bush
mandarin orange

Furniture

bar	door	chair	shelf	galley
bed	hall	chest	stool	garage
cot	loft	couch	study	garret
den	nook	decor	suite	larder
mat	oven	diner	table	lounge
pad	rack	divan	tapis	lowboy
pew	safe	duvet	alcove	luxury
rug	seat	lobby	bureau	mirror
ambo	sofa	piano	carpet	pantry
bath	ambry	porch	carver	remove
bunk	arras	press	castor	rocker
crib	attic	quilt	closet	ruelle
desk	blind	salon	day-bed	screen

FURNITURE

serdab
settee
settle
teapoy
veneer
almirah
antique
armoire
bedroom
bibelot
boudoir
boxroom
bunk bed
buttery
canteen
car port
chamber
charpoy
commode
curtain
dinette
dresser
epergne
furnish
kitchen
landing
library
nursery
ottoman
parlour
picture
tallboy
tearoom
whatnot
armchair
back door
ballroom
banister
barstool
basement
bedstead
bookcase
chair bed
chair-leg
corridor
hatstand
jalousie
love seat
mess hall
outhouse
pembroke
playroom
scullery
stairway
table-leg
table-top
tea-table
upstairs
vargueno
wall-safe
wardrobe
woodshed
apartment
bed-settee
bookshelf
brasserie
bric-a-brac
cane chair
card table
carpeting
carpet-rod
cloakroom
club chair
cookhouse
cubby-hole
davenport
deck chair
double bed
drum table
easy-chair
footstool
furniture
garden hut
glory-hole
grillroom
guest room
hallstand
high chair
household
house-room
inglenook
leaf-table
lunchroom
maid's room
marquetry
mezzanine
music room
parquetry
pierglass
pier-table
refectory
rice paper
sideboard
side table
spare room
sun lounge
top drawer
washstand

9/12 LETTERS

wing chair
balustrade
bucket seat
chiffonier
coal-cellar
dining hall
dining room
downstairs
dumb waiter
escritoire
featherbed
folding bed
four-poster
garden shed
lumber room
music stool
passageway
piano stool
public room
rumpus room
scatter rug
secretaire
sun parlour
swing chair
upholstery
Victoriana
wicker-work
wine cellar
basket chair
below stairs
bookshelves
cabriole leg
Chippendale
coffee table
dining table
drawing room
fireside rug
fold-away bed
furnishings
garden chair
Heppelwhite
kitchenette
laundry room
morning room
player piano
reading lamp
roll-top desk
sitting room
studio couch
summer-house
swivel chair
utility room
wicker chair
writing-desk
bedside table
chaise longue
chesterfield
console-table
contour chair
dressing room
Dutch dresser
emergency bed
fitted carpet
gate-leg table
inner sanctum
ironing table
kitchen table
kneehold desk
library table
nest of tables
regency chair
reproduction

FURNITURE

rocking|chair	airing|cupboard
sheepskin|rug	breakfastˌtable
spare|bedroom	central|heating
trestle|table	chest|of|drawers
upright|piano	French|polisher
Welsh|dresser	kitchen|cabinet
writing|table	kitchen|dresser
dressingˌtable	venetian|carpet
Louisˌquatorze	Axminster|carpet
Persian|carpet	cocktail|cabinet
receptionˌroom	diningˌroom|table
revolving|door	furniture|polish
room|with|a|view	gateˌlegged|table
skirting|board	occasional|table
umbrella|stand	soft|furnishings
washˌhand|basin	tables|and|chairs

Geography

air	fen	pap	arid	calm	duct
ait	fog	pit	bank	cape	dune
alp	gap	ria	beck	cave	dust
bed	gas	rip	belt	city	dyke
ben	GMT	sea	berg	clay	east
bog	har	sod	bill	crag	eyot
cay	jet	wad	bolt	dale	fall
col	jut	wax	bomb	damp	fell
cwm	map	wet	bore	dawn	firn
dam	mud	adit	brae	deep	floe
dew	nip	apex	burn	dell	flow
dip	oil	arch	bush	dirt	flux
eye	orb	area	calf	down	fold

fork
foss
gang
gill
glen
grit
hade
hail
halo
haze
head
high
hill
holm
home
hook
isle
kame
khor
lake
land
lias
lieu
limb
lime
linn
loam
loch
lord
mere
mesa
midi
mild
mire
mist
moor
moss
mull
naze
neck
ness
neve
node
ooze
park
pass
peak
peat
plat
pole
pond
pool
purl
race
rack
rias
rift
rill
ring
sand
scar
scud
seam
seat
sial
sill
silt
sima
site
slag
soil
spit
spot
spur
tarn
till
tilt
town
trap
vale
vane
veld
void
wadi
wane
ward
warm
wash
weir
well
west
wold
zoic
zone
abysm
abyss
adobe
amber
ambit
argil
atlas
azure
bayou
beach
bedew
bleak
bluff
boggy
bourn
brash
broad
broch
brogh
brook
brush
burgh
butte
campo
canal
canon
chain
chalk
chart
chase
chasm
chine
cliff
clime
close
coast
coomb
crack
craig
creek
crust
cycle
deeps
delta
ditch
downs
drift
drink
dross
druse
dunes
dwarf
eagre
earth
emery
erode
esker
ether
falls
fault
fauna
fiord
firth
fjord
flats
flint
flood
flora
fluor
focus
frith
froth
gelid
geode
geoid
ghyll
glare
globe
gorge
grail
grove
gully
heath
humus
inlet
islet
joint
karoo
knoll
kopje
kraal
lapse
layer
levee
level
llano
local
locus
loess
lough
magma
marge
marly
marsh
mould
mount
mouth
nodes
north
Notus
oasis
oxbow
ozone
place
plain
plash
playa
plaza
point
polar
range
rapid

reach
realm
Reich
ridge
right
river
rural
salse
sault
scale
scarp
scaur
scree
serac
shade
shaft
sheer
shelf
shire
slope
slush
smoke
solum
sough
south
spate
stack
state
stria
surge
swale
swamp
swirl
table
talus
tract
urban
vault
veldt
waste
weald
wilds
wilds
world
alpine
arctic
autumn
barrow
border
bottom
branch
broads
brough
burrow
canopy
canton
canyon
cavern
circle
cirque
clayey
clunch
colony
colure
common
corral
corrie
coulee
county
course
crater
defile
deluge
depths
desert
dew|bow
dingle
dolmen
domain
efflux
Empire
Eocene
eothen
ethnic
Europa
facies
famine
feeder
flurry
geodes
geyser
gravel
groove
grotto
ground
gulley
hamlet
hiatus
hiemal
hollow
Ice|age
icecap
icicle
influx
inland
island
jungle
karroo
lagoon
layers
levant
locale
lochan
lunate
map|out
margin
marshy
massif
menhir
mirage
morass
nation
native
nebula
Orient
outlet
pampas
parish
pebble
period
placer
plains
plasma
plenum
polder
puddle
quaggy
rapids
ravine
region
riding
rillet
ripple
rubble
runlet
runnel
rustic
saddle
salina
sarsen
schist
season
sector
shadow
sierra
sinter
skerry
slough
slurry
solano
source
sphere
splash
spring
steppe
strata
strath
stream
strial
suburb
summer
summit
sun|dog
swampy
tremor
trench
tropic
trough
tundra
tunnel

6/8 LETTERS

turnip
upland
valley
vernal
vortex
welkin
wester
window
winter
zenith
zephyr
alluvia
almanac
azimuth
barrens
bedding
bone|bed
bottoms
boulder
breaker
caldera
capture
cascade
chimney
clachan
cluster
commune
compass
conduit
conflux
contour
corcass
couloir
country
country
crannog
crevice
crystal
culvert
debacle
demesne
diurnal
dog|days
freshet
full|sun
geodesy
geogony
geology
glacial
glacier
habitat
hachure
harbour
hillock
hilltop
horizon
hummock
iceberg
ice|cave
icefall
ice|floe
ice|pack
ice|raft
incline
insular
isobase
isthmus
kingdom
lakelet
land|ice
lowland
machair
meander
mill|run
Miocene
mofette
mundane
Neogene
pot|hole
prairie
proctor
profile
quarter
quietus
radiant
rivulet
road|map
salband
salt|pan
savanna
section
settled
shingle
sky|line
snow|bed
snow|cap
souther
station
stratum
stretch
subsoil
suburbs
sunbeam
sundown
surface
terrain
the|line
thermal
tideway
topical
topsoil
torrent
trickle
tropics
uplands
village
volcano
West|end
worldly
affluent
alluvial
alluvion
alluvium
altitude
anabatic
autumnal
bearings
bone|cave
boom|town
boondock
borehole
boundary
brooklet
calciole
Cambrian
catacomb
cataract
causeway
cleavage
coal|mine
confines
corridor
crevasse
darkling

darkness
date line
detritus
diluvium
district
dominion
downtown
drainage
dustbowl
easterly
effluent
Eolithic
epifocal
eruption
exposure
fold axis
foreland
fountain
fracture
frontier
fumarole
granules
headland
headrace
hibernal
hick town
highland
hillside
homeland
Huronian
hypogene
hypogeum
ice blink
ice field
ice sheet
indented
indigent
interior
irrigate
isostasy
Jurassic
lakeland
land form
land mass
landslip
latitude
lava flow
left bank
lenticle
levanter
Lewisian
littoral
location
lodestar
lowlands
mainland
Menevian
Mesozoic
millpool
millrace
monolith
monticle
moorland
mountain
Nearctic
Near East
New World
Occident
Old World
on the map
ordnance
overfold
overhang
photomap
pinnacle
plateaux
Pliocene
polar cap
position
precinct
prospect
province
purlieus
quagmire
ring dyke
riparian
river bed
riverine
rotation
sabulose
salt lake
sandbank
sand dune
sandhill
sandspit
seaboard
sea level
seashore
sediment
seedtime
shallows
Silurian
snowball
snowland
snow line
spectrum
stagnant
Stone Age

suburban
syncline
tailrace
telluric
Tertiary
tide gate
tide race
time zone
township
Triassic
undertow
undulate
upheaval
vicinity
warm cell
warm wave
water gap
westerly
Wild West
workings
zastruga
adumbrate
affluence
anabranch
antarctic
anticline
antipodes
Armorican
avalanche
backwater
backwoods
billabong
Bronze Age
brushland
canicular
catchment
cisalpine
city-state
cliff-face
coalfield
coastland
coastline
concourse
continent
cornbrash
cosmology
curvature
dead water
detrition
down under
earth-wave
epicentre
esplanade
estuaries
estuarine
everglade
evolution
exosphere
foliation
foothills
foreshore
geography
ghost town
glacieret
green belt
highlands
Holarctic
homotaxis
hour angle
hypogaeum
ice action
inner city
intrusion
isoclinal
Kainozoic
lake basin
landscape
landslide
loadstone
longitude
low ground
macrocosm
maelstrom
magnitude
mare's-tail
marshland
mattamore
midstream
Neolithic
north east
northerly
north pole
North star
north west
obsequent
off the map
Oligocene
parallels
peneplain
peninsula
phacolith
phenomena
polar axis
pozzolana
precipice
quicklime
rainwater
refluence

relief|map
reservoir
right|bank
riverhead
riverside
rock|basis
salt|marsh
sand|dunes
satellite
Secondary
sheer|drop
shoreline
situation
snowdrift
snow|field
snowfield
snowscape
solfatara
solstices
south|east
southerly
south|land
south|pole
south|west
statehood
streamlet
streamway
subregion
summer|day
surveying
survey|map
tableland
tectonics
temperate
territory
tidal|bore
tidal|flow
tidal|flux
tide|gauge
tidewater
tornadoes
tributary
underfoot
unsettled
upcountry
volcanoes
vulcanism
wasteland
waterfall
water|flow
water|hole
watershed
waterside
whirlpool
wide|world
wind|blown
aerography
aerosphere
air|current
arable|land
arid|desert
atmosphere
barysphere
bathometer
body|of|land
borderland
borderline
Boreal|zone
bottom|land
bradyseism
breakwater
Caledonian
campestral
chalk|downs
chersonese
cismontane
colatitude
confluence
consequent
contortion
contour|map
cordillera
cosmic|dust
demography
denudation
deposition
depression
dreikanter
drosometer
druid|stone
earthlight
earthquake
earthshine
embankment
ephemerist
equatorial
escarpment
excavation
fatherland
fieldstone
floatstone
fore|shocks
fossilized
foundation
freshwater
geographer
geophysics
ground|mass

hard|winter
headstream
headwaters
hemisphere
high|ground
hinterland
homosphere
hot|springs
hour|circle
hypocentre
ice|crystal
insularity
inundation
irrigation
jet|streams
lacustrine
landlocked
large|scale
latent|heat
mappemonde
map|reading
market|town
meteor|dust
metropolis
micrometer
midchannel
Middle|East
millstream
morphology
motherland
narrow|seas
native|land
native|soil
natural|gas
no|man's|land
old|country

oppressive
Ordovician
orogenesis
outline|map
overshadow
overthrust
Palaeogene
Palaeozoic
phenomenon
plot|of|land
population
potamology
promontory
rain|forest
rift|valley
river|basin
rock|bottom
rock|desert
rock|pillar
rock|series
rupestrian
seismic|map
seismology
serpentine
settlement
small|scale
springtime
stalactite
stalagmite
steep|slope
still|water
stratiform
subsequent
subsidence
substratum
subterrene

subtropics
summertide
summertime
terra|firma
theodolite
topography
torrid|zone
trade|route
tramontana
undercliff
undulation
vegetation
visibility
waterflood
water|front
water|gauge
waterspout
water|table
weathering
wilderness
wintertide
wintertime
archipelago
Austral|zone
back|country
barrier|lake
bathysphere
bottom|glade
boulder|clay
buffer|state
capital|city
cartography
cataclastic
chorography
circumpolar
climate|zone

climatology
colorimetry
Continental
convergence
coral island
counterflux
counterglow
countryside
country town
crag and tail
drusy cavity
dust counter
earth pillar
earth's crust
earth-tremor
environment
equinoctial
exploration
fata Morgana
frontal wave
frozen north
fulmination
grain of sand
great circle
harvest time
ice-movement
ichnography
ignis fatuus
impermeable
indentation
isogeotherm
katabothron
Kelvin scale
lake dweller
land feature
land measure
land surface
lone prairie
monticolous
mountaintop
mural circle
nationality
native heath
native lands
open country
Palaearctic
passage beds
pile dweller
polar circle
polar region
Pre-Cambrian
prominences
raised beach
raw material
reclamation
rising coast
river course
river system
river valley
seismic zone
seismograph
spelaeology
stony ground
submergence
subtropical
swallow-hole
terrestrial
thrust-plane
torridonian
transalpine
transandine
transmarine
troposphere
true horizon
ultra-violet
underground
under the sun
universally
vulcanicity
vulcanology
warm springs
watercourse
water pocket
whereabouts
white cliffs
wind erosion
alluvial flat
arctic circle
artesian well
barren ground
biogeography
Black country
cartographer
commonwealth
compass point
conglomerate
cross-bedding
elevated area
evaporimeter
false bedding
false horizon
field of force
fountainhead
frozen tundra
geanticlinal
geochemistry
geographical
geomagnetism

geosynclinal
geotectonics
glacial drift
glacial epoch
glaciologist
granular snow
jack-o'-lantern
Lake District
lake dwelling
law of gravity
magnetic axis
magnetic pole
main sequence
marginal land
mean sea level
metamorphism
metasomatism
midcontinent
mountain pass
mountain peak
municipality
neighbouring
oceanography
one horse town
otherworldly
palaeobotany
Palaeolithic
parcel of land
polarization
principality
rising ground
running water
semi-diameter
sinking coast
stratigraphy
subcontinent
subterranean
transleithan
transmundane
transoceanic
tropical heat
tropical zone
unconformity
undercurrent
variable zone
volcanic cone
volcanic rock
will-o'-the-wisp
zoogeography
above sea-level
active volcano
cardinal point
cardinal point
catchment area
drainage basin
east-north-east
east-south-east
Latin-American
Mediterranean
mountain chain
North Atlantic
north-easterly
north-eastward
north-westerly
north-westward
seismographer
seismological
south-easterly
south-eastward
south-westerly
south-westward
temperate zone

GEOGRAPHY

transatlantic
arrondissement
cartographical
compass|bearing
compass|reading
ethnologically
geographically
north|eastwards
north|north|east
north|north|west
north|westwards
Ordnance|Survey
south|eastwards
south|south|east
south|south|west
south|westwards
Antarctic|Circle
biogeographical
north|eastwardly
north|westwardly
south|eastwardly
south|westwardly
topographically

Government

CD	HMS	brig	imam	poll	tana
MP	nob	bull	Inca	pomp	toft
PC	red	camp	jack	rack	Tory
PM	rex	clan	king	raja	tsar
UN	rod	czar	lady	rani	visa
act	SOS	dame	left	rank	vote
aga	tax	deed	levy	rent	ward
beg	UDI	demo	mace	rota	Whig
bey	UNO	diet	memo	rule	whip
bug	wet	dove	mute	sack	aegis
CID	ally	duke	nick	seal	agent
con	alod	duty	OHMS	seat	agora
dip	axis	earl	oyes	serf	alias
don	beat	emir	oyez	shah	amban
dot	bill	fief	pact	soke	baron
FBI	bloc	file	peer	sway	begum
Fed	bond	hawk	pink	tail	blimp

board	junto	sheik	debate	nonage
bonds	laird	slate	depute	notice
booty	liege	staff	deputy	nuncio
boule	lobby	thane	despot	office
bulla	major	tribe	digest	orator
burgh	manor	truce	domain	ordeal
cabal	mayor	trust	durbar	papacy
caste	minor	usurp	dynast	parage
cause	Mogul	voter	empire	patrol
chair	nabob	Whigs	eparch	patron
chief	nawab	agenda	exarch	pledge
civic	Neddy	aristo	Fabian	pogrom
class	negus	asylum	faggot	policy
co-opt	noble	ballot	fasces	polity
corps	noose	bandit	Fuhrer	pow-wow
count	panel	barony	gentry	prince
crown	party	brevet	holder	puisne
curia	pasha	bureau	homage	puppet
deeds	plebs	Caesar	induna	quorum
divan	poach	caliph	junker	ransom
doyen	polls	caliph	Kaiser	rapine
draft	Porte	caucus	keeper	rating
duchy	posse	censor	knight	recess
edict	power	census	leader	record
elder	proof	clause	legate	reform
elect	proxy	clique	Majlis	regent
elite	queen	coheir	master	regime
fence	rajah	colony	mayhem	reward
filch	rally	con-man	mikado	sachem
forum	realm	consul	milady	satrap
frame	rebel	copper	milord	sconce
front	regal	cordon	moiety	senate
graft	reign	Cortes	motion	shogun
guard	royal	county	mutiny	sircar
guild	ruler	curfew	Nazism	sirdar
junta	ruler	daimio	NIBMAR	socage

GOVERNMENT

soviet
speech
squire
status
sultan
summit
syndic
throne
ticket
tocsin
Tories
treaty
truant
Tyburn
tyrant
umpire
vassal
vizier
voting
warden
yeoman
abstain
adjourn
admiral
adviser
Aga Khan
amnesty
anarchy
annuity
armiger
autarky
band aid
baronet
biparty
borough
cabinet
cacique
canvass
capital
Capitol
captain
captive
Chamber
charter
closure
colonel
command
Commons
compact
con game
consort
coronet
corsair
council
counsel
czarina
deed box
diarchy
dictate
D notice
dowager
duarchy
duchess
dukedom
dyarchy
dynasty
earldom
elector
embargo
embassy
emperor
empress
enclave
esquire
faction
Fascism
Fascist
federal
general
Gestapo
grandee
harmost
hidalgo
his nibs
hot seat
infanta
khedive
Knesset
Kremlin
land tax
leftist
libelee
Liberal
lording
majesty
mandate
marquis
Marxism
Marxist
measure
mediate
militia
minutes
mob rule
mobsman
mobster
monarch
mormaor
neutral
New Deal
officer
pageant
patriot
peerage
peeress
pension
Pharaoh
pillage
plunder
poacher
podesta
politic
praetor
precept
prefect
Premier
primary
process
protest
proviso
purview
radical
reality
recount
red tape
referee
refugee
regency
regimen
returns
Rigsdag
Riksdag
royalet
royalty

sacking
samurai
sceptre
senator
settler
shyster
soapbox
Speaker
spy ring
station
statist
steward
sultana
Sun King
support
supremo
swear in
sworn in
tallage
Templar
toisech
torture
Toryism
tsarina
uniform
Vatican
viceroy
villain
villein
abdicate
abrogate
accolade
activism
alienate
alliance
archduke
argument
arrogate
aspirant
assassin
Assembly
assessor
atheling
autarchy
autonomy
averment
balloter
bankrupt
baronage
baroness
Bastille
bicamera
Black Rod
brass hat
campaign
caudillo
ceremony
chairman
chambers
champion
chartism
citation
civilian
claw-back
Conclave
congress
countess
danegeld
dead hand
delegate
demagogy
Democrat
diadochi
dictator
diplomat
division
doctrine
dominion
don't-know
election
embezzle
Fine Gael
flatfoot
freehold
free vote
fugitive
Gaullist
gendarme
genocide
governor
grilling
guardian
gynarchy
hanger-on
heckling
hegemony
heirloom
henchman
heritage
highness
home rule
hustings
imperial
in camera
incivism
Jingoism
John Bull
jointure
kingship
ladyship
left wing
legation
lobbying
lobbyist
lordship
loyalist
maharani
majority
mandarin
marauder
margrave
martinet
mayoress
mem-sahib
Minister
ministry
minority
monarchy
monition
movement
narratio
navicert
nihilism
nobility
nobleman
nonvoter
official
oligarch
overlord
overrule
pacifism
palatine
partisan
party man

passport
patentee
Pentagon
platform
politico
politics
polygamy
preamble
princess
protocol
puissant
put up job
question
quisling
reformer
regicide
regnancy
reigning
republic
royalist
sabotage
saboteur
Salic law
sanction
security
seigneur
shanghai
Sobranje
solatium
splinter
Stormont
suffrage
summitry
suzerain
tanaiste
taxation
thearchy
the chair
top brass
town hall
treasury
triarchy
ultraist
Uncle Sam
upper ten
vendetta
verbatim
vice king
viscount
wardmote
Whiggism
Wool Sack
abduction
absconder
accession
accessory
actionist
Admiralty
alarm bell
amendment
anarchist
annulment
apartheid
Areopagus
authority
autocracy
back bench
bailiwick
ballot box
black book
blood feud
blue blood
bodyguard
bolshevik
bourgeois
brain wash
buccaneer
Bundesrat
Bundestag
caliphate
candidate
capitular
captaincy
catchpole
centumvir
chain gang
chieftain
Chief Whip
class rule
coalition
collegian
colonelcy
Cominform
Comintern
commander
committee
communism
communist
complaint
concordat
constable
consulate
cosmocrat
coup d'etat
custodian
Dalai Lama
death blow
demagogue

democracy
desertion
desperado
diplomacy
dogmatist
enactment
espionage
exchequer
exciseman
executive
ex officio
extremist
feudalism
feudatory
fire alarm
first lady
first lord
Folketing
formality
franchise
frithgild
generalcy
grand duke
Grand Turk
high birth
impartial
imperator
incognito
incumbent
influence
Iron Guard
kingcraft
kingmaker
Labourite
landgrave
landslide
Landsting
lend-lease
liege lord
life owner
logroller
Lord Mayor
maharajah
maharanee
major-domo
majorship
manifesto
mayoralty
menshevik
mobocracy
moral code
next of kin
oligarchy
Ombudsman
pageantry
palsgrave
paramount
party line
party whip
patriarch
patrician
patronage
pendragon
plutocrat
Politburo
political
portfolio
potentate
power game
precedent
prescript
president
presidium
pretender
princedom
princelet
privateer
procedure
programme
protector
publicist
put in suit
queenship
quittance
red-tapism
registrar
remainder
represent
right wing
sanctions
sanhedrin
secretary
selectman
seneschal
sheriffry
socialism
socialist
sovereign
statement
statesman
straw poll
straw vote
supporter
synedrion
taoiseach
terrorism
tetrarchy
theocracy

think tank
tidal wave
top secret
treasurer
viscounty
waldgrave
walkabout
abdication
absolutism
aggression
allegiance
ambassador
annexation
arbitrator
aristarchy
aristocrat
autonomous
bureaucrat
Big Brother
bill of sale
birthright
Black Shirt
blood royal
blue murder
brevet rank
by-election
Caesarship
campaigner
canvassing
capitalist
capitulary
cashiering
casual ward
censorship
centralism
chancellor
Chauvinism
chrematist
city father
civil death
classified
commandant
commissary
commission
common weal
communiqué
conversion
coronation
corruption
councillor
councilman
counsellor
department
dispatches
dotted line
doubletalk
duumvirate
electorate
encyclical
Falangists
federation
Fianna Fáil
figurehead
filibuster
fiscal year
forfeiture
front bench
full pardon
Gallup poll
gas chamber
government
Grand Mufti
grass roots
Green Paper
handshaker
harman-beck
hatchet man
heteronomy
hold office
Home Office
imposition
inducement
in jeopardy
Inner House
invocation
king's peace
knighthood
land-pirate
leadership
left-winger
legitimacy
Liberalism
lieutenant
logrolling
lower house
mace-bearer
machinator
Magna Carta
maiden name
major party
man of straw
margravine
marquisate
matriarchy
memorandum
metrocracy
metropolis
militarism

minor party
mitigation
morganatic
mouthpiece
muckraking
mugwumpery
neutralism
neutrality
noble birth
noblewoman
no man's land
nomination
ochlocracy
on the fence
Ostpolitik
Outer House
palatinate
parliament
party-liner
patriarchy
plebiscite
plundering
plural vote
pocket veto
politician
Post Office
power-happy
pray a tales
presidency
princeling
procession
protection
proveditor
pursuivant
quarantine
quarter-day

queencraft
ransacking
ration book
real estate
referendum
reform bill
refutation
regulation
reparation
Republican
resolution
revolution
right of way
ringleader
sanctioned
search form
separation
settlement
single vote
speed limit
Square Deal
stadholder
statecraft
Statehouse
statistics
statute cap
strategist
straw voter
succession
suffragist
suspension
suzerainty
the Commons
the Royal we
third reich
throne room

trade union
underworld
upper class
upper crust
upper house
vigilantes
voters roll
White House
White Paper
adjournment
agrarianism
appointment
archduchess
aristocracy
authorities
backbencher
black-and-tan
body politic
buffer state
bureaucracy
burgomaster
Butskellism
candidature
capital city
casting vote
chairperson
chamberlain
civil rights
civvy street
co-existence
colonelship
colonialism
condominium
confederate
congressman
constituent

corporation
crowned head
crown prince
Dail Eireann
declaration
diplomatics
disarmament
dissolution
divine right
doctrinaire
duty officer
electioneer
empanelment
ergatocracy
fifth column
functionary
generalship
gentlewoman
geopolitics
gerrymander
good offices
grand vizier
gynecocracy
head of state
heir general
high sheriff
high society
high steward
House of Keys
hunger-march
imperialist
independent
in duplicate
inner circle
institution
intercessor
investiture
Iron Curtain
Kellogg pact
king's speech
Labour party
lieutenancy
limited veto
Machiavelli
maintenance
marchioness
meritocracy
ministerial
mudslinging
nationalism
Nationalrat
negotiation
nonpartisan
null and void
officialdom
officialism
Papal Nuncio
partisanism
partnership
party member
peace treaty
policy maker
politbureau
powermonger
power of veto
prerogative
proceedings
procuration
progressive
Prohibition
proletariat
protest vote
public enemy
public works
queen mother
rate-capping
reactionary
rear-admiral
right to vote
right-winger
Royal Assent
royal family
royal palace
royal pardon
royal person
rubber stamp
rule of thumb
ruling class
safe-conduct
sansculotte
secretariat
senatorship
ship of state
shore patrol
show of hands
sovereignty
speechmaker
squirearchy
stateswoman
statute book
stratocracy
suffragette
summit talks
sympathizer
syndicalism
Tammany Hall
technocracy
traffic duty

triumvirate
undersigned
vice-admiral
vindication
viscountess
voting paper
Westminster
wirepulling
absolute veto
administrate
after the fact
ancien regime
Board of Trade
civil defence
civil service
collectivism
Colonel Blimp
commissariat
commissioner
commonwealth
compensation
conscription
conservatism
Conservative
constituency
constitution
customs union
dictatorship
dominion rule
domino theory
Federal Union
feudal estate
feudal system
First Chamber
floating vote
gerontocracy
grand duchess
guardianship
heir apparent
House of Lords
House of Peers
Imperial Diet
independence
in triplicate
isolationism
Jack-in-office
knight-errant
laissez-faire
landed gentry
leading light
left of centre
Liberal party
lord temporal
lower chamber
lying-in-state
maiden speech
majority rule
majority vote
metropolitan
modus vivendi
municipality
office-bearer
officeholder
pantisocracy
party machine
peace officer
people's front
plural voting
point of order
politicaster
polling booth
popular front

powers|that|be
prescription
Prince|Regent
Privy|council
protectorate
protest|march
puppet|regime
queen|dowager
queen's|speech
question|time
registration
royal|charter
royal|command
run|for|office
security|risk
seignioralty
self|governed
split|the|vote
standing|army
status|symbol
stuffed|shirt
subcommittee
totalitarian
Traitor's|gate
upper|chamber
viscountship
welfare|state
worldly|goods
absolute|power
absolute|ruler
administrator
anti|marketeer
antisocialism
appropriation
associateship
authorisation
authoritarian
authoritative
branch|officer
British|Consul
bureaucratist
ceremonialism
chain|of|office
class|struggle
committee|room
committeeship
communist|bloc
confrontation
congressional
congresswoman
consideration
consul|general
contentiously
contravention
county|borough
court|circular
courtesy|title
cross|the|floor
crown|imperial
crown|princess
demonstration
devolutionist
diplomatic|bag
division|lobby
Downing|Street
election|fever
electoral|roll
establishment
fellow|citizen
filibustering
floating|voter
Foreign|Office

foreign|policy
founder-member
franchisement
governing|body
Home|Secretary
incomes|policy
Inland|Revenue
international
letters|patent
London|Gazette
Lord|President
Lord|Privy|Seal
minority|group
misgovernment
mismanagement
mother-country
nationalistic
order|of|the|day
parish|council
parliamentary
parliament|man
party|politics
peace|and|quiet
peacock-throne
plenary|powers
pocket-borough
power|politics
pressure|group
prime|minister
prince|consort
Prince|of|Wales
Princess|Royal
proconsulship
protectorship
public|records
Public|Trustee
quadrumvirate
questionnaire
royal|standard
second|chamber
second|reading
Secret|Service
secret|session
self-governing
shadow|cabinet
smear|campaign
snap|judgement
splinter|group
splinter|party
standing|order
statesmanlike
statesmanship
straight|fight
supranational
Supreme|Soviet
ten|minute|rule
three-line|whip
Treasury|bench
Triple|Entente
United|Kingdom
United|Nations
urban|district
valuation|roll
War|Department
accountability
administration
administrative
affairs|of|state
ambassadorship
antimonarchist
balance|of|power
banana|republic

British|embassy
chancellorship
committee|stage
communist|party
constitutional
controllership
corporate|state
council,chamber
credibility|gap
current|affairs
democratically
disenfranchise
early|day|motion
elder|statesman
electioneering
firm|government
foreign|affairs
general|council
go|to|the|country
government|whip
grace,and,favour
grace|and|favour
High|Commission
Home|Department
House|of|Commons
labour|movement
local|authority
Lords|spiritual
matters|of|state
multiracialism
national|anthem
New|Year|honours
non,involvement
official|secret
order|in|council
polling|station
Primrose|League
read|the|riot|act
registry|office
security|police
self,government
shadow|minister
silent|majority
social|contract
Social|Democrat
social|security
standing|orders
state|ownership
town,councillor
Triple|Alliance
trust|territory
under,secretary
vice,presidency
watch,committee
works|committee
Young|Pretender
absolute|monarch
Act|of|Parliament
antimonarchical
birthday|honours
cabinet,minister
chamberlainship
charge,d'affaires
clerk|of|the|house
Council|of|Europe
counter,movement
democratic|party
diplomatic|corps
director,general
district|council
dollar|diplomacy
emergency|powers

enfranchisement
equalitarianism
fellow traveller
full dress debate
General Assembly
general election
governor general
heir presumptive
Independence Day
insubordination
local government
Lord High Steward
mass observation
Minister of State
Ministry of Works
nationalisation
non intervention
opposition bench
overflow meeting
parliamentarian
parliament house
party government
peace conference
personality cult
Petition of Right
plenipotentiary
political asylum
political career
political office
political theory
Privy Councillor
public ownership
quarter sessions
regional council
republican party
Right Honourable
royal commission
Security Council
select committee
standing ovation
Stars and Stripes
State Department
the powers that be
vice chamberlain
white man's burden
working majority
world government

Heraldry

or	arms	coif	fret	lion	paly
bar	bard	Cork	gamb	lure	pean
orb	bend	coup	helm	Lyon	pile
rod	boss	flag	jack	orle	ring
ankh	coat	foot	jamb	pale	rose

Ross
seal
sign
sown
spur
toga
umbo
undy
vair
vert
wavy
York
aegis
azure
badge
cadet
chief
crest
crook
cross
crown
dance
dwale
fesse
field
fusil
giron
gules
gyron
label
luces
March
mitre
motto
order
paled
pales
pheon
plain
plate
razed
rebus
rowel
sable
scion
staff
stake
tenne
tiara
torse
visor
Albany
argent
armour
banner
beaver
bezant
billet
blazon
border
braced
burgee
camail
canton
casque
charge
cheeky
cleche
collar
couped
cuisse
device
dexter
diadem
dragon
Dublin
emblem
ensign
ermine
fillet
fitche
fitchy
flanch
fretty
fylfot
garter
gemels
gobony
gorget
guidon
heaume
helmet
herald
livery
lodged
lorica
mantle
mascle
morion
mullet
Norroy
patent
pellet
pennon
potent
raguly
rustre
salade
sallet
scutum
shield
signet
sleeve
spread
symbol
tabard
Ulster
uraeus
voided
wreath
wyvern
armiger
armoury
attired
basinet
bearing
bezants
bordure
buckler
bunting
Carrick
chaplet
charged
checker
Chester
chevron
cockade
college
colours
coronet
corslet
crozier
cuirass
dolphin

dormant
engrail
estoile
flanche
gardant
garland
grafted
greaves
griffon
gyronny
hauberk
heralds
impaled
labarum
leopard
lozenge
martlet
nombril
oak|leaf
pageant
panoply
parting
passant
pendant
pennant
pierced
quarter
rampant
regalia
roundel
salient
saltant
saltier
Saltire
sceptre
sixfoil
statant
surcoat
trefoil
unguled
unicorn
uniform
vermeil
Windsor
accolade
ancestor
armorial
banneret
bearings
blazoner
blazonry
brassard
caduceus
cantoned
chamfron
cheveron
cinqfoil
corselet
couchant
crescent
crosslet
dancetty
demi|lion
erminees
erminois
fan|crest
fountain
gauntlet
gonfalon
half|mast
heraldic
heraldry
herisson
indented
insignia
invected
Lord|Lyon
mill|rind
ordinary
powdered
Richmond
Rothesay
sanguine
scallops
segreant
siege|cap
sinister
Somerset
standard
streamer
swastika
tau|cross
tincture
tressure
trippant
vambrace
vexillum
armorials
assigning
assurgent
backplate
banderole
blackjack
blue|peter
cadet|line
embattled
epaulette
face|guard

flaunches
genealogy
gonfannon
Great Arms
great seal
habergeon
hatchment
head piece
Lancaster
nose guard
nose piece
oriflamme
pageantry
powdering
prick-spur
privy seal
quarterly
red ensign
regardant
rerebrace
royal coat
royal seal
scutcheon
sollerets
spear side
spur rowel
trappings
tricolour
Union Jack
assign arms
assignment
at half mast
blue ensign
Blue Mantle
brigandine
broad arrow

cap and gown
cinquefoil
Clarenceux
coat-armour
coat of arms
cockatrice
decrescent
dexter half
dexter side
difference
dovetailed
eagle crest
escutcheon
family tree
figurehead
fleur-de-lis
fleur-de-lys
gimmal ring
increscent
Jolly Roger
King of Arms
Lyon depute
ordinaries
parted arms
parted coat
plain cross
plain field
portcullis
pursuivant
quartering
quatrefoil
roll of arms
Rouge Croix
royal crown
signal flag
stall-plate

supporters
wavy border
achievement
ancient coat
assignments
bar sinister
bishop's lawn
breastplate
counterseal
countervair
crested helm
demi-leopard
differenced
dimidiation
display arms
distaff side
dormant lion
engrailment
flag officer
fleurs-de-lys
gilded spurs
grant of arms
Lion passant
lion rampant
lion salient
marshalling
mortarboard
pickelhaube
privy signet
rampant lion
robe of state
rod of empire
Rouge Dragon
spindle side
spread eagle
subordinary

triple|crown
triple|plume
true|colours
voided|cross
white|ensign
armorial|seal
bend|sinister
bishop's|apron
border|gobony
cadet's|shield
cardinal's|hat
charged|field
couchant|lion
cross|botonny
differencing
false|colours
grand|quarter
granting|arms
grants|of|arms
heraldic|seal
imperial|seal
inescutcheon
laurel|wreath
office|of|arms
parted|shield
paternal|arms
purple|ermine
rowelled|spur
sinister|half
sinister|side
tabard|of|arms
College|of|Arms
unscutcheoned
counter-passant
heraldic|colour
heraldic|device
heraldic|shield
herald's|college
Lyon|King|at|Arms
St|Andrew's|cross
St|George's|cross
St|Anthony's|cross

Household Items

bib	log	tin	door	iron	plug
box	mop	beam	ewer	jamb	safe
cup	mug	bell	flue	lamp	sash
fan	pan	bowl	fork	lift	seat
gas	peg	bulb	fuel	lock	sink
hob	pot	case	gong	oven	soap
jar	rug	coal	hi-fi	pail	soda
key	tap	dish	hose	pipe	sofa

HOUSEHOLD ITEMS

spit
tank
tidy
tile
tray
vase
zarf
apron
ashet
basin
bench
besom
bidet
blind
board
broil
brush
caddy
chore
cigar
clock
cloth
cover
crock
cruet
cruse
diota
doily
duvet
flask
frame
glass
grate
hinge
juice
knife

ladle
latch
linen
mixer
mural
paint
panel
plate
poker
quilt
radio
sheet
shelf
sieve
spoon
stove
straw
timer
tongs
torch
towel
trunk
whisk
aerial
ash|bin
ash|can
awning
basket
beaker
biggin
bleach
bluing
boiler
bucket
bunker
burner

candle
caster
coffer
colmar
cooker
cradle
damper
dishes
dolium
drawer
duster
egg|cup
fender
fiasco
fingan
flacon
flagon
fridge
frieze
gas|jet
gas|tap
geyser
grater
hamper
handle
hearth
heater
ice|box
jumble
kaross
kettle
ladder
lagena
lintel
locker
log|bin

louvre
mangle
menage
mincer
mobile
napkin
patina
pelmet
pillow
plaque
polish
pouffe
pulley
rhyton
salver
saucer
scales
sconce
shovel
shower
skewer
sponge
starch
string
switch
teapot
teaset
tea|urn
toybox
trivet
tureen
vessel
washer
window
wiring
adaptor

amphora
ashtray
bath tub
bedding
blanket
bolster
bouquet
cake tin
canteen
ceiling
chalice
chamois
chimney
chopper
cistern
cleaver
coaster
coconut
crystal
cushion
cutlery
deed box
dish mop
doorway
dustbin
dust-pan
faience
fitting
fixture
furbish
furnace
fuse box
gas-ring
griddle
hammock
heating
hickory
high tea
hip bath
holdall
keyhole
lacquer
lagging
lantern
lattice
matches
oil lamp
overall
padella
parquet
pass-key
pie-dish
pitcher
platter
play pen
pottery
ramekin
roaster
samovar
sanctum
service
serving
shelves
skillet
spatula
spy-hole
stamnos
steamer
stewpot
sundial
sweeper
tankard
tea-cosy
tea tray
thermos
thimble
ticking
toaster
Toby jug
tool kit
transom
trellis
trolley
tumbler
utensil
valance
varnish
washday
washtub
worktop
wringer
atomiser
ballcock
barbecue
bassinet
bath cube
bath soap
bed cover
bed linen
bell pull
billy can
bird bath
bookends
cache-pot
canister
casement
cauldron
cigar box
colander
coverlet
cream jug
crockery
cupboard
cuspidor
cut glass
decanter
doorbell
doorknob
doorpost
doorstep
doorstop
driptray
eggslice
eggspoon
eggtimer
eggwhisk
emulsion
fanlight
filament
fireside
firewood
fixtures
flat iron
flour bin
fly paper
food-mill
fuse-wire
gallipot
gas-meter
handbell
handrail
hangings
hip flask
Hollands

HOUSEHOLD ITEMS

homespun
hot-plate
immerser
jelly bag
jewel box
kickshaw
kindling
linoleum
matchbox
mattress
meatsafe
monogram
moth ball
moulding
new broom
ornament
ovenware
painting
pannakin
paraffin
patty pan
pendulum
pipe rack
polisher
portrait
pot plant
radiator
rosebowl
saucepan
scissors
scrubber
shoehorn
shredder
shutters
side-door
sink unit
sitz bath
skylight
slop bowl
slop pail
snuff box
soap dish
soapsuds
soft soap
solarium
spice jar
spittoon
squeezer
strainer
sunblind
surround
tablemat
tapestry
tea chest
tea cloth
teaspoon
trapdoor
underlay
wainscot
water jug
water tap
wig-block
wireless
Yale lock
Ansaphone
auto-timer
baking tin
barometer
bath salts
bath towel
bay window
bedspread
beer glass
blank door
cakestand
cantharus
casserole
chinaware
cigarette
clepsydra
coffee cup
container
corkscrew
crossbeam
cullender
demitasse
desk light
detergent
directory
dishcloth
dish towel
distemper
dog basket
doorplate
drainpipe
dust-sheet
Dutch oven
Dutch wife
egg beater
egg slicer
eiderdown
facecloth
face towel
fire alarm
fireguard
fire irons
firelight
fireplace

fish|knife
fish|slice
flower|pot
foodmixer
front|door
fruit|bowl
fruit|dish
frying|pan
gas|burner
gas|cooker
girandole
glass|door
gold|plate
gravy|boat
hand|towel
hourglass
housewife
housework
japanning
jewel|case
joss|stick
lamplight
lampshade
lampstand
letterbox
light|bulb
log|basket
loving|cup
master|key
mousetrap
objet|d'art
panelling
partition
patchwork
phone|book
pie|funnel

place|card
porcelain
porringer
punchbowl
radiogram
safety|pin
salad|bowl
sauceboat
serviette
shakedown
shoeblack
shower|cap
side|light
slop|basin
soup|plate
soup|spoon
spin|drier
sponge|bag
staircase
statuette
steam|iron
steel|wool
storm|door
stovepipe
sugar|bowl
swing|door
table|lamp
tableware
tea|kettle
tea|waggon
telephone
threshold
timepiece
tinder|box
tin|opener
toast|rack

toilet|bag
underfelt
wall|clock
wall|light
wallpaper
washbasin
washboard
water|butt
water|cock
water|pipe
water|tank
wax|polish
whitewash
window|box
wine|glass
abstergent
alarm|clock
anthracite
apple|cover
baking|bowl
baking|tray
bedclothes
bedsprings
bellarmine
boot|polish
bread|board
breadknife
butter|dish
candelabra
cassolette
chafing|pan
chandelier
chopsticks
clothes|peg
clothes|pin
coal|bucket

HOUSEHOLD ITEMS

coal bunker
coat hanger
coffee mill
curtain rod
deep freeze
dinner gong
dishwasher
doorhandle
drawing pin
Dutch clock
featherbed
finger bowl
fire basket
fire escape
firescreen
fish kettle
floor cloth
forcing bag
fruit knife
glass cloth
gramophone
grand piano
hollow ware
knickknack
lamp socket
letter rack
loose cover
matchstick
milk bottle
mixing bowl
musical box
mustard pot
napkin ring
night light
nutcracker
oven gloves
paint brush
paper knife
pepper mill
percolator
Persian rug
persiennes
photograph
pillowcase
pillow slip
pilot light
pin cushion
plate glass
plate piece
pot scourer
pot scraper
power point
rain barrel
ration book
rolling pin
rose window
salt cellar
sealing wax
silverware
soap flakes
soap powder
spirit lamp
step ladder
storage jar
strip light
tablecloth
table knife
table linen
tablespoon
tea service
television
thermostat
time switch
tobacco jar
toilet roll
toilet soap
toothbrush
toothpaste
transistor
trinket box
vanity lamp
ventilator
waffle iron
wall socket
warming pan
washbasket
watch glass
water clock
whisk broom
window pane
window sash
window seat
window sill
wine basket
wine cooler
wine bottle
wooden ware
work basket
worry beads
airtight jar
baking sheet
bead curtain
broom handle
butter knife
candelabrum
candlestick
centrepiece
chafing dish

cheese board
china figure
Chinoiserie
clothes line
clothes pole
coal scuttle
cookery book
cooling tray
counterpane
cuckoo clock
curtain hook
curtain rail
curtain ring
dessert fork
door knocker
earthenware
eating irons
elbowgrease
family album
firelighter
first aid box
floor polish
French chalk
garden party
garden swing
hearth brush
kitchen sink
kitchen unit
laundry room
light switch
linen basket
loving spoon
mantelpiece
meat chopper
meat cleaver
metal polish
non stick pan
oil painting
Oriental rug
paperweight
picture rail
plant holder
pocket flask
primus stove
pudding bowl
pumice stone
record album
roasting tin
rotary whisk
sauce bottle
scouring pad
serving dish
shopping bag
shower cloth
silver plate
silver spoon
skeleton key
sliding door
spring clean
storm window
table napkin
tape measure
tea strainer
thermometer
vacuum flask
vinaigrette
washing line
washing soap
washing soda
wassail bowl
water closet
water heater
window blind
window frame
window light
wintergreen
wooden spoon
work surface
wrought iron
adhesive tape
antimacassar
apron strings
ball of string
bedside light
bottle opener
bottom drawer
candleholder
candle sconce
carpet beater
carriage lamp
carving knife
cheese grater
chiming clock
chimney piece
chimney stack
cigarette box
clothes brush
clothes drier
clothes horse
companion set
convex mirror
cooking range
dessert spoon
disinfectant
double boiler
electric fire
electric iron
electric lamp

HOUSEHOLD ITEMS

extractor|fan
firelighters
fireside|seat
flower|holder
French|polish
hot|water|tank
ironing|board
kettleˌholder
labourˌsaving
light|fitting
lookingˌglass
lunch|counter
magazine|rack
mulligatawny
paraffin|lamp
passeˌpartout
perambulator
picnic|basket
picnic|hamper
picture|frame
placeˌsetting
pudding|basin
radiant|plate
recordˌplayer
reel|of|cotton
reel|of|thread
refrigerator
serving|hatch
serving|spoon
sewing|needle
shopping|list
silver|polish
stain|remover
standard|lamp
swizzle|stick
table|lighter
table|service
talcum|powder
tapeˌrecorder
thermos|flask
toasting|fork
turkish|towel
userˌfriendly
visiting|card
washing|board
washing|cloth
backscratcher
blanket|stitch
blotting|paper
candle|snuffer
carpet|sweeper
carriage|clock
choppingˌblock
choppingˌboard
clothes|basket
cocktail|stick
darningˌneedle
dinner|service
draught|screen
electric|mixer
electric|razor
emulsion|paint
feather|duster
fireˌresistant
food|processer
household|gods
hurricane|lamp
lawn|sprinkler
microwave|oven
mowingˌmachine
petrol|lighter
pinkingˌshears

13/15 LETTERS

preserving pan
Saratoga trunk
sewing machine
smoothing iron
soldering iron
storage heater
vacuum cleaner
venetian blind
washing powder
water softener
cartridge paper
casement window
central heating
Chinese lantern
cocktail shaker
coconut matting
corrugated iron
cut-throat razor
electric cooker
electric kettle
electric shaver
hot-water bottle
hot-water system
household goods
household linen
insulating tape
kitchen utensil
knitting needle
knives and forks
luncheon basket
pair of scissors
patchwork quilt
pressure cooker
scrubbing brush
spring cleaning
spring mattress
washing machine
cigarette holder
combination lock
corrugated paper
electric blanket
electric toaster
immersion heater
knitting machine
pencil sharpener
photograph album
weighing machine

Insects

ant	eft	bley	gila	mite	slug
asp	fly	cleg	gnat	moth	tick
bee	nit	comb	grig	newt	wasp
bug	web	croc	grub	pest	wing
dor	bike	flea	lice	pupa	worm

INSECTS

adder
agama
aphid
aphis
aweto
brize
chirp
cobra
croak
culex
drone
emmet
fluke
gecko
genus
guana
imago
krait
larva
leech
limax
louse
mamba
midge
nymph
sedge
skink
snail
snake
sting
swarm
vespa
viper
acarus
anguis
ant cow

apiary
aranea
bedbug
bee fly
beetle
botfly
breeze
burnet
chafer
chigoe
chinch
cicada
cicala
cocoon
dayfly
dipsas
dorfly
earwig
ellops
gadfly
gavial
hop fly
hornet
iguana
insect
jigger
lizard
locust
looper
maggot
mantid
mantis
maybug
mayfly
motuka
mugger

nereid
palolo
python
red ant
sawfly
scarab
slough
sow bug
sphinx
spider
teredo
thrips
tipula
tsetse
tunnel
turtle
weevil
anguine
annelid
antenna
antheap
ant hill
ant lion
army ant
axolotl
bat tick
bean fly
bee hive
beeline
bee moth
blowfly
boat fly
carabus
cat flea
cestoid
chigger

cricket
cutworm
deer fly
earworm
echidna
emperor
firefly
flyblow
frog fly
gallfly
glowfly
goldbug
hive bee
hop flea
hornbug
hornfly
ice worm
June bug
June fly
katydid
lacerta
ladybug
lady cow
ladyfly
lampfly
lobworm
lugworm
mawworm
monitor
ophidia
papilio
phasmid
pill bug
pinworm
pismire
prepupa

pyralis
ratflea
reptile
rosebug
sandfly
saurian
serpent
shadfly
strigil
syrphus
termite
tuatara
vespoid
waxmoth
webworm
woodant
yardant
anaconda
antennae
apterous
arachnid
armyworm
avicular
basilisk
blackant
blackfly
bollworm
booklice
bookworm
caseworm
cerastes
cranefly
curculio
ephemera
firebrat
fireworm
flatworm
fleshfly
frothfly
fruitfly
gallgnat
gallwasp
glowworm
goatmoth
goldwasp
greenfly
hairworm
hawkmoth
helminth
honeybee
hookworm
horntail
hornworm
horsefly
houseant
housebug
housefly
inchworm
itchmite
lacewing
ladybird
linkworm
matamata
mealworm
mealybug
moccasin
mosquito
mudpuppy
myriapod
nightfly
nurseant
oakeggar
ophidian
parasite
pitviper
pussmoth
queenant
queenbee
sanddart
sandflea
sandwasp
scarabee
scorpion
seasnake
shipworm
silkworm
slaveant
slowworm
stonefly
subimago
tapeworm
tubeworm
vespiary
viperish
viperous
wallnewt
waterboa
waterbug
waterfly
wheateel
wheatfly
whiteant
whitefly
wireworm
woodlice
woodmite
woodtick
woodwasp

woodworm
alligator
amazon|ant
angleworm
ant|patrol
aphid|pest
arachnoid
bee|beetle
berg|adder
birdlouse
blindworm
book|louse
brandling
breeze|fly
brimstone
bull|snake
bumble|bee
butterfly
caddis|fly
candle|fly
canker|fly
cantharis
centipede
chaetopod
chameleon
cheesefly
chinch|bug
chrysalis
cicindela
clavicorn
cochineal
coffee|bug
corn|borer
corncrake
cuckoo|fly
earthworm
ephemerid
flour|moth
forest|fly
fruit|moth
gall|midge
gipsy|moth
grain|moth
gregarine
gypsy|moth
hawksbill
hemiptera
hodmandod
horned|bug
hornet|fly
humble|bee
king|cobra
king|snake
milk|snake
millepede
millipede
orange|tip
paper|wasp
peripatus
plume|moth
potato|bug
pterosaur
puff|adder
red|spider
reptilian
rhynchota
ring|snake
robber|fly
rock|snake
roundworm
sand|mason
satin|moth
sea|turtle
sheep|tick
snakelike
spillworm
spinneret
squash|bug
swift|moth
tiger|moth
tree|snake
trematode
tsetse|fly
tumblebug
turnip|fly
velvet|ant
wasp's|nest
wheatmoth
wheatworm
wood|borer
woodlouse
worker|ant
worker|bee
worm|eaten
anguifauna
bird|spider
black|snake
black|widow
blister|fly
bluebottle
boll|weevil
buffalo|bug
burnet|moth
bushmaster
cabbage|fly
caddice|fly
caddis|worm
canker|worm

carpet moth
clam shrimp
cockatrice
cockchafer
codlin moth
coleoptera
congo snake
copperhead
copperworm
coral snake
corn beetle
deathwatch
digger wasp
drosophila
dung beetle
fire beetle
flea beetle
flycatcher
fritillary
froghopper
galleyworm
gasteropod
glass snake
grass snake
green drake
green snake
guinea worm
hairstreak
hanging fly
harvest bug
hessian fly
horse leech
jigger flea
June beetle
kitten moth
lady beetle
lantern fly
lappet moth
leafcutter
leaf hopper
leaf insect
musk beetle
palmer worm
phylloxera
pine beauty
pine beetle
pine chafer
red admiral
ribbon worm
Roman snail
rose beetle
rose chafer
rove beetle
sand lizard
scarabaeus
serpentine
sheep louse
sidewinder
social wasp
soldier ant
soldierfly
Spanish fly
sphinx moth
spider's web
stag beetle
Syrphus fly
tiger snake
tomato worm
turn turtle
vinegar fly
wall lizard
water snake
web spinner
wheat midge
winter moth
wolf spider
assassin bug
beehawk moth
black beetle
bloodsucker
bristletail
cabbage moth
cabbage worm
caterpillar
clothes moth
coconut moth
codling moth
constrictor
corn earworm
cottonmouth
crocodilian
desert snail
drinker moth
emperor moth
fence lizard
flour weevil
Gila monster
grain beetle
grasshopper
green bottle
horned snake
insectarium
leatherback
lepidoptera
meadow brown
painted lady
phantom gnat
rattlesnake

rhopalocera
ringed snake
scale insect
scissor tail
scolopendra
scorpion fly
sea-longworm
Skye terrier
snout beetle
stick insect
tiger beetle
tobacco worm
tussock moth
vine fretter
water beetle
wood fretter
xylophagous
beaded lizard
book scorpion
buzzard clock
cabbage-white
carpenter ant
carpenter bee
carpet python
cecropia moth
cinnabar moth
cucumber flea
December moth
diving beetle
dragon lizard
flying lizard
garden spider
ground-beetle
hellgrammite
horned lizard
lightning bug
limnophilous
marbled white
mosquito hawk
queen termite
radish maggot
salamandrian
serpentiform
social insect
spring beetle
Suffolk punch
tropical moth
vapourer moth
walking-stick
waterboatman
water strider
white admiral
winged insect
worm's eye view
arachnologist
daddy-long-legs
entomological
harvest-spider
herpetologist
leather-jacket
praying mantis
boa constrictor
Colorado beetle
herpetological
entomologically

Islands

Als
Cos
Vis
Aran
Bali
Cebu
Coll
Cuba
Eigg
Elba
Gozo
Guam
Iona
Java
Jura
Muck
Mull
Oahu
Rhum
Sark
Skye
Unst
Arran
Barra
Capri
Chios
Corfu
Crete
Delos

Haiti
Ibiza
Islay
Lewis
Leyte
Luzon
Malta
Naxos
Nevis
Panay
Rugen
Samar
Samoa
Samos
Samso
Sumba
Texel
Timor
Tiree
Tonga
Aegina
Amager
Andros
Azores
Bangka
Bikini
Borneo
Cyprus
Euboea

Hainan
Hawaii
Honshu
Ischia
Ithaca
Jersey
Kyushu
Lemnos
Lesbos
Midway
Quemoy
Rhodes
Saipan
Sicily
Skyros
Staffa
Tahiti
Taiwan
Thasos
Tobago
Ushant
Amboina
Andaman
Antigua
Bahamas
Bahrein
Bermuda
Celebes
Corsica

Curacao
Cythera
Formosa
Gotland
Grenada
Iceland
Ireland
Iwo Jima
Jamaica
Lismore
Madeira
Majorca
Mindoro
Molokai
Oceania
Okinawa
Orkneys
Palawan
Rathlin
Re, Ile de
Reunion
Salamis
Shikoku
Socotra
St Kilda
St Kitts
St Lucia
Sumatra
Sumbawa

ISLANDS

Surtsey
Tenedos
Zealand
Zeeland
Abu Dhabi
Akimiski
Alcatraz
Alderney
Anglesey
Anguilla
Antilles
Barbados
Belitung
Beveland
Bornholm
Canaries
Colonsay
Cyclades
Dominica
Fair Isle
Foulness
Guernsey
Hebrides
Hokkaido
Hong Kong
Jan Mayen
Malagasy
Mindanao
Moluccas
Sakhalin
Sardinia
Scillies
Sporades
Sri Lanka
St Helena
St Martin
St Pierre
Tasmania
Tenerife
Trinidad
Zanzibar
Aleutians
Ascension
Balearics
Benbecula
Ely, Isle of
Falklands
Greenland
Innisfree
Manhattan
Man, Isle of
Mauritius
Melanesia
Nantucket
New Guinea
Polynesia
Rarotonga
Runnymede
Shetlands
Singapore
St Vincent
Uist, North
Uist, South
Vanua Levi
Walcheren
Ailsa Craig
Cephalonia
Dodecanese
Dogs, Isle of
East Indies
Fernando Po
Grenadines
Heligoland
Hispaniola
Holy Island
Long Island
Madagascar
Martinique
Montserrat
New Zealand
Puerto Rico
Samothrace
Seychelles
Wake Island
Yap Islands
Fiji Islands
Florida Keys
Grand Canary
Guadalcanal
Lindisfarne
New Hebrides
Philippines
Rhode Island
San Salvador
Spitzbergen
Wight, Isle of
Baffin Island
Bougainville
British Isles
Canvey Island
Cocos Islands
Devil's Island
Easter Island
Farne Islands
Faroe Islands
Great Britain
Mont St Michel
New Caledonia

Newfoundland
South Georgia
Spice Islands
Staten Island
Thanet, Isle of
Cayman Islands
Ellice Islands
Ionian Islands
Kurile Islands
Lipari Islands
New Providence
Purbeck, Isle of
Sheppey, Isle of
Virgin Islands
Channel Islands
Frisian Islands
Gilbert Islands
Leeward Islands
Lofoten Islands
Maldive Islands
Nicobar Islands
Pitcairn Island
Solomon Islands
Tierra del Fuego
Tristan da Cunha
Christmas Island
Falkland Islands
Friendly Islands
Marshall Islands
Severnaya Zemlya
Vancouver Island
Windward Islands

Jewellery

gem
gold
jade
onyx
opal
ruby
sard
agate
amber
beads
beryl
bijou
cameo
carat
charm
clasp
coral
ivory
jewel
lapis
paste
pearl
topaz
bangle
brooch
diadem
fibula
garnet
gewgaw
jargon
jasper
pearls
plasma
sequin
silver
spinel
zircon
abraxas
adamant
coronet
diamond
earring
emerald
jacinth
jargoon
olivine
sautoir
spangle
aigrette
amethyst
bracelet
carcanet

JEWELLERY

churinga
crucifix
diamante
filigree
fire|opal
gemstone
girasole
necklace
platinum
sapphire
sardonyx
sunstone
black|onyx
black|opal
brilliant
cairngorm
carbuncle
carnelian
cornelian
gemmology
guard-ring
jadestone
jewellery
moonstone
morganite
moss|agate
seed|pearl
tremblant
turquoise
water|opal
adder|stone
black|pearl
bloodstone
chalcedony
chrysolite
lucky|charm
paste|jewel
rhinestone
ring-brooch
rose|quartz
signet-ring
spinel|ruby
tourmaline
bishop's|ring
chrysoberyl
chrysoprase
lapis|lazuli
slave|bangle
wedding|ring
eternity|ring
link|bracelet
mourning|ring
semi-precious
charm|bracelet
cultured|pearl
diamond|brooch
mother-of-pearl
precious|stone
cairngorm-stone
diamantiferous
engagement|ring
precious|metals
string|of|pearls
cultivated|pearl
diamond|merchant
diamond|necklace
emerald|bracelet
emerald|necklace
imitation|pearls

Lakes

Bala
Kyoga
Aral|Sea
Dead|Sea
Dead|Sea
Tuz,|Lake
Van,|Lake
Chad,|Lake
Como,|Lake
Earn,|Loch
Erie,|Lake
Eyre,|Lake
Fyne,|Loch
Grasmere
Holy|Loch
Kivu,|Lake
Long,|Loch
Ness,|Loch
Tana,|Lake
Tonle|Sap
Azov,|Sea|of
Derg,|Lough
Erne,|Lough
Garda,|Lake
Huron,|Lake
Leven,|Loch
Maree,|Loch
Mweru,|Lake
Nyasa,|Lake

Taupo,|Lake
Thirlmere
Ullswater
Wastwater
Albert,|Lake
Baikal,|Lake
Brienz,|Lake
Caspian|Sea
Geneva,|Lake
Great|Lakes
Kariba,|Lake
Ladoga,|Lake
Linnhe,|Loch
Lomond,|Loch
Lugano,|Lake
Malawi,|Lake
Peipus,|Lake
Windermere
Corrib,|Lough
Katrine,|Loch
Lucerne,|Lake
Nipigon,|Lake
Ontario,|Lake
Rannoch,|Loch
Balkhash,|Lake
Derwentwater
Galilee,|Sea|of
Maggiore,|Lake
Manitoba,|Lake

LAKES

Michigan, Lake	Coniston Water
Superior, Lake	Constance, Lake
Tiberias, Lake	Great Bear Lake
Titicaca, Lake	Great Salt Lake
Victoria, Lake	Maracaibo, Lake
Wakatipu, Lake	Trasimene, Lake
Winnipeg, Lake	Great Slave Lake
Champlain, Lake	Tanganyika, Lake

Law

JP	case	nick	bribe	judge
KC	cell	oath	brief	jurat
QC	code	oyer	by-law	juror
act	dent	plea	canon	lease
bar	dock	rape	choky	legal
cop	doge	silk	claim	libel
feu	eyre	stir	clink	licit
jug	feod	suit	court	Mafia
jus	feud	swag	crime	mores
lag	fiat	thug	crook	mufti
law	fine	tort	dower	mulct
lex	gaol	veto	dowry	pinch
rob	gyve	will	ephor	plead
soc	hang	writ	felon	Provo
sue	heir	aggro	feoff	quash
try	jail	alibi	fraud	reeve
wig	jury	annat	garda	reset
bail	just	arson	gavel	rider
beak	kadi	bench	guilt	right
bill	lien	birch	hakim	screw
cadi	lord	bobby	in-law	Solon

swear
theft
thief
trial
trust
ulema
usher
vakil
visne
abjure
action
appeal
archon
arrest
asylum
bailie
bigamy
breach
bye-law
caveat
censor
charge
clause
cooler
decree
delate
delict
denial
dharma
dictum
dogate
emptor
entail
equity
estate
felony
fetter
fiscal
forger
gaoler
guilty
gunman
harman
heriot
holdup
honour
indict
infamy
jailer
junior
jurant
jurist
kidnap
laches
Lammas
lawful
lawman
lawyer
leaser
legacy
legist
lessee
lessor
lethal
lictor
mollah
motive
murder
octroi
old lag
on oath
outlaw
pardon
parole
peeler
piracy
pirate
police
prison
remand
report
rip-off
robber
rozzer
rubric
ruling
search
simony
speech
stocks
suitor
sultan
tenant
tenure
tie-wig
warder
abscond
accused
accuser
adjourn
alcalde
alimony
alodium
amnesty
arbiter
arraign
assault
assizes
autopsy
bailiff
Beltane
bencher
bequest
binding
borstal
bribery
burglar
case-law
cashier
caution
charter
chattel
circuit
codicil
cojuror
convict
coroner
counsel
custody
damages
defence
delator
demesne
deodand
deposit
divorce
dossier
dragnet
dungeon
enfeoff
escheat
estover
estreat
fair cop

fee|tail
felonry
feoffee
feu|duty
footpad
foreman
forfeit
forgery
frame-up
gallows
garotte
grassum
hanging
hangman
harbour
hearing
hearsay
heiress
heritor
illicit
impeach
inquest
inquiry
jeofail
John|Doe
jury|box
juryman
justice
ladrone
larceny
latitat
law-list
law-lord
lawsuit
legatee
legator
looting
mafioso
manacle
marshal
nonsuit
offence
on|trial
parolee
penalty
perjury
pillory
pinched
pleader
probate
proctor
provost
purloin
questor
Riot|Act
robbery
shackle
sheriff
slander
soccage
statute
stick-up
stretch
summons
suspect
swear|in
swindle
sworn|in
tenancy
testate
testify
traitor
treason
tribune
trustee
turnkey
Tynwald
verdict
warrant
witness
abductor
accusant
adultery
advocate
amortise
articled
articles
attorney
backlash
bastardy
black|cap
burglary
calendar
canon|law
chancery
chantage
civil|law
claimant
contempt
contract
copyhold
criminal
crown|law
cursitor
deedpoll
defender
delictum
demurrer
deponent
detainee
distrain
distress
domicile
embracer
eviction
evidence
executor
findings
forensic
foul|play
game|laws
gangster
garrotte
gravemen
Gray's|Inn
green|bag
homicide
hung|jury
informer
innocent
Interpol
jailbird
judgment
judicial
law|agent
law|court
lawgiver
lawmaker
lay|judge
legal|aid
legalism
legality
libelant
litigant

litigate
loophole
lynching
lynch|law
mandamus
messuage
mistrial
mittimus
mortgage
mortmain
mortuary
Mounties
nomology
offender
on|the|run
outlawry
panda|car
peculate
penal|law
penology
petition
picaroon
pleading
porridge
precinct
prisoner
promisor
quaestor
rebuttal
receiver
recorder
reprieve
Roman|law
scaffold
scot|free
sentence
sergeant
sessions
Sing|Sing
smuggler
speed|cop
squad|car
stealage
stealing
subpoena
sub|poena
swindler
take|silk
talesman
tenement
tenendum
testamur
test|case
the|Bench
thievery
thirlage
tipstaff
trespass
tribunal
true|bill
vice|ring
Wool|Sack
acquittal
ademption
affidavit
appellant
appellate
Areopagus
attainder
attestant
avizandum
barmaster
barrister
blackmail
body|of|law
bound|over
bridewell
brief|case
bring|suit
Bumbledom
case|lists
cassation
cell|block
champerty
civil|case
civil|list
civil|suit
common|law
coparceny
copyright
court|list
court|roll
courtroom
cracksman
death|duty
defendant
detective
detention
direct|tax
discharge
disseisin
disseizin
distraint
doing|time
drug|squad
embezzler
embracery
enactment

equity bar
ex-convict
execution
exonerate
extortion
fair trial
fee simple
felonious
feudal law
feudal tax
frithborh
grand jury
Great Seal
guardroom
handcuffs
heir-at-law
High Court
hit-and-run
Identi-kit
income tax
indemnity
injustice
inspector
intestate
inventory
Jack Ketch
jailbreak
judge-made
judgement
judicator
judiciary
jungle law
jurywoman
justiciar
kidnapper
law reform
law report
law school
leasehold
legal heir
legal term
legal year
licitness
litigator
litigious
matricide
mercy seat
miscreant
moot court
moot point
mortgagee
mortgager
Mosaic Law
Mr Justice
nisi prius
not guilty
not proven
novo damus
objection
Old Bailey
ombudsman
open court
ordinance
oubliette
parricide
patrimony
patrol car
patrolman
peculator
penal code
petit jury
petty jury
pilfering
plaintiff
pleadings
police car
police dog
policeman
police van
polyandry
portreeve
probation
prolicide
pronounce
prosecute
public law
racketeer
recaption
receiving
red-handed
registrar
remission
represent
reprimand
resetting
riot squad
Royal seal
rule of law
sanctions
smuggling
solicitor
stamp duty
statement
stuff gown
sub judice
suit at law
suit in law
summing-up

testament
testatrix
testifier
testimony
title|deed
trial|jury
truncheon
uxoricide
vice|squad
vigilante
violation
wanted|man
witch|hunt
accomplice
accusation
aid|and|abet
allegation
amercement
arbitrator
bank|robber
Black|Maria
Black|Power
breath-test
certiorari
chancellor
circuiteer
code|of|laws
confession
confiscate
conspiracy
constraint
contraband
contravene
conveyance
conviction
coparcener
corregidor
courthouse
court|of|law
court|order
court|usher
crime|sheet
crime|squad
death|chair
decree|nisi
delinquent
deposition
disherison
entailment
estate|tail
eye|witness
find|guilty
fratricide
fraud|squad
freebooter
free|pardon
glasshouse
grand|juror
guardhouse
guillotine
gunrunning
hamesucken
hard|labour
highwayman
hold|a|brief
illegality
impediment
in|articles
in|chancery
indictment
injunction
jus|commune
justiciary
King's|bench
land-tenure
law-abiding
lawbreaker
lawfulness
law|officer
Law|Society
legal|right
legislator
litigation
magistracy
magistrate
Magna|Carta
mail|robber
martial|law
mass|murder
Murphy's|law
nomography
out|of|court
palliation
papal|brief
Papal|Court
peccadillo
petitioner
petty|juror
petty|theft
pickpocket
point|of|law
postliminy
post|mortem
praesidium
prefecture
private|law
prize|court
procurator

prosecutor
punishment
purloining
put on trial
recidivist
recognitor
regulation
remand home
respondent
Richard Roe
sergeantcy
serve a writ
shoplifter
sneak thief
state trial
statute law
stillicide
third party
title deeds
trafficker
undress wig
usurpation
witness box
written law
your honour
appeal court
arbitration
arm of the law
arraignment
assumed name
attestation
bag snatcher
bank robbery
bear witness
bill chamber
blackmailer
black market
breathalyse
burglarious
cattle thief
civil arrest
civil rights
Common Pleas
complainant
compurgator
confinement
contract law
contractual
conveyancer
coparcenary
corroborate
county court
criminal law
criminology
delinquency
diet of proof
digest of law
double cross
embracement
enfeoffment
engrossment
equity court
escheatment
estate in fee
examination
exculpation
executioner
exoneration
extenuation
extradition
factory acts
fair hearing
false arrest
fieri facias
fingerprint
firing squad
flying squad
foreclosure
found guilty
gallows bird
garnishment
grave robber
guilty party
higher court
high treason
house arrest
impeachment
impoundment
incarcerate
incriminate
inculpation
indirect tax
infanticide
inheritance
Inner Temple
Inns of Court
inquisition
insufflator
jury process
last request
law and order
lawbreaking
lawlessness
law merchant
legal action
legal battle
legal estate
legal record

legal reform
legal remedy
legal tender
legislation
legislative
legislature
lese majeste
libel action
lie detector
Lincoln's Inn
long stretch
Lord Justice
magisterial
malpractice
man on the run
military law
mosstrooper
murder squad
omnibus bill
open verdict
patent-right
patent rolls
pathologist
penal reform
pettifogger
police court
police force
police judge
police squad
police state
policewoman
prosecution
Provisional
puisne judge
Queen's bench
Queen's peace
questioning
ransom money
reformatory
safecracker
shanghaiing
sheriffwick
shoplifting
Star Chamber
statute book
stolen goods
stool pigeon
take to court
tenant-right
testamental
third degree
train robber
trial by jury
under arrest
ward of court
writ of error
your worship
adjudication
amicus curiae
amortisement
appeal motion
apprehension
bar of justice
bench warrant
Bill of Rights
breathalyser
bring charges
burglar alarm
carpet-bagger
cause celebre
cause in court
chattels real
Chief Justice
circuit court
circuit judge
codification
common lawyer
compurgation
condemnation
condemned man
confiscation
constabulary
conveyancing
coroner's jury
court martial
court of wards
criminal code
criminal suit
cross-examine
death penalty
death warrant
debtor's court
den of thieves
dispensation
divorce court
dressing down
ducking stool
embezzlement
estate at will
estate in tail
false witness
first offence
frankalmoign
grand juryman
grand larceny
Habeas corpus
hanging judge
hereditament

housebreaker
House|of|Lords
imprisonment
incriminator
in|litigation
intromission
investigator
jail|sentence
judge|and|jury
judge-made|law
judgment|debt
judgment|hall
judgment|seat
judicial|oath
jurisdiction
jurisprudent
Justice-clerk
King's|counsel
King's|Proctor
Land|Registry
law|of|the|land
legal|adviser
legal|aid|fund
legal|fiction
legal|history
legally|bound
legal|redress
legal|science
life|sentence
Lord|Advocate
magistrature
maiden|assize
manslaughter
mercy|killing
misdemeanour
pass|sentence

Patent|Office
penitentiary
petty|juryman
petty|larceny
plain|clothes
plea|for|mercy
police|cordon
police|office
police|patrol
prison|warder
probate|court
probate|judge
reform|school
rent|tribunal
resist|arrest
rest|one's|case
right|of|entry
rough|justice
safe|breaking
safe|cracking
scene|of|crime
Scotland|Yard
secret|police
sergeantship
sheriff|court
silk-gownsman
smash|and|grab
strait|jacket
summary|trial
supreme|court
tenant|at|will
thirdborough
unwritten|law
violent|death
whipping|post
witness|stand

word of honour
against the law
articled clerk
assassination
break the peace
break the rules
burden of proof
call the police
cast-iron alibi
cat-o'-nine-tails
chief of police
code of conduct
common assault
company lawyer
condemned cell
coroner's court
corroboration
corroborative
countercharge
counterfeiter
Court of Appeal
courts-martial
criminal trial
criminologist
cross-question
Dean of Faculty
electric chair
expert witness
expropriation
extra-judicial
false evidence
first offender
flying pickets
funny business
High Constable
house breaking
hunger marcher
hunger striker
impersonation
incarceration
interrogation
investigation
investigative
jiggery-pokery
judge-advocate
jurisprudence
juvenile court
kangaroo court
King's evidence
knuckleduster
licensing laws
litigiousness
mental cruelty
moonlight flit
mounted police
non-appearance
non-attendance
non-compliance
non-fulfilment
non-observance
parking ticket
Petty Sessions
poetic justice
police officer
police station
Queen's counsel
race relations
read for the bar
reinstatement
rightful owner
right of appeal
rogues gallery

search|warrant
seat|of|justice
security|check
sharp|practice
sheep|stealing
sheriff|depute
sitting|tenant
Special|Branch
the|law|is|an|ass
under|sentence
unlawful|entry
watching|brief
absolute|decree
according|to|law
action|for|libel
Act|of|Indemnity
aggressiveness
bring|to|justice
Chancery|Office
Chief|Constable
Children's|Panel
citizen's|arrest
civil|liberties
code|of|practice
commit|for|trial
commit|to|prison
Common|Sergeant
conjugal|rights
court|of|inquiry
court|of|justice
Court|of|Session
court|procedure
crime|of|passion
crime|passionel
criminal|charge
criminal|lawyer
criminal|record
customs|barrier
customs|officer
decree|absolute
defence|counsel
defence|witness
detention|order
devil's|advocate
disinheritance
driving|licence
false|pretences
finders|keepers
finger|printing
forbidden|fruit
general|amnesty
general|damages
guilty|of|murder
habit|and|repute
high|court|judge
highway|robbery
hostile|witness
identification
identity|parade
incident|centre
Inns|of|Chancery
lack|of|evidence
lawful|occasion
law|of|the|jungle
learned|counsel
legal|liability
legally|binding
legal|ownership
legal|procedure
letter|of|the|law
licensing|court
loaded|question

Lord Chancellor
McNaghten rules
member of the bar
military police
monkey business
naturalisation
non-cooperation
parish register
partner in crime
penal servitude
pillar of the law
plead not guilty
presiding judge
prohibitionism
prohibitionist
provost-marshal
Queen's evidence
question of fact
read the riot act
receiving order
registry office
sheriff-officer
silence in court
special damages
special licence
sworn statement
thick as thieves
verbal evidence
ward in chancery
ward of the court
Attorney-General
bankruptcy court
barrister's clerk
blunt instrument
breach of promise
bring in a verdict
capital sentence
clerk of the court
commit an offence
confidence trick
conscience money
contempt of court
coroner's inquest
coroner's verdict
counsel's opinion
counter-evidence
decree of nullity
detention centre
disorderly house
false accusation
full-bottomed wig
inadmissibility
indecent assault
insurrectionist
judgment summons
judicial trustee
laughter in court
legal department
legal profession
legal settlement
long arm of the law
majority verdict
my learned friend
Newgate calendar
performing right
plain-clothes man
police constable
police inspector
positive vetting
power of attorney
protection money
provost-sergeant

reinterrogation
rent|restriction
scales|of|justice
scene|of|the|crime
sentence|of|death
sentence|to|death
shotgun|marriage
statement|on|oath
stay|of|execution
under|lock|and|key

Length, Area, Volume, Speed

are
ell
mph
rod
acre
area
foot
hand
inch
knot
link
mile
pace
pole
rood
rule
step
tape
yard
broad
chain
cubit
depth
folio
gauge
metre
perch
ruler
stere
toise
ton,up
arpent
bovate
decare
fathom
finger
height
league
length
linear
micron
oxgang
oxgate
oxland
parsec
sector
square
volume
coulomb
deciare
furlong
granule
hectare
virgate
calipers
carucate
centiare
distance
dividers
inchmeal
inch|tape
land|mile
quadrant
board,foot
callipers
cubic|foot
cubic|inch
cubic|mile
cubic|yard
decametre
decastere
decimetre

dekametre
kilometre
light|year
milestone
size|stick
thickness
try|square
yardstick
centimetre
centistere
planimeter
square|feet
square|foot
square|inch
square|mile
square|yard
tachometer
cable|length
square|metre
statute|mile
tape|measure
hairsbreadth
measured|mile
miles|per|hour
nautical|mile
cruising|speed
full|sped|ahead
full|speed|ahead
middle|distance
rod,|pole|or|perch

Literary Characters

Eva
Rat
Aida
Dido
Elsa
Iago
Ilia
Ko|Ko
Loge
Lulu
Mime
Mimi
Pooh
Puff
Smee
Alice
Baloo
David
Fagin
Gilda
Mabel
Marco
Norma
Oscar
Osmin
Senta
Smike
Sneer
Taper
Tessa
Tosca
Venus
Wotan
Abessa
Aeneas
Ayesha
Barkis
Bumble
Carmen
Cassio
Daland
Eeyore
Figaro
Gretel
Hansel
Hassan
Isolde
Jeeves
Jenufa
Kundry
Lenski
Merlin
Mole,|Mr
Mowgli
Otello
Pamina
Piglet
Pinkie
Pogner
Rabbit
Rosina
Salome
Sophie
Stalky
Tamino
Thisbe
Toad,|Mr
Turnus
Ulrica
Yum|Yum

LITERARY CHARACTERS

Absalom
Aladdin
Amneris
Ariadne
Azucena
Belinda
Colline
Dandini
Darcy, Mr
Despina
Don Jose
Faninal
Gunn, Ben
Kai Lung
Kala Nag
Leonora
Manrico
Masetto
Musetta
Peachum
Pelleas
Phyllis
Pooh-Bah
Radames
Raffles
Rodolfo
Salieri
Scarpia
Susanna
Tadpole
Tatiana
Tristan
Walther
Wolfram
Wozzeck
Zerlina
Abanazar
Alberich
Amfortas
Amonasro
Anchises
Apollyon
Badger, Mr
Bede, Adam
Belmonte
Bly, Nelly
Brangane
Claggart
Clorinda
Dangle, Mr
Dixon, Jim
Eyre, Jane
Falstaff
Ferrando
Flashman
Frederic
Gianetta
Giuseppe
Grose, Mrs
Gunga Din
Hiawatha
Idomeneo
Iolanthe
Jekyll, Dr
Jokanaan
Jones, Tom
Klingsor
Kurwenal
Lucretia
Macavity
MacHeath
Marcello
Nanki-Poo
Octavian
Papagena
Papageno
Parsifal
Patience
Pervaneh
Peter Pan
Pinch, Tom
Ridd, John
Sarastro
Slightly
Strephon
Svengali
Tom, Uncle
Turandot
Violetta
Wardle, Mr
Water Rat
Watson, Dr
Battle, Ben
Budd, Billy
Cherubino
Cio-Cio-San
Constanze
Desdemona
Don Carlos
Donna Anna
Dorabella
Elisabeth
Escamillo
Gamp, Sarah
Grundy, Mrs
Guglielmo
Guinevere
Gurnemanz

Hieronimo
Janos, Hary
Josephine
Leporello
Lohengrin
Manette, Dr
Marke, King
Melisande
Minnehaha
Ochs, Baron
Paget, Jean
Pinkerton
Podsnap, Mr
Point, Jack
Pross, Miss
Proudie, Dr
Rigoletto
Sachs, Hans
Sawyer, Tom
Schaunard
Siegfried
Sieglinde
Sikes, Bill
Wegg, Silas
Weller, Sam
Zenocrate
Achitophel
Allan a Dale
Aram, Eugene
Arrowsmith
Aschenbach
Aylmer, Rose
Bardell, Mrs
Bard of Avon
Beckmesser
Brunnhilde
Clare, Angel
Collatinus
Dartle, Rosa
Dombey, Paul
Don Alfonso
Don Basilio
Doone, Lorna
Drood, Edwin
Eliot, Lewis
Fiordiligi
Gargery, Joe
Gilpin, John
Gray, Dorian
Hawkins, Jim
Holy Willie
Jellyby, Mrs
Jessel, Miss
Lampton, Joe
Leigh, Amyas
Magnus, King
Marguerite
McGregor, Mr
Miniver, Mrs
Monostatos
Mulliner, Mr
Nogood Boyo
Pangloss, Dr
Poste, Flora
Quint, Peter
Rabbit, Brer
Remus, Uncle
Robin, Fanny
Sharp, Becky
Tannhauser
Tapley, Mark
Tinker Bell
Willy Nilly
Zerbinetta
Ahab, Captain
Bedivere, Sir
Billows, Lady
Brown, Father
Butler, Rhett
Cavaradossi
Charles, Nick
Cratchit, Bob
Dawkins, Jack
Don Giovanni
Donna Elvira
Don Pasquale
Doone, Carver
Dormouse, The
Finn, Phineas
Garter, Polly
Grimes, Peter
Hook, Captain
Kipps, Arthur
Lancelot, Sir
Legree, Simon
Linton, Edgar
Machin, Denry
Mad Margaret
Malaprop, Mrs
Malatesta, Dr
Marner, Silas
Miller, Luisa
Mitty, Walter
Morgan, Organ
Mudjekeewis
Noggs, Newman
Oakroyd, Jess
Orford, Ellen

Paris, Judith
Pecksniff, Mr
Polly, Alfred
Pooter, Lupin
Porter, Jimmy
Quilp, Daniel
Rabbit, Peter
Rochester, Mr
Scobie, Henry
Sparafucile
Spenlow, Dora
Stone, Rodney
Tamburlaine
Tam o Shanter
Traddles, Tom
Tulliver, Tom
Tupman, Tracy
Twist, Oliver
Varden, Dolly
Vere, Captain
Absolute, Jack
Baggins, Bilbo
Bland, Pigling
Bloom, Leopold
Borgia, Caesar
Carton, Sydney
Cheeryble, Ned
Claypole, Noah
Cuff, Sergeant
Datchery, Dick
Despair, Giant
Dracula, Count
Flanders, Moll
Green, Verdant
Havisham, Miss
Higgins, Henry
Humpty Dumpty
Jarndyce, John
Jimson, Gulley
Jingle, Alfred
Jorrocks, John
La Creevy, Miss
Magwitch, Abel
Manette, Lucie
March Hare, The
Merrilies, Meg
Millamant, Mrs
M'Turk, William
Norris, Arthur
Omnium, Duke of
Peachum, Polly
Pooter, Carrie
Probert, Rosie
Reece, Captain
Rudge, Barnaby
Smith, Winston
Traill, Archie
Troy, Sergeant
Waters, Esther
Wilkes, Ashley
Willcox, Henry
Worthing, John
Almaviva, Count
Bartolo, Doctor
Benyon, Butcher
Blake, Franklin
Bountiful, Lady
Bracknell, Lady
Bultitude, Paul
Cruncher, Jerry
Darnay, Charles
Dashwood, Henry

13/15 LETTERS

Defarge, Madame
Dobson, Zuleika
Forsyte, Jolyon
Forsyte, Soames
Greystoke, Lord
Grimes, Captain
Hannay, Richard
Herring, Albert
Holmes, Mycroft
Honeycomb, Will
Jenkins, Rev Eli
Languish, Lydia
Mock Turtle, The
Nickleby, Ralph
Oakapple, Robin
O'Hara, Scarlett
Peggotty, Clara
Perrin, Vincent
Pirate King, The
Poirot, Hercule
Pooter, Charles
Skimbleshanks
Sneerwell, Lady
Tolloller, Earl
Winnie-the-Pooh
Winslow, Ronnie
Woffington, Peg
Wooster, Bertie
Allnutt, Charlie
Battle, Mrs Sarah
Beynon, Gossamer
Borgia, Lucretia
Buzfuz, Sergeant
Collins, William
Crusoe, Robinson
Dedalus, Stephen
Dingo, Yellow Dog
Doolittle, Eliza
Fairfax, Colonel
Flyte, Sebastian
Germont, Alfredo
Holmes, Sherlock
Hunter-Dunn, Joan
Jollifant, Inigo
Madam Butterfly
Marschallin, The
Mephistopheles
Nutkin, Squirrel
Prince Charming
Rabbit, The White
Rackstraw, Ralph
Rikki-tikki-tavi
Salteena, Alfred
Shandy, Tristram
Silver, Long John
Teazle, Sir Peter
Tiggy-Winkle, Mrs
Trotwood, Betsey
Tulliver, Edward
Tulliver, Maggie
Wickfield, Agnes
Absolute, Anthony
Bennet, Catherine
Bennet, Elizabeth
Commendatore, The
Corcoran, Captain
Cratchit, Tiny Tim
Crummles, Vincent
Doolittle, Alfred
Earnshaw, Hindley
Finn, Huckleberry
Harlowe, Clarissa

LITERARY CHARACTERS

Hawk,|Sir|Mulberry
Hentzau,|Rupert|of
Knightley,|George
Little|Buttercup
Micawber,|Wilkins
Mountararat,|Earl
Murdstone,|Edward
Plazo|Toro,|Duke|of
Porter,|Sir|Joseph
Prufrock,|J|Alfred
Queen|of|the|Night
Scrooge,|Ebenezer
Smollett,|Captain
Squeers,|Wackford
Steerforth,|James
Tarzan|of|the|Apes
Trelawney,|Squire
Valiant|for|Truth
Wimsey,|Lord|Peter
Wotton,|Lord|Henry

Literature

Ed	pen	copy	mora	root	yarn
em	pie	dash	muse	ruby	acute
en	pun	dele	myth	rune	adage
MS	rag	demy	note	saga	affix
op	saw	edit	noun	scan	album
ps	set	epic	opus	slip	annal
ABC	anas	epos	page	slug	argot
act	anon	font	part	song	arsis
ana	bard	foot	past	star	atlas
bar	beat	gest	pica	stem	axiom
cap	bold	hack	plan	stet	bible
dot	book	hero	play	tale	blurb
gem	bull	iamb	plot	term	books
ink	cant	idea	poem	text	brace
lay	card	joke	poet	tome	breve
log	case	leaf	puff	type	brief
mot	Clio	line	pull	verb	canon
ode	code	mode	quad	word	canto
pad	coin	mood	read	work	caret

codex
colon
comic
comma
cover
daily
devil
diary
ditto
divan
draft
drama
dummy
elegy
envoi
envoy
epode
essay
extra
fable
farce
final
folio
forel
fount
genre
geste
ghost
gloss
gnome
grave
heads
ictus
idiom
idyll
index

Ionic
irony
issue
lingo
lyric
maxim
metre
moral
motto
Muses
novel
odist
organ
paean
paper
parse
pearl
phone
piece
plume
poesy
point
press
prime
print
proem
proof
prose
prosy
quill
quote
rebus
recto
reply
rhyme
Roman

runes
runic
scald
scene
sci|fi
scrip
serif
set|up
sheet
skald
slang
slant
slate
space
spell
stamp
story
study
style
summa
tense
thema
theme
tilde
title
topic
tract
trope
twist
usage
verse
verso
voice
vowel
words
works

abrege
accent
action
adverb
Alcaic
Aldine
annals
annual
aorist
apercu
Apollo
author
ballad
bathos
binder
bon|mot
browse
burden
byword
chorus
clause
cliche
climax
colour
column
comedy
copula
crambo
critic
dactyl
dagger
dative
delete
depict
dictum
diesis

digest
dipody
doodle
editor
em|quad
ending
eponym
epopee
errata
etymon
eulogy
expose
fabler
favour
figure
flimsy
folder
future
galley
gender
gerund
gnomic
Gothic
gradus
heroic
hiatus
homily
hybrid
hyphen
iambic
iambus
impose
italic
jacket
jargon
jingle

LITERATURE

leader
legend
letter
lyrist
mackle
macron
macule
make|up
manual
margin
matter
memoir
metric
minion
monody
morgue
neuter
notice
number
obelus
object
octave
octavo
offcut
offset
old|saw
pathos
patois
pencil
penman
penned
pen|pal
period
person
phrase
poetry
postil
potted
praxis
precis
prefix
primer
prolix
pundit
purist
quarto
quotes
reader
recant
record
relate
remark
report
resume
Reuter
review
revise
rhymer
rhymic
rondel
run|off
satire
saying
scheme
scrawl
screed
scribe
script
scrive
scroll
sequel
serial
series
seriph
sermon
sestet
sextet
simile
sketch
sonnet
spread
stanza
strain
stress
Strine
stylus
suffix
syntax
tablet
tercet
theory
thesis
tongue
truism
umlaut
uncial
vellum
verbal
volume
weekly
writer
zeugma
abridge
account
acronym
addenda
adjunct
anagram
antique
antonym
apostil
article
autonym
ballade
binding
bookery
book|fed
bookish
booklet
Boswell
brevier
bucolic
caconym
caesura
calamus
capital
capsule
cedilla
chapter
classic
codices
coinage
comment
compend
compose
context
copyman
coterie
couplet
creator
dash|off
daybook
decline
delenda

7 LETTERS

demotic
descant
dialect
diamond
dimeter
distich
eclogue
edition
elegiac
English
enstamp
epigram
episode
epistle
epitaph
epithet
epitome
eponymy
erratum
excerpt
extract
fabliau
factual
fad|word
fantasy
feature
fiction
flowers
fluency
flyleaf
garland
gazette
georgic
grammar
graphic
handout
heading
Helicon
heroine
history
Homeric
homonym
huitain
idyllic
imagery
impress
imprint
initial
in|print
insight
italics
journal
jussive
justify
laconic
lampoon
leaders
leaflet
Leonine
letters
lexicon
library
literal
litotes
log|book
lyrical
Marchen
meaning
measure
mémoirs
message
metonym
missive
monthly
morceau
mystery
narrate
neology
newsman
new|word
nominal
nookman
notepad
novella
obelisk
octapla
old|joke
omnibus
on|paper
opuscle
outline
overrun
oxytone
pandect
papyrus
parable
paradox
paragon
parsing
passage
pen|name
perfect
phoneme
playlet
Pléiade
poetess
poetics
poetise
portray
preface
prelims
present
printed
printer
profile
pronoun
proofer
prosaic
prosody
proverb
publish
quadrat
recount
refrain
reissue
release
reprint
reverso
reviser
rewrite
rhyming
romance
rondeau
roundel
sagaman
Sapphic
sarcasm
scaldic
scholia
section
sestina
shocker
sorites
special

spondee
storied
strophe
subject
summary
synesis
synonym
tabloid
telling
textual
themata
the|Nine
tragedy
treat|of
trilogy
triolet
triplet
tripody
triseme
trochee
typeset
verbose
versify
virelay
virgule
vocable
western
wordage
write|up
writing
written
ablative
abstract
acrostic
allegory
allusion
alphabet
analecta
analects
analogue
analysis
anapaest
anaphora
anecdote
annalist
annotate
antihero
aphorism
apodosis
apologia
apologue
apothegm
appendix
archaism
archives
asterisk
Atticism
autotype
ballader
banality
biweekly
boldface
bold|hand
bookcase
book|club
book|ends
book|mark
bookrack
book|read
bookrest
bookroom
bookshop
bookworm
bout|rime
brackets
brochure
bulletin
buzz|word
cacology
calendar
Calliope
causerie
chapbook
chestnut
chiasmus
choliamb
circular
city|desk
city|room
classics
clerihew
co|author
colophon
compiler
composer
construe
contents
copybook
copy|desk
creative
critique
cuttings
dactylic
describe
despatch
dispatch
document
doggerel
dramatic
elegiast
ellipsis
enallage
end|paper
end|rhyme
epanodos
epic|poet
epigraph
epilogue
epitasis
epopoeia
essayist
eulogium
euphuism
excerpta
excursus
exegesis
extracts
eye|rhyme
fabulist
fabulous
fair|copy
fascicle
feminine
folk|tale
foolscap
footnote
fragment
fullface
full|stop
genitive
glossary
Good|Book
graffiti
graffito

8 LETTERS

handbook
headline
hexapody
hieratic
historic
hornbook
humorist
ideogram
idyllist
inkstand
inscribe
inscroll
Irishism
jongleur
kyrielle
laconics
language
laureate
libretto
ligature
limerick
link|verb
linotype
lipogram
literacy
literate
logogram
logotype
longhand
love|poem
madrigal
magazine
malaprop
measured
metaphor
metonymy
metrical
minstrel
misnomer
misprint
misusage
modifier
molossus
monotype
morpheme
mot|juste
mythical
narrator
notation
notebook
novelist
obituary
octapody
offprint
old|story
open|book
opuscule
original
oxymoron
palinode
pamphlet
parabole
paradigm
paragoge
paragram
particle
password
pastoral
pencraft
Pierides
Pindaric
playbook
pleonasm
poethood
poetizer
poet|king
poetling
poetship
polyglot
post|card
pressman
printers
printery
printing
prologue
prosaism
protasis
put|to|bed
quatrain
rare|book
read|copy
ready|pen
relation
reporter
rescript
reviewer
revision
rhapsode
rhapsody
rhetoric
romancer
romantic
root|word
ruby|type
satirist
scanning
scansion
scholion
scholium
scribble
sentence
skeleton
slip|case
slipslop
solecism
spelling
spondaic
subtitle
syllable
syllabus
symploce
synopsis
synoptic
textbook
thematic
the|Press
thriller
toponymy
tractate
treasury
treatise
tribrach
trigraph
trimeter
tristich
trochaic
trouvere
trouveur
type|face
type|page
type|size
verbatim
verbiage
verselet

verseman
versicle
vignette
vocative
web|press
whodunit
wordbook
word|form
yearbook
accidence
acrostics
adjective
adventure
adverbial
allograph
amoebaean
ampersand
amphigory
anacrusis
anecdotal
annotator
anonymous
anthology
anti-novel
antispast
apostille
assonance
Athenaeum
Attic|salt
attribute
authoress
autograph
ballpoint
battology
bimonthly
biography
blackface
bold-faced
bookboard
book|cloth
book|cover
bookcraft
booklover
bookmaker
bookshelf
bookstall
bookstand
bookstore
book|token
book|trade
bourgeois
brilliant
bucoliast
cap|rhymes
cap|verses
catalogue
catch|line
catchword
character
chronicle
clarendon
classical
clippings
coin|a|word
collector
collotype
columnist
comic|book
commenter
composing
condensed
conjugate
consonant
conundrum
copy|chief
copy|paper
copyright
criticism
crossword
cuneiform
Decameron
depiction
depictive
descanter
diaeresis
diphthong
directory
discourse
dithyramb
dramatist
editorial
emphasize
end-reader
ephemeris
epic|verse
epithesis
epizeuxis
eponymism
epopoeist
etymology
euphemism
exegetics
expositor
expounder
extrabold
fairy|tale
fictional
folk|story

fragments
free|lance
free|verse
full|faced
gazetteer
gerundive
ghost|word
gleanings
go|to|press
great|work
guidebook
hair|space
half|title
hard|cover
headlines
heptapody
heteronym
hexameter
hexastich
historian
historify
holograph
hypallage
hyperbole
idiomatic
idioticon
Indian|Ink
in|measure
intensive
Irish|bull
late|extra
Leavisite
legendary
lettering
librarian
life|story
lightface
limp|cover
lithotype
livraison
local|room
logogriph
logomachy
love|story
lower|case
macaronic
major|poet
majuscule
masculine
Meliboean
melodrama
Menippean
minor|poet
minuscule
monograph
monostich
mythmaker
narration
narrative
necrology
neologism
neoterism
newspaper
newsprint
nonce|word
nonpareil
note|paper
novelette
octastich
onomastic
page|proof
palillogy
paper|back
parabolic
paragraph
parchment
Parnassus
partitive
past|tense
pen|and|ink
penscript
pentapody
personify
philology
phonemics
phonetics
phonology
phototypy
pictorial
platitude
poetaster
poetastry
poetcraft
poeticule
Poet's|Poet
portrayal
potboiler
potential
predicate
pressroom
presswork
preterite
print|shop
prolative
prolepsis
prolixity
proofread
proofroom

pseudonym
publicist
punch|line
punctuate
qualifier
quarterly
quodlibet
quotation
raconteur
rationale
recountal
recounter
reference
reflexive
represent
retelling
rhymester
rigmarole
romancist
rotograph
roundelay
round|hand
runesmith
sans|serif
satirical
scholiast
scribbler
scription
scrivener
scrivenry
secretary
secret|ink
selection
semanteme
semantics
semicolon
semiotics
sgraffito
sheetwork
shorthand
signature
slip|cover
small|pica
soft-cover
songsmith
sonneteer
spin|a|yarn
statement
stenotype
storiette
story|book
story|line
strike|off
subeditor
substance
summarize
sumpsimus
syllabary
syllepsis
symbolism
symposium
tail|rhyme
tall|story
tetrapody
tetraseme
thesaurus
thin|space
title|page
treatment
triticism
true|story
type|mould
upper|case
vade-mecum
verbalism
verbarian
verbosity
verse|form
versifier
vers|libre
vocabular
vogue|word
vulgarism
witticism
wordiness
write|upon
zincotype
abridgment
accusative
active|verb
adaptation
adjectival
adversaria
alliterate
amanuensis
amphibrach
amphimacer
anapaestic
anastrophe
anecdotage
anecdotist
Anglo-Saxon
annotation
antecedent
anticlimax
antithesis
apocalypse
apostrophe

atmosphere
authorship
background
back|number
bad|grammar
battledore
best|seller
bibliology
bibliomane
bibliopegy
bibliopole
bibliosoph
bibliothec
billet|doux
biographer
blank|verse
Bloomsbury
bookbinder
bookdealer
bookholder
book|jacket
book|loving
bookmaking
bookmonger
book|review
bookseller
bookwright
brain|child
broadsheet
bucket|seat
cacography
catalectic
chapel|text
chromotypy
chronicler
circumflex
classicism
collection
colloquial
colportage
colporteur
comic|strip
commentary
common|noun
compendium
compositor
conspectus
continuity
copulative
copyholder
copying|ink
copyreader
corruption
cradle|book
cryptogram
curate's|egg
cyclopedia
dead|letter
dead|matter
declension
dedication
definition
denotation
derivation
diaskeuast
dictionary
discourser
dissertate
dust|jacket
embroidery
epanaphora
epic|poetry
exposition
expression
fairy|story
feuilleton
fictionist
figurative
filing|room
finite|verb
funeral|ode
ghost|story
glossarist
glossology
glottology
grammarian
hack|writer
Heptameron
heptameter
heptastich
historical
house|organ
hybrid|word
hyperbaton
imperative
imposition
impression
incunabula
indicative
infinitive
inflection
ink|slinger
job|printer
journalese
journalism
journalist
lame|verses
lead|pencil

letter card
lexicology
lexiconist
librettist
light-faced
light verse
literature
live matter
logorrhoea
long accent
long primer
love letter
macaronics
magazinist
magnum opus
make a proof
make-up room
manuscript
metalepsis
metaphrase
metathesis
metrically
miscellany
mock-heroic
morphology
neuter verb
news editor
newsletter
news writer
nom-de-plume
nominative
non-fiction
noun clause
obligative
obsoletism
open letter
orismology
ottava rima
palaeotype
palimpsest
palindrome
palinodist
paper tiger
paraphrase
Parnassian
participle
pen pushing
pentameter
pentastich
periodical
permissive
plate proof
playwright
pleonastic
pluperfect
poet-artist
poetastery
poet-farmer
poet-priest
possessive
prenominal
press proof
production
proof sheet
proper noun
prosaicism
prospectus
publishers
publishing
put to press
recounting
rhapsodist
rhyme royal
round robin
runic verse
schoolbook
scratch pad
scribbling
scriptural
scrivening
sealed book
set in print
shibboleth
short story
slim volume
socio-drama
soubriquet
spoonerism
stereotype
storiology
storymaker
subheading
Swan of Avon
synecdoche
syntactics
taleteller
tell a story
tetrameter
tetrastich
thick space
transitive
troubadour
true to life
type matter
typescript
typesetter
typewriter
typography

verbal note
verbal noun
vernacular
versecraft
versemaker
versesmith
villanelle
vocabulary
word-coiner
word-seller
writership
abecedarian
active voice
acute accent
adversative
alexandrine
alphabetics
anachronism
anacoluthia
Anacreontic
antiphrasis
antispastic
antistrophe
antonomasia
attributive
authorcraft
author's copy
ballad maker
bastard type
bibliolater
bibliophage
bibliophile
bibliotheca
biographist
black comedy
black letter
bookbinding
bookishness
book-learned
Book of books
book of verse
book printer
book selling
book support
bring to book
catachresis
catch phrase
circulation
cliff hanger
collectanea
commentator
compendious
compilation
composition
concordance
conditional
confessions
conjugation
conjunction
conjunctive
connotation
contributor
correlative
corrigendum
counterterm
crabbed hand
crambo-clink
cub reporter
description
descriptive
disjunctive
dissertator
dissyllable
dithyrambic
dithyrambus
dittography
electrotype
Elzevir book
enchiridion
engrossment
exclamation
festschrift
first person
Fleet Street
flow of words
fortnightly
fountain pen
future tense
galley proof
ghostwriter
glottal stop
grammatical
grave accent
great primer
gutter press
handwriting
happy ending
heroic verse
incunabulum
inscription
inspiration
interviewer
letter paper
letter press
library book
linguistics
literary man
litterateur

local|colour
logographer
lucubration
lyric|poetry
malapropism
memorabilia
memorialist
miracle|play
miscellanea
monographer
Mrs|Malaprop
Mrs|Slipslop
nom|de|guerre
novelettist
nursery|tale
onomasticon
onomatology
orthography
pamphleteer
paragrapher
parenthesis
participial
Passion|play
passive|verb
past|perfect
patent|space
penny-a-liner
perissology
phrasemaker
phraseology
picture|book
Pindaric|ode
play|on|words
poetic|prose
poetic|works
poet-patriot
poet-pilgrim
poet-thinker
poet-warrior
point|tenses
preposition
press|revise
printed|word
printer's|ink
proofreader
psychodrama
publication
public|press
punctuation
reading|room
real|meaning
retold|story
rhyme|scheme
rotary|press
rotogravure
sad|to|relate
scriptorial
semantology
semasiology
short|accent
solid|matter
stenography
storyteller
story|writer
subjunctive
substantive
superscribe
tachygraphy
taletelling
terminology
the|Good|Book
third|person
tragi-comedy
transcriber
translation
true|meaning
type|foundry
typesetting
typographer
typographic
unfold|a|tale
verbigerate
versemaking
vers|librist
war|reporter
word|history
word|painter
word|picture
written|word
yarn|spinner
Yellow|press
abbreviation
abbreviature
abstract|noun
adherent|noun
advance|proof
alliteration
author's|proof
balladmonger
ballpoint|pen
bedtime|story
bibliography
bibliologist
bibliomaniac
bibliopegist
bibliopolist
bibliotheque
binder's|title

block|capital
book|learning
book|reviewer
bookstitcher
brachygraphy
calligrapher
chrestomathy
chronography
classicalism
collaborator
collectarium
commentation
complete|work
complication
condensation
construction
dead|language
deponent|verb
direct|object
direct|speech
disquisition
dissertation
double|dagger
early|edition
elegiac|verse
encyclopedia
epigrammatic
fat|faced|type
first|edition
foundry|proof
fourth|estate
frontispiece
gnomic|aorist
gobbledegook
gossip|column
halting|rhyme
hermeneutics
hieroglyphic
Hudibrastics
indelible|ink
initial|rhyme
instrumental
interjection
intransitive
introduction
invisible|ink
king's|English
leader|writer
letter|writer
lexicography
literary|hack
literary|lion
logodaedalus
man|of|letters
metaphorical
metrical|foot
metrical|unit
monkish|Latin
monosyllable
morality|play
mother|tongue
newspaperman
nomenclature
nursery|rhyme
onomatopoeia
palaeography
paragraphist
part|of|speech
passive|voice
pastoral|poet
perfect|rhyme
perfect|tense

plain English
poetastering
poetic genius
poet laureate
poet-novelist
poet-satirist
polysyllable
present tense
press release
question mark
quill driving
rhyming slang
Rosetta stone
second person
slanting hand
slip of the pen
society verse
space fiction
speedwriting
spelling book
stock of words
story telling
strip cartoon
turn of phrase
typeprinting
uncial letter
versemongery
word painting
writer's cramp
writing paper
yarn spinning
alpha and omega
anagrammatist
autobiography
back-formation
belles-lettres
bibliographer
bibliophilist
book of the film
book of the play
border ballads
boustrophedon
colloquialism
conquistadors
correspondent
double meaning
epigrammatist
gerund-grinder
Homeric simile
internal rhyme
lexicographer
literary agent
mixed metaphor
nonsense verse
palaeographer
palaeontology
penny dreadful
pidgin English
pocket edition
poetical works
poetic licence
poetry reading
polysyllabism
prehistorical
purple passage
put pen to paper
reading matter
reference book
romantic novel
Shakespearean
spring-cleaner
structuralism

subject matter
subject-object
tongue-twister
versification
work of fiction
ancient history
archaeological
apple of discord
autobiographer
bowdlerisation
circumlocution
circumlocutory
collected poems
concrete poetry
correspondence
covering letter
cross-reference
Dear John letter
detective novel
detective story
early Victorian
epigrammatical
etymologically
figure of speech
four-letter word
glossy magazine
grammaticaster
imperative mood
imperfect tense
indicative mood
indirect object
indirect speech
interpretation
inverted commas
Kailyard school
limited edition
living language
locus classicus
masculine rhyme
mistranslation
Norman Conquest
past participle
Pilgrim Fathers
pre-reformation
principal parts
relative clause
rhyming couplet
science fiction
shaggy dog story
Shakespeareana
sonnet-sequence
subject-heading
transitive verb
ancient monument
bibliographical
Bloomsbury group
character sketch
cloud-cuckoo-land
coffee-table book
complex sentence
creative writing
definite article
exclamation mark
higher criticism
historical novel
Hundred Years War
naughty nineties
palaeontologist
personal pronoun
portmanteau word
proof correcting
punctuation mark

LITERATURE

relative|pronoun
shilling|shocker
spelling|mistake
split|infinitive
standard|English
subjunctive|mood
thumbnail|sketch

Machinery

bar	case	lock	vice	drain	panel
cam	cell	loom	wire	drier	pedal
car	cock	luff	yale	earth	pivot
cog	coil	mast	yoke	edges	plant
fan	cowl	mike	anode	Ernie	plate
gin	dial	mill	anvil	fence	press
gun	drum	mine	Asdic	fiche	prong
hub	duct	mule	baler	flare	pylon
jet	flex	nail	bevel	forge	quill
jib	flue	pile	block	frame	quoin
key	fuse	pipe	brake	gauge	radar
nut	gear	plug	brush	gland	radio
ram	grab	pump	cable	guide	razor
rig	grid	rack	chain	hoist	relay
tap	hasp	reel	chase	inlet	rifle
vat	hi-fi	rule	choke	jenny	rivet
bank	horn	seal	clamp	ladle	robot
bolt	iron	shoe	clock	lance	rotor
bomb	kiln	skip	crane	laser	screw
boom	knob	slur	crank	lathe	shaft
bore	last	sump	crate	litho	shank
boss	lead	tank	davit	meter	shunt
buff	lens	till	diode	mixer	sieve
bush	lift	tube	dolly	motor	spool
butt	link	vane	dowel	mould	spray

stick
still
stove
strut
thole
timer
tooth
torch
tower
train
truck
TV set
valve
wheel
winch
xerox
abacus
aerial
baffle
barrel
barrow
beacon
big end
binder
blower
bobbin
boiler
brayer
breech
broach
buffer
burton
bus bar
camera
caster
castor
clutch
collar
con rod
cooker
cooler
cutout
device
diesel
dredge
dynamo
engine
etcher
faggot
filter
flange
galley
gantry
garnet
gasket
G clamp
grader
ground
gutter
handle
heater
hopper
jumper
keyway
klaxon
leader
magnet
matrix
mincer
monkey
mortar
muzzle
needle
nipple
nozzle
oil rig
outlet
pharos
pickup
pinion
pintle
pistol
piston
platen
pulley
ram jet
reglet
riddle
rocket
rounce
rudder
runner
saddle
scales
seeder
siphon
sleeve
sluice
smithy
socket
spring
square
stator
stroke
switch
tackle
Tannoy
tappet
ticker
torque
trepan
triode
tripod
trivet
turret
tympan
volery
washer
woofer
airlock
air pump
antenna
arc lamp
arsenal
balance
ballast
battery
bearing
bellows
bindery
blanket
blender
booster
caisson
cannery
capstan
cathode
chamber
charger
chassis
chatter
circuit
combine
compass

control
decoder
derrick
dredger
dry|cell
ejector
encoder
exciter
exhaust
factory
fanbelt
ferrule
flare|up
foghorn
foundry
frisket
fulcrum
furnace
fuse|box
gearbox
grommet
hydrant
lighter
limiter
locknut
magneto
measure
monitor
muffler
network
overlay
padlock
palette
pattern
pentode
planter
pottery
push|rod
ratchet
reactor
sawmill
scanner
shackle
shutter
sleeper
smelter
speaker
spindle
starter
stirrer
sweeper
tannery
televox
terebra
toaster
tracker
tractor
treadle
trigger
trolley
turbine
tweeter
utensil
welding
wet|cell
winding
wing|nut
wringer
absorber
actuator
air|brake
air|motor
armament
armature
backlash
ballista
bearings
bloomery
blowpipe
bosshead
camshaft
cogwheel
cold|weld
colliery
computer
controls
conveyor
coupling
crucible
cylinder
Davy|lamp
demister
detector
dip|stick
dynamite
earphone
elevator
fail|safe
filament
fly|press
flywheel
fork|lift
fuse|wire
gadgetry
garrotte
gaslight
governor
gyrostat
hardware
hemostat
hose|pipe
hotplate
ignition
impeller
intercom
iron|lung
isolator
laser|gun
lift|pump
linotype
lock|gate
lock|weir
logotype
manifold
monotype
neon|tube
outboard
pendulum
pinwheel
pipeline
pulse|jet
radiator
radio|set
receiver
recorder
refinery
register
repeater
resistor
rheostat
scaffold
selector
shredder
silencer

slip ring
smithery
software
sprocket
spur gear
teetotum
teletype
template
terminal
thole-pin
thresher
throttle
time bomb
track rod
turbofan
turbojet
underlay
vibrator
web press
windlass
windmill
wind pump
wireless
X-ray tube
Yale lock
zoom lens
air-engine
alarm bell
altimeter
amplifier
apparatus
aspirator
automatic
automaton
autopilot
bar magnet
bevel gear
bilge pump
booby trap
brake drum
brake shoe
bulldozer
burnisher
capacitor
clockwork
component
condenser
contactor
converter
cotton gin
crankcase
crosshead
diaphragm
disc brake
disc valve
disc wheel
drop forge
drop press
electrode
escalator
explosive
face lathe
fire alarm
flash bulb
flash lamp
floodgate
flour mill
flow valve
focus lamp
food-mixer
foot-brake
footstick
force pump
fumigator
fuseboard
fuse links
gas engine
gas-holder
gasometer
gear lever
gear train
gearwheel
generator
gyroplane
gyroscope
half shaft
hand-brake
harvester
headlight
hydrofoil
incubator
indicator
inlet port
insulator
interlock
jackscrew
jet engine
land rover
light bulb
limelight
liquefier
lithotype
loadstone
mechanism
milk churn
mill wheel
milometer
monoscope

neon|light
oiling|can
overdrive
page|gauge
periscope
piston|rod
plug|point
pneumatic
power|line
power|pack
preheater
projector
propeller
propshaft
prototype
punch|card
punch|tape
pyrometer
radiogram
rectifier
reflector
regulator
rotary|gap
sandpaper
separator
sidelight
skyrocket
small|bore
solar|cell
sound|unit
spin|drier
spotlight
stamp|mill
star|drill
steel|mill
stink|bomb
stop|light
strip|mill
sump|guard
tabulator
tail|light
telephone
thyristor
tool|chest
top|burton
treadmill
turbopump
turntable
type|mould
water|cock
watermill
wattmeter
wood|screw
worm|wheel
yardstick
zincotype
aero|engine
alarm|clock
alternator
angle|block
angle|board
angle|brace
angle|plate
arc|welding
attachment
automation
automobile
bench|drill
calculator
centrifuge
chain|block
chain|drive
check|valve
cine|camera
cobalt|bomb
coffee|mill
commutator
compressor
controller
corking|pin
cotton|mill
crankshaft
crown|wheel
crystal|set
depth|gauge
dictaphone
dishwasher
diving|bell
donkey|pump
drum|sander
dry|battery
duplicator
earth|mover
economiser
emery|board
emery|wheel
escapement
explosives
filter|pump
fire|engine
flare|light
flashlight
floodlight
gas|turbine
grindstone
gudgeon|pin
guillotine
hearing|aid

heat|engine
hectograph
hovercraft
humidifier
hydroplane
incendiary
inductance
laundromat
lighthouse
lock|washer
locomotive
luff|tackle
Machine|Age
magnet|core
marker|buoy
masonry|pin
microfiche
micrometer
microphone
mimeograph
miner's|lamp
motorcycle
oil|derrick
oscillator
osmium|lamp
oxygen|tent
paramagnet
pari-mutuel
percolator
petrol|pump
photoflash
photoflood
piledriver
pilot|light
piston|pump
piston|ring
power|brake
power|drill
power|press
push|button
quartz|lamp
respirator
road|roller
robot|pilot
rose|engine
rotary|pump
sack|barrow
safety|fuse
safety|lamp
serve|valve
servomotor
shunt|motor
silk|screen
slide|valve
sluice|gate
snowplough
spring|lock
stay|tackle
stenograph
stereotype
strip|light
sunray|lamp
suppressor
suspension
switchgear
tachometer
television
thermistor
thermostat
ticker|tape
time|switch
timing|gear
transducer
twin|triode
typewriter
vacuum|pump
vacuum|tube
vapour|lamp
ventilator
water|clock
water|gauge
water|tower
water|wheel
wind|tunnel
yard|tackle
zircon|lamp
accelerator
accumulator
afterburner
aftercooler
anchor|light
atomic|power
autostarter
ball|bearing
barrel|scale
battery|lamp
beam|antenna
beam|balance
bevel|square
bicycle|pump
brake|lining
cam|follower
carbon|light
carburettor
caterpillar
choking|coil
cold|welding
compensator

comptometer
cooling coil
dark lantern
depth charge
distributor
dolly camera
dynamometer
echo sounder
electric arc
electric eye
electrotype
engine block
engine of war
exhaust pipe
exhaust port
feeler gauge
Ferris wheel
field magnet
filing block
hair trigger
interrupter
ironmongery
jumper cable
junction box
letterpress
lie detector
limit switch
loud-speaker
machine-made
machine shop
machine work
memory tubes
mercury lamp
microswitch
mortice lock
offset litho
offshore rig
oil refinery
on-off switch
platen press
pop-rivet gun
preselector
pulley block
radio beacon
range finder
relief valve
road scraper
rocket motor
rolling mill
rotary press
safety valve
scaffolding
searchlight
self-starter
series motor
signal light
slot machine
snatch block
solar engine
speedometer
spirit level
steam engine
steam roller
stirrup pump
stock ticker
storage cell
stuffing box
suction pump
switchboard
synchromesh
tackle block
teleprinter
totalisator
track rod end
transceiver
transformer
transmitter
tumble drier
type foundry
weighbridge
X-ray machine
aerial camera
arithmometer
assembly line
balance wheel
barrel plater
battery plate
binding screw
blast furnace
blinker light
burglar alarm
capstan lathe
cash register
control panel
control valve
conveyor belt
cooling tower
copying press
cylinder head
depth sounder
diesel engine
differential
donkey engine
driving force
electric cord
electric fire
electric wire
filament lamp

flame-thrower
flashing lamp
forge foundry
fruit machine
grease nipple
grinding mill
high fidelity
landing light
lightning rod
machine ruler
magic lantern
magnetic tape
marine engine
micro circuit
mine detector
mobile camera
monkeywrench
national grid
nuclear power
pair of scales
petrol engine
photocathode
piston engine
potter's wheel
power station
pressure mine
pulley tackle
radial engine
radio compass
record player
refrigerator
resuscitator
rocket engine
rubber hammer
short circuit
signal beacon
signal rocket
single tackle
solar battery
sound limiter
sparking plug
spring washer
steam turbine
steering gear
supercharger
tantalum lamp
tape recorder
telecomputer
transmission
tungsten lamp
walkie-talkie
wheel bearing
aerodynamical
air compressor
box the compass
concrete mixer
connecting-rod
counter-motion
cylinder block
electric drill
electric motor
engine failure
fuel injection
Heath Robinson
hydraulic jack
jet propulsion
manufacturing
mechanisation
mowing machine
oceanographer
power-assisted
printing-press

rack|and|pinion
remote|control
sewing|machine
spinning|jenny
spinning|wheel
admiralty|chart
butterfly|screw
compound|engine
Davis|apparatus
design|engineer
hydraulic|brake
pneumatic|drill
production|line
propeller|shaft
starting|handle
three|speed|gear
universal|joint
companion|ladder
drilling|machine
knitting|machine
perpetual|motion
printing|machine
weighing|machine

Marine

bay
ebb
sea
cove
eddy
foam
gulf
kyle
main
neap
reef
surf
tide
wave
atoll
basin
beach
bight
briny
ocean
shoal
shore
sound
spume
swell
eddies
marine
roller
sea|air
sea|bed
sea|fog
seaway
strait
strand
benthos
breaker
catspaw
channel
coastal
current
deepsea
ebb|tide
euripus
harbour
high|sea
low|tide
narrows
oceanic
pelagic
riptide
sandbar
sea|loch
sea|mist
shingle
straits
wavelet
becalmed
cerulean
doldrums
full|tide
heavy|sea
high|seas
high|tide
littoral
low|water
mainsail
mainsail
maritime

8/15 LETTERS

mean tide
millpond
neap tide
ocean bed
offshore
rough sea
sandbank
sand reef
seaboard
sea floor
seascape
seashore
sounding
tidal rip
choppy sea
coastline
coral reef
flood tide
high water
marigraph
quicksand
salt water
sea breeze
sea margin
seven seas
tidal wave
choppiness
ebb and flow
heavy swell
sea breezes
spring tide
arm of the sea
deep blue sea
echo sounder
ground swell
hydrography
hydrosphere
neritic zone
ocean depths
wave erosion
white horses
drift current
oceanography
opposite tide
the seven seas
tidal current
fall overboard
high-water mark
master mariner
ship's register
starboard side
circumnavigate
herring fishery
starboard watch
any port in a storm
circumnavigable
circumnavigator

Mathematics

pi	trig	prism	Euclid
add	unit	radii	eureka
arc	zero	radix	factor
cos	acute	ratio	figure
cot	angle	rhomb	finite
nil	bevel	rider	fluent
sec	chord	ruler	heptad
sin	conic	solid	loglog
sum	cosec	table	matrix
tan	count	tenth	minute
apex	cubed	tithe	moduli
axes	cubic	triad	nonary
axis	curve	value	nought
cone	datum	X-rays	number
cosh	digit	abacus	oblong
cube	equal	adding	octant
cusp	field	alidad	pentad
data	graph	apogee	radian
half	helix	binary	radius
line	index	binate	secant
lune	lemma	bisect	sector
node	locus	circle	senary
plot	minus	cosine	series
plus	octad	cosinh	sphere
root	octet	cuboid	square
sine	plane	cyclic	tables
sinh	point	degree	tetrad
sums	power	denary	trigon
surd	prime	divide	ungula

vector
versin
vertex
volume
abaxial
algebra
alidade
aliquot
analogy
angular
bearing
bracket
compass
complex
counter
cubical
cycloid
decagon
decimal
diagram
digital
divided
divisor
ellipse
figures
flexure
fluxion
formula
fulcrum
hexagon
indices
inertia
integer
isochor
isotype
lattice
minuend
modulus
nonuple
nothing
null|set
numeral
numeric
oblique
octagon
octuple
ordinal
per|cent
polygon
problem
product
pyramid
quinary
radiant
rhombic
rhombus
scalene
segment
sextant
squared
tabular
tangent
ternary
ternion
theorem
totient
trapeze
unitary
accuracy
addition
algorism
aliquant
analogue
argument
binomial
brackets
calculus
cardinal
centrode
centroid
centuple
constant
cosecant
cube|root
cubiform
cylinder
decimate
diagonal
diameter
dihedral
dividers
division
dynamics
empty|set
exponent
figurate
fluxions
formulae
fraction
function
geometer
geometry
gradient
helicoid
heptagon
hexagram
infinity
integral

MATHEMATICS

isogonic
mantissa
matrices
monomial
multiple
multiply
negative
nonenary
numerary
octonary
one|sided
parabola
parallel
pentagon
prismoid
quadrant
quadrate
quantity
quotient
rational
repetend
rhomboid
septimal
septuple
sequence
sextuple
spheroid
subtract
sum|total
tetragon
totitive
triangle
trigonal
trochoid
variable
variance
velocity
vicenary
vinculum
aggregate
algebraic
algorithm
bipyramid
callipers
chiliagon
cochleate
compasses
cotangent
curvature
decagonal
dimension
directrix
duodenary
eccentric
ellipsoid
equipoise
Euclidean
figure|out
fluxional
hemicycle
hexagonal
histogram
hyperbola
increment
inversion
isosceles
logarithm
mechanics
Newtonian
numbering
numerator
numerical
octagonal
parameter
perimeter
polygonal
pyramidal
quadruple
quintuple
reckoning
rectangle
reduction
re|entrant
rhombical
set|square
slide|rule
summation
tabulator
tetragram
trapezium
trapezoid
trinomial
algebraist
arithmetic
asymmetric
biquadrate
calculator
cancellate
centesimal
complement
concentric
co|ordinate
cross|staff
decahedron
difference
duodecimal
elongation
estimation

fractional
half|circle
hemisphere
heptagonal
hexahedral
hexahedron
hexangular
holohedral
hypotenuse
irrational
mathematic
multiplier
numeration
octahedral
octahedron
orthogonal
pantograph
pentagonal
percentage
polyhedral
polyhedron
protractor
quadrangle
quadratrix
quadrature
quadricone
quadriform
quaternary
reciprocal
relativity
rhomboidal
right|angle
semicircle
square|root
statistics
subalgebra
subtrahend
tetragonal
triangular
trilateral
triplicate
unilateral
versed|sine
aliquot|part
binary|digit
binary|scale
bipartition
biquadratic
calculation
coefficient
combination
comptometer
computation
co-ordinates
cubic|system
denominator
directrices
dodecagonal
enumeration
equidistant
equilibrium
equilateral
heptahedron
holohedrism
icosahedron
integration
latus|rectum
locus|vector
logarithmic
mathematics
mensuration
metaphysics
mirror|image
mixed|number
Napier's|rods
number|field
obtuse|angle
pentahedral
pentahedron
permutation
prime|factor
prime|number
progression
proposition
rectangular
reflex|angle
right|angled
right|angles
round|number
rule|of|three
sesquialter
simple|curve
solution|set
submultiple
subtraction
tetrahedron
trapezoidal
whole|number
arithmograph
arithmometer
chiliahedron
combinations
common|factor
conic|section
critical|path
decimal|point
differential
dodecahedron

eccentricity
geometrician
hyperalgebra
line|geometry
long|division
metric|system
mixed|decimal
multiangular
multilateral
multiplicand
Napier's|bones
oblique|angle
open|sentence
orthorhombic
Platonic|body
pons|asinorum
quadrangular
quadrinomial
rhombohedron
serial|number
straight|line
substitution
tally|counter
tetrahedroid
trigonometry
vernier|scale
antilogarithm
apportionment
approximately
approximation
arithmetician
associativity
beyond|measure
circumference
commutability
complementary
complex|number
computational
concentricity
corresponding
differentiate
dihedral|angle
disproportion
exponentially
exterior|angle
geometrically
geometric|mean
golden|section
hydrodynamics
indeterminate
interior|angle
irrationality
mathematician
parallelogram
perfect|number
perpendicular
Platonic|solid
quadratic|mean
quadrilateral
quantum|number
ready|reckoner
short|division
standard|error
statistically
alphanumerical
arithmetically
asymmetrically
asymptotically
axis|of|symmetry
cardinal|number
common|multiple
decimalisation

14/15 LETTERS

head|for|figures
infinite|number
linear|equation
mathematically
miscalculation
multiplication
multiplicative
natural|numbers
paralellopiped
proper|fraction
rational|number
transformation
two-dimensional
vulgar|fraction
decimal|notation
differentiation
Fibonacci|series
golden|rectangle
identity|element
imaginary|number
proportionately
pure|mathematics
square|the|circle
trigonometrical
unknown|quantity

Measurement

amp
BTU
cab
erg
ohm
rad
rem
atom
BThU
dyne
iota
mole
norm
phon
phot
size
volt
watt
angle
curie
cycle
dozen
farad
fermi
gauge
gross
henry
hertz
joule
level
lumen
meter
plumb
score
therm
third
ampere
armful
calory
degree
kilerg
megohm
minute
myriad
photon
proton
radian
second
chiliad
compass
decibel
geodesy
gilbert
hundred
kiloton
lambert
maximum
maxwell
minimum
modicum
neutron
pelorus
poundal
quarter

MEASUREMENT

rontgen
sextant
sixfold
tenfold
twofold
umpteen
vernier
zillion
angstrom
electron
fivefold
fourfold
fraction
gas meter
kilovolt
kilowatt
magneton
megavolt
megawatt
microbar
milliard
molecule
ninefold
odometer
particle
roentgen
standard
thousand
viameter
watt-hour
astrolabe
barometer
eightfold
geodesist
graticule
hodometer
kilocycle
manometer
megacurie
megacycle
minometer
nonillion
osmometer
pedometer
pinchbeck
potometer
pyrometer
set square
sevenfold
slide rule
surveying
telemeter
telemetry
threefold
umpteenth
vicesimal
vigesimal
anemometer
audiometer
bathometer
brinometer
Centigrade
clinometer
cyclometer
densimeter
depth gauge
Fahrenheit
goniometer
goniometry
gravimeter
heliometer
hygrometer
hypsometer
micrometer
multicurie
nitrometer
odorimetry
ombrometer
pantometer
piezometer
planimeter
planimetry
protractor
pyknometer
radiometer
radiometry
Rutherford
spirometer
tachometer
tachymetry
theodolite
tintometer
twelvefold
viscometer
voltameter
volt-ampere
actinometer
baker's dozen
calibration
calorimeter
calorimetry
candle power
chronometry
dynamometer
gradiometer
mensuration
polarimeter
polarimetry

quantometer
salinometer
spirit level
thermal unit
thermometer
undecennary
undecennial
cathetometer
decimal point
declinometer
electrometer
electronvolt
extensometer
golden guinea
inclinometer
kilowatt hour
magnetometer
metric system
microohmeter
millirontgen
psychrometer

respirometer
spectrometer
thousandfold
alcoholometer
alcoholometry
anticlockwise
common measure
dead reckoning
made to measure
measuring tape
quadruplicate
tablespoonful
as the crow flies
commensuration
counterbalance
countermeasure
mismeasurement
third dimension
antepenultimate
drop in the bucket
fourth dimension

Medicine

Dr	bed	ENT	hip	oil	sty
GP	cup	eye	ill	pep	tea
MD	cut	fat	jaw	pox	tic
MO	doc	fit	lab	pus	toe
os	DTs	flu	LDS	rib	vet
TB	ear	gas	leg	rub	wan
ail	ECG	gum	lip	sac	wen
arm	EEG	gut	LSD	spa	abed

MEDICINE

ache	face	lint	shin	aorta	croup
acne	fade	lips	shot	atomy	dagga
ague	fall	lisp	sick	aural	dandy
AIDS	flux	lobe	skin	bathe	death
back	foot	lung	slim	baths	decay
bald	gall	maim	sole	belch	digit
balm	game	malt	sore	birth	dizzy
band	gash	mask	spot	blain	donor
bile	germ	mole	stab	bleed	drain
body	gout	mute	stye	blind	drill
boil	grip	nail	swab	blood	drops
bone	guts	nape	tent	bolus	dying
bubo	hair	nape	turn	bomoh	edema
burn	halt	neck	ulna	borax	elbow
burp	hand	noma	umbo	botch	ether
calf	harm	nose	vein	bowel	faint
case	head	numb	vena	brace	femur
cast	heal	oral	wale	brain	fever
cell	heel	otic	wall	brash	fibre
chin	hemp	pain	ward	break	flesh
clot	hips	pale	wart	build	flush
cold	home	palm	weal	bulla	fossa
coma	hurt	pang	welt	bursa	frame
corn	hypo	pest	wilt	canal	fugue
cure	ilia	pill	wits	catch	Galen
cusp	iris	plug	womb	chafe	gauze
cyst	iron	pock	Xray	cheek	gland
daze	itch	pons	yawn	chest	gonad
deaf	junk	pore	yaws	chest	gored
diet	kibe	rash	acute	clava	gouty
dope	kink	rest	agony	colic	graft
dose	knee	ribs	algid	colon	graze
drip	lame	roof	alive	conch	gripe
drug	lens	root	ancon	cough	gumma
duct	limb	scab	ankle	cramp	gyrus
dumb	limp	scar	anvil	crick	heart

5/6 LETTERS

helix
herbs
hilum
hives
hyoid
ictus
ileum
ilium
incus
inion
inlay
jerks
joint
jowls
lance
lazar
leech
leper
liver
local
locum
lungs
lymph
lysis
mamma
medic
medic
miasm
molar
mouth
mumps
nasal
navel
nerve
nevus
nurse

opium
organ
ovary
palsy
panel
pinna
plate
polio
polyp
probe
psora
pulse
pupil
purge
quack
rabid
ramus
raphe
renal
rheum
salts
salve
scalp
seedy
senna
serum
shell
shock
sight
sinew
sinus
skull
sleep
sling
smart
sopor

sound
spasm
spine
stall
sting
stupe
sweat
swoon
tabes
tabid
taint
talus
teeth
thigh
throb
throe
thumb
tibia
tired
tonic
tooth
torso
trace
tract
treat
trunk
tummy
ulcer
ulnar
uncus
unfit
urine
uvula
vagus
valve
villi

virus
vomer
vomit
waist
wheal
whelk
wince
wound
wreck
wrist
aching
addict
ailing
albino
alexia
amytal
anemia
anemic
angina
anoint
antrum
apnoea
areola
armpit
arnica
artery
asthma
ataxia
atocia
attack
aurist
axilla
balsam
bedpan
benign
biceps

binder
biopsy
blanch
bowels
bracer
breast
breath
bruise
bulimy
bunion
caecum
caligo
callus
cancer
canker
caries
carpus
cavity
cervix
chafed
chiasm
choler
chorea
clavus
clinic
clonus
coccyx
codein
coelom
comedo
concha
corium
cornea
corpse
cortex
coryza

MEDICINE

costal
cow|pox
crisis
crusta
crutch
cuboid
cuneus
damage
dartre
deadly
defect
demise
dengue
dental
dermis
doctor
dorsum
dosage
dossil
dropsy
eczema
elixir
embryo
emetic
engram
eschar
eyelid
fascia
fester
fibula
figure
fillip
finger
foetus
fornix
fundus
fungus
gargle
goitre
gripes
grippe
growth
gullet
hallux
hammer
healer
health
hearty
hernia
heroin
humour
immune
infirm
injury
in|pain
instep
insula
intern
iodine
kidney
labial
labour
laid|up
lambda
lancet
lappet
larynx
lavage
lesion
lichen
lipoma
lobule
lotion
lumber
lunula
maimed
malady
marrow
matron
measly
meatus
medico
medius
megrim
member
meninx
mentum
miasma
midrib
mongol
morbid
mucous
muscle
mutism
myopic
naevus
nasion
nausea
needle
neuron
nipple
oculus
opiate
osteal
palate
pallor
papule
pelvis
peptic
phlegm
phobia
physic
pimple
plague
plasma
pleura
plexus
poison
poorly
potion
ptisan
puncta
pyemia
queasy
quinsy
rabies
rachis
radial
ranula
reflex
relief
remedy
retina
rhesus
rictus
robust
roller
sacrum
saliva
scrape
scurvy
seeing
senses
sepsis
septic
serous
sicken
sickly
simple
sister
slough
sneeze
spatum
spinal
spleen
splint
spotty
sprain
squint
stapes
stasis
stigma
stitch
strium
stroke
struma
stupor
stylet
suffer
suture
tablet
tampon
tarsus
temple
tender
tendon
tetter
thorax
throat
throes

thrush
thymus
ticker
tingle
tisane
tissue
tongue
tragus
tremor
trepan
trocar
troche
tumour
twinge
unwell
ureter
vector
vesica
vessel
villus
viscus
vitals
vomica
voyeur
weaken
weakly
wrench
writhe
xyster
zygoma
abdomen
abscess
acidity
aconite
adrenal
ailment

airsick
alcohol
allergy
allheal
ampulla
anaemia
anaemic
analyst
anatomy
anodyne
antacid
antigen
aphasia
aphonia
apraxia
arcanum
aspirin
assuage
atebrin
atrophy
auricle
autopsy
bacilli
bandage
bedfast
bedsore
bilious
bismuth
bladder
blister
booster
bow-legs
bromide
bubonic
bulimia
cadaver

calcium
calomel
camphor
cannula
capsule
carcass
cardiac
carious
carrier
carsick
cascara
catarrh
cautery
chalone
chancre
chemist
chiasma
cholera
chorion
choroid
chronic
ciliary
cocaine
cochlea
colicky
colitis
condyle
cordial
coroner
cranium
cricoid
cripple
cupping
cure-all
cuticle
deathly

decease
decline
deltoid
dentist
derange
disease
draught
earache
eardrum
ear-lobe
earshot
epithem
erosion
ethmoid
eyeball
eyebrow
eyewash
failing
fantasy
fatigue
febrile
feel-ill
feeling
femoral
fibroid
fidgets
filling
fimbria
fistula
flushed
foramen
forceps
forearm
frailty
freckle
frontal

MEDICINE

game|leg
gastric
glasses
gumboil
haggard
hashish
heal|all
healing
healthy
hearing
hipbone
history
hormone
hospice
hot|bath
humerus
hygiene
icterus
illness
incisor
innards
insides
insulin
invalid
ischium
jawbone
jejunum
jugular
kneecap
kneepan
laid|low
lanolin
lazaret
lentigo
leprosy
leprous
linctus
lockjaw
lozenge
lumbago
malaise
malaria
malleus
massage
masseur
mastoid
maxilla
measles
medical
medulla
menthol
microbe
midwife
milk|leg
mixture
myringa
nail|bed
nervous
nostril
nostrum
obesity
occiput
oculist
omentum
operate
orbital
orderly
organic
osseous
ossicle
otology
ovaries
panacea
papilla
paresis
parotid
passage
pass|out
patella
patient
pessary
phalanx
pharynx
pigment
pill|box
pinkeye
placebo
plaster
pledget
podagra
pterion
punctum
pustule
putamen
pyaemia
pylorus
pyramid
pyretic
pyrexia
quassia
quinine
regimen
relapse
removal
reviver
ribcage
rickets
rubella
rubeola
run|down
rupture
saccule
sarcoma
scabies
scalpel
scapula
scratch
seasick
seconal
section
seizure
seltzer
sensory
sick|bay
sickbed
sinking
skin|man
soother
spastic
spitoon
springs
stammer
sterile
sternum
stirrup
stomach
stutter
sublime
sulphur
sun|bath
sun|lamp
surgeon
symptom
syncope

syntone
syntony
syringe
tactile
taenial
take ill
talipes
tampion
tapetum
tear-bag
tetanus
theatre
theriac
thermae
thyroid
toenail
tonsils
tormina
toxemia
trachea
travail
triceps
trional
typhoid
unction
unguent
unsound
urethra
utricle
vaccine
vapours
variola
veronal
verruca
vertigo
viscera

vitamin
whitlow
witless
zymotic
abnormal
abortion
abrasion
accident
acidosis
acromion
adenoids
adhesion
agar-agar
agraphia
albinism
allergic
allopath
alopecia
amputate
analysis
anatomic
antibody
antidote
aperient
apoplexy
aposteme
appendix
appetite
arteries
Asian flu
asphyxia
assuager
asthenia
atropine
autacoid
bacillus

backache
backbone
bacteria
baldness
barbital
beriberi
bicuspid
bifocals
bile duct
bistoury
black eye
black-out
bleeding
blind eye
blockage
brachial
break out
bulletin
caffeine
cannabis
carditis
casualty
cataract
catching
catheter
cathexis
cephalic
cerebral
cervical
choleric
cicatrix
clavicle
clinical
club-foot
cockeyed
cold sore

collapse
comatose
compress
confined
contract
coronary
critical
crutches
curative
cyanosis
cynanche
dandruff
deathbed
debility
decrepit
delicate
delirium
delivery
dentures
diabetes
diagnose
digestif
diplegia
disabled
diseased
disgorge
disorder
dispense
diuretic
dog tired
dosology
dressing
drop dead
druggist
drumhead
ductless

MEDICINE

duodenum
ecraseur
edgebone
embolism
emulsion
enceinte
engramma
entrails
epidemic
epilepsy
epiploon
eruption
erythema
etiology
excision
exit|dose
exposure
eye|drops
eye|patch
eyesalve
eyesight
eye|tooth
face|lift
first|aid
flat|feet
follicle
forehead
fracture
freak|out
frenulum
fumigant
furuncle
gallipot
ganglion
gangrene
glaucoma
glycerin
grand|mal
hair|ball
handicap
hard|drug
hay|fever
headache
heat|lamp
heat|spot
heel|bone
hemostat
hip|joint
holotony
homesick
hospital
hot|flush
houseman
immunity
impetigo
impotent
incision
infected
inflamed
inhalant
inner|ear
insomnia
internal
iron|lung
irritant
jaundice
languish
laudanum
laudanum
lavement
laxative
lenitive
lethargy
leukemia
ligament
ligature
lincture
liniment
lip|salve
lobotomy
lordosis
love|drug
malarial
mal|de|mer
mandible
marasmus
masseter
masseuse
maturant
medicate
medicine
membrane
midbrain
migraine
morphine
muscular
mycology
naked|eye
narcosis
narcotic
necrosis
nembutal
neoplasm
neuritis
nosogeny
nosology
novocain
numbness
ointment
olive|oil
operator
otoscope
overdose
pancreas
pandemia
papillae
parasite
parietal
paroxysm
pectoral
peduncle
pellagra
perspire
petit|mal
phalange
pharmacy
philtrum
phthisis
physical
physique
pia|mater
pick|me|up
pisiform
placenta
pleurisy
podagric
podiatry
posology
poultice
practice
pregnant
premolar
prenatal
procaine

prostate
pulmonic
pump room
purblind
pus basin
pyorrhea
reaction
receptor
Red Cross
remedial
resident
rest cure
ringworm
roborant
salivary
sanatory
scaphoid
scarring
sciatica
scrofula
secretin
sedation
sedative
senility
serology
shinbone
shingles
shoulder
sick abed
sickling
sickness
sickroom
sinapism
skeletal
skeleton
skin-deep

skin dose
smallpox
smarting
soft drug
somatist
soothing
soreness
sore spot
specimen
speculum
sphenoid
sphygmus
splenium
stinging
stitches
striatum
subacute
sudarium
sufferer
surgical
swelling
take sick
tear drop
tear duct
teething
temporal
teratoma
thalamus
the bends
thin skin
thoracic
thyroxin
tingling
tocogony
tocology
toponymy

trachoma
traction
trephine
true skin
tubercle
tumerous
tympanum
ulcerous
unciform
uroscopy
vaccinia
valerian
variolar
vascular
vaseline
vena cava
venotomy
vertebra
vesicant
vitality
vomiting
wall-eyed
wandered
weakling
wet nurse
admission
adrenalin
aitchbone
alcoholic
alkalizer
alleviate
allopathy
amaurosis
ambulance
analeptic
analgesia

MEDICINE

analgesic
anamnesis
anklebone
ankylosis
antenatal
antihelix
antiserum
antitoxin
arthritis
aspirator
assuasive
audiology
auriscopy
bacterium
bandaging
barbitone
bath|chair
bedridden
bellyache
birthmark
blackhead
blindness
blind|spot
blood|bank
blood|bank
blood|test
blue|blood
body|odour
boric|acid
bow|legged
brain|cell
breakdown
broken|arm
broken|leg
Caesarean
calenture
callipers
callosity
calmative
calvities
cankerous
carbuncle
carcinoma
cartilage
caruncula
case|sheet
castor|oil
catalepsy
cataplasm
cataplexy
catatonia
catatonic
catch|cold
catharsis
cathartic
cauterize
cheekbone
chilblain
chin|cough
chiropody
cicatrice
cirrhosis
claustrum
cleansing
collyrium
complaint
condition
conscious
contagion
contusion
corpuscle
cortisone
cough|drop
crash|diet
cretinism
cross|eyed
cuneiform
curvature
dead|faint
dead|tired
defective
delirious
demulcent
dentistry
depth|dose
diagnosis
diaphragm
diarrhoea
diathermy
dichotomy
diet|sheet
digitalis
discharge
dispenser
distemper
dizzy|turn
dosimeter
dosimetry
drain|tube
dropsical
dura|mater
dysentery
dyspepsia
dyspeptic
dystrophy
echolalia
electuary
emaciated

9 LETTERS

embrocate
emergency
emollient
endocrine
endolymph
energumen
ephedrine
epidermis
epileptic
epiphyses
esotropia
exotropia
extremity
eye|doctor
eyelashes
faith|cure
fallopian
fallotomy
false|ribs
febrifuge
febrility
festering
fetishism
fever|heat
fever|ward
flatulent
fore-brain
frostbite
fumigator
fungosity
funny|bone
gastritis
gathering
geriatric
germicide
give|birth
gladiolus
glandular
glycerine
halitosis
hammer|toe
hamstring
heartbeat
heartburn
histamine
homeopath
horehound
hunchback
idiopathy
ill-health
impatient
incubator
incurable
infection
infirmary
infirmity
influenza
ingestion
inhalator
injection
injection
inoculate
in|plaster
invalided
iron|pills
iron|tonic
isolation
jail|fever
king's|evil
knee|joint
labyrinth
lachrymal
lazaretto
leucocyte
life|force
long|sight
lymphatic
malar|bone
malignant
malleolus
manubrium
marihuana
marijuana
maternity
maxillary
medicated
medicinal
mesentery
mesocolon
middle|ear
midwifery
milk|teeth
mongolism
morbidity
mortified
mouthwash
nappy|rash
narcotics
nasal|duct
nauseated
near-sight
nebulizer
neophobia
nephritis
nerve|cell
neuralgia
neurology
neuropath

noncompos
nutrition
nux|vomica
nystagmus
occipital
off|colour
officinal
olfactory
on|the|mend
operation
optic|disc
optometry
osteology
osteopath
otologist
pacemaker
paralysis
paregoric
parotitis
pathology
perilymph
pertussis
pesthouse
phagocyte
phalanges
phlebitis
phrenetic
physician
pin|and|web
pituitary
pneumeter
pneumonia
poisoning
pollution
precuneus
premature
prescribe
prognosis
prophasis
psoriasis
pulmonary
purgative
purifying
quadratus
rachidial
radiogram
radiology
resection
sartorius
sassafras
sauna|bath
sclerosis
sclerotic
sebaceous
secretion
seediness
semi-lunar
sensorium
sinusitis
skingraft
soporific
spare-part
splay|feet
squeamish
squinting
sterilize
stiff|dose
stiff|neck
stillborn
stimulant
stretcher
subsultus
sudorific
suffering
sunstroke
suppurant
sweat|bath
syntectic
taste|buds
tear|gland
tegmentum
thanatoid
therapist
thighbone
thyrotomy
toothache
toothpick
trapezium
trapezius
treatment
tricuspid
tummy-ache
umbilical
umbilicus
unguentum
unhealthy
urticaria
vaccinate
varicella
varicosis
venectomy
ventricle
vermifuge
vertibrae
vestibule
vulnerary
washed|out
waste|away

water cure
wax glands
wellbeing
wristbone
xeroderma
X-ray plate
zoophobia
zooplasty
abirritant
abreaction
acetabulum
acrophobia
Adam's apple
aerophobia
affliction
afterbirth
algophobia
alimentary
amputation
anesthesia
ankle joint
antibiotic
antipoison
antisepsis
antiseptic
antitragus
apoplectic
apothecary
applicator
astragalus
barium meal
batophobia
belladonna
Black Death
blood count
blood donor
blood group
bloodstain
bloody flux
bonesetter
brain fever
breastbone
breathless
broken bone
broken dose
broken nose
bronchitis
buccinator
canker rash
castration
catalepsis
catholicon
cerebellum
chickenpox
chloroform
chromosome
cibophobia
collarbone
commissure
common cold
compulsion
concussion
consultant
contagious
convalesce
convulsion
corn doctor
corrective
cotton wool
cough syrup
cyclothyme
cynophobia
cystectomy
cystoscope
dandy fever
danger list
deathwatch
dentifrice
dermatitis
dim-sighted
diphtheria
dipsomania
dirty nurse
disability
discomfort
disfigured
dispensary
dizzy spell
doraphobia
draw breath
drop serene
drug addict
ear trumpet
ectodermal
elbow joint
emaciation
embonpoint
embryology
emplastrum
enclampsia
entodermal
epispastic
epithelium
Epsom salts
ergophobia
erotomania
eructation
euthanasia

extraction
faith|curer
false|teeth
farsighted
feebleness
fever|pitch
fibrositis
fine|fettle
fingernail
five|senses
flatulence
fonticulus
foot|doctor
gallstones
gamophobia
gastrotomy
geriatrics
gripe|water
haunch|bone
healing|art
health|farm
hearing|aid
heatstroke
hemaglobin
hematology
hemiplegia
hemisphere
hemophilia
hemophobia
homeopathy
hot|springs
hypodermic
hypodermis
idiopathic
immunology
Indian|hemp
indisposed
infectious
inhibition
insolation
inspirator
instrument
interferon
internship
intestines
invalidate
invalidism
invalidity
irritation
kill|or|cure
kiss|of|life
knock|knees
laboratory
laceration
laparotomy
laryngitis
lassa|fever
last|breath
lazar|house
leechcraft
lethal|dose
loss|of|life
lymph|gland
main|stream
medical|man
medicament
medicaster
medication
meningitis
mesogaster
metabolism
metacarpus
metatarsus
microscope
monophobia
mutilation
nail|matrix
narcissist
nauseation
nerve|fibre
nettle|rash
neuropathy
night|float
night|nurse
nosophobia
obstetrics
odontogeny
oesophagus
optic|nerve
optic|tract
orthopraxy
orthoscope
ossiferous
osteoblast
osteoclast
osteopathy
out|of|sorts
outpatient
overweight
oxygen|mask
oxygen|tank
oxygen|tent
padded|cell
paediatric
painkiller
palliative
paraphasia
paraplegia

10/11 LETTERS

paronychia
pathognomy
pediatrics
pediatrist
penicillin
periosteum
peritoneal
peritoneum
pestilence
pharmacist
phenacetin
phlebotomy
physiology
pigeon toed
pineal body
plague spot
podiatrist
polychrest
polyclinic
poor health
post mortem
premaxilla
presbyopia
prevention
preventive
prognostic
protective
public ward
pyretology
radiograph
radiometer
radioscopy
radium bath
ray therapy
recuperate
regression
resistance
respirator
rheumatics
root sheath
rude health
salivation
salt cellar
sanatorium
sanitarian
saucer eyes
scarlatina
scrofulous
semeiology
semeiotics
sense organ
septicemia
serologist
short sight
sick as a dog
sickliness
sixth sense
soft palate
somatology
sore throat
specialist
spectacles
sphacelate
spinal cord
spirograph
spirometer
splanchnic
squint eyes
staff nurse
sterilizer
strabismus
strict diet
strychnine
sublingual
suprarenal
sweat gland
teratology
thrombosis
tonic spasm
toothpaste
toponymics
tourniquet
toxicology
transplant
traumatism
trochanter
truth serum
tumescence
ulceration
urinalysis
varicotomy
vesicotomy
veterinary
Vichy water
vital force
vital spark
vocal cords
wheel chair
witch hazel
wonder drug
xenophobia
yellow jack
yellow spot
abnormality
abortionist
airsickness
amphetamine
anaesthesia

MEDICINE

anaesthetic
an apple a day
antifebrile
antipyretic
aphrodisiac
application
arteriotomy
astigmatism
auscultator
bactericide
barbiturate
basket cells
blood stream
blood stroke
blood-vessel
booster dose
breaking out
caesarotomy
canine tooth
cardiograph
carminative
car-sickness
case history
cephalalgia
chemiatrist
chiroplasty
chiropodist
chiropraxis
choroid coat
circulation
cleft palate
coconscious
cod liver oil
cold therapy
colour blind
confinement
conjunctiva
consumption
consumptive
contact lens
convolution
convulsions
corn plaster
decrepitude
deep therapy
deobstruent
dermaplasty
dermatology
diagnostics
diaphoretic
dislocation
dull-sighted
eccrinology
Elastoplast
elixir vitae
embrocation
endocardium
examination
exoskeleton
expectorant
extremities
face lifting
facial nerve
famine fever
fatty tissue
fibre optics
fingerstall
floating rib
fluoroscope
fomentation
gall-bladder
gastrectomy
gerontology
gild the pill
gnawing pain
gold therapy
granule cell
growing pain
gynaecology
haemorrhage
handicapped
healthiness
health salts
heart attack
hebephrenia
hectic fever
hectic flush
heteropathy
Hippocratic
hormonology
horse doctor
hospital bed
hospitalize
hydrophobia
indigestion
inoculation
internal ear
intravenous
ipecacuanha
irradiation
isodose line
jugular vein
kidney basin
laparoscopy
laughing gas
locum tenens
long-sighted
lycanthropy

malfunction
median nerve
medicine man
miracle drug
miscarriage
mitral valve
mortal wound
musculature
nasopharynx
naturopathy
nearsighted
nerve ending
nerve supply
neurologist
neuroplasty
neutralizer
nursing home
nyctophobia
observation
obstruction
obtometrist
orthodontia
orthopaedic
orthopedics
orthopedist
palpitation
Pandora's box
parathyroid
parturition
pathologist
pelvic colon
peptic ulcer
pericardium
peristaltic
peritonitis
pharyngitis
physiognomy
plaster cast
prickly heat
private ward
probationer
prognostics
prophylaxis
quack remedy
quacksalver
rabbit fever
radiography
radiologist
radiopraxis
radiothermy
respiration
restorative
rheumaticky
rhinoplasty
rigor mortis
roentgen ray
running nose
sal-ammoniac
sal volatile
schizoidism
seasickness
senile decay
skin disease
solar plexus
stethoscope
stirrup bone
stomach-ache
stomach-pump
stomatology
sudden death
suppuration
surgeon's saw
temperature
therapeutic
thermometer
the sniffles
tonsillitis
tooth powder
transfusion
trench fever
trench mouth
tumefaction
Turkish bath
unconscious
vaccination
venesection
warm springs
water canker
wisdom tooth
X-ray machine
X-ray therapy
yellow fever
aero-embolism
alexipharmic
alpha blocker
anaesthetist
anthropotomy
appendectomy
appendicitis
aquapuncture
at death's door
athlete's foot
auscultation
bacteriology
balm of Gilead
bill of health
bismuth salts
black and blue

bloodletting
breath|of|life
casualty|ward
central|canal
chemotherapy
chiropractic
chiropractor
cold|compress
come|down|with
complication
conditioning
constipation
consultation
convalescent
coronary|vein
cough|mixture
countervenom
court|plaster
critical|list
curietherapy
debilitation
dietotherapy
disinfectant
electrolysis
elixir|of|life
emergency|bed
encephalitis
endoskeleton
faith|healing
fallen|arches
family|doctor
felinophobia
fever|blister
feverishness
formaldehyde
friar's|balsam
gastric|juice
gastroplasty
geriatrician
grinding|pain
gynecologist
hair|follicle
hair|restorer
health|resort
heart|disease
heart|failure
hydropathist
hydrotherapy
hypertension
hysterectomy
iatrochemist
iatrophysics
immunization
immunologist
inflammation
integral|dose
intoxication
island|of|Reil
knock|out|drop
laser|surgery
light|therapy
lock|hospital
lose|one's|head
lose|strength
loss|of|memory
major|surgery
malnutrition
mammary|gland
minor|surgery
morbid|growth
muscle|fibres
natural|death
neurasthenia
obstetrician
optic|chiasma
orthodiagram
orthodontics
orthodontist
orthopaedics
orthopaedist
ossification
palpitations
parasitology
parietal|bone
parotid|gland
pediatrician
pelvic|girdle
perspiration
pestilential
pharmaceutic
pharmacology
pharmacopeia
phlebotomist
phototherapy
pigmentation
prescription
preventative
prophylactic
psychrometer
purblindness
radiosurgery
radiotherapy
radiotherapy
reflex|action
rehabilitate
resectoscope
respirometer
resuscitator

robust|health
rubber|gloves
scarlet|fever
serum|therapy
sesamoid|bone
shaking|palsy
shock|therapy
shooting|pain
shortsighted
simple|reflex
sleep|inducer
sleeping|pill
sleepwalking
slimming|diet
solar|therapy
somnambulism
sphygmograph
sphygmometer
spinal|column
spotted|fever
stabbing|pain
straitjacket
streptomycin
student|nurse
St|Vitus|dance
subcutaneous
surgical|boot
suture|needle
therapeutics
therapeutist
thyroid|gland
tonsillotomy
trained|nurse
tranquillize
tuberculosis
turn|a|deaf|ear
varicose|vein
violent|death
vitreous|body
water|blister
word|deafness
zinc|ointment
actinotherapy
adenoidectomy
anaphrodisiac
anastigmatism
anticoagulant
antihistamine
antiscorbutic
bacteriolysin
bacteriolysis
bacteriolytic
bacteriophage
blood|pressure
brainsickness
bubonic|plague
cardiac|arrest
cardiographer
cauterisation
confined|to|bed
contraception
contraceptive
convalescence
dental|surgery
dentist's|chair
dermatologist
diagnostician
Down's|syndrome
encephalogram
endocrinology
fertility|drug
fever|hospital

MEDICINE

field dressing
field hospital
food poisoning
gentian violet
German measles
group practice
gynaecologist
haematologist
healthfulness
health service
health visitor
heat treatment
homoeopathist
indisposition
intensive care
kidney machine
medicine chest
paediatrician
pharmaceutics
pharmaceutist
pharmacopoeia
physicianship
physiognomist
physiotherapy
poliomyelitis
psychotherapy
second opinion
smelling salts
styptic pencil
tonsillectomy
tranquilliser
whooping-cough
X-ray apparatus
antaphrodisiac
anticonvulsant
antilymphocyte
antiseptically
appendicectomy
blood poisoning
breathlessness
Bright's disease
carcinogenesis
carcinological
cardiovascular
conjunctivitis
consulting room
contagiousness
cross infection
cystic fibrosis
dangerously ill
encephalograph
family planning
hole in the heart
housemaid's knee
house physician
infectiousness
medical officer
medical student
medicine bottle
milk of magnesia
national health
night blindness
operating table
pasteurisation
pharmaceutical
pharmacologist
phenobarbitone
pins and needles
plastic surgeon
plastic surgery
pneumoconiosis
rheumatic fever

14/15 LETTERS

surgical|spirit
travel|sickness
ankylostomiasis
anorexia|nervosa
antenatal|clinic
aversion|therapy
blackwater|fever
cerebrovascular
clearing|station
cottage|hospital
counter-irritant
delirium|tremens
dental|treatment
dressing|station
falling|sickness
gastroenteritis
general|practice
Hippocratic|oath
manic-depressive
morning|sickness
physiotherapist
psychotherapist
sleeping|draught
sticking|plaster
third|degree|burn

Meteorology

ice
icy
low
blow
cold
gale
gust
haar
heat
hoar
rain
rime
smog
snow
thaw
warm
wind
blast
blowy
chill
clime
cloud
Eurus
foggy
front
frost
gusty
hoary
humid
misty
muggy
rains
rainy
sleet
storm
sunny
windy
Aeolus
aurora
boreal
Boreas
breeze
breezy
brumal
chilly
cirrus
cloudy
degree
dry|air
flatus
fogbow
freeze
haboob
hot|air
hot|day
isobar
isohel
nimbus
red|sky
samiel
serein
simoom
squall
stormy

stuffy
sultry
trades
aeolian
air|mass
aureola
backing
blue|sky
bluster
chinook
clement
climate
cold|air
cumulus
current
cyclone
drizzle
drought
element
freshen
gregale
grey|sky
ice|cold
icy|wind
ill|wind
isohyet
khamsin
mistral
monsoon
nebulae
pea|soup
rainbow
raining
showery
sirocco
sizzler
squally
subzero
sweltry
tempest
the|blue
thunder
tornado
typhoon
veering
warm|air
washout
weather
Beaufort
black|ice
blizzard
blow|over
clear|day
clear|sky
climatic
cloud|cap
cold|snap
cold|wave
cold|wind
cyclonic
dew|point
doldrums
downpour
east|wind
elements
Favonius
favonian
fireball
firebolt
fohn|wind
forecast
freezing
fresh|air
haziness
head|wind
heat|haze
heatwave
heavy|sky
high|wind
humidity
ice|storm
isobront
isocheim
isocryme
isothere
isotherm
libeccio
low|cloud
moderate
occluded
overcast
pressure
rain|belt
rain|drop
rainfall
rainy|day
scorcher
snowfall
sunburst
sunlight
sunshine
west|wind
wind|belt
wind|cock
wind|cone
wind|vane
anemology
anemostat

barometer
baroscope
below|zero
blue|skies
bourasque
brilliant
cloud|bank
cloud|over
cold|front
cold|spell
corposant
dust|devil
dust|storm
fogginess
frostbite
gale|force
hailstone
hailstorm
hard|frost
harmattan
heavy|rain
high|cloud
hoar|frost
hurricane
inclement
Jack|Frost
lapse|rate
levin|bolt
lightning
London|fog
midday|sun
mild|spell
mistiness
nephology
nimbosity
nor'easter
north|wind
nor'wester
occlusion
overcloud
rain|cloud
rain|gauge
rainspout
rainstorm
rime|frost
sand|blast
sand|devil
sandspout
sandstorm
snowflake
snowstorm
snow|under
sou'easter
south|wind
sou'wester
trade|wind
turbulent
warm|front
weak|front
whirlwind
williwaws
wind|gauge
windiness
windscale
wind|speed
windstorm
windswept
anemometer
antitrades
atmosphere
black|frost
Cape|doctor
clear|skies
cloud|atlas
cloudburst
cloudiness
coastal|fog
cool|breeze
driven|snow
drying|wind
Euroclydon
frontal|low
gentle|wind
glaciation
hailstones
hot|weather
hyetograph
hyetometer
hygrometer
insolation
nebulosity
nubilation
ombrometer
powder|snow
radiosonde
sharp|frost
snow|flurry
snow|squall
stormblast
storm|cloud
storm|track
strong|wind
summer|heat
turbulence
weather|eye
weatherman
weather|map
wet|weather

wind sleeve
anticyclone
arctic front
cats and dogs
cirrus cloud
cold weather
driving rain
evening mist
flaming June
fresh breeze
frigid zones
frontal zone
frozen stiff
frozen water
gale warning
ground frost
harvest moon
hunter's moon
hydrometeor
hyperborean
light breeze
lowering sky
low pressure
mackerel sky
meteorology
monsoon wind
northeaster
northwester
pluviometer
pouring rain
precipitate
rainy season
sheet of rain
snow blanket
snow crystal
southeaster
southwester
spell of rain
storm centre
temperature
tempestuous
thermograph
thermometer
thunderball
thunderbolt
thunderclap
thunderpeal
weathercock
weathervane
bitterly cold
blow up a storm
cirro-cumulus
cirro-stratus
cumulo-cirrus
cumulo-nimbus
cumulus cloud
etesian winds
freezing cold
high pressure
Indian summer
keraunograph
macroclimate
meteorograph
microclimate
migratory low
moderate wind
nephelometer
offshore wind
piercing wind
pressure belt
pressure wave
rainy weather

12/15 LETTERS

snow|blizzard
thundercloud
thunderstorm
volcanic|wind
weather|chart
weather|gauge
weatherglass
wind|velocity
Beaufort|scale
climatography
climatologist
cumulostratus
electric|storm
meteorologist
thunder|shower
weather|report
weather|symbol
aurora|borealis
further|outlook
meteorological
roaring|forties
sheet|lightning
weather|prophet
weather|station
bolt|from|the|blue
forked|lightning
prevailing|winds
rain|cats|and|dogs
summer|lightning
tropical|climate
weather|forecast

Military Leaders

Lee
Byng
Foch
Haig
Slim
Blake
Clive
Dayan
Drake
Keyes
Moore
Tromp
Wolfe
Alfred
Attila
Balboa
Beatty
Caesar
Cortes
Franco
Gordon
Halsey
Ireton
Jervis
Moltke
Nelson
Patton
Petain
Pompey
Raglan
Rodney
Rommel
Rupert
Wavell
Allenby
Blucher
Bradley
Doenitz
Dowding
Fairfax
Raleigh
Saladin
Sherman
Tirpitz
Wallace
Wingate
Agricola
Aurelian
Burgoyne
Cardigan
Crockett
Cromwell

MILITARY LEADERS

Hannibal
Jellicoe
Lawrence
Leonidas
Montcalm
Montrose
Napoleon
Pershing
Potemkin
Runstedt
Stilwell
Woodward
Alexander
Bonaparte
Glendower
Grenville
Hasdrubal
Joan of Arc
Kitchener
MacArthur
Montezuma
Trenchard
Abercromby
Alanbrooke
Belisarius
Caractacus
Clausewitz
Cornwallis
Eisenhower
Kublai Khan
Montgomery
Wellington
Charlemagne
Collingwood
Genghis Khan
Marlborough
Mountbatten
Chiang kai Shek

Minerals

gem
ore
tin
coal
clay
gold
iron
jade
lava
lead
lode
marl
mica
onyx
opal
rock
ruby
salt
spar
talc
tufa
tuff
vein
zinc
agate
alloy
beryl
borax
coral
flint
fluor
gault
ingot
magma
metal
ochre
shale
slack
slate
sleet
steel
stone
topaz
wacke
basalt
bronze
cerium
chrome
cobalt
copper

erbium
flinty
Flysch
gabbro
galena
gangue
garnet
gneiss
gypsum
indium
iolite
jargon
jasper
kaolin
maltha
marble
molten
morion
nickel
oroide
osmium
pewter
pumice
pyrite
quarry
quartz
radium
rutile
scoria
silica
silver
spinel
zircon
adamant
apatite
asphalt
azurite
bauxite
biotite
bornite
breccia
cadmium
calcite
calcium
cat's eye
chuckie
citrine
diabase
diamond
diorite
emerald
epidote
felspar
gallium
girasol
gothite
granite
hafnium
holmium
hyalite
igneous
iridium
iron ore
iron pan
jacinth
jargoon
kerogen
kyanite
lignite
lithium
lithoid
mercury
mineral
niobium
olivine
peridot
pig iron
pyrites
realgar
rhenium
sulphur
terbium
thorium
thulium
tin mine
tripoli
uranium
wolfram
yttrium
zeolite
zincite
amethyst
amygdule
antimony
argonite
asbestos
autunite
basanite
brookite
cast iron
chlorite
chromite
chromium
cinnabar
corundum
cryolite
dendrite
dibstone
diggings
dolerite
dolomite
epsomite
europium
euxenite
feldspar
fineness
fire opal
fluorite
gemstone
girasole
gold dust
gold mine
gold rush
graphite
gritrock
hematite
idocrase
ilmenite
inkstone
iron clay
lazurite
limonite
liparite
lutecium
metallic
monazite
mudstone
mylonite
nephrite
obsidian
platinum
plumbago
polonium
porphyry

pumicite
pyroxene
rhyolite
rock|salt
rubidium
samarium
sapphire
sardonyx
scandium
selenite
siderite
smelting
steatite
stibnite
sunstone
tantalum
thallium
tinstone
titanium
trachyte
traprock
tungsten
vanadium
volcanic
xenolith
alabaster
aluminium
americium
amphibole
anglesite
aragonite
argentite
base|metal
beryllium
blacklead
brilliant
brimstone
burrstone
cairngorm
carbuncle
carnelian
carnotite
china|clay
diatomite
dripstone
elaterite
flagstone
fluorspar
fool's|gold
freestone
gemmology
germanium
goldstone
granulite
gritstone
haematite
ironstone
jackstone
jadestone
kaolinite
laccolite
laccolith
lanthanum
lapideous
limestone
lithology
magnesite
magnesium
magnetite
malachite
manganese
marcasite
marlstone
metalloid
microlite
milkstone
mispickel
moonstone
morganite
neodymium
ozocerite
palladium
pegmatite
periclase
petroleum
petrology
petrology
phenolite
plutonium
quartzite
rhodonite
ruthenium
sandstone
scheelite
semimetal
slabstone
soapstone
spodumene
strontium
tellurium
turquoise
uraninite
vulcanite
wulfenite
ytterbium
zirconium
adamantine
adder|stone

aquamarine
aventurine
bloodstone
brownstone
chalcedony
chalkstone
chessylite
chrysolite
clinkstone
common salt
copper mine
drakestone
dysprosium
eaglestone
gadolinium
glauconite
globulites
graptolite
greenstone
heliotrope
hornblende
lead glance
lithomarge
meerschaum
metallurgy
mica schist
mineralogy
mineral oil
molten lava
molybdenum
noble metal
ore deposit
orthoclase
peacock ore
pitchstone
promethium
rare metals
rose quartz
sheet metal
silver mine
slingstone
smokestone
snakestone
spinel ruby
stinkstone
technetium
touchstone
tourmaline
wolframite
alexandrite
cassiterite
chrysoberyl
chrysoprase
clinochlore
country rock
earth metals
gravelstone
hatchettite
igneous rock
iron pyrites
lapis lazuli
layer of rock
lithosphere
Lydian stone
mineral coal
mineral salt
mineral vein
molybdenite
native stone
peristalith
petrography
pissasphalt

pitchblende
potter's|clay
quarrystone
quicksilver
rock|crystal
sarsen|stone
schistosity
stone|circle
vermiculite
vesuvianite
volcanic|ash
alkali|metals
anthraconite
argillaceous
arsenopyrite
black|diamond
chalcopyrite
coal|measures
duraluminium
electroplate
fuller's|earth
metal|fatigue
mineral|pitch
native|metals
oriental|opal
praesodymium
protactinium
red|sandstone
residual|clay
star|sapphire
wollastonite
carboniferous
chrome|plating
cinnamon|stone
copper|pyrites
metalliferous
metallurgical
millstone|grit
mineralogocal
petrification
Portland|stone
quartz|crystal
smokeless|fuel
copper,bottomed
electroplating
metallographer
mineral|deposit
mineral|kingdom
open,cast|mining
plaster|of|Paris
Portland|cement
quartz|porphyry
stainless|steel
Old|Red|Sandstone

Money

as
bit
bob
écu
mag
mil
pie
sen
sol
sou
yen
anna

bean
buck
cash
cent
chip
coin
dime
doit
kyat
lira
mark
merk
mill
mint
mite
obol
peso
plum
pony
quid
rand
real
reis
rial
ryal
thou
angel
asper
belga
colon
conto
crown
daric
dinar
ducat
eagle
fiver
franc
grand
groat
krona
krone
louis
mohur
noble
obang
paolo
pence
penny
piece
pound
rupee
sceat
semis
soldo
sucre
toman
verso
aureus
bawbee
copeck
copper
denier
dollar
drachm
escudo
florin
guinea
gulden
kopeck
lepton
monkey
nickel
peseta
rouble
scudos
sequin
shekel
solidi
specie
stater
stiver
tenner
tester
teston
thaler
cordoba
crusado
denarii
drachma
exergue
guilder
ha'penny
milreis
moidore
nummary
obverse
pfennig
piastre
red cent
reverse
sawbuck
sceatta
sextans
smacker
solidus
ten spot
testoon

- two|bits
- base|coin
- cruzeiro
- denarius
- didrachm
- doubloon
- farthing
- gold|coin
- groschen
- louis|d'or
- napoleon
- new|pence
- new|penny
- picayune
- planchet
- quadrans
- semissis
- semuncia
- shilling
- short|bit
- sixpence
- ten|cents
- tuppence
- twopence
- zecchino
- dupondius
- fourpence
- fourpenny
- gold|crown
- gold|penny
- gold|piece
- half-crown
- half-eagle
- half-noble
- halfpenny
- pistareen
- rose-noble
- schilling
- sovereign
- tremissis
- yellow|boy
- zwanziger
- reichsmark
- sestertius
- threepence
- double|eagle
- silver|penny
- sixpenny|bit
- base|shilling
- imperial|coin
- piece|of|eight
- quarter-noble
- silver|dollar
- brass|farthing
- half|sovereign
- pieces|of|eight
- ten-dollar|bill
- almighty|dollar
- coin|of|the|realm
- debased|coinage
- decimal|coinage
- half-a-sovereign
- half-pennyworth
- fifty-pence|piece
- handful|of|silver

Mountains

K2
Alps
Jura
Altai
Andes
Eiger
Ghats
Hekla
Urals
Ararat
Exmoor
Kunlun
Pamirs
Pindus
Vosges
Brocken
Helicon
Mendips
Nan Ling
Nan Shan
Rockies
Skiddaw
Snowdon
Sudeten
Caucasus
Cevennes
Cheviots
Chirripo
Cotopaxi
Dartmoor
Demavend
Hymettus
Ida, Mount
Jungfrau
Krakatoa
Nevis, Ben
Pennines
Pyrenees
Tien Shan
Vesuvius
Aconcagua
Allegheny
Apennines
Catskills
Chilterns
Cook, Mount
Cotswolds
Dolomites
Erzebirge
Etna, Mount
Grampians
Helvellyn
Himalayas
Hindu Kush
Huascaran
Meru, Mount
Mont Blanc
Mont Cenis
Monte Rosa
Nanda Devi
Pikes Peak
Puy de Dome
Ras Dashan
Ruwenzori
Stromboli
Zugspitze
Arakam Yoma
Cader Idris
Cairngorms
Chimborazo
Coast Range
Dent du Midi
Elgon, Mount
Kenya, Mount
Khyber Pass
Sinai, Mount
St Gotthard
Adirondacks
Brenner Pass
Brooks Range
Carmel, Mount
Drakensberg
Elbert, Mount
Elbrus, Mount
Erebus, Mount
Hermon, Mount
Katmai, Mount

MOUNTAINS

Kazbek, Mount
Kilimanjaro
Koryak Range
Lammermuirs
Mendip Hills
Nanga Parbat
Scafell Pike
Sierra Madre
Simplon Pass
Appalachians
Cheviot Hills
Gran Paradiso
Illampu, Mount
Kanchenjunga
Monte Cassino
Olympus, Mount
Palomar, Mount
Peak District
Popocatépetl
Rainier, Mount
Roraima, Mount
Ruapehu, Mount
Schiehallion
Sierra Nevada
Triglav, Mount
Whitney, Mount
Blue Mountains
Brecon Beacons
Cameroun, Mount
Chiltern Hills
Cotswold Hills
Grossglockner
Harz Mountains
Kinabalu, Mount
Massif Central
McKinley, Mount
Mitchell, Mount
Mount of Olives
move mountains
Riesengebirge
Sierra Maestra
Stanovoi Range
Sulaiman Range
Table Mountain
Black Mountains
Cleveland Hills
Galty Mountains
Karakoram Range
Kosciusko, Mount
Ozark Mountains
Parnassus, Mount
Snowy Mountains
White Mountains
Mourne Mountains
Taurus Mountains
Zagros Mountains

Muses

Clio	Urania	Melpomene
Erato	Euterpe	Polyhymnia
Thalia	Calliope	Terpsichore

Music

A	me	hay	sax	blow	harp
B	op	hey	ska	brio	hi-fi
C	pp	hit	soh	clef	horn
D	re	hum	sol	coda	hymn
E	sf	jig	tie	dash	jack
f	te	key	uke	disc	jazz
F	ut	kit	wax	disk	jive
G	act	lah	alap	diva	jota
p	air	lay	alto	drum	juba
DC	bar	lip	arco	duet	keen
do	bop	lur	aria	dump	lead
DS	bow	nut	ayre	fife	lied
EP	cat	ode	band	fine	lilt
fa	cue	ped	bard	flat	lira
ff	doh	pes	base	flue	lure
fp	dot	pop	bass	form	lute
gu	duo	rag	beat	fret	lyra
la	fah	ray	bell	glee	lyre
LP	gue	run	bind	gong	mass

MUSIC

mode
mood
mute
neck
node
noel
note
oboe
open
opus
part
peal
pick
port
Prom
raga
rank
reed
reel
rest
rock
roll
root
rote
scat
sing
slur
solo
song
stop
time
tone
toot
trio
tuba
tuck

tune
turn
vamp
viol
wait
wind
wood
work
ad lib
album
A side
assai
atone
banjo
basso
baton
bebop
bells
belly
blues
bones
brass
brawl
breve
B side
bugle
canon
canto
carol
cello
chant
chime
choir
chord
close
comma

corno
crook
croon
dance
desto
dirge
disco
ditty
dolce
drone
drums
elegy
Erato
etude
fancy
farce
fifer
fifth
final
flute
forte
fugue
galop
gamba
gamut
gigue
grace
grave
ictus
idyll
jazzy
jodel
kyrie
large
largo
lento

luter
lyric
major
march
melic
metre
mezzo
minim
minor
modal
motet
motif
musak
music
naker
nebel
neume
ninth
nonet
notes
octet
odeon
opera
organ
paean
pause
pavan
pedal
piano
piece
piper
pitch
pleno
pluck
point
polka

proms
psalm
pulse
quint
range
rebec
reeds
regal
resin
rondo
rosin
round
rumba
runic
scale
scena
score
segno
segue
shake
sharp
shawm
siren
sixth
slide
snare
sol fa
sordo
sound
space
staff
stave
Strad
strum
study
suite

swell	accent	damper	legato	rounds
swing	accord	decani	Lieder	rubato
tabla	adagio	diesis	lutist	scorer
table	almain	direct	lyrist	second
tabor	almand	do-re-mi	manual	sempre
tacet	answer	double	maxixe	septet
tambo	anthem	drones	medley	sestet
tango	Apollo	dulcet	melody	sextet
tempo	arioso	ecbole	minuet	shanty
tenor	a tempo	eighth	monody	shofar
theme	atonal	encore	motion	singer
third	aubade	euphon	motive	snatch
throb	ballad	fading	musico	sonata
thrum	ballet	fiddle	needle	spinet
tonic	bolero	figure	neumes	stanza
touch	bowing	finale	nobile	strain
triad	bridge	firing	nowell	string
trill	bugler	fourth	oboist	subito
troll	burden	fugato	octave	syrinx
trope	cadent	giusto	off-key	tabret
tuned	can-can	graces	ottava	tampon
tutti	cantor	grazia	pavane	tam-tam
up bow	cantus	great C	period	tattoo
valse	catchy	guitar	phrase	temper
valve	catgut	hammer	pipe up	tenor C
verse	chanty	harper	piston	tenuto
vibes	chimes	hepcat	player	tercet
viola	choral	horner	presto	terzet
voice	chorus	hymnal	quaver	timbal
volta	cither	hymner	racket	timbre
volte	citole	in tune	rattle	tom-tom
waits	cornet	jingle	rebeck	tooter
waltz	corona	keener	record	top ten
winds	cue-ing	kettle	reggae	treble
woods	cymbal	lament	repeat	tromba
yodel	da capo	leader	rhythm	troppo

MUSIC

tucket
tune|up
tuning
tymbal
tympan
unison
up|beat
vielle
violin
vivace
voices
waxing
zambra
zither
zufolo
agitato
allegro
althorn
andante
animato
arietta
arrange
art|song
attacca
attuned
bagpipe
ballade
bandman
bandore
bar|beat
bar|line
baryton
bassist
bassoon
battery
battuta
bazooka
bellows
bombard
bourdon
bourrée
brasses
bravura
buccina
cadence
cadency
cadenza
calando
calypso
cantata
canzona
canzone
caprice
carioca
celesta
cellist
cembalo
chanson
chanter
chantry
chikara
chiming
chorale
chorine
chorist
cithara
cithern
cittern
clapper
clarion
classic
clavier
codetta
compass
compose
con|brio
concert
concord
conduct
con|moto
consort
cornett
cornist
coupler
Cremona
crooner
curtall
cymbals
descant
discord
double|C
doubles
down|bow
drummer
episode
euphony
Euterpe
fagotto
fanfare
fermata
fiddle|G
fiddler
flutina
fluting
flutist
forlana
fox|trot
furioso
furlana
fuzzbox
gavotte
giocoso
gradual
G|string
halling
harmony
harpist
hautboy
hit|song
hit|tune
hornist
hot|jazz
humming
hymnist
hymnody
intrada
introit
ivories
juke|box
keening
key|note
Landler
lullaby
maestro
mandola
mandora
marcato
marimba
mazurka
measure
mediant
melisma
melodia
melodic

middle C
mixture
mordent
morendo
musette
musical
natural
ocarina
octette
offbeat
one-step
organum
Orpheus
pandora
pandore
pandura
Panpipe
partial
passage
pas seul
pesante
piacere
pianist
pianola
pibroch
piccolo
piffero
pomposo
pop song
potlids
prelude
Psalter
quartet
quintet
ragtime
recital
refrain
reprise
requiem
respond
ribible
ripieno
romance
rondeau
rondino
rosalia
roulade
sackbut
salicet
sambuca
samisen
Sanctus
saxhorn
saxtuba
scherzo
scoring
septuor
serpent
service
seventh
singing
skiffle
soloist
song hit
soprano
sordino
stopped
stretto
strings
subject
syncope
taborer
taboret
tambura
tangent
the Nine
theorbo
timbrel
timpani
tirasse
toccata
top note
tracker
treble C
tremolo
triplet
tritone
trumpet
tuneful
two-step
ukelele
ukulele
upright
vespers
vibrato
vihuela
violist
violone
warbler
war song
wassail
whistle
ziganka
Agnus Dei
alto clef
alto horn
alto viol
antiphon
a piacere
archlute
arpeggio
arranger
Ave Maria
bagpiper
bagpipes
bandsman
banjoist
baritone
barytone
base clef
base note
base viol
bass drum
bass horn
bass oboe
beat time
berceuse
boat song
bouffons
Calliope
canticle
canticum
cantoris
canzonet
carillon
cavatina
chaconne
chanting
choirboy
choirman
choragus
choregus
clappers
clarinet

MUSIC

col|legno
composer
con|amore
concerto
continuo
coronach
courante
cromorna
cromorne
crooning
crotchet
cylinder
dal|segno
diapason
diapente
diatonic
doh-ray-me
doloroso
dominant
downbeat
doxology
drumbeat
drumhead
drumskin
duettino
duettist
dulciana
dulcimer
emphasis
ensemble
entr'acte
faburden
falderal
falsetto
fandango
fantasia

fantasie
flautist
flip|side
flourish
flue-pipe
flue-work
folderol
folk|rock
folk|song
galliard
gemshorn
glee|club
habanera
half|rest
hand|bell
harmonic
harp|lute
hornpipe
humstrum
hymeneal
hymn|tune
in|accord
in|chorus
interval
in|unison
jazz|band
jazzed|up
jew's|harp
jongleur
Jubilate
keyboard
key-bugle
last|post
lay|clerk
lay|vicar
left|hand

leggiero
libretto
ligature
love|song
low|pitch
lutanist
madrigal
maestoso
maggiore
major|key
mazourka
mean-tone
measured
melodeon
melodica
melodics
melodist
minor|key
minstrel
moderato
monotone
movement
musicale
music|box
musician
nocturne
notation
open|note
operatic
operetta
oratorio
organist
ornament
ostinato
overtone
overture

Panpipes
parallel
parlando
parlante
part|song
pastoral
phantasy
phrasing
pianette
pianiste
Pierides
pipe|tune
plangent
plectron
plectrum
pop|group
pop|music
post|horn
postlude
psalmody
psaltery
raga-rock
ragtimer
recorder
reed|pipe
reed|stop
register
response
reveille
rhapsody
rigadoon
ritenuto
saraband
scordato
semitone
semplice

septette
sequence
serenade
serenata
sextette
sextolet
side drum
sing-song
sliphorn
sol-faist
solo stop
sonatina
songbird
song book
songplay
songster
sour note
spianato
spinette
squiffer
staccato
strike up
strummer
strummer
swan song
swell-box
symphony
tamboura
tenor cor
tenoroon
terzetto
the Muses
threnody
tonalist
tonality
tone deaf
tone down
tone poem
tone poet
tonguing
tonic key
triangle
trombone
trouvere
tunester
tympanon
una corda
vamp horn
Victrola
virginal
virtuosa
virtuosi
virtuoso
vocalion
vocalism
vocalist
Vorspiel
warbling
wind band
woodwind
yodeller
zambomba
zarzuela
a cappella
accompany
accordion
acoustics
adagietto
ad libitum
alla breve
allemande
andantino
antiphony
arabesque
archilute
aria buffa
baby grand
bagatelle
balalaika
ballerina
band major
bandstand
banjolele
barcarole
blow a horn
blues song
bombardon
bow fiddle
brass band
bugle call
bugle horn
cacophony
cantabile
cantilena
capriccio
carolling
castanets
celestina
chalumeau
chantress
charivari
choralist
chorister
chromatic
citharist
clarionet
classical
claviharp

concentus
conductor
consonate
contralto
cornopean
crescendo
croon song
cymbalist
dance band
dance form
dead march
death song
diaphonia
dithyramb
double bar
drone bass
drum corps
drum major
drumstick
dulcitone
duple time
echo organ
ecossaise
entrechat
epicedium
epinicion
euphonium
execution
extempore
farandole
figurante
fine-toned
fingering
flageolet
flute-a-bec
folk dance
folk music
fugue form
full close
full organ
full score
glissando
grace note
grandioso
Gregorian
guitarist
half-close
handbells
hand organ
harmonica
harmonics
harmonist
harmonium
harmonize
head voice
hexachord
high pitch
hit-parade
homophony
hymnology
imitation
impromptu
improvise
inflexion
interlude
invention
inversion
jazz stick
jitterbug
kent-bugle
krummhorn
langspiel
larghetto
leger line
Leitmotiv
lyric bass
lyrichord
major mode
malaguena
mandoline
mediation
melodious
melodrama
melomania
metronome
mezza voce
minor mode
modulator
monochord
monophony
music hall
music roll
music room
music wire
mute pedal
obbligato
octachord
offertory
open notes
open score
orchestra
organ stop
orpharion
out of tune
overtones
part music
pas de deux
passepied

pasticcio
pastorale
pedal|note
performer
piacevole
piangendo
piano|keys
pianolist
piano|wire
pipe|organ
pitch|pipe
pizzicato
plainsong
play|by|ear
polonaise
polychord
polyphony
pop|record
potpourri
precentor
principal
programme
prolation
promenade
quadrille
quartette
quintette
quodlibet
recording
reed|organ
remote|key
rendering
rendition
resonance
rhythmics
ricercare
right|hand
rondo|form
roundelay
saxcornet
saxophone
scherzoso
scrape|gut
semibreve
semitonic
seraphine
serenader
sforzando
shantyman
siciliana
signature
singspiel
sink|a|pace
slow|march
smerzando
soap|opera
soft|pedal
solfeggio
solo|organ
song|sheet
sonometer
sostenuto
sotto|voce
sound|hole
sound|post
spiritoso
spiritual
stockhorn
succentor
swing|band
symphonic
tablature
tabor|pipe
tail|piece
tambourin
tempo|mark
tenor|clef
tenor|drum
tenor|horn
tenor|tuba
tenor|viol
tessitura
theme|song
theorbist
time|value
timpanist
top|twenty
torch|song
transpose
tremulant
triangles
trumpeter
tuning|bar
tympanist
tymp|stick
undertone
variation
viola|alto
violin|bow
violinist
virginals
virtuosic
vocalizer
voice|part
Volkslied
voluntary
vox|humana
waltz|time

MUSIC

whole|note
whole|rest
whole|step
whole|tone
wind|chest
wind|music
wind|trunk
woodwinds
wrestpins
wrong|note
xylophone
zitherist
accidental
adaptation
added|sixth
affettuoso
allargando
allegretto
alteration
antiphoner
attunement
background
ballad|horn
band|leader
band|master
band|waggon
barcarolle
basset|horn
basset|oboe
bassoonist
bell|ringer
Benedictus
binary|form
bottom|note
brass|winds
bridal|hymn
bull|fiddle
cancionero
cancrizans
canto|fermo
canzonetta
chest|voice
chime|bells
chitarrone
choir|organ
chorus|girl
cinquepace
clavichord
coloratura
comic|opera
common|time
concertina
concertino
concertist
concordant
conducting
consonance
con|sordini
contrabass
cor|anglais
cornettist
Coryphaeus
cradlesong
dance|music
diminuendo
diminution
disc|jockey
dissonance
doodlesack
dotted|note
double|bass
double|flat
double|time
drummer|boy
dulcetness
Eisteddfod
enharmonic
euphonious
exposition
expression
five|finger
Flugelhorn
folk|singer
fortepiano
fortissimo
French|harp
French|horn
golden|disc
grace|notes
gramophone
grand|opera
grand|piano
great|organ
great|stave
Greek|modes
grind|organ
ground|bass
harmonicon
harmonizer
homophonic
hornplayer
horse|opera
humoresque
hurdy|gurdy
incidental
instrument
intermezzo
intonation

jam session
kettledrum
leger lines
light music
light opera
long player
lyre guitar
lyric drama
lyric tenor
mainstream
major chord
major scale
major sixth
major third
major triad
manuscript
marimbaist
melody part
mezzo forte
mezzo piano
minor canon
minor chord
minor scale
minor sixth
minor third
minor triad
minstrelsy
mixed times
modal scale
modern jazz
modulation
mouth music
mouth organ
mouthpiece
musical bow
musical box

musical ear
music lover
music maker
musicology
music paper
music stand
oboe d'amore
opera buffa
opera score
ophicleide
orchestral
organ point
patter song
pedal board
pedal organ
pedal point
pentachord
pentatonic
percussion
perdendosi
phonograph
pianissimo
pianoforte
pianologue
piano score
piano stool
piccoloist
plagal mode
Polyhymnia
polyphonic
ponticello
pop concert
popular air
portamento
prima donna
proportion

quick march
recitalist
recitative
recitativo
related key
repertoire
repetition
resolution
responsory
rhapsodist
ritardando
ritornelle
ritornello
round dance
sacred Nine
salicional
saltarello
saxotromba
scherzando
scordatura
Scotch snap
seguidilla
semichorus
semiquaver
set to music
shaped note
sheet music
short score
silver disc
simple time
sonata form
song leader
songstress
songwriter
sound board
sousaphone

speaker|key
squeeze|box
Stradivari
strathspey
street|band
stringendo
submediant
supertonic
suspension
swell|organ
swell|pedal
symphonion
symphonist
syncopated
syncopator
tambourine
tarantella
tetrachord
tin|whistle
tone|poetry
tonic|chord
tonic|major
tonic|minor
tonic|sol-fa
transcribe
transition
treble|clef
treble|viol
tremolando
triple|time
trombonist
troubadour
tuning|fork
tuning|pipe
tuning|wire
tweedledee
tweedledum
twelve|note
union|pipes
variations
vibraphone
villanella
vocal|music
vocal|score
accelerando
accompanist
Aeolian|harp
alla|tedesca
arrangement
ballad|maker
ballad|opera
barrel|organ
bass|passage
beat|a|tattoo
beat|the|drum
bell|ringing
blues|singer
broken|chord
calliophone
campanology
canned|music
capriccioso
cat's|concert
chansonette
chanterelle
choirmaster
clarinetist
clarion|call
clavicymbal
common|chord
compact|disc
composition
concertante
concert|band
concert|hall
consecutive
contrapunto
contredanse
counterbase
damper|pedal
decrescendo
descant|viol
discography
discotheque
divided|stop
dominant|key
Dorian|modes
dotted|minim
double|chant
double|fugue
double|sharp
double|touch
dulcet|tones
ear|for|music
English|horn
equal|voices
eurhythmics
extemporize
faux|bourdon
fiddlestick
fife|and|drum
figured|bass
finger|board
fipple|flute
first|fiddle
first|violin
French|pitch
French|sixth

fundamental
funeral song
German flute
German sixth
golden-toned
graphophone
great octave
half cadence
harmonizing
harpsichord
hunting horn
inscription
in the groove
keyed guitar
leading note
long-playing
Lydian modes
madrigalist
major second
mandolinist
mellifluent
mellifluous
mellisonant
Minnesinger
minor second
mixed voices
morris dance
musica ficta
musical copy
musical joke
musical note
music lesson
music-loving
music school
nickelodeon
normal pitch
opera ballet
opera bouffe
orchestrate
orchestrion
organophone
organ player
over blowing
Pandean pipe
partial tone
part playing
part singing
part writing
passacaglia
passing-bell
passing note
percussives
performance
piano player
piano-violin
pitch accent
plagal modes
player piano
polyphonism
popular tune
preparation
prestissimo
progression
psalm singer
quarter note
quarter rest
ragtime band
rallentando
relative key
Requiem mass
retardation
rock and roll
sacred music
saxophonist
scat singing
Schottische
Scotch catch
short octave
silver-toned
singing sand
small octave
solmization
soprano clef
sound in tune
square piano
Stabat Mater
stopped pipe
street organ
street piano
string music
string plate
subdominant
sweet-voiced
synchronism
syncopation
temperament
tempo giusto
ternary form
Terpsichore
time pattern
Tin Pan Alley
tonic accent
torch singer
transposing
tunefulness
tuning slide
vicar choral
viola d'amore

viol|da|gamba
violin|piano
violoncello
vivacissimo
voix|celeste
wedding|song
willow|pipes
acciaccatura
accompanyist
accordionist
acoustic|bass
agogic|accent
anticipation
appassionata
appoggiatura
augmentation
balladmonger
ballad|singer
banjo,ukelele
bass|baritone
bass|clarinet
bass|trombone
beat|a|retreat
boogie,woogie
brass|section
chamber|music
chamber|organ
changing|note
chest|of|viols
chorus|singer
clavicembalo
comedy|ballet
compound|time
concert|grand
concertinist
concert|music
concert|pitch
Concertstuck
conservatory
contrapuntal
counterpoint
counter|tenor
country|dance
cushion|dance
divertimento
dominant|note
dotted|quaver
drinking|song
extended|play
extravaganza
false|cadence
fiddlesticks
fiddlestring
florid|phrase
funeral|march
glockenspiel
gravicembalo
harmonichord
harmonic|tone
hidden|fifths
hurdy,gurdist
hymnographer
improvisator
instrumental
introduction
inverted|turn
Italian|sixth
ivory|thumper
ivory|tickler
jazz|musician
key|signature
less|semitone
light|harmony
lyric|cantata
major|seventh
marching|song
martial|music
mean|semitone
medieval|mode
mellifluence
melodic|minor
mezzo,soprano
military|band
minor|seventh
minstrel|song
mixed|cadence
monochordist
musical|scale
musical|score
musicianship
musicologist
mutation|stop
opening|notes
opera|comique
orchestra|pit
orchestrator
organ|grinder
parlour|grand
passion|music
penny|whistle
perfect|fifth
perfect|pitch
philharmonic
Phrygian|mode
piobaireachd
pipe|and|tabor
polytonality
popular|music

reciting note
record player
registration
repercussion
rhythmic mode
sarrusophone
sesquialtera
sing in chorus
skiffle group
slow movement
speaking stop
steam whistle
Stradivarius
street singer
stress accent
symphonic ode
tape recorder
theatre organ
thorough-bass
tintinnabula
tone measurer
tone painting
top of the pops
tromba marina
trumpet major
upper partial
upright piano
viola da gamba
vocalization
wedding march
wind musician
Zigeunerlied
accompaniment
American organ
capellmeister
cello concerto
choir practice
choral society
choreographer
concrete music
conductorship
conservatoire
contrabassoon
contrafagotto
contrapuntist
cornet-a-piston
corps de ballet
electric organ
Gregorian mode
harmonic scale
kapellmeister
kettle-drummer
meistersinger
melodiousness
music mistress
musicological
orchestration
piano concerto
recorded music
rhythm section
signature tune
singing-master
staff notation
string quartet
string quintet
symphonic poem
time signature
transposition
twelve-tone row
violoncellist
ballet-mistress
chromatic scale

MUSIC

classical|music
concerto|grosso
contrary|motion
demisemiquaver
double,stopping
electric|guitar
male|voice|choir
musical|prodigy
music|publisher
negro|spiritual
open,air|concert
piano,accordion
plantation|song
reed|instrument
smoking,concert
violin|concerto
wind|instrument
Bachelor|of|Music
background|music
Christy|minstrel
concert|overture
concert|platform
electronic|music
flutter,tonguing
incidental|music
instrumentalist
instrumentation
Moog|synthesiser
perfect|interval
string|orchestra
symphony|concert

Mythology

Anu	Gog	nis	Sol	Adad	Ares
Ate	Hel	nix	Sri	Aeon	Argo
Aya	Hob	Nox	Tem	Afer	Askr
Bel	Ida	Nut	Tiu	Agni	Aten
Bor	imp	Nyx	Tiw	Ajax	Aton
Cos	Ino	obi	Tum	Alea	Auge
dea	Ira	Ops	Tyr	Amen	Baal
Dia	Leo	Ore	Ull	Amor	Bast
Dis	Ler	Oya	Vac	Amun	Bora
elf	Lok	Pan	Van	Anax	Bran
Eos	Lug	Ran	Zan	Anna	Bron
fay	Mab	Seb	Zio	Anta	Buto
god	Mot	Set	Ziu	Apis	Ceto

4/5 LETTERS

Ceyx	Hera	Ment	Tiki	Atlas	Dione
Civa	Hero	Mors	Troy	Atman	Diral
Clio	Hler	Muse	tyro	Baldr	Dirce
Cora	Hodr	Nabu	Ullr	Batea	Donar
deil	Hora	Naga	Upis	Belus	Dorus
deus	Hoth	Nana	Urth	Bhaga	Draco
Deva	huma	Nebo	Vach	bogey	dryad
Devi	icon	Neph	Vale	Bragi	Durga
Dewa	idol	Nike	Vali	Brute	dwarf
Dian	Idun	Nona	Vans	Cabal	Dyaus
Dido	Ilus	Norn	Vayu	Cacus	Dylan
Dike	Inar	Nott	Vili	Canis	Dymas
Echo	Iole	Odin	Wate	Capta	Egill
Edda	Iris	ogre	Yama	Caria	Ehlis
Eden	Isis	peor	yeti	Carpo	elves
Enyo	jinn	peri	Ymir	Ceres	Enlil
Erda	jinx	Ptah	Zemi	Cerus	Epona
Eric	joss	Puck	Zeus	Cetus	Erato
Eris	Jove	Rahu	Zion	Chaos	Erlik
Eros	juju	Rama	Aegir	charm	Etara
Erua	Juno	Rhea	aegis	Circe	Eurus
Fate	Kali	Rind	Aegle	Coeus	fable
Faun	Kama	Saga	Aeson	Comus	Fagus
Fons	kami	Sati	afrit	coven	fairy
Frey	Kapi	seer	Algol	Creon	Fauna
Fria	Leda	Seth	Ammon	Creus	Faust
Frig	Leto	Shri	angel	Crius	fetch
Fury	Loke	Siva	Arcas	Cupid	fiend
Gaea	Loki	Soma	Arges	Dagda	Flora
Gaia	Luna	Spes	Argos	Dagon	Freya
Gerd	Lyra	Styx	Argus	Damia	Frigg
Gere	magi	tabu	Ariel	Danae	Gauri
Goll	Maia	Tara	Aries	deify	genie
Hapi	mana	Tare	Arion	deity	ghost
Hebe	Mara	Thea	Artio	Devil	ghoul
hell	Math	Thor	Athor	Diana	giant

Gibil
gnome
Grace
Gyges
Hadad
Hades
Harpy
Hatra
haunt
Helen
Helle
Herse
Hoder
Holda
Horae
Horus
houri
Hyads
Hydra
Hylas
Hymen
Iasus
ichor
Idmon
Iliad
Indra
Irene
Irmin
Istar
Ister
Janus
Jason
jinni
Karna
kelpy
Komos
Kotys
Laius
lamia
Lamos
Lares
larva
Lepus
Lethe
Liber
Libra
limbo
Lupus
Lycus
Lydia
Magog
magus
Marut
Mazda
Medea
Metis
Midas
mimic
Minos
Moira
Momos
Momus
Morna
Morta
naiad
Nanna
Nerio
Ninos
Niobe
nisse
nixie
Njord
Notus
nymph
obeah
Orcus
oread
Orion
ouphe
Paean
pagan
Pales
Parca
Paris
Pitys
pixie
Pluto
Poeas
Priam
Remus
Robur
Satan
satyr
shade
Sheol
Shiva
Shree
Sibyl
Sinon
siren
Siris
spell
spook
Surya
sylph
taboo
Terra
Theia
theos
Thoth
Thrym
Thule
Titan
totem
Troad
troll
Tyche
Uriel
Vanir
Varah
Venus
Vesta
Vidar
Virgo
Vithi
Wabun
weird
Wodan
Woden
Wotan
Yasna
zombi
Adonai
Adonis
Aeacus
Aeetes
Aegeus
Aegina
Aeneas
Aeneid
Aeolus
Aethra
afreet
Agenor
Aglaia
Alecto
Alseid
Amazon
Amen-Ra
Amenti
Amores
amulet
Anubis
Anytus
Apollo
Aquila
Arthur
Asgard
Assama
astral
Athena
Athene
Atreus
Attica
Auriga
Aurora
Auster
Avalon
avatar
Azrael
Babbar
Balder
Baldur
Baucis
Belial
Beulah
Bootes
Boreas
Brahma
brewer

6 LETTERS

Buddha	Freyia	Isolde	Nereus	Saturn
Cabiri	Freyja	Ithunn	Nergal	Sciron
Cadmus	Frigga	jinnee	Nessus	Scylla
Cancer	Ganesa	jumart	Nestor	sea god
Castor	Garuda	kelpie	Nimrod	Sekume
Chandi	Gawain	kobold	numina	Selene
Charis	Gemini	kraken	Oberon	Semele
Charon	genius	Kronos	obi man	seraph
cherub	Geryon	Laputa	occult	Simios
Chiron	goblin	Libera	Oeneus	Sinbad
Clotho	Gorgon	Lilith	ogress	Sirius
Corona	Graces	Locris	Oileus	sky god
Corvus	Graeae	Lucina	Old Ned	Somnus
Crater	Haemon	Lugaid	Ondine	Sparta
Creusa	Hathor	maenad	oracle	Sphynx
Cronus	heaven	Mammon	Ormuzd	spirit
Crotus	Hebrus	manito	Osiris	sprite
Cybele	Hecate	Marduk	Ossian	Stator
Cygnus	Hector	Marmar	Pallas	Stheno
daemon	Hecuba	mascot	panisc	Strymo
Danaus	Hekate	Medusa	panisk	sun god
Daphne	Helios	Megara	Parcae	syrinx
Decuma	Hermes	Memnon	Peleus	Tammuz
dragon	Hobbit	Mentor	Pelias	Taurus
durgan	Hoenir	Merlin	Pelops	Tellus
Egeria	hoodoo	merman	Phocis	Tethys
Eirene	Hyades	Merope	Phoebe	Teucer
Epirus	Hyllus	Mithra	Pisces	Thalia
Erebus	Iasion	Moerae	Placia	Thallo
Erinys	Iasius	Moirai	Pollux	Thebus
Erotes	Icarus	Molech	Pontus	Themis
Etolia	Indara	Moloch	Pothos	Thetis
Europa	Iolcus	Myrrha	Psyche	thrall
Euryte	Iseult	nectar	Pythia	Thunor
Faunus	Ishtar	Neleus	Python	Titans
fetish	Ismene	Nereid	Rhodus	Tithon

MYTHOLOGY

Tityus
Tonans
Tophet
Triton
Tydeus
Typhon
undine
Urania
Uranus
Utopia
Varuna
Vesper
Victor
Vishnu
vision
voodoo
Vulcan
war god
wizard
wraith
Wyvern
Yahweh
ye gods
Zephyr
Zethus
zombie
Abaddon
Achalia
Achates
Acheron
Actaeon
Ahriman
Aladdin
Alcaeus
Alcmene
Alcyone
Ali Baba
Amphion
Antaeus
Antenor
Anteros
Antiope
Aquilon
Arallis
Arcadia
Argolis
Ariadne
Artemis
Astarte
Athamas
Atropos
Avallon
Avernus
Axierus
Azapane
Bacchus
bad luck
bad peri
banshee
Bellona
bewitch
Bifrost
Boeotia
boggart
Bona Dea
Brontes
brownie
bugaboo
bugbear
Cabeiri
Calydon
Calypso
Camelot
cantrip
Capella
Cecrops
centaur
Cepheus
Cercyon
charmer
Chemosh
chimera
Chloris
Cisseus
Clymene
Cocytus
Curetes
cyclops
Cynthia
Cyzicus
Deasura
Deipyle
Demeter
demigod
dervish
dog star
Echidna
Electra
Eleusis
Elysian
Epigoni
Erginus
Erinyes
erlking
Eubulus
Eunomia
Eupheme
Euryale
Eurytus
Euterpe
evil eye
Evil One
Faustus
fire god
Fortuna
Gabriel
Galahad
Galatea
Gehenna
giantry
Glaucus
Glitnir
goat god
goddess
godling
gremlin
griffin
griffon
half god
Hanuman
Harpies
Helenus
hellion
heroine
Hesione
Himeros
Horatii
Hygieia
Iacchus
Iapetus
Icarius
Illyria
incubus
inferno

Iuturna
Jocasta
Jupiter
Krishna
Laertes
Lakshmi
Laocoon
Laodice
Laputan
Leander
limniad
Lorelei
Lucifer
Lynceus
Marsyas
Megaera
Mercury
mermaid
Michael
Midgard
Miletus
Minerva
Mordred
Mycenae
Nariman
Nemesis
Nephele
Neptune
Nerthus
Niflhel
Nirvana
Nisroch
nymphet
Oceanid
Oceanus
Oedipus
Old Nick
Olympus
Omphale
Orestes
Orpheus
Orthrus
Ouranos
Pandion
Pandora
Panthus
Pegasus
Penates
Perseus
Pervati
Phaedra
phantom
Philtre
Phineus
Phoebus
Phoenix
Phorcys
Phryxus
Pleione
Pluvius
Procris
Procyon
Proteus
Pylades
Pyrrhus
rain god
Raphael
Rig Veda
Romulus
Sagitta
Sammael
sandman
Savitri
Scorpio
sea maid
Serapis
Serpens
serpent
Shaitan
Shamash
Sigmund
Silenus
sorcery
spectre
sylphid
Taygete
Telamon
Thaumus
the gods
Theseus
Titania
Tristan
Troilus
Ulysses
unicorn
vampire
warlock
Wieland
wind god
Zadkiel
Absyrtus
Achelous
Achernar
Achilles
Acrisius
Adrastus
Aegyptus
Aganippe
Aidoneus
ambrosia
Ameinias
Anchises
Antigone
Apollyon
Aquarius
Arcturus
Argestes
Argonaut
Arimaspi
Asmodeus
Asterope
Astraeus
Astyanax
Astyoche
Atalanta
Atlantis
Baalpeor
bacchant
bad fairy
black art
Briareus
Cabeirus
caduceus
Calliope
Callisto
Capareus
Castalia
Cephalus
Cerberus
Charites
cherubim
chimaera
Chrysaor
chthonic

Cimmerii
Clymenus
Cockayne
colossus
Corythus
Cretheus
Curiatii
Cyclopes
Cynosura
Daedalus
Danaides
Dardanus
Deiphyle
demiurge
demonism
Despoina
devaloka
devil god
Diomedes
Dionysus
Dioscuri
dream god
earth god
El Dorado
elf child
Epicaste
Eridanus
Erinnyes
Eriphyle
Erytheia
Eteocles
Eurayale
Eurydice
exorcise
exorcism
fabulous
false god
Favonius
folklore
Ganymede
giantess
Glasberg
good luck
gramarye
grimoire
Harmonia
Harpinna
hell fire
Hellotis
Heracles
Hercules
Hesperis
Hiawatha
Himantes
Horatius
Hyperion
Iphicles
Juventas
Kalevala
Lachesis
Laconica
Lancelot
Laomedon
Laputian
Leiriope
libation
Lilliput
limoniad
Lycurgus
Lyonesse
magician
Mahadeva
Marathon
Marnaran
Melampus
Meleager
Menelaus
Mephisto
Merodach
Messenia
Minotaur
morganes
Morpheus
Myrtilus
Nauplius
Nephthys
Niflheim
Odysseus
Oenomaus
Old Harry
Old Horny
Olympian
paganism
Pan pipes
Pantheon
Paradise
Pasiphae
Penelope
Pentheus
Percival
Pergamus
Periboea
Persides
Peter Pan
Phaethon
Philemon
Philotis
Pierides

Pittheus
Pleiades
Podarces
Polyxena
Portunus
Poseidon
Quirinus
revenant
Sabazius
Sarpedon
Satanism
sea nymph
Sharrapu
Sisyphus
Sleipnir
sorcerer
Steropes
succubus
talisman
Tantalus
Tartarus
Teraphim
Thanatos
the Deuce
the Muses
the Seven
Thyestes
Tithonus
Tristram
Tristran
Valhalla
Valkyrie
werefolk
werewolf
Ygdrasil
Zephyrus
zoolater
zoolatry
Acarnania
Aegisthus
Agamemnon
Agapemone
Aigialeus
Aldebaran
Alexander
Amphiarus
Andromeda
Anticleia
Aphrodite
archangel
archfiend
Argus-eyed
Aristaeus
Asclepiad
Asclepios
Asclepius
Ashtaroth
Assaracus
Astydamia
Atalantis
Atargatis
Atlantica
Attic salt
Autolycus
Axiocersa
bacchante
Beelzebub
bewitcher
Black mass
brimstone
Britannia
cacodemon
Cassandra
Centaurus
Cephissus
Charybdis
chthonian
Cimmerian
Cleopatra
cloudland
Cockaigne
Concordia
cupbearer
Cupidines
Davy Jones
Deianeira
Delphinia
Delphinus
Dendrites
Deucalion
devil lore
diablerie
diabolism
Discordia
dreamland
Electryon
enchanter
Eumenides
Euphorbus
Excalibur
fairyfolk
fairyland
fairy ring
Friar Tuck
Gilgamesh
golden age
golden egg
good fairy

Great|Bear
Guenevere
Guinevere
hamadryad
Heimdallr
Hippocoon
Hippolyte
Hobgoblin
Holy|Grail
Houyhnymn
Hyppolita
Ilmarinen
Immortals
Jagannath
Kumarpish
labyrinth
Launcelot
love|charm
lucky|bean
Lycomedes
Lyonnesse
maelstrom
magic|wand
magic|word
Marspiter
Meilanion
Melpomene
Mnemosyne
Myrmidons
Narcissus
occultism
Palamedes
Palladium
Pandareus
Parnassus
Parthenon
Phantasus
Philomelo
pied|piper
Polydorus
purgatory
pyrolater
pyrolatry
Robin|Hood
Ruritania
Sangarius
Sarasvati
Shangri|la
sorceress
Sthenelus
Strategis
Teiresias
Telegonus
the|Furies
Tisiphone
totem|pole
tree|nymph
Trojan|War
Tyndareus
Ursa|major
Ursa|minor
Valkyries
Valkyriur
winged|cap
wood|nymph
Yggdrasil
Zernebock
Zeus|Pater
Alexandros
Amphiaraus
Amphitrite
Amphitryon
Andromache
apotheosis
apparition
Arion's|lyre
Armageddon
Axiocersus
bewitchery
black|magic
broomstick
Callirrhoe
Canis|major
Cassiopeia
cast|a|spell
changeling
Chrysippus
cloven|foot
Cockatrice
Coriolanus
cornucopia
Cretan|Bull
Demogorgon
demonology
Electryone
Epimetheus
Erechtheus
Euphrosyne
Euroclydon
Eurystheus
evil|genius
evil|spirit
fairy|queen
Gargantuan
ghost|dance
Greek|Fates
hagiolatry
Happy|Isles

10/11 LETTERS

heathen god
heliolater
heliolatry
Hellespont
Hephaestus
Hesperides
Hippocrene
hippogriff
hippogryph
Hippolytus
hippomanes
Hippomenes
Hitopadesa
hocus-pocus
Hyacinthus
idolatrous
idolomancy
invocation
ivory tower
Juggernaut
Juno Lucina
King Arthur
leprechaun
Little Bear
Little John
lucky charm
lucky piece
magic spell
Maid Marion
Melicertes
Memnonides
Menestheus
Midas touch
minor deity
mumbo-jumbo
myrmidones
Nebelkappe
necromancy
Nemean lion
ocean nymph
Oedipus Rex
old soldier
open sesame
Orion's belt
Pantagruel
Peripheles
Persephone
Pheidippes
Phlegethon
Phosphoros
phylactery
pipes of Pan
Polydectes
Polydeuces
Polyhymnia
Polymestor
Polyneices
Polyphemus
Procrustes
Prometheus
Proserpina
rabbit-foot
River of woe
round table
salamander
Samothrace
Santa Claus
Saturnalia
Schamander
sixth sense
soothsayer
St Nicholas
sun worship
Telemachus
the Dickens
the Tempter
Thruthvang
Triangulum
underworld
Vardhamana
water nymph
water witch
white magic
wishing cap
witchcraft
Wonderland
Yggdrasill
abracadabra
Aesculapius
amphisbaena
Aonian fount
Aonian mount
Aristomenes
bedevilment
Bellerophon
Britomartis
Brobdingnag
Capricornus
charmed life
demigoddess
demonolatry
enchantment
fetch-candle
fire worship
flower nymph
Gog and Magog
Golden Bough
golden goose

MYTHOLOGY

Gorgon's head
Happy Valley
Helen of Troy
hippocampus
Hypermestra
Juno Curitis
Kabibonokka
kingdom come
Locrian Ajax
lotus-eaters
lycanthrope
magic carpet
magic circle
meadow nymph
mecromancer
medicine man
Megapenthes
moon goddess
Morgan le Fay
mother earth
Mudjekeavis
Neoptolemus
nether world
Nymphagetes
Orion's hound
Orion's sword
Pallantides
Pandemonium
Pandora's box
pastoral god
patron saint
Persephassa
Philippides
Philoctetes
poltergeist
Polymnestor
Prester John
Rosicrucian
Sagittarius
Scamandrius
second sight
Shawandasee
spellbinder
Stygian oath
sylvan deity
Symplegades
Terpsichore
the black art
three Graces
thunderbolt
Triptolemos
Trojan horse
tutelary god
ultima Thule
under a spell
ware-animals
water spirit
water sprite
wishing well
witch-doctor
wooden horse
Achilles heel
Aesop's fables
Aladdin's lamp
Amphion's lyre
Arcadian hind
Athena Pallas
Augean stable
avenging fury
Bower of Bliss
Bull Poseidon
Chrysomallus
Clytemnestra
Doppelganger
Dyanean rocks
Erichthonius
exsufflation
Garden of Eden
golden apples
golden fleece
Golden Legend
heavenly host
Hesperethusa
hippocentaur
horn of plenty
household god
Hyperboreans
Isle of Apples
Juno Quiritis
Kriss Kringle
Laestrygones
Lake Tritonis
Land o the Leal
lap of the gods
Lernean Hydra
little people
Marathon bull
Mount Helicon
Mount Olympus
ordeal by fire
Pallas Athene
Parthian shot
Periclymenus
Promised Land
Rhadamanthus
Serpentarius
Stygian creek
Stygian gloom

supernatural
thaumaturgus
Thesmophorus
vestal|virgin
Wandering|Jew
Weird|Sisters
Will|Scarlett
wishing|stone
witches|coven
Augean|stables
Elysian|fields
metamorphosis
Phoebus|Apollo
apple|of|discord
Jupiter|Pluvius
mythologically
Never|Never|Land
Walpurgis|Night
Father|Christmas
Gotterdammerung
Homeric|laughter
sword|of|Damocles

Occupations

AB	dux	bard	feed	peon	adult
BA	fan	beak	firm	poet	agent
CA	guy	bear	girl	pope	baker
DD	job	beau	G-man	sage	belle
GP	kid	boss	hack	salt	boots
MA	lad	bull	hand	seer	bosun
MC	man	chap	head	serf	boxer
MD	Mrs	char	hero	silk	buyer
MO	nun	chef	hobo	star	caddy
MP	pay	cook	host	task	cadet
Mr	rep	crew	lass	tyro	canon
PA	sir	cure	lead	wage	chief
PM	spy	dean	magi	ward	chips
BSc	tar	demy	maid	whip	chore
CID	vet	dick	miss	work	clerk
deb	aide	diva	monk	abbot	coach
doc	babe	doxy	page	actor	crier
don	baby	dyer	peer	ad-man	crone

OCCUPATIONS

crony	luter	sewer	bandit	codist
crook	madam	slave	banker	coheir
decoy	major	smith	barber	consul
demon	maker	sower	bargee	coolie
devil	Maori	staff	barker	cooper
diver	mason	tenor	barman	copier
donor	mayor	thief	batman	copper
doyen	medic	tiler	batter	costar
dummy	miner	tommy	beadle	coster
dutch	minor	trade	bearer	couper
elder	model	tramp	beater	cowboy
envoy	nanny	tuner	beggar	Creole
extra	navvy	tutor	beldam	critic
fakir	nurse	uhlan	Berber	curate
felon	odist	usher	bishop	cutler
fence	owner	valet	boffin	cutter
fifer	padre	vicar	bookie	damsel
friar	party	viner	bowman	dancer
Galen	pilot	wages	broker	deacon
garbo	pinup	wench	bugler	dealer
ghost	piper	witch	bursar	debtor
gipsy	posse	woman	busker	deputy
grass	prior	yokel	butler	divine
guard	proxy	youth	cabbie	docker
guest	pupil	abbess	caddie	doctor
guide	quack	admass	caller	double
hewer	quill	airace	camper	dowser
issue	rabbi	airman	cantor	draper
judge	racer	albino	captor	drawer
juror	rider	alumna	career	driver
laird	rishi	archer	carter	drudge
limey	rival	artist	carver	duenna
local	rover	aupair	casual	editor
locum	saver	aurist	censor	ensign
loser	sawer	author	cleric	escort
lover	scout	backer	client	Eskimo

etcher
expert
fabler
factor
feeder
fellow
fitter
flunky
flyman
forger
friend
fuller
gaffer
gagman
ganger
gaoler
garcon
gaucho
German
gigolo
gillie
glazer
glover
golfer
graver
grocer
grower
gunman
gunner
hatter
hawker
healer
helper
herald
hermit
het|man

high|up
hippie
hosier
hunter
hussar
hymner
ice|man
inmate
intern
jailer
jester
jet|set
jobber
jockey
joiner
jumper
junior
junker
keener
keeper
killer
lackey
lancer
lascar
lawyer
leader
lector
legate
lender
lessee
Levite
limner
living
lodger
lutist
lyrist

mahout
maiden
marine
marker
master
matron
medico
medium
member
menial
mentor
mercer
mikado
miller
minion
mister
moiler
monger
moppet
mortal
mummer
munshi
musico
mystic
nannie
native
Norman
notary
novice
nudist
nuncio
oboist
odd|job
office
oilman
optime

oracle
orator
ostler
outlaw
packer
parson
pastor
patron
pedlar
penman
pen|pal
picket
pieman
pirate
pitman
plater
player
Pommie
porter
potter
prater
priest
punter
purser
ragman
ranger
rating
reader
reaper
rector
regius
rhymer
rigger
ringer
rioter
robber

rookie
runner
sailor
sapper
sartor
savage
savant
sawyer
scorer
scouse
scribe
sea|dog
sealer
seaman
second
seller
senior
sentry
server
sexton
shadow
sheila
shower
shrink
singer
sister
skater
skivvy
skyman
slater
slavey
slayer
sleuth
smoker
sniper
soutar

souter
sowter
sparks
squire
status
stoker
suitor
sutler
tailor
talent
tanner
Tartar
taster
tatter
teller
tenant
Teuton
tiller
tinker
tinner
toiler
trader
truant
turner
tycoon
typist
tyrant
umpire
urchin
usurer
valuer
vanman
vendor
verger
victor
Viking

waiter
walk-on
warden
warder
weaver
welder
whaler
winner
wizard
worker
wright
writer
yeoman
abetter
abigail
acolyte
acrobat
actress
actuary
admiral
adviser
almoner
alumnus
amateur
analyst
apostle
arbiter
artisan
artiste
assayer
athlete
attache
auditor
aviator
bailiff
ballboy

bandman
barmaid
baronet
bassist
Bedouin
beldame
bellboy
bellhop
big name
big shot
bit-part
blender
boarder
boatman
bookman
bouncer
breeder
brigand
builder
burglar
bushman
butcher
buttons
callboy
calling
cambist
captain
captive
carrier
cashier
caulker
caveman
cellist
chemist
chindit
chorist

citizen
cleaner
climber
clippie
coalman
cobbler
cockney
colleen
collier
colonel
commere
company
compere
comrade
convert
convict
co-pilot
copyist
copyman
coroner
corsair
Cossack
counsel
courier
cowherd
cowpoke
creator
crofter
crooner
cropper
curator
custode
cyclist
danseur
daysman
debater

denizen
dentist
diviner
dominie
doorman
dragoon
drayman
dresser
driller
drummer
dustman
elogist
embassy
entrant
equerry
escapee
escaper
esquire
farceur
farcist
farrier
fiddler
fighter
fireman
flagman
flapper
flesher
florist
footboy
footman
footpad
foreman
founder
frogman
furrier
gambler
gate man
general
ghillie
glazier
gleaner
grown up
gun moll
gymnast
handler
hangman
harpist
haulier
head boy
headman
heckler
heiress
heroine
hipster
histrio
hostess
hymnist
imagist
invalid
Jack tar
janitor
jemedar
juggler
junkman
justice
knacker
knitter
know how
learner
lineman
linkboy
linkman
lockman
look out
lorimer
maestro
magnate
mailman
manager
mariner
marshal
masseur
matador
matelot
meatman
midwife
milkman
mobsman
mobster
modiste
monitor
moulder
mourner
mudlark
navarch
newsboy
newsman
oarsman
oculist
officer
old salt
omnibus
oratrix
orderly
page boy
painter
partner
passman
patient
patroon
pearler
peasant
pianist
picador
pierrot
pilgrim
pioneer
planner
planter
plumber
poacher
poetess
pollman
poloist
pontiff
poor man
pop idol
pop star
post boy
postman
prefect
prelate
premier
presser
primate
printer
privado
private
proctor
proofer
prophet
protege
provost
prowler

OCCUPATIONS

puddler
punster
pursuer
railman
rancher
rat race
realtor
redskin
referee
refugee
regular
remover
rentier
rescuer
reserve
retinue
rich man
routine
rustler
saddler
sagaman
samurai
sandman
scalper
scenist
scholar
scraper
sea cook
sea king
sea lord
sea wolf
seminar
senator
servant
service
settler
sharper
shearer
sheriff
shopman
shopper
showman
skinner
skipper
soldier
soloist
soprano
spartan
speaker
spinner
sponsor
spotter
stand by
starlet
starman
starter
station
steward
stipend
student
supremo
surgeon
swagman
tapster
teacher
tipster
tourist
trainee
trainer
trapper
trawler
tripper
trooper
trouper
tumbler
turfman
veteran
viceroy
vintner
visitor
warrior
webster
whipper
wiseman
witness
wolf cub
woodman
woolman
workman
abductor
adherent
adjutant
advocate
aeronaut
alderman
alienist
allopath
ambivert
anchoret
armorist
armourer
arranger
assassin
assessor
attacker
attorney
axemaker
bagmaker
banjoist
bankrupt
banksman
bargeman
baritone
beadsman
bedesman
bedmaker
beginner
benefice
bigamist
blackleg
blind man
boardman
Bohemian
bondsman
boniface
borrower
botanist
bowmaker
boxmaker
boy scout
brakeman
brunette
bummaree
business
cabin boy
call girl
canoness
cardinal
castaway
ceramist
chairman
chambers
champion
chandler

8 LETTERS

chaperon
chaplain
choirboy
cicerone
cicisbeo
civilian
claimant
clansman
classman
clerkess
clothier
co-author
comedian
commando
commoner
compiler
composer
conjurer
convener
corporal
coryphee
cottager
courtier
coxswain
creditor
croupier
cupmaker
cutpurse
dairyman
danseuse
dead-head
deck hand
delegate
deserter
designer
detainee
dictator
diet cook
diocesan
diplomat
director
disciple
dogsbody
domestic
dragoman
druggist
duettist
educator
elegiast
embalmer
emeritus
emigrant
emissary
employee
engineer
engraver
epic poet
essayist
eulogist
examinee
executor
explorer
exponent
fabulist
factotum
falconer
fanfaron
fanmaker
farm hand
ferryman
figurant
film idol
filmstar
finalist
finisher
fishwife
flatfoot
flautist
floorman
forester
forgeman
freshman
front-man
fugitive
fusilier
gangsman
gangster
gaolbird
gardener
garroter
gendarme
goatherd
governor
gownsman
graduate
guardian
guerilla
gunmaker
gunsmith
ham actor
handmaid
handyman
hatmaker
hawkshaw
haymaker
head cook
head girl
headship
Hebraist
helmsman
henchman
herdsman
hijacker
hired gun
hired man
hireling
home help
horseman
hotelier
houseboy
hula girl
huntsman
identity
idyllist
importer
inceptor
informer
initiate
inkmaker
inventor
investor
islander
jailbird
jet pilot
jeweller
jongleur
juvenile
knife-boy
labourer
land girl
landlady
landlord
landsman
lapidary

law agent
lawgiver
law maker
laywoman
lecturer
licensee
life peer
life work
linesman
linguist
listener
logician
loiterer
looker on
lumberer
luminary
lyricist
magician
mandarin
mapmaker
marauder
marksman
masseuse
mechanic
mediator
melodist
mercator
merchant
milkmaid
millgirl
millhand
milliner
minister
ministry
minstrel
mistress
modeller
moralist
motorist
muleteer
muralist
murderer
musician
narrator
naturist
neophyte
netmaker
newcomer
news hawk
nightman
Norseman
novelist
objector
observer
occupant
official
onlooker
op artist
operator
opponent
optician
oratress
ordinand
organist
overlord
overseer
pardoner
parodist
party man
passer by
patentee
penmaker
perfumer
perjurer
picaroon
pilferer
pillager
plagiary
poetling
poisoner
polisher
pontifex
position
potmaker
practice
preacher
pressman
prioress
prisoner
prizeman
producer
promoter
prompter
psychist
publican
pugilist
purveyor
quarrier
radar man
rag trade
ragwoman
receiver
recorder
reformer
reporter
research
resident
retailer
retainer
reveller
revenant
reviewer
rewriter
rifleman
rivetter
road gang
rotarian
rugmaker
saboteur
salesman
salvager
satirist
sawbones
sawsmith
sciolist
scullion
sculptor
seafarer
seedsman
selector
sentinel
sergeant
servitor
shepherd
shipmate
shopgirl
showgirl
side kick
sidesman
silk gown
sinecure
sketcher
sky scout
small fry

smuggler
solitary
songster
sorcerer
spaceman
spearman
speed|cop
sprinter
stageman
star|turn
stockman
storeman
stowaway
stranger
stripper
stroller
stunt|man
superior
superman
supplier
surveyor
survivor
swagsman
tallyman
taxpayer
teddy|boy
teenager
thatcher
Thespian
thurifer
tin|miner
tinsmith
Tom|Thumb
tone|poet
top|brass
toreador
torturer
townsman
trainman
trappist
tripeman
tunester
unionist
union|man
vagabond
valuator
vanguard
virtuoso
vocalist
vocation
waitress
ward|maid
wardress
watchman
waterman
wayfarer
wet|nurse
wheelman
whiphand
whipjack
whittler
wig|maker
woodsman
workfolk
workgirl
workhand
wrangler
wrestler
yodeller
aborigine
absconder
aerialist
alchemist
anatomist
anchoress
anchorite
annotator
announcer
annuitant
antiquary
apologist
applicant
appraiser
arch|enemy
architect
archivist
art|critic
art|dealer
artificer
assistant
associate
astronaut
attendant
authoress
authority
automaton
axlesmith
balladist
ballerina
bargainer
barrister
barrow|boy
beefeater
bee|keeper
beermaker
beggarman
bellmaker
biologist

OCCUPATIONS

bit|player
boatswain
bodyguard
bodymaker
boilerman
boltsmith
bookmaker
bootblack
bootmaker
brass|hats
brigadier
buccaneer
bunny|girl
bus|driver
bush|pilot
byrewoman
bystander
cab|driver
cabin|crew
cafe|owner
cakemaker
cameraman
candidate
canvasser
cardsharp
caretaker
carpenter
casemaker
celebrity
cellarman
centurion
chain|gang
chartered
charterer
charwoman
chauffeur
choralist
chorus|boy
clergyman
clinician
clogmaker
coadjutor
coal|miner
coenobite
colleague
collector
columnist
combatant
commander
commodore
companion
concierge
concubine
conductor
confessor
confidant
conqueror
conscript
constable
contender
contralto
cornerboy
cosmonaut
cost|clerk
costumier
court|fool
couturier
covergirl
crackshot
cracksman
crayonist
cricketer
cupbearer
custodian
cutthroat
cymbalist
daily|help
day|labour
deaconess
dean|of|men
debutante
decorator
defendant
dependent
designate
desk|clerk
detective
dialogist
dietician
dispenser
dog|walker
dollmaker
dramatist
drum|major
drysalter
ecologist
economist
embezzler
emolument
enamelist
enchanter
engrosser
entourage
errand|boy
espionage
estimator
exchanger
exchequer

9 LETTERS

exciseman
executive
eye|doctor
fieldwork
figurante
film|actor
film|extra
film|maker
financier
fire|guard
first|mate
fisherman
foreigner
foundling
free|lance
freemason
fruiterer
furnisher
garreteer
garrotter
gas|fitter
gazetteer
gem|cutter
geologist
girl|guide
gladiator
gluemaker
go|between
goldsmith
gondolier
governess
grapevine
grenadier
guarantor
guardsman
guerrilla
guest|star
guitarist
gunrunner
hand|sewer
harbinger
harbourer
hard|graft
harlequin
harmonist
harpooner
harvester
head|clerk
herbalist
hillbilly
hired|hand
hired|help
historian
home|maker
homeopath
Hottentot
house|dick
housemaid
husbandry
hypnotist
immigrant
increment
incumbent
innkeeper
inscriber
in|service
inside|man
inspector
interview
ironminer
ironsmith
jay|walker
jitterbug
jobholder
key|worker
kidnapper
lacemaker
lady's|maid
lampmaker
lampooner
land|agent
land|force
landowner
landreeve
land|shark
larcenist
launderer
laundress
lawmonger
lay|figure
lay|reader
lay|sister
legionary
lensmaker
librarian
lifeguard
life's|work
linotyper
liontamer
lip|reader
liveryman
loan|agent
lockmaker
locksmith
log|roller
lord|mayor
lowlander
lumberman

machinist
major|domo
major|poet
make-up|man
male|model
male|nurse
man-at-arms
man|Friday
medallist
mendicant
mercenary
mesmerist
messenger
middleman
minor|poet
model|girl
monitress
moonraker
mortician
muscle-man
musketeer
mythmaker
navigator
neighbour
newsagent
newshound
nursemaid
occultist
odd|job|man
office|boy
old|master
old|stager
ombudsman
operative
osteopath
otologist
outfitter
panellist
pantomime
paparazzo
part-owner
passenger
patrolman
patroness
paymaster
paysagist
pedagogue
pen|friend
pen|pusher
pensioner
performer
personage
personnel
phone|girl
physician
physicist
picksmith
Pierrette
pistoleer
pitwright
plaintiff
plasterer
ploughboy
ploughman
plunderer
poetaster
policeman
pop|artist
pop|singer
portrayer
portreeve
possessor
postulant
postwoman
poulterer
precentor
precursor
prelector
presbyter
president
priestess
principal
privateer
professor
profiteer
prud'homme
publicist
publisher
puppeteer
raconteur
rainmaker
ransacker
ranzelman
ratefixer
ratepayer
recordist
reference
registrar
residency
rhymester
ringsider
roadmaker
rocketeer
rocket|man
ropemaker
roundsman
rum|runner
rural|dean

9/10 LETTERS

sackmaker
safemaker
sailmaker
sales girl
sales team
sassenach
scarecrow
scaristan
scavenger
scenarist
scientist
scrapegut
scribbler
scrivener
sea lawyer
secretary
seneschal
sentryman
seraskier
serenader
sermonist
servitude
shoemaker
signaller
signalman
situation
skin diver
solicitor
songsmith
sonneteer
sophister
sophomore
sorceress
soubrette
space crew
speedster
spider man
spokesman
sportsman
stagehand
stage idol
star gazer
statesman
stationer
steersman
stevedore
strike pay
subaltern
sub editor
suffragan
swineherd
tablemaid
tailoress
tap dancer
tax evader
tentmaker
test pilot
therapist
timberman
toolsmith
town clerk
towncrier
tradesman
traveller
tribesman
troubador
trumpeter
tympanist
undergrad
usherette
vigilante
violinist
volunteer
wassailer
waxworker
weekender
wheelsman
winemaker
woodreeve
workwoman
yachtsman
youngster
zitherist
zoologist
able seaman
accomplice
accountant
advertiser
aeronomist
agrologist
agronomist
aide de camp
air hostess
air steward
amanuensis
ambassador
Anglo Saxon
anvilsmith
apothecary
apprentice
arbitrator
archbishop
archdeacon
archpriest
aristocrat
astrologer
astronomer
auctioneer

audit|clerk
au|pair|girl
babe|in|arms
baby|sitter
ballet|girl
ballplayer
bandmaster
bank|robber
baseballer
bassoonist
bear|leader
beautician
bellringer
benefactor
billbroker
billposter
biochemist
biographer
blacksmith
bladesmith
blockmaker
bludgeoner
bluebottle
bluejacket
boatwright
bogtrotter
bombardier
bonesetter
bonus|clerk
bookbinder
book|dealer
bookfolder
bookholder
bookkeeper
bookseller
bookwright
bootlegger
brain|drain
brakemaker
brass|smith
breadmaker
bricklayer
brickmaker
broom|maker
brushmaker
bulb|grower
bumbailiff
bureaucrat
burlesquer
camera|team
campaigner
cartoonist
cat|breeder
cat|burglar
catechumen
cavalryman
ceramicist
chainmaker
chairmaker
chancellor
changeling
chargehand
charity|boy
chauffeuse
chorus|girl
chronicler
cider|maker
cigar|maker
claim|agent
clapper|boy
cloakmaker
clockmaker
clocksmith
clog|dancer
cloisterer
cloistress
clothmaker
clubmaster
coachmaker
coastguard
co|director
collar|work
coloratura
colporteur
comedienne
commandant
commission
competitor
compositor
concertist
consultant
contestant
contractor
controller
copyreader
copywriter
corn|doctor
cornettist
coryphaeus
councillor
counsellor
country|boy
countryman
couturiere
cover|agent
crackbrain
cultivator
customs|man

cytologist
day|tripper
demoiselle
dilettante
dirty|nurse
disc|jockey
discounter
discoverer
dishwasher
dispatcher
dog|breeder
donkey|work
doorkeeper
dramatizer
dramaturge
dressmaker
drug|pusher
drummer|boy
dry|cleaner
duty|roster
early|riser
empiricist
employment
equestrian
evangelist
experience
eye|witness
fabricator
faith|curer
farmer's|boy
fellmonger
fictionist
film|editor
firemaster
fire|raiser
fishmonger
flag|bearer
flight|crew
flower|girl
folk|singer
footballer
foot|doctor
forecaster
forerunner
forty|niner
frame|maker
freebooter
fund|raiser
gamekeeper
game|warden
garage|hand
gatekeeper
gatewright
geisha|girl
geneticist
geochemist
geographer
glassmaker
glossarist
goalkeeper
gold|beater
gold|digger
goldworker
grammarian
grand|prior
grindstone
groceryman
gubernator
gunslinger
hall|porter
handmaiden
handshaker
hatchet|man
headhunter
headmaster
head|porter
head|waiter
hedgesmith
henchwoman
highjacker
highlander
high|priest
highwayman
hitchhiker
holy|orders
honorarium
horn|player
horologist
house|agent
husbandman
impresario
incendiary
incumbency
inhabitant
inquisitor
instructor
ironmaster
ironmonger
ironworker
jewel|thief
job|hunting
job|printer
journalist
junk|dealer
kennelmaid
kitchenboy
kitchenman
knifesmith

land|holder
land|jobber
landlubber
land|pirate
land|waiter
lapidarist
laundryman
law|officer
lay|brother
leading|man
legislator
liberty|man
librettist
licentiate
lieutenant
lighterman
lime|burner
linotypist
livelihood
lobsterman
lock|keeper
loggerhead
loomworker
lumberjack
machineman
magistrate
mail|robber
management
manageress
manicurist
manservant
medical|man
medicaster
message|boy
midshipman
militiaman
millwright
mind|curist
mind|healer
mindreader
ministress
missionary
model|maker
monopolist
moonshiner
motley|fool
mouthpiece
naturalist
nautch|girl
naval|cadet
negotiator
neutralist
newscaster
news|editor
newsvendor
newswriter
night|float
night|nurse
notability
nurseryman
obituarist
occupation
oil|painter
pallbearer
pantomimic
pantry|maid
papermaker
park|keeper
park|ranger
pastrycook
pathfinder
pawnbroker
peacemaker
pearl|diver
pearly|king
pedestrian
pediatrist
pedicurist
penologist
perruquier
petitioner
pharmacist
piano|tuner
piccoloist
pickpocket
piermaster
plagiarist
platelayer
playbroker
playwright
playwriter
poet|artist
poet|farmer
poet|priest
politician
postmaster
prebendary
priesthood
prima|donna
private|eye
procurator
profession
programmer
prolocutor
proprietor
prospector
proveditor
questioner

quizmaster
railwayman
raw recruit
recitalist
researcher
retirement
revenue man
revivalist
rhapsodist
ringmaster
roadmender
ropedancer
ropewalker
safeblower
sales clerk
sales force
saleswoman
saltworker
sand-dancer
schoolma'am
scrutineer
sculptress
sea-captain
seamstress
second mate
seminarian
sempstress
serologist
serviceman
session man
shanghaier
shipwright
shopfitter
shopkeeper
signwriter
sinologist
songstress
sound mixer
spacewoman
specialist
speculator
spy catcher
staff nurse
starmonger
steelmaker
step dancer
stewardess
stick-up man
stockrider
stocktaker
stonemason
storesmith
strategist
submariner
subscriber
substitute
supercargo
supervisor
supplicant
swordsmith
symphonist
syncopator
tally clerk
tallywoman
taskmaster
taxi driver
technician
technocrat
televiewer
tenderfoot
third party
tilewright
timekeeper
trafficker
translator
tripehound
tripewoman
trombonist
tweedledee
tweedledum
typesetter
typing pool
underagent
understudy
undertaker
vegetarian
versemaker
versesmith
veterinary
vice-consul
vice-master
victualler
vine grower
wage earner
wage worker
wainwright
watchmaker
water guard
wharfinger
wholesaler
winebibber
winewaiter
wireworker
woodcarver
woodcutter
woodworker
wool carder
wool comber

wool|sorter
wool|winder
workfellow
working|man
workmaster
workpeople
worshipper
abecedarian
academician
accompanist
actor's|agent
antiquarian
appointment
army|officer
astrologist
astronomist
audio|typist
backroom|boy
bag|snatcher
bank|cashier
bank|manager
bargemaster
basketmaker
beauty|queen
bell|founder
beneficiary
billsticker
bingo|caller
bird|fancier
bird|watcher
board|member
body|builder
body|servant
boilermaker
boilersmith
breadwinner
bridgemaker
broadcaster
bronzesmith
bullfighter
bushfighter
businessman
candlemaker
car|salesman
chamberlain
chambermaid
charcoalist
cheerleader
cheesemaker
chiropodist
choirmaster
clairvoyant
clergywoman
coachwright
co-authoress
coffinmaker
cognoscenti
commentator
congressman
conspirator
contributor
conveyancer
co-ordinator
coppersmith
court|jester
crane|driver
crimewriter
crown|lawyer
cub|reporter
cypher|clerk
day|labourer
dean|of|women
delivery|man
demographer
distributor
double|agent
draughtsman
drill|master
drug|peddler
duty|officer
electrician
embroiderer
enlisted|man
entertainer
estate|agent
etymologist
executioner
extortioner
factory|hand
faith|healer
field|worker
fifth|column
fighting|man
filing|clerk
fingersmith
fire|brigade
fire|watcher
flag|captain
flag|officer
flat|dweller
flying|squad
foot|soldier
fruit|picker
funambulist
functionary
galley|slave
games|master
gentlewoman

ghostwriter
ginger group
glass blower
glass cutter
grave digger
greengrocer
gunman's moll
haberdasher
hairdresser
hair stylist
hammersmith
handservant
hardwareman
head teacher
hedgepriest
high sheriff
high society
home crofter
horse doctor
horse trader
housekeeper
housemaster
housemother
housewright
ice-cream man
illuminator
illusionist
illustrator
infantryman
interpreter
interviewer
iron founder
kitchenmaid
lamplighter
landscapist
land steward
laundrymaid
leading lady
leaseholder
ledger clerk
lifeboatman
locum tenens
lollipop man
Lord Provost
lorry driver
madrigalist
maidservant
mandolinist
manipulator
masquerader
master baker
matinee idol
mechanician
medicine man
memorialist
merchantman
metalworker
method actor
military man
millionaire
mimographer
miniaturist
money lender
moonlighter
mother's help
mountaineer
music critic
naval rating
needlewoman
neurologist
night hunter
night porter
night sister
night worker
novelettist
numismatist
office party
onion Johnny
optometrist
ornamentist
orthopedist
palaestrian
pamphleteer
panelbeater
panel doctor
papal nuncio
paperhanger
paragrapher
parish clerk
parlourmaid
pathologist
pearlfisher
pearly queen
penny-a-liner
petrologist
philatelist
philologist
philosopher
phonologist
piece worker
police cadet
policewoman
portraitist
predecessor
prizewinner
probationer
protagonist
proof reader

purseholder
questionist
quill|driver
radiologist
rag|merchant
rank|and|file
rear|admiral
relic|monger
research|man
resignation
rhetorician
river|keeper
roadsweeper
rocket|pilot
rugby|player
safebreaker
safecracker
sandwichman
saxophonist
school|nurse
scorekeeper
scoutmaster
scrap|dealer
scythesmith
search|party
secret|agent
semanticist
semaphorist
semi,skilled
senior|clerk
sharebroker
sheep|farmer
shepherdess
shipbuilder
ship's|cooper
ship's|tailor
ship's|writer
shop|steward
silversmith
sister|tutor
slaughterer
slave|labour
slave|trader
smallholder
sociologist
space|doctor
spacewriter
speechmaker
stage|player
stagewright
stallholder
steeplejack
stenotypist
stereotyper
stipendiary
stockbroker
stockfarmer
stockjobber
stonecutter
storekeeper
storyteller
straight|man
stripteaser
subordinate
surrebutter
swordmaster
talent|scout
taxidermist
telegrapher
telepathist
telephonist
terpsichore
testimonial
ticket|agent
toastmaster
tobacconist
Tommy|Atkins
tooth|doctor
tooth|drawer
town|planner
toxophilite
train|bearer
train|robber
transcriber
travel|agent
tree|surgeon
truck|farmer
typographer
upholsterer
van|salesman
versemonger
vice,admiral
vine|dresser
viola|player
war|reporter
washerwoman
water|doctor
water|finder
welfare|work
whalefisher
wheelwright
white,collar
white|hunter
witch|doctor
woodchopper
wool|stapler
working|girl
workmanlike

xylophonist
youth leader
actor-manager
advance party
air commodore
aircraftsman
air-sea rescue
ambulance man
anaesthetist
armour bearer
artilleryman
balladmonger
ballad singer
ballet dancer
bibliologist
bibliopegist
board meeting
body snatcher
booking clerk
bookstitcher
border sentry
bottlewasher
boulevardier
bridgemaster
brigade major
brinkmanship
cabinet maker
calligrapher
camp follower
candlewright
caricaturist
carpet bagger
carpet fetter
cartographer
casual labour
cattle lifter
cerographist
check-weigher
chicken thief
chief cashier
chief justice
chief mourner
chief of staff
chimney sweep
chirographer
chiropractor
churchwarden
circuit rider
civil servant
civil service
clarinettist
clerk of works
coachbuilder
collaborator
commissioner
confectioner
conquistador
contemporary
corn chandler
costermonger
customs clerk
deep-sea diver
demonstrator
desk sergeant
doctor's round
dramaturgist
ecclesiastic
electrotyper
elocutionist
entomologist
entrepreneur
equestrienne
escapologist
exhibitioner
experimenter
ex-service man
exterminator
family doctor
father figure
field-marshal
field officer
figure dancer
filibusterer
film director
film producer
first officer
first reserve
flying column
flying doctor
footplateman
garret master
general agent
geriatrician
globetrotter
grandstander
group captain
guest speaker
gynecologist
headmistress
headshrinker
heir apparent
high official
hockey player
holidaymaker
hotel manager
housebreaker
housepainter
hydropathist

immunologist
impersonator
improvisator
in conference
inseparables
instructress
intermediary
jazz musician
junior rating
juvenile lead
king's counsel
kitchen staff
knifegrinder
knifethrower
lady superior
landed gentry
land surveyor
law stationer
lay-out artist
leader writer
leathernecks
legal adviser
letter writer
lexicologist
line sergeant
literary hack
literary lion
lithographer
longshoreman
loss adjuster
maid of honour
maitre d'hotel
major-general
make-up artist
man of letters
man of science
manual worker
manufacturer
mass-producer
master-at-arms
mastersinger
metallurgist
metropolitan
mezzo soprano
mineralogist
money-changer
monographist
motorcyclist
musicologist
naval officer
newspaperman
notary public
nutritionist
obstetrician
office bearer
office junior
pastoral poet
patent office
pediatrician
penitentiary
petty officer
photographer
physiologist
plant manager
ploughwright
plumber's mate
poet laureate
post graduate
postmistress
practitioner
press officer
principal boy
prison warder
prison worker
quarrymaster
racing driver
radiodontist
radiographer
receptionist
remuneration
restaurateur
retaining fee
sales manager
scene-painter
scene-shifter
schoolmaster
screenwriter
scriptwriter
scullery maid
sister german
site engineer
snake-charmer
social worker
soil mechanic
sole occupant
special agent
speechwriter
spiritualist
sports master
sportscaster
sportswriter
staff officer
stage manager
statistician
steel erector
stenographer
stereotypist
stonedresser

stormtrooper
street-trader
tax-collector
technologist
telegraph boy
telephone man
tennis player
test engineer
theatre nurse
ticket holder
ticket writer
top executive
trained nurse
trichologist
trick-cyclist
troutbreeder
undermanager
vaudevillist
vice-director
vice-governor
warehouseman
water-diviner
wind musician
wine merchant
wood-engraver
worker priest
working party
workmistress
works manager
alongshoreman
antique dealer
archaeologist
articled clerk
audio-engineer
barber-surgeon
campanologist
church officer
civil engineer
coastguardman
common law wife
contortionist
contrabandist
cook-housemaid
cotton spinner
counter-jumper
craftsmanship
cryptographer
dancing master
dental surgeon
district nurse
feature editor
fellow-servant
fencing master
fortune-teller
guardian angel
gynaecologist
harbour master
health visitor
industrialist
lady-in-waiting
lift attendant
lighthouseman
livery servant
livery servant
lollipop woman
maid-of-all-work
master builder
master mariner
night watchman
office manager
old-clothes man
poultry farmer

printer's devil
prison visitor
process server
rag-and-bone man
rent collector
scrap merchant
ship's chandler
shop assistant
shop detective
skeleton staff
skilled worker
still-room maid
street sweeper
toastmistress
traffic warden
universal aunt
window cleaner
window dresser
accomplishment
apprenticeship
audiometrician
black marketeer
bus conductress
busman's holiday
casual labourer
charcoal burner
chimney sweeper
clerical worker
coastguardsman
commissionaire
common informer
dramatic critic
elder statesman
gentleman usher
hotel detective
house decorator
house detective
king's messenger
labour exchange
maintenance man
market gardener
marriage broker
matron of honour
mining engineer
munition worker
naval architect
nursing officer
opposite number
prison governor
research worker
Reverend Mother
ship's carpenter
sports reporter
stage carpenter
stamp collector
standard bearer
station manager
store detective
street musician
superintendent
tobacco planter
troubleshooter
turf accountant
valet de chambre
blastfurnaceman
Bow Street runner
colliery manager
commission agent
crossing sweeper
customs official
district visitor
Father Christmas

15 LETTERS

funeral director
gentleman farmer
gossip columnist
Jack of all trades
old age pensioner
one parent family
ophthalmologist
planning officer
police constable
police inspector
programme seller
Queen's messenger
research chemist
shorthand typist
shorthand writer
slave trafficker
stamp collection
stretcher bearer
surrogate father
surrogate mother
surrogate parent
ticket collector
tightrope walker
undercover agent
youth club leader

Oceans and Seas

Aegean
Arctic
Baltic
Red Sea
Aral Sea
Dead Sea
Java Sea
Kara Sea
Oresund
Ross Sea
Sulu Sea
Wash, The
Adriatic
Atlantic
Black Sea
Bosporus
Coral Sea
Kattegat
Korea Bay
Minch, The
North Sea
Spithead
Timor Sea
Azov, Sea of
Bantry Bay
Foxe Basin
Hudson Bay
Ionian Sea
Scapa Flow
Skagerrak
Solent, The
Yellow Sea
Zuider Zee
Aden, Gulf of
Andaman Sea
Arabian Sea
Bass Strait
Caspian Sea
Celebes Sea
Cook Strait
Delagoa Bay
Fundy, Bay of
Oman, Gulf of
Palk Strait
Riga, Gulf of
Siam, Gulf of
Aqaba, Gulf of
Beaufort Sea

OCEANS AND SEAS

Bengal,|Bay|of
Bismarck|Sea
Cabot|Strait
Dardanelles
Indian|Ocean
Korea|Strait
Lions,|Gulf|of
Menai|Strait
Persian|Gulf
Plenty,|Bay|of
Saronic|Gulf
Solway|Firth
Benin,|Bight|of
Darien,|Gulf|of
East|China|Sea
Greenland|Sea
Guinea,|Gulf|of
Mannar,|Gulf|of
Marmora,|Sea|of
Mexico,|Gulf|of
Panama,|Gulf|of
Tonkin,|Gulf|of
Torres|Strait
Bothnia,|Gulf|of
Corinth,|Gulf|of
Finland,|Gulf|of
Fonseca,|Gulf|of
Mediterranean
Pentland|Firth
South|China|Sea
Taranto,|Gulf|of
Tyrrhenian|Sea
Van|Diemen|Gulf
Albemarle|Sound
Bristol|Channel
English|Channel
Macassar|Strait
Magellan|Strait
Malacca,|Strait|of
Messina,|Strait|of

Physical Sciences

AU
amp
erg
lab
ray
wow
atom
beam
cell
coil
core
echo
flex
flux
foam
foci
fuse
heat
lens
mass
phon
pile
pion
pole
rays
rule
tone
unit
volt
wane
watt
wave
X|ray
anion
anode
curie
cycle
field
flame
focus
force
gauss
henry
hertz
laser
light
meson
optic
orbit
phase
polar
power
quark
radar

relay	siphon	density	science
solve	solder	diagram	Sputnik
sound	stress	Doppler	tensile
spark	syphon	dry cell	tension
steam	theory	elastic	torsion
A blast	thrust	entropy	vernier
aerial	torque	EURATOM	voltage
albedo	vacuum	fall out	aerology
ampere	vortex	fatigue	aerostat
atomic	weight	fissile	alpha ray
baffle	actinon	fission	angstrom
boffin	adaptor	gilbert	anode ray
bolide	aerator	gimbals	antinode
cation	airlock	gravity	armature
charge	air pump	heating	atmology
degree	ammeter	impulse	atomizer
dipole	aneroid	inertia	Avogadro
dynamo	angular	isotone	beta rays
energy	antenna	isotope	betatron
Geiger	aphotic	kiloton	bevatron
H blast	atomics	megaton	cassette
ignite	atomism	missile	constant
isobar	aureole	monitor	delta ray
kation	azimuth	neutron	detector
magnet	battery	nuclear	deuteron
megohm	beta ray	nucleon	dew point
metric	binocle	nucleus	electron
micron	bipolar	off peak	enthalpy
mirror	capsule	ohmeter	equation
nuclei	cathode	physics	eutectic
opaque	chamber	positon	excitant
optics	circuit	project	fast pile
proton	control	quantum	filament
quasar	crystal	radical	formulae
radome	current	reactor	freezing
sensor	decibel	rontgen	friction

fuel|cell
gamma|ray
gas|laser
half-life
harmonic
heat|sink
hologram
ignition
impeller
inductor
infra-red
injector
ion|drive
ionizing
iriscope
klystron
laser|gun
magic|eye
mesotron
molecule
momentum
negative
negatron
neutrino
nucleate
ohmmeter
overload
paradigm
particle
peak|load
physical
pinacoid
polarity
positive
positron
power|cut
pressure
radiator
reaction
reactive
receiver
recorder
red|shift
research
resistor
rheostat
roentgen
scanning
scissile
sine|wave
slow|pile
Space|age
spectrum
sub-atoms
thruster
unit|cell
velocity
watt-hour
wave|form
X-ray|tube
zoetrope
zoom|lens
acoustics
activated
activator
adiabatic
advection
air|pocket
altimeter
amplitude
annealing
aperiodic
apparatus
atom|blast
atomicity
atomology
barograph
barometer
baroscope
binocular
blast|wave
bolometer
Boyle's|law
canal|rays
capacitor
capillary
cold|short
condenser
conductor
converter
cosmic|ray
cosmogony
cosmology
cosmotron
countdown
cryoscope
ctyogenic
cyclotron
dead|point
deflector
deionizer
detonator
dineutron
discharge
elastance
electrode
equipoise
explosion

field|coil
flotation
flow|meter
focimeter
frequency
galvanize
gamma|rays
gyroscope
heat|index
heliostat
holograph
hydration
hydrostat
hygrostat
indicator
induction
inelastic
inventory
isosteric
kilohertz
laser|beam
Leyden|jar
libration
light|wave
light|year
long|waves
lubricant
Mach|front
macrodome
magnetism
magnetron
magnifier
manometer
mechanics
megacurie
megacycle
megascope
mesic|atom
mesotrons
microfilm
microtron
microwave
moderator
molecular
monatomic
multipole
Newtonian
phonemics
photocell
physicist
pitot|tube
plumb|line
pneumatic
polar|axis
potential
power|pack
proton|gun
radiation
radiology
radio|rays
recording
reflector
reservoir
resonance
scientist
scintilla
short|wave
side-chain
sound|wave
spaceship
spacesuit
spacewalk
stability
stop|clock
subatomic
telephony
telescope
threshold
time-clock
tolerance
triatomic
video|tape
voltmeter
wattmeter
wave|guide
wire|gauge
wire|photo
air-cooling
amphoteric
antiproton
atmosphere
atomic|mass
atomic|pile
atomic|unit
atom|rocket
battery|jar
biophysics
bleep|bleep
Bohr|theory
calorifier
carbonated
carbon|atom
catenation
cathode|ray
Centigrade
centrifuge
cine|camera
cobalt|bomb

collimator
combustion
compressor
controller
convection
corrugated
cryogenics
curiescopy
deep|freeze
degaussing
desiccator
Dewar|flask
distortion
elasticity
electronic
elongation
energetics
epithermal
estimation
evaporator
excitation
experiment
Fahrenheit
filter|pump
filter|tube
geophysics
gravimeter
heat|shield
horse|power
hydraulics
hypothesis
hypsometer
inductance
ionosphere
isonuclear
isothermal

laboratory
latent|heat
light|valve
Mach|number
macroprism
magnet|pole
mass|defect
mass|energy
mass|number
megaparsec
megascopic
metacentre
microcurie
micrograph
microphone
microscope
millicurie
multicurie
nanosecond
nucleonics
pentatomic
polycyclic
power|plant
projectile
pronucleus
propellant
propulsion
radiogenic
radiometer
radiometry
radioscope
radioscopy
radio|sonde
reactivity
reluctance
resilience

resistance
resolution
rutherford
scientific
short|waves
space|craft
spallation
stabilizer
step|rocket
supersonic
synchroton
tagged|atom
technology
telegraphy
television
tetratomic
thermistor
thermopile
thermostat
three|phase
time|switch
transistor
transition
triniscope
trochotron
voltameter
volt|ampere
water|gauge
water|level
wave|length
white|light
wind|tunnel
xerography
X|radiation
zwitterion
accelerator

accumulator
achromatism
actinic rays
actinometer
anticathode
antineutron
atom counter
atomic clock
atomologist
atom smasher
Auger effect
baffle plate
barycentric
bifocal lens
capillarity
carnot cycle
cathode rays
coefficient
conductance
crystalline
cytophysics
diffraction
dynamometer
echo sounder
Einsteinium
electricity
electrolyte
electronics
engineering
epidiascope
fast breeder
fibre optics
fissionable
fluorescent
fluoroscope
fluoroscopy
free radical
gravitation
gravity cell
ground state
heat barrier
high-voltage
iridescence
irradiation
isochronism
kinetic body
landing beam
light shield
lyophilizer
macroscopic
manipulator
opeidoscope
open circuit
photography
photosphere
polarimeter
polarimetry
polarograph
positive ray
primary cell
quantum jump
radiant heat
radioactive
radio beacon
radiologist
reactor pile
regenerator
retro-rocket
Rontgen rays
rule of thumb
space rocket
stroboscope
supercooled
technocracy
temperature
thermionics
thermoduric
thermograph
thermometer
transformer
transmitter
tripod stand
troposphere
ultrasonics
vacuum flask
acceleration
acceptor atom
actinic glass
aerodynamics
afterburning
Angstrom unit
antineutrino
antiparticle
astronautics
astrophysics
atomic energy
atomic number
atomic theory
atomic weight
atom-smashing
boiling point
burning glass
burning point
carat balance
central force
chain reactor
cloud chamber
condensation

critical|mass
crystallites
deceleration
deflagration
displacement
electric|cell
electric|lamp
electron|pair
electronvolt
electroscope
experimental
extranuclear
fluorescence
galvanometer
geomagnetism
high|fidelity
hyperphysics
iatrophysics
infra-red|lamp
interference
law|of|gravity
luminescence
macrophysics
microammeter
microphysics
millerontgen
mirror|nuclei
nuclear|force
nuclear|power
optical|laser
oscilloscope
photofission
photoneutron
polarization
positive|rays
power|reactor
power|station
quantization
radio|compass
reactivation
refrigerator
Roentgen|rays
scintillator
selenium|cell
short|circuit
smash|the|atom
solar|battery
solar|physics
space|station
specific|heat
split|the|atom
stereophonic
stereopticon
stratosphere
thermoscopic
transmission
unified|field
Van|Allen|belt
vaporization
wave|function
X-ray|spectrum
amplification
Appleton|layer
astrophysical
Auger|electron
camera|obscura
chain|reaction
compressed|air
critical|angle
decompression
demonstration
direct|current

discharge tube
Doppler effect
electric field
electric light
electric meter
electromagnet
electrostatic
ferromagnetic
freezing point
Geiger counter
graticulation
heat-resistant
high frequency
hydroelectric
kinetic energy
magnetic field
magnetic north
magnetic poles
magnetisation
non-conducting
photo-electric
quantum theory
radioactivity
radiolocation
semiconductor
spring balance
telephoto lens
thermonuclear
tracer element
under pressure
anacoustic zone
applied science
astrophysicist
audio-frequency
bioelectricity
breeder reactor
cathode-ray tube
circuit breaker
counter-current
disintegration
eigenfrequency
electronically
heavier than air
Heaviside layer
magnetic needle
microcomponent
nuclear fission
nuclear physics
nuclear powered
nuclear reactor
phantom circuit
printed circuit
radio telescope
surface tension
thermodynamics
torsion balance
transverse wave
trickle charger
tuner amplifier
centre of gravity
crystallography
electrification
electroanalysis
electrodynamics
electrokinetics
electromagnetic
horseshoe magnet
magneto-electric
microtechnology
nuclear reaction
optical illusion
Planck's constant

potential|energy
specific|gravity
specific|gravity
ultra|violet|rays

Plants

bur
fog
hay
ivy
mow
poa
rue
sod
tea
balm
bent
bixa
burr
cane
culm
dill
dock
fern
flax
gale
gall
hemp
herb
jute
kelp
lawn
leaf
ling
lint
mint
moly
moss
otto
peat
rape
reed
rhea
rush
rust
sage
soma
star
tare
taro
tuft
turf
weed
woad
abaca
abrus
algae
anise
aspic
basil
blade
bract
camas
canna
caper
clary
clove
couch
cumin
cycad
dagga
dulse
erica
fitch
frond
fucus
fungi
gemma
gloom
grass
halfa
heath
lemna
liana
musci
orpin
osier
panic
plant
radix
ramie
rubia
scrub
sedge
senna
sisal
sprig
starr
stoma
sward
tansy
thyme
umbel
vetch
wrack
yeast
yucca
acacia
agaric
albino
arabis
aralia
balsam
bamboo
borage
bryony
burnet
cacoon
cactus
camass
catnip
caulis
clover
cockle
coffee
corkir
cotton
crotal
croton
cummin
darnel
eringo
fescue
fucoid
fungus
hedera
hyssop
indigo
jungle
kiss|me
knawel

lalang	twitch	dogbane	seaweed
lichen	acerose	esparto	seedbox
madder	alecost	foxtail	sorghum
mallee	alfalfa	frogbit	spignel
manioc	alkanet	genista	spurrey
maquis	all|heal	ginseng	statice
marram	amanita	guarana	stipule
marrum	aniseed	guayule	tanghin
medick	armilla	hawk|bit	tarweed
myrica	auricle	hayseed	tendril
nettle	benthos	heather	thistle
nostoc	bistort	hemlock	timothy
origan	bogbean	henbane	tobacco
orpine	bog|moss	herbage	trefoil
oxalis	bracken	hogweed	truffle
pampas	bugloss	honesty	tussock
pappus	bulrush	labiate	vanilla
phylum	burdock	linseed	verdant
raffia	calamus	lucerne	verdure
ramson	caltrop	lycopod	vervain
redtop	cambium	mayweed	zedoary
sapium	caraway	melilot	zizania
seamat	carline	milfoil	abutilon
sesame	cassava	mudwort	acanthus
simple	catmint	mustard	angelica
sobole	cat's|ear	opuntia	asphodel
sorrel	clivers	osmunda	bedstraw
spurge	clotbur	papyrus	bignonia
spurry	cowbane	pinguin	bindweed
squill	cow|weed	red|root	blueweed
stolon	creeper	rhizome	bog|grass
storax	crinoid	rootage	buckbean
sun|dew	crottle	saguaro	canaigre
tangle	curcuma	sampire	cardamom
teasel	deutzia	sea|reed	cat's|foot
thrift	dittany	sea|tang	cat's|tail

caulicle
centaury
charlock
cleavers
clubmoss
clubrush
cocculus
conferva
costmary
cow|grass
cow|plant
cow|wheat
cut|grass
death|cap
death|cup
dicentra
dock|leaf
dog|grass
dog|wheat
dropwort
duckweed
eel|grass
egg|plant
fernshaw
fireweed
flaxseed
gas|plant
glory|pea
goatweed
greenery
gulfweed
hedgerow
hepatica
hibiscus
honeydew
ice|plant
knapweed
knapwood
knotweed
lady|fern
licorice
mandrake
marjoram
medicago
meristem
milkweed
milkwort
moonwort
mushroom
offshoot
origanum
peat|moss
phyllome
pillwort
pinkroot
plantage
plantain
plant|pot
plantule
plumbago
pokeweed
pondweed
puffball
purslane
ratsbane
red|algae
reed|mace
ribgrass
rockweed
root|knot
ryegrass
saltwort
samphire
sargasso
seaberry
sea|blite
sea|grape
sea|holly
sea|wrack
seedcase
seed|leaf
shamrock
soapwort
spergula
spigelia
spikelet
starwort
take|root
tamarisk
tarragon
toad|flax
tree|fern
tree|lily
tree|moss
tremella
tuberose
turmeric
valerian
vasculum
waybread
xanthium
acrospire
arrowhead
arrowroot
arrowroot
artemisia
astrofell
baldmoney

9 LETTERS

bearberry
beech fern
bent grass
bird's foot
bird's nest
birthwort
bloodroot
bluegrass
bog myrtle
bog orchid
bracteole
broomrape
cane sugar
carrageen
catchweed
centaurea
chain fern
chickweed
China root
cockscomb
coral root
coriander
crab grass
crazyweed
crosswort
cryptogam
cup lichen
desert pea
dittander
dock cress
duck's meat
dyer's weed
earth star
euphorbia
fairy ring
fenugreek
flagellum
fly agaric
galingale
gama grass
gemmation
germander
glasswort
goosefoot
gramineae
greenweed
ground ivy
groundsel
hair grass
halophyte
herbarium
holly ferm
holy grass
horehound
hornwrack
horsetail
house leek
idioblast
involucre
Irish moss
knotgrass
laserwort
leaf mould
lemon weed
liquorice
liverwort
luxuriant
lyme grass
mare's tail
marijuana
marsh fern
marshwort
mesophyte
milk vetch
mistletoe
monk's hood
musk plant
navelwort
overgrown
pellitory
pennywort
plant life
poison ivy
polygonum
portulaca
quillwort
reed grass
rocambole
rock brake
rockcress
rock plant
royal fern
sand grain
sand grass
scale moss
screw pine
seabottle
sea girdle
sea tangle
silk grass
sisal hemp
smartweed
snakeroot
snowplant
spearmint
spikenard
star grass
stinkweed

PLANTS

stonecrop
stonewort
sugar cane
sun spurge
sweet flag
sweetgale
tear grass
toadstool
toothwort
vernation
water fern
water leaf
water vine
waterweed
wire grass
worm grass
aftergrass
arrow grass
aspidistra
beard grass
bitterroot
brown algae
bunch grass
butterwort
Canada rice
China grass
couch grass
cow chervil
cow parsley
cow parsnip
dead nettle
dog parsley
dog's fennel
dyer's broom
elecampane
glasshouse
goat's beard
golden seal
goosegrass
grama grass
grasswrack
green algae
greenhouse
greensward
hemp nettle
herb garden
Indian hemp
indigenous
Jimson weed
lemon grass
lycopodium
maidenhair
maidenweed
malaguetta
mandragora
Manila hemp
manna grass
motherwort
musk mallow
new mown hay
nipplewort
orangeroot
penny cress
pennyroyal
peppermint
pepperwort
photometry
planthouse
plume grass
restharrow
sand binder
sea burdock
sea lettuce
sea whistle
second crop
seed vessel
semination
shield fern
sisal grass
slime mould
spear grass
spiderwort
springwort
stitchwort
strike root
sword grass
thale cress
transplant
tree mallow
tumbleweed
vegetation
wall pepper
waterbloom
wilderness
wild indigo
willow weed
Adam's needle
alpine plant
bellheather
blue thistle
bur marigold
canary grass
chanterelle
chive garlic
cotton grass
cotton plant
cruciferous
cypress knee

dame's violet
dog's mercury
dyer's rocket
false acacia
finger grass
French berry
fuller's herb
garden stuff
germination
giant cactus
graft hybrid
green dragon
guinea grass
hart's tongue
horseradish
Iceland moss
kidney vetch
lady's finger
leopardbane
luxuriation
manna lichen
marram grass
myrtle grass
oyster plant
pampas grass
peppergrass
potting shed
pullulation
ribbon grass
Roman nettle
root climber
rubber plant
salad burnet
scurvy grass
sea furbelow
sea lavender
sea milkwort
sea purslane
sesame grass
Spanish moss
swallowwort
switch grass
thistledown
tree creeper
viper's grass
water meadow
water pepper
water violet
wintergreen
witches meat
bladderwrack
buffalo grass
climbing fern
conservatory
esparto grass
feathergrass
fool's parsley
forcing house
green fingers
hassock grass
hound's tongue
Jacob's ladder
lady's fingers
lady's thistle
orchard grass
sheep's fescue
skunk cabbage
snuffbox bean
Spanish cress
Spanish grass
staghorn moss
Timothy grass

PLANTS

tobacco plant	Scotch thistle
umbelliferae	water crowfoot
Venus fly-trap	chincherinchee
waterhemlock	circumnutation
watermilfoil	classification
white heather	evergreen plant
zantedeschia	flowering plant
elephant grass	mountain sorrel
golden thistle	Shepherd's purse
horse mushroom	wood nightshade
lady's bedstraw	Virginia creeper
meadow saffron	virgin territory
noli-me-tangere	woody nightshade

Political Leaders

Fox	Bevan	Caesar	Allende
Blum	Bevin	Carson	Ataturk
Eden	Botha	Castro	Baldwin
Grey	Derby	Cripps	Balfour
Hess	Heath	Curzon	Bolivar
Marx	Laval	Dulles	Canning
Meir	Lenin	Franco	Goering
More	Nehru	Ghandi	Hampden
Nagy	North	Hitler	Hertzog
Peel	Obote	Kaunda	Himmler
Pitt	Peron	Mobutu	Kosygin
Tito	Smuts	Nasser	Luthuli
Tojo	Spaak	Pelham	Mandela
Banda	Attlee	Stalin	Masaryk
Benes	Brandt	Wilson	Menzies
Beria	Bright	Wolsey	Molotov

7/11 LETTERS

Nkrumah
Nyerere
Parnell
Reynaud
Russell
Salazar
Trotsky
Trudeau
Walpole
Aberdeen
Adenauer
Andropov
Augustus
Bismarck
Bonar Law
Brezhnev
Bulganin
Burghley
Caligula
Cosgrave
Cromwell
Crossman
de Gaulle
de Valera
Disraeli
Goebbels
Kenyatta
Kruschev
Malenkov
McCarthy
Napoleon
Perceval
Pericles
Poincaré
Rosebery
Thatcher

Verwoerd
Ben Gurion
Bonaparte
Chou en Lai
Churchill
Gaitskell
Garibaldi
Gladstone
Gorbachev
Ho Chi Minh
Kissinger
Lafayette
Liverpool
Macdonald
Macmillan
Melbourne
Mussolini
Richelieu
Salisbury
Shelburne
Stevenson
Vishinsky
Alcibiades
Che Guevara
Clemenceau
Mao Tse tung
Metternich
Palmerston
Ribbentrop
Stresemann
Talleyrand
Castlereagh
Chamberlain
Demosthenes
Douglas Home
Machiavelli

POLITICAL LEADERS

Robespierre	Bandaranaike	Mendes France
Shaftesbury	Julius Caesar	Themistocles

Presidents of the USA

Ford	Pierce	Coolidge
Polk	Reagan	Fillmore
Taft	Taylor	Garfield
Adams	Truman	Harrison
Grant	Wilson	McKinley
Hayes	Harding	Van Buren
Nixon	Jackson	Cleveland
Tyler	Johnson	Jefferson
Arthur	Kennedy	Roosevelt
Carter	Lincoln	Eisenhower
Hoover	Madison	Washington
Monroe	Buchanan	

Relations

ma
pa
dad
kin
mum
son
aunt
heir
kith
sire
twin
mater
mummy
niece
pater
scion
sonny
twins
uncle
widow
agnate
auntie
cousin
father
fiancé
frater
godson
infant
junior
mother
nephew
nuncle
orphan
parent
senior
sister
spouse
suitor
best man
brother
cognate
consort
dowager
fiancée
heiress
husband
kindred
kinsman
mankind
partner
progeny
sibling
stepson
widower
ancestor
bachelor
children
daughter
divorcee
grandson
helpmeet
relation
relative
son-in-law
spinster
triplets
boy friend
firstborn
forebears
godfather
godmother
grand-aunt
great-aunt
kid sister
kinswoman
next of kin
offspring
patriarch
antecedent
babe in arms
bridegroom
bridesmaid
forefather
grandchild
grand-niece
grand-uncle
grass widow

great-uncle
half-sister
kid brother
kith and kin
maiden aunt
seventh son
son and heir
stepfather
stepmother
stepsister
sweetheart
blood sister
father-in-law
first cousin
foster child
grandfather
grandmother
grandnephew
grandparent
half brother
mother-in-law
sister-in-law
step-brother
blood brother
brother-in-law
cousin-german
Darby and Joan
foster-father
foster-mother
foster-parent
foster-sister
heir apparent
natural child
near relation
second cousin
stepdaughter
blood brothers
blood relation
Bob's your uncle
brotherliness
close relative
consanguinity
daughter-in-law
direct descent
distant cousin
family reunion
first-begotten
flesh and blood
foster-brother
granddaughter
great-grandson
identical twin
intermarriage
marriage lines
materfamilias
progenitorial
fairy godmother
foster-daughter
husband and wife
identical twins
in loco parentis
mother and child
mother's darling
distant relative
every mother's son
great-grandchild
honeymoon couple
mother and father
rude forefathers
surrogate father
surrogate mother
surrogate parent
wife and children

Religions

alb
ark
goy
pew
pie
pye
pyx
RIP
see
sin
vow
alms
ambo
amen
apse
bell
bema
bier
bull
cant
cell
cope
cowl
cure
dean
dome
fast
font
guru
halo
harp
Hell
holy
hymn
icon
idol
joss
keen
kirk
lama
mass
monk
naos
nave
oath
pall
Pope
pray
pyre
raga
rite
robe
rood
sect
seer
sext
soul
text
tomb
tope
veil
vows
wake
zeal
abbey
abbot
agape
aisle
Allah
almug
Alpha
altar
ambry
amice
angel
apron
apsis
banns
beads
Bible
bigot
bless
cairn
canon
carol
cella
chant
chela
choir
cotta
credo
creed
cross
crypt
curse
demon
Devil
dogma
druid
dulia
elder
ephod
exile
extol
faith
fanon
feral
Flood
friar
frock
glebe
glory
goyim
grace
grail
grave
Hades
Islam
Jewry
judge
knell
Koran
lauds
laver
leper
Logos
magus
Maker
manna
manse
Mazda
Mecca
Medes
Media
mitre
motet
mound
myrrh
Negeb
nones
Omega
padre
paean
pagan
paten

RELIGIONS

piety
pious
prior
psalm
rabbi
relic
saint
Satan
scarf
Solon
spire
staff
stall
stole
stoup
stupa
Sumer
synod
taber
tiara
Torah
tract
tunic
vault
vicar
abbess
amulet
anoint
anthem
armlet
barrow
beadle
bishop
Brahma
Buddha
burial
cantor
casket
censer
chapel
cherub
chimer
chrism
church
clergy
cleric
coffin
corban
curacy
curate
deacon
Deluge
devout
diadem
divine
dolmen
Easter
embalm
eunuch
famine
fannel
Father
flamen
gospel
hallow
hearse
Heaven
Hebrew
heresy
hermit
homage
homily
Israel
Jesuit
Jewish
Jordan
Josiah
josser
jubbah
keener
latria
lector
lemuel
litany
litany
magian
manger
mantle
mantra
manual
martyr
matins
maundy
missal
Mormon
Moslem
mosque
mullah
mystic
nimbus
nipter
novena
novice
office
ordain
orison
pagoda
palace
papacy
parish
parson
pastor
plague
postil
prayer
preach
priest
primus
priory
pulpit
Quaker
rector
ritual
rochet
rosary
rubric
sacred
satrap
schism
Scribe
sedile
Semite
sermon
sexton
shaman
shrine
shroud
sinner
sister
stalls
Sunday
suttee
tablet
talent

sanctum
sandals
Saviour
sceptic
scourge
secular
sedilia
Semitic
serpent
service
session
Shammah
sistrum
soutane
steeple
stipend
tonsure
Trinity
tumulus
tunicle
unction
Vatican
vespers
Vulgate
worship
aetheist
agnostic
Akeldama
Almighty
anathema
Anglican
antipope
Apostles
Ave|Maria
basilica
beadroll

beadsman
bedesman
believer
blessing
bless|you
bondmaid
brethren
breviary
Buddhist
canonics
canonize
canticle
capuchin
cardinal
catholic
cemetery
cenotaph
ceremony
chaplain
chasuble
cherubim
choirboy
chrismal
cincture
cloister
compline
conclave
corporal
covenant
Creation
credence
credenda
cromlech
crucifix
Crusader
dalmatic

delubrum
disciple
divinity
doctrine
doxology
druidess
embolism
Emmanuel
Epiphany
Epistles
evensong
exegesis
exequial
exequies
exorcism
faithful
funerary
funereal
Gentiles
God's|acre
Good|Book
governor
Hail|Mary
hallowed
hecatomb
here|lies
hic|jacet
High|Mass
holiness
holy|city
holy|coat
Holy|Land
holyrood
Holy|Week
Holy|Writ
Huguenot

hymn|book
idolater
idolatry
Immanuel
inner|man
Jonathan
lamasery
lay|vicar
lich|gate
Lord's|day
Lutheran
marabout
Mass|book
mediator
megalith
memorial
menology
minister
ministry
monachal
monastic
monolith
monument
mourning
mozzetta
neophyte
Noah's|Ark
obituary
oblation
offering
orthodox
Paradise
Parousia
Passover
penitent
Pharisee

pontifex
praise be
preacher
predella
prie-dieu
province
psaltery
publican
pyx cloth
religion
Romanism
rood-loft
sacellum
sacristy
sanctity
scapular
seraphic
seraphim
Shepherd
skullcap
Son of Man
surplice
tenebrae
theology
thurible
thurifer
transept
versicle
vestment
viaticum
vicarage
Wesleyan
ziggurat
Aaron's rod
adoration
Allelujah
altar desk
altar rail
Apocrypha
archangel
arch-druid
arch-enemy
arch-fiend
Ascension
atonement
baldachin
barbarian
Beatitude
Beelzebub
black mass
blasphemy
Calvinist
canonical
cantharus
canticles
Carmelite
carpenter
cartulary
catacombs
catechism
cathedral
celebrant
cerecloth
cerements
Christian
churchman
claustral
clergyman
cloisters
coadjutor
Communion
concubine
confessor
converted
cremation
cupbearer
deaconess
decalogue
dei gratia
desecrate
devotions
dignitary
dog-collar
dogmatics
Dominican
embalming
episcopal
episcopus
Eucharist
exchanger
family pew
firmament
firstborn
firstling
fisherman
footstone
godfather
godliness
godmother
godparent
good works
gospeller
graveside
graveyard
hagiarchy
hagiology
headstone
Hereafter

heterodox
Hexateuch
hierarchy
hierology
high|altar
holocaust
holy|cross
Holy|Ghost
Holy|Grail
holy|table
holy|water
incumbent
interment
Israelite
Jerusalem
joss|house
joss|stick
Judas|kiss
Lamb|of|God
land|of|Nod
last|rites
laudation
lay|reader
lay|sister
loincloth
Lost|Sheep
mactation
Magdalene
martyrdom
mausoleum
mercy|seat
Methodist
monastery
Monsignor
mortcloth
Mosaic|law
mummy|case
Mussulman
mysticism
obsequial
obsequies
offertory
officiant
orthodoxy
ossuarium
Palestine
papal|bull
Paraclete
parchment
parsonage
patriarch
pay|homage
Pentecost
prayer|mat
prayer|rug
precentor
presbyter
priestess
prime|song
profanity
proselyte
proseuche
prothesis
psalmbook
reliquary
reverence
righteous
rood|stair
rood|tower
rural|dean
sackcloth
sacrament
sacrarium
sacrifice
sacrilege
sacristan
sainthood
saintship
salvation
Samaritan
sanctuary
scapegoat
scapulary
schoolman
Scripture
sepulchre
sepulture
shewbread
Shintoist
shovel|hat
spiritual
suffragan
synagogue
Synoptics
testament
tombstone
triforium
undersong
unfrocked
Unitarian
unworldly
venerable
Zoroaster
zucchetta
zucchetto
absolution
allocution
allotheist

almsgiving
altar cloth
altar front
altar mound
altarpiece
amen corner
Anabaptist
antichrist
Apocalypse
archbishop
archdeacon
arch-flamen
arch-priest
Armaggedon
Band of Hope
baptistery
bar mitzvah
battle hymn
Beatitudes
benedicite
benefactor
Bible class
birthright
blind faith
canonicals
Carthusian
catafalque
catechumen
chartulary
choirstall
Church Army
church bell
churchgoer
churchyard
Cistercian
clearstory
clerestory
cloistered
collection
Colossians
confession
consecrate
conversion
dedication
diaconicon
divination
doctrinism
Douay Bible
encyclical
entombment
episcopacy
episcopant
Evangelist
Evil Spirit
exaltation
false piety
fellowship
Franciscan
funeral ode
funeral urn
godfearing
golden calf
goody-goody
gravestone
hagiolatry
hagioscope
Hallelujah
Heptateuch
hierolatry
hieromancy
hierophant
high church
high places
high priest
Holy Family
Holy Father
Holy Orders
Holy Spirit
Holy Willie
House of God
hyperdulia
iconoclast
idolatrous
immolation
incumbency
inhumation
in memoriam
irreligion
Jacob's Well
Lady chapel
Last Supper
lay brother
lectionary
lie in state
lip service
Lord's house
Lord's table
magnificat
mantellone
Mark of Cain
missionary
Mohammedan
Mount Sinai
Mount Tabor
necropolis
Needle's eye
pallbearer
papal brief

RELIGIONS

Papal|Court
paraphrase
Pentateuch
Pharisaism
Philistine
phylactery
pilgrimage
pontifical
poor|sinner
praetorium
prayer|bead
prayer|book
prebendary
Presbytery
priesthood
procurator
prophetess
Protestant
Providence
regenerate
Revelation
Roman|Curia
rood|screen
Sabbath|day
sacerdotal
sacredness
sacrosanct
sanctimony
Scepticism
Schismatic
scholastic
Scriptures
secularism
Septuagint
sepulchral
shibboleth
soothsayer
superaltar
synthronus
tabernacle
tartuffery
temperance
temptation
theo-logian
theologist
unbeliever
undertaker
veneration
watch|night
widow's|mite
wilderness
worshipper
Wycliffite
agnosticism
altar|carpet
altar|facing
apologetics
arch-heretic
arch-prelate
aspergillum
Augustinium
Benedictine
benediction
bishop's|ring
bitter|herbs
blasphemous
body|and|soul
Book|of|Books
burning|bush
Catholicism
chapel|royal
choir-stalls
Christendom
christening
church|court
church|mouse
City|of|David
commandment
communicant
conventicle
Convocation
crematorium
crucifixion
Curia|Romana
decanal|side
Divine|right
Epistle|side
eschatology
family|bible
first-fruits
funeral|pile
funeral|pyre
Geneva|bands
Geneva|cloak
good|tidings
graven|image
Greek|Church
hagiographa
hagiologist
hierography
incarnation
irreligious
Kingdom|Come
kirk|session
last|offices
lawn|sleeves
Lord|of|Hosts
Lord's|prayer

Lord's supper
missal stand
monasterial
Nicene Creed
nullifidian
original sin
parish clerk
paternoster
patron saint
pillar saint
pontificals
pontificate
prayer wheel
Prodigal Son
protomartyr
pure in heart
reading desk
Reformation
religiosity
remembrance
requiem mass
rest in peace
river Jordan
Sacred Heart
saintliness
Sanctus bell
sarcophagus
soteriology
take the veil
theological
triple crown
Vatican City
vine of Sodom
Virgin's Well
Wise Virgins
Annunciation
burial ground
canonization
cardinal's hat
chancel table
chapel of ease
chapter house
charnel house
Charterhouse
Chosen People
Christianity
church living
churchmaster
church nation
church parade
churchwarden
City of Refuge
collectarium
Commandments
Common Prayer
confessional
confirmation
congregation
consecration
Coptic church
Damascus road
Day of the Lord
denomination
ecclesiastic
enshrinement
fiery serpent
frankincense
Garden of Eden
Good Shepherd
hagiographer
herald angels
Holy Alliance

RELIGIONS

Holy of Holies
Holy Thursday
hot gospeller
Jacob's ladder
jot and tittle
Judgment Hall
Judgment Seat
Last Judgment
major prophet
marriage vows
minor prophet
money changer
New Testament
Old Testament
prayer carpet
Promised Land
resting place
Resurrection
Rose of Sharon
sacred ground
sacrilegious
Sea of Galilee
Second Coming
Sunday school
thanksgiving
theologician
Three Wise Men
Tower of Babel
ultramontane
wear the cloth
winding sheet
Abraham's bosom
aggiornamento
Ancient of days
Anglo-Catholic
anthroposophy
Apostles creed
archbishopric
archidiaconal
beatification
bidding prayer
bottomless pit
church officer
church service
communion card
co-religionist
day of judgment
divine justice
divine service
ecumenicalism
eschatologist
excommunicate
high churchman
holy innocents
household gods
household gods
incense burner
infant baptism
Lambeth degree
light of nature
moral theology
morning prayer
nonconformist
nonconformity
pantheistical
pantheologist
pectoral cross
prayer meeting
reincarnation
Salvation Army
Zarathustrism
Anglican church

6/7 LETTERS

Talmud
temple
tierce
tippet
unholy
vakass
verger
vestry
vigils
vision
zealot
acolyte
Alcoran
almoner
angelic
angelus
apostle
ascents
atheist
Babylon
baptism
Baptist
biretta
blessed
bondage
bondman
brother
burying
buskins
cabbala
calotte
Cantuar
capuche
cassock
chancel
chantry
chaplet
chapman
chapter
charity
charnel
chimere
chorale
collect
complin
convent
convert
cortege
Creator
crosier
crozier
crusade
daysman
Dead Sea
deanery
deodate
devotee
diocese
diptych
diviner
doubter
Dry Mass
Eleazar
epitaph
Essenes
fanatic
fasting
frontal
funeral
gaiters
gentile
glorify
godhead
good man
gradino
heathen
Hebrews
heretic
holy day
holy see
holy war
Hosanna
hymnary
Ichabod
impiety
impious
incense
infidel
introit
Jehovah
jubilee
Judaism
keening
Lambeth
Lebanon
lectern
lection
liturgy
Low Mass
maniple
mastaba
memoria
Messiah
Messias
minaret
minster
miracle
mission
mourner
muezzin
mummify
narthex
nunnery
obelisk
oratory
ossuary
pallium
papyrus
parable
periapt
pietism
pilgrim
piscina
pontiff
prayers
prebend
prelate
primate
profane
prophet
psalter
Puritan
pyramid
pyx veil
rabboni
raiment
Ramadan
Rameses
rectory
religio
requiem
reredos
retable
Sabbath

apostolic vicar
archiepiscopal
beatific vision
cardinal virtue
church militant
communion bread
communion table
Dean and chapter
denominational
devil's advocate
ecclesiastical
eschatological
evangelicalism
extreme unction
fisherman's ring
forbidden fruit
high priesthood
intercommunion
Latter-day saint
mark of the Beast
morning service
mother superior
Orthodox Church
pastoral letter
recording angel
reformed church
Revised Version
sabbatarianism
sabbath breaker
sign of the cross
Society of Jesus
Tridentine Mass
Zoroastrianism
anthropomorphic
anticlericalism
archiepiscopacy
archiepiscopate
articles of faith
chapter and verse
Christadelphian
Church of England
confessionalist
devil worshipper
divine messenger
episcopalianism
excommunication
General Assembly
harvest festival
Holy Roman Empire
Jehovah's witness
laying on of hands
Moral Rearmament
new English Bible
odour of sanctity
Plymouth brother
Presbyterianism
religious belief
seven deadly sins
synoptic gospels
ten commandments
transfiguration

Rivers

Ob	Lena	Congo	Rhone	Ganges
Po	Maas	Douro	Saône	Hudson
Si	Main	Drava	Seine	Humber
Bug	Milk	Dvina	Siang	Iguaçú
Dee	Nile	Forth	Snake	Ijssel
Don	Oder	Foyle	Snowy	Irtysh
Ems	Ohio	Green	Somme	Japura
Esk	Oise	Havel	Spree	Jhelum
Exe	Ouse	Indus	Swale	Jordan
Han	Oxus	Ishim	Tagus	Kolyma
Lys	Para	James	Tiber	Leitha
Oka	Prut	Jumna	Torne	Liffey
Red	Saar	Jurua	Trent	Medway
Tay	Spey	Kasai	Tweed	Mekong
Usk	Suir	Lagan	Vitim	Mersey
Wye	Swan	Liard	Volga	Moldau
Aire	Taff	Loire	Volta	Murray
Arno	Tana	Marne	Weser	Neckar
Avon	Tees	Meuse	Xingú	Neisse
Ebro	Tyne	Negro	Yukon	Orange
Eden	Ural	Niger	Abdiel	Ottawa
Elan	Vaal	Osage	Amazon	Parana
Elbe	Wear	Peace	Angara	Ribble
Gila	Yalu	Pearl	Atbara	Sabine
Göta	Adige	Pecos	Chenab	Salado
Juba	Aisne	Piave	Danube	Sambre
Kama	Argun	Plate	Donets	Severn
Kura	Boyne	Purus	Fraser	St John
Lech	Clyde	Rhine	Gambia	Struma

6/9 LETTERS

Sutlej
Thames
Tigris
Vilyui
Wabash
Wharfe
Alabama
Berbice
Bighorn
Darling
Derwent
Dnieper
Dubawnt
Garonne
Helmand
Hooghly
Hwang Ho
Krishna
Lachlan
Limpopo
Madeira
Maritsa
Moselle
Orinoco
Pechora
Potomac
Roanoke
Salween
Scheldt
Senegal
Shannon
Si Kiang
Tsangpo
Uruguay
Vistula
Waikato
Waitaki
Yangtze
Yenisei
Zambezi
Amu Darya
Arkansas
Cheyenne
Chindwin
Colorado
Columbia
Delaware
Dniester
Dordogne
Eastmain
Flinders
Godavari
Hamilton
Illinois
Missouri
Paraguay
Parnaiba
Putumayo
Savannah
Suwannee
Wanganui
Athabaska
Churchill
Euphrates
Irrawaddy
Mackenzie
Macquarie
Magdalena
Murchison
Porcupine
Rio Grande
Tennessee

RIVERS

Wisconsin	Brahmaputra	Murrumbidgee
Republican	Mississippi	Saskatchewan
Sacramento	Yellowstone	
St Lawrence	Guadalquivir	

Shakespearean Characters

Ely	Jamy	Bigot	Feste	Philo
Nym	John	Blunt	Flute	Pinch
Say	Juno	Boult	Froth	Poins
Adam	Kent	Boyet	Ghost	Priam
Ajax	Lear	Bushy	Goffe	Regan
Anne	Luce	Butts	Gower	Robin
Bawd	Lucy	Caius	Green	Romeo
Bona	Moth	Casca	Helen	Rugby
Cade	Page	Celia	Henry	Sands
Cato	Peto	Ceres	Hymen	Snare
Davy	Puck	Cinna	Julia	Snout
Dick	Ross	Cleon	Lafeu	Speed
Dion	Snug	Corin	Lewis	Timon
Dull	Vaux	Court	Lovel	Titus
Eros	Wart	Cupid	Lucio	Tubal
Fang	York	Curan	March	Varro
Fool	Aaron	Curio	Maria	Viola
Ford	Alice	Denny	Melun	Adrian
Grey	Angus	Derby	Menas	Aegeon
Hero	Anjou	Diana	Mopsa	Aeneas
Hume	Ariel	Edgar	Osric	Albany
Iago	Bagot	Egeus	Paris	Alonso
Iden	Bates	Elbow	Percy	Amiens
Iras	Belch	Essex	Peter	Angelo
Iris	Bevis	Evans	Phebe	Antony

6/7 LETTERS

Armado
Arthur
Audrey
Banquo
Basset
Bianca
Blanch
Blount
Boleyn
Bottom
Brutus
Bullen
Cadwal
Caesar
Caphis
Cassio
Chiron
Cicero
Cimber
Clitus
Cloten
Cobweb
Curtis
Dennis
Dorcas
Dorset
Dromio
Duncan
Edmund
Edward
Elinor
Emilia
Exeter
Fabian
Feeble
Fenton

Gremio
Grumio
Gurney
Hamlet
Hecate
Hector
Helena
Hermia
Horner
Imogen
Isabel
Jaques
Juliet
Launce
LeBeau
Lennox
Lovell
Lucius
Marina
Morgan
Morton
Mouldy
Mutius
Nestor
Oberon
Oliver
Olivia
Orsino
Oswald
Oxford
Pandar
Pedant
Philip
Pistol
Pompey
Portia

Quince
Rivers
Rumour
Scales
Scarus
Scroop
Seyton
Shadow
Silius
Silvia
Simple
Siward
Strato
Surrey
Talbot
Tamora
Taurus
Thaisa
Thomas
Thurio
Tranio
Tybalt
Ursula
Verges
Vernon
Wolsey
Abraham
Aemilia
Afriana
Agrippa
Alarbus
Alencon
Antenor
Antonio
Arragon
Aumerle

Bedford
Berowne
Bertram
Bourbon
Brandon
Calchas
Caliban
Camillo
Capulet
Cassius
Catesby
Cerimon
Charles
Chatham
Claudio
Conrade
Costard
Cranmer
deBurgh
Dionyza
Douglas
Dumaine
Eleanor
Escalus
Escanes
Flavius
Fleance
Francis
Gallius
Goneril
Gonzalo
Gregory
Helenus
Herbert
Holland
Horatio

SHAKESPEAREAN CHARACTERS

Hotspur
Iachimo
Jessica
Laertes
Lavache
Lavinia
Leonato
Leonine
Leontes
Lepidus
Lorenzo
Lucetta
Luciana
Lymoges
Macbeth
Macduff
Malcolm
Marcade
Marcius
Mardian
Mariana
Martext
Martius
Messala
Michael
Miranda
Montano
Montjoy
Morocco
Mowbray
Nerissa
Nicanor
Norfolk
Octavia
Ophelia
Orlando
Orleans
Othello
Paulina
Perdita
Phrynia
Pisanio
Proteus
Provost
Publius
Quintus
Richard
Rutland
Salanio
Sampson
Shallow
Shylock
Silence
Silvius
Simpcox
Slender
Solinus
Stanley
Suffolk
Theseus
Thyreus
Titania
Travers
Tressel
Troilus
Tyrrell
Ulysses
Urswick
Valeria
Varrius
Vaughan
Warwick
William
Abhorson
Achilles
Aemilius
Aufidius
Auvergne
Baptista
Bardolph
Bassanio
Beatrice
Beaufort
Belarius
Benedick
Benvolio
Berkeley
Bernardo
Borachio
Bullcalf
Burgundy
Campeius
Canidius
Capucius
Carlisle
Charmian
Clarence
Claudius
Clifford
Cominius
Cordelia
Cornwall
Cressida
Cromwell
Dercetas
Diomedes
Dogberry
Don Pedro
Eglamour
Falstaff
Florence
Florizel
Fluellen
Gadshill
Gargrave
Gertrude
Grandpre
Gratiano
Griffith
Harcourt
Hastings
Hermione
Isabella
Jack Cade
Jourdain
Laurence
Leonardo
Leonatus
Ligarius
Lodovico
Lucentio
Lucilius
Lucullus
Lysander
Maecenas
Malvolio
Margaret
Marullus
Menelaus
Menteith
Mercutio
Montague
Mortimer
Overdone

Pandarus
Pandulph
Panthino
Parolles
Patience
Pembroke
Pericles
Philario
Philemon
Philotus
Pindarus
Polonius
Polydore
Prospero
Rambures
Ratcliff
Reignier
Reynaldo
Richmond
Roderigo
Rosalind
Rosaline
Salarino
Seleucus
Somerset
Stafford
Stephano
Thaliard
Timandra
Titinius
Trinculo
Violenta
Virgilia
Volumnia
Whitmore
Williams
Woodvile
Agamemnon
Aguecheek
Alexander
Antigonus
Antiochus
Apemantus
Archibald
Arvigarus
Autolycus
Balthasar
Balthazar
Bassianus
Biondello
Boatswain
Bourchier
Brabantio
Caithness
Calpurnia
Cambridge
Cassandra
Chatillon
Cleomenes
Cleopatra
Coleville
Constance
Cornelius
Cymbeline
Dardanius
Deiphobus
Demetrius
Desdemona
Dolabella
Donalbain
Elizabeth
Enobarbus
Erpingham
Ferdinand
Fitzwater
Flaminius
Francisca
Francisco
Frederick
Glansdale
Glendower
Guiderius
Guildford
Helicanus
Hippolyta
Hortensio
Katharina
Katharine
Lancaster
Lychorida
Macmorris
Mamillius
Marcellus
Nathaniel
Patroclus
Petruchio
Polixenes
Posthumus
Rotherham
Rousillon
Salisbury
Sebastian
Servilius
Simonides
Southwell
Thersites
Trebonius
Valentine

SHAKESPEAREAN CHARACTERS

Ventidius
Vincentio
Voltimand
Volumnius
Worcester
Young|Cato
Alcibiades
Andromache
Andronicus
Anne|Boleyn
Antipholus
Apothecary
Barnardine
Brakenbury
Buckingham
Coriolanus
Duke|of|York
Euphronius
Fortinbras
Gloucester
Holofernes
Hortensius
Jaquenetta
Longaville
Lysimachus
Margarelon
Mark|Antony
Menecrates
Montgomery
Proculeius
Saturninus
Sempronius
Somerville
Starveling
Touchstone
Willoughby

Abergavenny
Artemidorus
Bolingbroke
Brackenbury
Caius|Lucius
John|of|Gaunt
Lady|Capulet
Mayor|of|York
Mustardseed
Philostrate
Plantagenet
Rosencrantz
Young|Siward
Decius|Brutus
Guildenstern
Julius|Caesar
Junius|Brutus
Marcus|Brutus
Peaseblossom
Popilius|Lena
Sir|Toby|Belch
Titus|Lartius
Westmoreland
Doll|Tearsheet
Faulconbridge
Joan|la|Pucelle
Young|Clifford
Christopher|Sly
Launcelot|Gobbo
Metellus|Cimber
Northumberland
Octavius|Caesar
Sextus|Pompeius
Tullus|Aufidius
Menenius|Agrippa
Mistress|Quickly

15 LETTERS

Robin|Goodfellow
Titus|Andronicus
Sicinius|Velutus

Sports, Games and Pastimes

KO	jig	away	deck	hand	lido
PT	kit	bail	dice	hank	lift
TT	lap	bait	dive	heat	lock
ace	lbw	ball	doll	hike	loom
aim	leg	bank	drag	hold	loop
bat	let	base	draw	hole	love
bet	lie	beat	duck	home	ludo
bid	lob	bend	duel	hook	luge
bow	loo	bias	epee	hoop	lure
box	net	bike	fall	hunt	mall
bye	par	bind	fare	hype	meet
cap	peg	blow	file	iron	meld
cat	pin	blue	fish	I|spy	mile
cox	Pit	bout	fist	jack	nock
cue	pot	bowl	foil	jape	Oaks
cup	run	brag	fore	jest	oars
dan	set	buck	form	jive	odds
die	shy	calx	foul	joke	Oval
DIY	ski	card	gaff	judo	over
fan	tag	chip	gala	jump	pace
fun	tie	chop	game	kail	pack
gin	ton	club	gate	kill	pass
gym	top	coup	gear	king	pawn
hit	toy	crew	goal	kite	play
hop	try	dart	golf	lane	polo
jab	win	dash	grid	lark	pool
jeu	ante	deal	grip	leap	port

SPORTS, GAMES AND PASTIMES

puck
putt
quiz
race
raft
reel
reel
ring
rink
rook
ruck
ruff
rule
sail
seat
seed
shot
side
skat
skid
skip
skis
slam
slip
snap
solo
spin
spot
suit
sumo
swim
tack
team
tice
toss
trap

trot
turf
walk
whip
wide
wing
wire
wood
yo-yo
alley
angle
arena
arrow
baffy
bathe
baths
baton
bingo
blade
blind
bluff
board
bogey
bound
bower
bowls
boxer
break
bully
caber
caddy
cadge
canoe
caper
cards
carom

catch
chase
check
chess
chips
chute
climb
clubs
coach
conge
count
coupe
court
craps
crawl
cycle
dance
darts
debut
decoy
Derby
deuce
diver
divot
dormy
drive
dummy
eagle
evens
event
eyass
fault
feint
field
fight
final

fives
fling
frame
going
grass
green
guard
guide
gully
halma
heave
hobby
inner
jetty
joker
joust
kails
kayak
kendo
kitty
knave
links
lists
loose
loser
lotto
lunge
mambo
march
match
medal
mid-on
miler
monte
morra
no-bid

notch
ombre
ouija
pairs
parry
pilot
pique
pitch
piton
pivot
point
poker
polka
pools
prank
pro-am
punto
quart
queen
racer
rally
range
relay
rouge
rough
round
rover
rugby
rules
rumba
rummy
sabre
samba
scent
score
screw

scrum
scull
serve
shaft
shoot
sight
skier
skiff
slide
slips
smash
spear
spoon
sport
stake
stalk
steer
strip
sweep
swing
sword
tally
tango
tarot
title
ton up
touch
track
trick
trump
twist
valse
venue
wager
waltz
wedge

whist
abseil
akimbo
anchor
angler
anorak
archer
ascent
at ease
attack
bailer
banker
bidder
birdie
bishop
bisque
blocks
bookie
borrow
boston
bowled
bowler
bowman
boxing
bracer
bricks
bridge
bulger
bumper
bunker
caddie
can can
cannon
canter
car run
casino

castle
centre
cestus
cha cha
chasse
cherry
chukka
circus
conker
corner
course
cradle
crambo
crease
crosse
cruise
cup tie
curler
dealer
dedans
diving
dog leg
dormie
driver
dry fly
eleven
equipe
euchre
fencer
fisher
flight
flying
gallop
gambit
gaming
glider

glider
gobang
gobble
go kart
golfer
googly
ground
gutter
hammer
hand in
hazard
header
hearts
helmet
hiking
hockey
honour
hooker
hookey
hoop la
hurdle
hurley
ice axe
jesses
jigsaw
jockey
jostle
jumper
karate
knight
lariat
leader
leg bye
mallet
manege
marble

marina
mascot
mashie
maxixe
merils
mid off
minuet
misere
morris
mud pie
murder
nelson
no ball
opener
paddle
pelota
period
piquet
player
plunge
pocket
pommel
popgun
puppet
putter
puzzle
quarry
quarte
quinze
quoits
rabbit
racing
racket
raffle
ramble
rapids

rapier
rave-up
record
remise
replay
result
rhumba
riddle
riding
roll-in
roquet
rowing
rubber
rugger
runner
safari
savate
scorer
sculls
seance
second
seesaw
shimmy
shinny
shinty
shorts
skater
skiing
slalom
sledge
soccer
spades
spikes
spiral
sports
sprint
squash
stakes
stance
sticks
stilts
strike
stroke
stroll
stumps
stymie
sweeps
swivel
tackle
target
tarots
tennis
threes
thrust
thwart
tickle
tipcat
tiptoe
tivoli
torero
touche
toy gun
trophy
truant
TT race
umpire
versus
volley
wicket
willow
winger
winner
yoicks
yorker
ace high
acrobat
address
also-ran
amateur
angling
archery
arm hold
arm lock
assault
athlete
back row
bad calx
balance
ballast
balloon
bar bell
bathing
batsman
beguine
bezique
bicycle
bidding
big game
bivouac
bladder
blaster
boating
bonfire
bowling
box-kite
bracing
bran tub
brassie
bubbles
camp bed
camping
captain
capture
carioca
cassino
catcher
century
charade
charter
Chicago
chicane
chimney
chipper
chukker
circuit
classic
compass
couloir
counter
crampon
creases
cricket
croquet
cue ball
curb bit
curling
cushion
cutlass
cycling
cyclist
dancing
day trip
decider
declare

defence
descent
diabolo
diamond
dicebox
discard
doubles
drawing
dribble
driving
endgame
endplay
enprise
entrant
fairway
fanclub
fencing
fielder
fifteen
fineleg
finesse
fishing
fixture
flyhalf
footbow
formula
forward
foxhunt
foxtrot
freehit
Frisbee
frogman
funfair
gallery
gavotte
gliding
goggles
golfbag
golfing
golftie
goodfun
grounds
guyrope
gymnast
hacking
hairpin
handoff
harpoon
harrier
hawking
holster
honours
hunting
hurdler
hurling
icepick
icerink
ikebana
infield
innings
jackpot
j'adoube
javelin
jogging
joyride
jujitsu
keepfit
kickoff
knockup
lancers
landing
lastlap
leghold
legside
letball
lineout
longbow
longhop
longleg
lottery
marbles
matador
maypole
mazurka
meccano
melding
midiron
netball
netcord
niblick
ninepin
notrump
oarsman
offside
oldmaid
onestep
onguard
overarm
overpar
paddock
pallone
partner
passade
passado
pastime
penalty
picador
picquet
pinball
pinfall
pinhigh
pinocle
pitcher
pitstop
playoff
poloist
pontoon
potshot
pressup
prowess
pyramid
quarter
rackets
ragdoll
rebound
referee
regatta
reserve
ripcord
riposte
rockers
rosette
rowlock
rubicon
running
sailing
sandpie
sandpit
scooter
scratch
service
sevenup
shotput
shuffle

shuttle
singles
singlet
skating
skid-lid
snaffle
snooker
snorkel
society
soft|toy
sparrer
squails
stadium
stamina
starter
stirrup
St|Leger
striker
stumped
sub-aqua
sun|bath
tacking
tactics
take-off
tally|ho
tangram
tantivy
tenpins
tent|peg
The|Oaks
The|Oval
throw-in
tie|game
tilting
toe|hold
tombola
Torpids
tourney
trainer
tumbler
twosome
two-step
vantage
vaulter
walking
war|club
war|game
workout
wrestle
ziganka
aerobics
all-fours
approach
apres-ski
aqualung
aquatics
armguard
away|game
baccarat
backhand
backheel
backspin
bail|ball
balk|line
ball|game
baseball
baseline
beagling
biathlon
biathlon
blocking
boat|race
body|blow
bonspiel
boundary
brackets
bullring
bull's|eye
bully|off
cakewalk
campfire
camp|site
canoeing
card|game
carnival
carousel
car|rally
castling
catapult
cat|stick
champion
charades
checkers
chequers
chessman
chess|set
chin|hold
chip|shot
climbing
coasting
contract
cottabus
counters
coursing
coxswain
crap|game
cribbage
crossbar
cross-bat
cruising
cup|final
dark|blue
dead|ball
dead|heat
deadlock
dead|shot
delivery
diamonds
dominoes
doubling
dragster
draughts
draw|lots
dressage
drop|goal
drop|kick
drop|shot
dumb|bell
even|keel
even|odds
exercise
face|card
fair|play
falconer
falconry
fandango
fast|ball
field|day
finalist
firework
fistiana
fivepins
flapping
flat|race

8 LETTERS

flippers
floating
foilsman
foothold
foot race
footwork
forehand
forfeits
foul goal
foul line
foul play
foursome
foxhound
free kick
fretwork
front row
full back
full draw
full toss
gambling
gamester
gauntlet
gin rummy
goal kick
goalpost
golfball
golf club
golliwog
good calx
good shot
gridiron
guarding
gymkhana
gym shoes
habanera
halfback
half-ball
half-blue
half-mile
half-shot
half-time
handball
handicap
hat trick
haymaker
headlock
helmsman
high dive
high jump
holed out
hole high
home game
hornpipe
horseman
how's that
hula hoop
hula-hula
huntsman
hurdling
ice yacht
Irish jig
iron shot
jiu-jitsu
joystick
knock out
korfball
lacrosse
lawn game
leapfrog
left back
left half
left hook
left wing
leg break
leg guard
lifeline
linesman
long game
long jump
long odds
long rush
long shot
long stop
lost ball
love game
lucky bag
lucky dip
mah-jongg
marathon
marksman
marriage
monopoly
motorist
multi-gym
napoleon
natation
ninepins
nosedive
no trumps
off break
off drive
Olympiad
open file
opponent
outfield
outsider
oval ball
paddling
pall-mall
pass line
pass roll
patience
pike dive
ping pong
pinochle
pin table
playmate
playroom
plunging
polo ball
polo pony
pony trek
pool room
port tack
pugilism
pugilist
pushball
pyramids
quintain
quiz game
racegoer
radio ham
rambling
reaching
recovery
red cloak
redouble
ricochet
rink polo
rope ring
roulette
rounders
rucksack
runner up

SPORTS, GAMES AND PASTIMES

Ruy|Lopez
sack|race
sand|iron
sand|trap
saraband
sardines
Scrabble
scramble
scrum|cap
sculling
selector
set|point
shell|out
shooting
short|leg
side,blow
side|line
skin|game
ski|slope
ski|stick
skittles
sledging
slow|ball
snapshot
snowball
snow|line
softball
southpaw
sparring
speedway
spoon|oar
sporting
sprinter
stalking
stand|off
stand|pat
stations
stoccado
stock|car
stop|shot
straddle
straight
tap|dance
team|game
tent|pole
The|Ashes
the|field
third|man
thole|pin
tie|break
toreador
Totopoly
tracking
trailing
training
train|set
tug,of,war
underarm
undercut
under|par
upper|cut
vaulting
venation
walkover
wall|game
wing|area
wood|club
wood|shot
wrestler
yachting
acey,deucy
advantage
all,comers
all|square
anchor|man
arabesque
arrow|shot
astrodome
athletics
Aunt|Sally
back|court
back|edges
back|swing
badminton
bagatelle
bandalore
bandy|ball
barn|dance
baulk|line
beach|ball
best|bower
biathlete
big|dipper
billiards
black|belt
blackjack
black|pawn
bladework
boarhound
boar|spear
bobsleigh
body|check
body|punch
bossa|nova
bowstring
brown|belt
caddie|car
camel|spin

card|trick
cartwheel
cavalcade
cha-cha-cha
chair|lift
challenge
checkmate
chess|game
clock|golf
clog|dance
closing|in
club|house
collector
combatant
conjuring
contender
cotillion
court|card
crackshot
cricketer
crossjack
crossword
cycle|race
cycle|tour
dance|step
dartboard
decathlon
decoy|duck
disengage
dog|racing
doll's|pram
drawn|game
dribbling
enclosure
en|passant
en|tout|cas
equalizer
exercises
extra|time
face|guard
favourite
field|game
fieldsman
first|half
first|seed
first|slip
fisherman
fisticuff
five-a-side
fletching
flight|bow
flyweight
foot|fault
fore|royal
forty-love
free|reach
freestyle
freewheel
full|house
galleries
game|point
gardening
gladiator
goalposts
go-karting
gold|medal
golf|links
golf|range
golf|shoes
golf|widow
good|loser
good|sport
grand|prix
grand|slam
gum|shield
gymnasium
handstand
hard|court
high|jinks
hill|climb
hitch|hike
hit|wicket
hopscotch
horseback
horseplay
horse|race
ice|hockey
ice|skates
infielder
jackknife
judo|throw
kennelman
king's|rook
lawn|bowls
left|bower
left|inner
leg|before
leg|spread
light|blue
long|loser
long|tacks
loose|ball
loose|maul
loose|rein
love|forty
love|match
low|volley
match|play

medallist
medal play
mid mashie
motocross
music hall
Newmarket
Nuts in May
orienteer
pacemaker
palaestra
panel game
pantomime
paper doll
parachute
party game
paso doble
passepied
Paul Jones
pelmanism
pen friend
penthouse
philately
pickaback
pilot ball
pinch draw
pirouette
pitch camp
plaything
pogo stick
poker dice
pole vault
polonaise
potholing
puissance
punchball
push parry
quadrille
quickstep
race track
racing car
relay race
relay team
right back
right half
right hook
right wing
ringsider
rock climb
roundelay
round game
round trip
rover hoop
safety net
sand yacht
sauna bath
schnorkel
score card
scrapbook
screw dive
scrimmage
scrum half
scrummage
second row
semi-final
shaftment
shamateur
shinguard
short game
short odds
shortstop
shrimping
signal gun
silver cup
singleton
skin diver
sky diving
small bore
snow climb
solitaire
solo whist
spectator
speedboat
spin parry
split shot
spoon bait
sports day
sportsman
spot dance
square leg
stable boy
stalemate
starboard
steersman
step-dance
stopwatch
stud poker
surfboard
sweatband
swordplay
swordsman
teddy bear
tennis net
terracing
test match
the sticks
three-jump
threesome
three-turn

tight rein
tip-and-run
torch race
touchdown
touch goal
touchline
track suit
trump card
trump suit
turnstile
twenty-one
twist dive
vingt-et-un
water polo
whirligig
white pawn
wristlock
yacht club
yacht race
yachtsman
youth club
acrobatics
aerobatics
agility mat
agonistics
backgammon
backmarker
backstroke
balneation
banderilla
basketball
battledore
beekeeping
betting man
binoculars
blind poker
blood sport
booby prize
boxing ring
catch a crab
cat's cradle
centre half
challenger
changeover
charleston
checkpoint
chessboard
Chinese box
christiana
clay pigeon
coconut shy
competitor
contestant
contractor
counted out
cover point
cricket bat
cricket net
crown green
cyclo-cross
daily dozen
decathlete
deck quoits
deck tennis
discobolus
diving bell
doll's house
dolly catch
double axle
double game
double peel
draw stumps
drop cannon
drop volley
equitation
Eskimo roll
fairground
fantoccini
fast bowler
feathering
fianchetto
field event
field sport
first blood
fishing net
fishing rod
flat racing
fly fishing
flying mare
flying shot
footballer
forced move
foundation
fox hunting
free-for-all
full nelson
gambit pawn
ghost train
goal circle
goal crease
goalkeeper
goal tender
golf course
grandstand
gymnastics
half bisque
half nelson
half volley

halieutics
halved hole
handspring
hard tackle
Harrow game
hazard side
headhunter
health club
health farm
heel and toe
high diving
hitch hiker
hobbyhorse
hockey team
hog hunting
horseshoes
horsewoman
hunting bow
ice dancing
ice skating
Indian club
Indian file
indoor golf
injury time
inside home
inside lane
inside left
inside lock
in the rough
in training
isometrics
jackstones
jackstraws
Jockey Club
jump the gun
karate chop
kewpie doll
kite flying
kriegspiel
lansquenet
lawn tennis
league game
little slam
loaded dice
loose scrum
love-thirty
maiden over
marionette
marker buoy
mashie iron
match point
middle spot
minor piece
non-starter
object ball
off the hook
opening bat
open season
open target
Ouija board
outfielder
pancration
pancratium
paper chase
par contest
pari-mutuel
passed pawn
penalty try
pentathlon
philatelic
pigeon loft
planchette
playground
point of aim
poker chips
polo ground
potato race
prize fight
prize money
punch drunk
push stroke
queen's pawn
queen's rook
racecourse
racing cars
ratcatcher
real tennis
recreation
relaxation
relegation
rifle range
right bower
right inner
right swing
ring-o roses
rod and reel
roundabout
round dance
rowing boat
royal flush
rubber ball
rubber duck
rugby union
rumpus room
run through
rush stroke
sand castle
scoreboard

second half
second slip
seconds out
second wind
seven-a-side
short tacks
show jumper
sidesaddle
side stroke
silly mid-on
silly point
single file
single game
skateboard
ski jumping
skin diving
ski running
sky jumping
slow bowler
somersault
speed trial
spike shoes
spin bowler
sportswear
spot stroke
square ring
stamp album
stock cards
stop thrust
strathspey
strike camp
stroke play
submission
substitute
sun bathing
surf riding
suspension
sweepstake
switchback
sword dance
take a trick
tarantella
team spirit
tennis ball
tennis shoe
thirty-love
thrown goal
tiger badge
timekeeper
time thrust
tin soldier
title fight
toe scratch
tournament
tour skiing
toy soldier
track event
trampoline
trial match
triple jump
triple peel
true to form
tumble turn
turkey trot
twelfth man
vantage set
Vardon grip
volleyball
water wings
whippers in
whist drive
wilful foul
willow wand
win by a head
winning gun
Yarborough
young entry
accumulator
baseball bat
bearbaiting
bellringing
Bengal spear
betting ring
biased bowls
big game hunt
boating pond
Bombay spear
bow and arrow
boxing match
bronze medal
bull baiting
canoe slalom
casual water
Channel swim
chariot race
cheer leader
cinder track
class racing
close season
compact disc
country walk
county match
coup de grace
court tennis
crash helmet
crawl stroke
cricket ball
cricket pads

croquet arch
croquet ball
croquet hoop
croquet lawn
cross swords
curling pond
curling rink
cycle racing
daisy cutter
deck of cards
deep fine leg
direct party
diving board
diving dress
double check
double fault
downhill run
driving iron
egg and spoon
envelopment
eurhythmics
false attack
fencing mask
Ferris wheel
field events
fifteen-love
figure eight
first attack
first eleven
fishing line
flick stroke
flying start
football fan
forced error
forward line
forward pass

fox and geese
free skating
fun and games
gambit piece
gambling man
gaming house
gaming table
garden party
glove puppet
gone fishing
good innings
grand salute
groundsheet
hairpin bend
half passage
halfway line
heavyweight
hide-and-seek
hitch-hiking
hockey match
hockey stick
home and away
horse racing
horse riding
ice yachting
inside right
jumping bean
king's bishop
king's knight
lap of honour
league table
lightweight
lock forward
loop the loop
love-fifteen
malibu board

modern waltz
morris dance
motor racing
mountaineer
mystery tour
nailed boots
neck and neck
offside rule
Olympic team
out of bounds
outside home
outside left
pack of cards
pair skating
palaestrian
pancake race
pancratiast
parlour game
pawn and move
penalty area
penalty goal
penalty kick
penalty line
photo finish
picture card
pigeon flier
pigeon house
pigeon timer
pig sticking
pillow fight
piscatology
pitch and run
playing card
playing line
play the game
pole vaulter

prizewinner
prop|forward
public|games
pyramid|spot
quarterback
rabbit|punch
race|meeting
racing|craft
racing|shell
racket|court
record|break
riddle-me-ree
Roman|candle
rouge|et|noir
round|of|golf
royal|tennis
rugby|league
Schottische
seam|bowling
self-defence
service|grip
service|hold
service|line
service|side
shinty|stick
shovelboard
show|jumping
shuttlecock
sightseeing
silver|medal
simple|parry
singing|game
skating|rink
skiing|field
sleeping|bag
slow|foxtrot
snow|glasses
snowshoeing
soft|landing
spade|mashie
speculation
spinning|top
sportswoman
spreadeagle
springboard
square|dance
square|tango
squash|court
staghunting
starting|gun
straight|bat
striker|ball
sudden|death
swallow|dive
sweep|rowing
table|tennis
target|arrow
tennis|court
tennis|match
tent|pegging
Terpsichore
theatregoer
the|Olympics
third|player
three-legged
tiddlywinks
time|sharing
tobogganing
totalisator
touring|club
toxophilite
track|record
training|run
transfer|fee
triple|crown
Turkish|bath
waiting|game
walking|race
water|hazard
water|skiing
water|sports
Western|roll
wine|tasting
wing|forward
winning|post
winning|time
win|on|points
wooden|horse
world|record
youth|hostel
anchor|cannon
approach|shot
back|straight
bantamweight
batting|order
beachcombing
Becher's|brook
billiard|ball
billiard|hall
billiard|room
billiard|spot
bingo|session
bird|watching
body|building
bowling|alley
bowling|green
boxing|gloves
break|dancing

break the bank
breast stroke
bull fighting
butterfly net
callisthenic
century break
championship
change bowler
change of ends
changing room
checkerboard
classic races
climbing rope
cockfighting
consequences
country dance
cradle cannon
crapshooting
cricket boots
cricket pitch
croquet court
cross-country
curling stone
cut and thrust
dead ball line
deep sea diver
direct cannon
directors box
disqualified
do-it-yourself
double sculls
doubles match
double threes
dressing room
earth stopper
Eton wall game
fast and loose
field glasses
figure skater
first defence
first innings
first reserve
first service
flying tackle
foursome reel
freewheeling
French boxing
fruit machine
game of chance
game of points
gamesmanship
gone to ground
ground stroke
guessing game
handicap race
head scissors
hill climbing
home straight
homing pigeon
horsemanship
housey housey
hundred yards
hunting groom
in the running
investigator
jack-in-the-box
kaleidoscope
knucklebones
lampadedromy
landing stage
level pegging
London Bridge
long distance
loose forward
losing hazard
maiden stakes
marathon race
medicine ball
melding score
merry-go-round
mincing steps
mixed doubles
National Hunt
nature ramble
noble science
nursery slope
obstacle race
old-time dance
Olympic games
Olympic title
Olympic torch
opposing side
ordinary foul
orienteering
orienteering
outside right
paddling pool
parallel bars
penalty bully
penalty throw
physical jerk
pigeon flying
ping-pong ball
pitch and putt
pitch and toss
playing cards
playing field
pleasure trip

12 LETTERS

point to point
pole position
pony trekking
prize fighter
professional
Punch and Judy
punto reverso
putting green
quarter final
queen's bishop
queen's knight
raffle ticket
receiving end
record holder
redoublement
referee's hold
return crease
ride to hounds
riding school
rock climbing
rocking horse
roller skates
running strip
sand yachting
sand yachting
scissors jump
second attack
second eleven
second player
shadow boxing
sharpshooter
short pinocle
shove ha'penny
shrimping net
shuffleboard
side chancery
simple attack
single combat
single sculls
singles match
skating boots
skipping rope
slice service
slippery pole
soapbox derby
speed skating
sporting life
sport of kings
stabbing blow
stand off half
starting grid
starting post
steeplechase
sticky wicket
stilt walking
straddle jump
stranglehold
strong finish
Sunday driver
sweep oarsman
swimming gala
swimming pool
sword fencing
table turning
tennis player
tennis racket
tennis stroke
three quarter
tiddleywinks
toss the caber
train spotter
trapshooting

treasure hunt
treble chance
trick cyclist
trigger happy
tunnel of love
umpire's chair
vantage point
Virginia reel
weightlifter
welterweight
wicket keeper
winter sports
all-in wrestler
auction bridge
beauty contest
big game hunter
billiard table
blanket finish
blind man's buff
bowling crease
callisthenics
centre forward
change ringing
chequered flag
climbing frame
coarse fishing
county cricket
cribbage board
cruiser weight
double or quits
equestrianism
featherweight
figure of eight
figure skating
finishing post
fishing tackle
follow through
football match
football pools
funny peculiar
ghetto blaster
Grand National
half-time score
hare-and-hounds
helter-skelter
hide-and-go-seek
Highland fling
Highland games
hunting ground
international
mashie niblick
mixed foursome
nightwatchman
nursery slopes
peace offering
physical jerks
popping crease
prisoner's base
prizefighting
return service
rollerskating
rough shooting
rugby football
Russian ballet
second innings
shooting range
shooting stick
sitting target
skateboarding
sleight of hand
Space Invaders
sportsmanlike

sportsmanship
sports stadium
square-dancing
squash rackets
stalking horse
starting price
starting stall
steeplechaser
straight flush
surface worker
table skittles
tenpin bowling
three-day event
train spotting
ventriloquism
ventriloquist
vulnerability
weight lifting
aerobic dancing
approach stroke
bathing costume
bathing machine
billiard marker
catherine wheel
champion jockey
channel swimmer
cock-a-doodle-doo
conjuring trick
contract bridge
country dancing
crown and anchor
fancy-dress ball
follow-my-leader
football ground
football league
golf tournament
greyhound Derby
grouse shooting
halloween party
high cockalorum
hop, skip and jump
hunt-the-slipper
marathon runner
master of hounds
mountaineering
nine-men's-morris
nineteenth hole
opening batsman
pig-in-the-middle
prima ballerina
putting the shot
ride a cock-horse
shove halfpenny
sit on the splice
smoking concert
solitaire board
spectator sport
speedway racing
squash racquets
starting blocks
starting stalls
steeplechasing
stock-car racing
supporters club
three-card trick
winter Olympics
wrestling match
amusement arcade
appearance money
Australian rules
bodyline bowling
catch-as-catch-can

SPORTS, GAMES AND PASTIMES

cross-country run
crossword puzzle
duplicate bridge
egg-and-spoon race
fancy-dress dance
firework display
game, set and match
glorious Twelfth
hit below the belt
Indian rope trick
king-of-the-castle
leg before wicket
nursery handicap
odds-on favourite
pipped at the post
puss-in-the-corner
rain stopped play
Roger de Coverley
Royal and Ancient
Russian roulette
shooting gallery
sparring partner
sports equipment
stable companion
stamp collecting
stamp collection
swimming costume
three-day eventer
three-legged race
three-ring circus
throw in the towel
women's institute

Theatre

act	foil	solo	enact	stagy
bit	fool	spot	extra	stall
bow	gods	star	farce	stand
box	grid	tail	flies	still
cue	hall	text	floor	stunt
fan	hero	turn	focus	usher
gag	idol	tutu	foots	wings
ham	joke	unit	foyer	absurd
hit	lead	wing	front	acting
mug	line	zany	heavy	action
pit	loft	actor	house	act|out
rag	loge	ad|lib	lines	appear
rep	mask	agent	mimer	backer
run	mime	angel	mimic	ballet
set	mute	arena	odeum	barker
tab	part	aside	on|cue	Big|Top
bill	play	barre	opera	boards
bowl	plot	break	piece	border
busk	prop	buffo	props	buskin
cast	rant	cloth	Punch	chaser
clap	rave	clown	put|on	chorus
dais	ring	comic	queue	circle
diva	role	corps	revue	circus
dock	rush	debut	rodeo	claque
dots	shot	decor	scena	comedy
drop	show	drama	scene	critic
epic	side	drill	score	dancer
flat	skit	dry|up	spout	depict
flop	sock	eclat	stage	direct

THEATRE

effect	review	callboy	manager
encore	ring up	casting	marquee
Equity	satire	cat call	matinee
exodus	scenic	cat walk	mimicry
farcer	script	charade	miracle
feeder	season	chorine	mummery
filler	singer	circuit	musical
finale	sketch	clapper	mystery
floats	speech	close-up	New Wave
flyman	stager	comedia	No drama
gagman	stalls	commere	on stage
guiser	stanza	company	overact
jester	stooge	compere	pageant
Kabuki	talent	costume	perform
lights	teaser	cothurn	Pierrot
limber	Thalia	coxcomb	play-act
lyceum	ticket	curtain	playing
make-up	tights	dancing	playlet
masque	timing	danseur	pop idol
method	tragic	deadpan	pop star
motley	troupe	dress up	portray
mummer	up left	drive-in	present
number	walk-on	fan club	preview
one act	warm-up	farceur	produce
on tour	writer	farcist	proverb
patron	acrobat	gallery	re-enact
patter	act-drop	gate man	rep show
person	actress	grimace	Roscius
pit man	all-star	ham it up	rostrum
player	artiste	heroine	scenery
podium	balcony	histrio	scenist
prompt	benefit	ingenue	showman
puppet	bit part	last act	show off
relief	booking	leg show	soapbox
repeat	buffoon	leotard	spieler
re-take	cabaret	long run	stadium

7/8 LETTERS

stagery
staging
stand by
stand in
stardom
starlet
support
tableau
theatre
the gods
Thespis
tragedy
trouper
tumbler
up right
upstage
vehicle
antimask
applause
audience
audition
backdrop
balletic
big scene
Broadway
burletta
business
carnival
clapping
claqueur
clowning
coliseum
comedian
conjuror
coryphee
costumer
coulisse
danseuse
dialogue
Dionysus
director
disguise
down left
dramatic
dumb show
duologue
entr'acte
entrance
epilogue
epitasis
exit line
farceuse
farcical
fauteuil
festival
figurant
filmgoer
film unit
first act
front row
funny man
gridiron
grimacer
ham actor
headline
interval
juvenile
libretto
live show
location
magician
morality
off stage
operatic
operetta
overture
paradise
parterre
pastoral
peep show
pit stall
platform
playbook
playgoer
playland
playwork
practice
premiere
producer
prologue
prompter
property
protasis
rehearse
ring down
scenario
sceneman
set piece
showboat
side show
smash hit
stagedom
stageman
stage set
star turn
stasimon
straight
stroller

THEATRE

subtitle
take a bow
the dance
Thespian
the stage
third act
tragical
travesty
typecast
usheress
wardrobe
wigmaker
wireless
absurdist
animation
announcer
arabesque
astrodome
backcloth
backstage
ballerina
bandstand
barnstorm
bit player
box office
breakaway
burlesque
carpenter
character
chorus boy
chorus man
cinematic
clip joint
Colosseum
Columbine
costumier

cothurnus
criticism
cyclorama
dead stage
direction
discovery
down right
downstage
dramatics
dramatist
dramatize
drop scene
entertain
entrechat
epirrhema
featuring
figurante
floor show
greenroom
guest star
ham acting
harlequin
headliner
heavy lead
hoardings
horseshoe
incognito
interlude
left stage
limelight
live stage
love scene
low comedy
major role
make-up man
melodrama

Melpomene
menagerie
minor role
monodrama
monologue
music hall
night club
old stager
orchestra
panel game
pantaloon
pantomime
parabasis
pas de deux
patronage
patroness
performer
personage
Pierrette
pirouette
play actor
playhouse
portrayal
programme
prompt box
publicity
punch line
raw comedy
rehearsal
repertory
represent
scenarist
scene plot
second act
side scene
slapstick

9/10 LETTERS

soliloquy
soubrette
spectacle
spectator
spotlight
stage|door
stagehand
stageland
stage|name
stage|play
staginess
superstar
take|a|part
tap|dancer
theatrics
the|big|top
the|boards
title|role
tragedian
triologue
usherette
wisecrack
act|curtain
act|the|goat
act|the|part
afterpiece
appearance
apron|stage
arena|stage
auditorium
bandwaggon
buffoonery
chorus|girl
chorus|show
clog|dancer
clown|white
comedienne
comic|opera
continuity
coryphaeus
costumiere
crowd|scene
denouement
disc|jockey
drama|group
dramalogue
dramatizer
dramaturge
dramaturgy
engagement
exhibition
expository
fantoccini
first|house
first|night
footlights
get|the|bird
high|comedy
hippodrome
histrionic
impresario
impression
intermezzo
in|the|round
in|the|wings
leading|man
legitimate
librettist
management
marionette
masquerade
microphone
milk|a|scene
mimologist
motley|fool
mountebank
music|drama
on|the|stage
opera|buffa
opera|house
pantomimic
pass|holder
performing
play|acting
playbroker
playreader
playwright
playwriter
presenting
prima|donna
production
promptbook
properties
proscenium
Pulcinella
puppet|show
put|on|a|show
rave|notice
repertoire
right|stage
Scaramouch
shadow|show
socio-drama
stage|boxes
stagecraft
stage|fever
step|dancer
strip|tease

THEATRE

substitute
tap dancing
tear jerker
theatre box
theatreman
theatrical
the critics
the unities
tragicomic
trial scene
understudy
utility man
variety act
vaudeville
walk-on part
actor's agent
actor's lines
all-star bill
all-star cast
a star is born
bag of tricks
balletomane
barnstormer
black comedy
broad comedy
cap and bells
catastrophe
charity show
cliff hanger
comedy drama
comic relief
commentator
concert hall
curtain call
drama school
dramatic art
dramaticism
dramaturgic
dress circle
drop curtain
electrician
entertainer
exeunt omnes
fire curtain
galanty show
grease paint
Greek chorus
histrionics
histrionism
illusionist
impersonate
jackpudding
kitchen sink
leading lady
light comedy
low comedian
make-believe
matinee idol
merry andrew
method actor
mimographer
miracle play
mise en scene
off Broadway
on the boards
pantomimist
pas de quatre
Passion play
performance
personality
personation
play actress
play the fool
play the part
practicable
protagonist
psychodrama
Punchinello
scene change
scenewright
set designer
set the scene
set the stage
showmanship
show stopper
Simon Legree
skirt dancer
sound effect
spectacular
stage design
stage effect
stage fright
stage player
stage school
stagestruck
stageworthy
stagewright
star billing
star quality
star studded
star vehicle
straight man
strip teaser
talent scout
terpsichore
theatregoer
theatreland
theatricals

theatrician
Thespian art
tragedienne
tragic drama
tragicomedy
upper circle
ventriloquy
waiting line
walking part
walk-through
word perfect
academy award
acting device
actor manager
advance agent
amphitheatre
ballet dancer
balletomania
booking agent
borderlights
characterize
character man
choreography
comedy ballet
concert party
dramatic play
dramaturgist
dressing room
entrepreneur
extravaganza
first-nighter
Grand Guignol
Greek theatre
harlequinade
hold the stage
impersonator
introduction
juvenile lead
make-up artist
masked comedy
melodramatic
method acting
minstrel show
modern ballet
morality play
old stage hand
opera glasses
orchestra pit
Pepper's ghost
presentation
principal boy
publicity man
Punch and Judy
scene painter
sceneshifter
scene stealer
scenic effect
screenwriter
season ticket
show business
show must go on
song and dance
sound effects
stage manager
stage setting
stage whisper
standing room
starring role
steal the show
stock company
stole the show
straight part

take|the|floor
theatrecraft
theatromania
top|of|the|bill
vaudevillian
vaudevillist
curtain|raiser
curtain|speech
dramatic|irony
dramatisation
emergency|exit
entertainment
impersonation
melodramatist
musical|comedy
one,night|stand
pantomime|dame
safety|curtain
theatre|school
theatricalism
walking,on|part
world|premiere
character|actor
dramatic|critic
dress|rehearsal
open,air|theatre
orchestra|stall
pantomime|horse
prima|ballerina
property|master
proscenium|arch
smoking|concert
speech|training
stage|carpenter
stage|direction
supporting|cast
supporting|part
supporting|role
touring|company
variety|theatre
behind|the|scenes
dramatic|society
gala|performance
legitimate|drama
National|Theatre
orchestra|stalls
raise|the|curtain
shadow|pantomime
situation|comedy
slapstick|comedy
strolling|player
tightrope|walker

Time

AD	mo	ago	due	eld	ere
am	pm	aye	e'en	Eos	eve
BC	age	day	e'er	era	May

3/6 LETTERS

oft
old
sec
ult
yet
aeon
ages
anon
ante
date
dawn
dial
dusk
even
ever
fall
fast
fore
Ides
inst
jiff
July
June
late
Lent
moon
morn
next
Noel
noon
once
over
past
post
prox
slow
soon
span
term
then
tick
tide
till
time
unto
week
when
Xmas
year
yore
Yule
again
annum
April
as yet
brief
clock
cycle
daily
dekad
delay
diary
early
epact
epoch
fasti
flash
jiffy
later
March
matin
month
never
night
nonce
often
passe
pause
point
prime
prior
Purim
ready
shake
sharp
short
since
so far
space
spell
still
style
sunup
tempo
today
trice
until
watch
while
years
young
youth
actual
advent
always
annual
at once
August
Aurora
autumn
Bairam
brumal
coeval
coming
crisis
curfew
decade
dotage
during
Easter
elapse
ere now
extant
ferial
Friday
future
gnomon
heyday
hiemal
hourly
Ice age
in time
jet age
Julian
Lammas
lapsed
lately
latest
latish
lustre
manana
May day
midday
minute

modern
moment
Monday
morrow
new day
o'clock
off-day
of late
old age
one day
on time
period
presto
pre-war
prompt
pronto
pro tem
rarely
recent
season
second
seldom
sooner
spring
sudden
summer
Sunday
sunset
timely
to date
update
vernal
vesper
weekly
whilst
winter
yearly
yester
abiding
ack emma
ageless
ages ago
all over
almanac
already
ancient
anytime
archaic
at night
bedtime
belated
betimes
boyhood
by-and-by
calends
century
chiliad
current
dawning
daylong
day-peep
daytime
diurnal
dog days
earlier
elapsed
endless
epochal
equinox
estival
evening
exactly
expired
extinct
fast day
flag day
forever
for good
for life
harvest
high day
history
holiday
holy day
infancy
instant
interim
Iron Age
January
journal
jubilee
just now
kalends
Lady day
long ago
long run
lustrum
manhood
manhour
matinal
mid-week
monthly
morning
newborn
New Year
nightly
noonday
October
one-time
overdue
pending
pip emma
postwar
present
proximo
quarter
quondam
Ramadan
ripe age
Sabbath
secular
shortly
sine die
some day
stretch
Sukkoth
sundial
sundown
sunrise
teenage
tertian
this day
time-lag
time was
tonight
too late
too soon
Tuesday
twinkle
two two's
unready
up to now
usually
weekday

7/8 LETTERS

weekend
whereon
whitsun
abruptly
a long day
antedate
as soon as
biannual
biennial
birthday
biweekly
blue moon
Brumaire
calendar
darkling
date line
daybreak
daylight
deadline
December
Derby day
directly
dogwatch
doomsday
duration
egg-timer
enduring
entr'acte
Epiphany
eternity
eventide
evermore
every day
evil hour
fast time
feast day

February
fleeting
foredawn
forenoon
formerly
frequent
gain time
gloaming
half hour
half past
Hanukkah
hereunto
hibernal
high time
hitherto
Hogmanay
holy days
Holy week
horology
ill-timed
in a flash
in a trice
infinity
in future
in no time
in season
interval
juncture
keep time
kill time
lang syne
last time
last week
lateness
latterly
leap year

lifelong
life-span
lifetime
livelong
long time
Lord's day
lose time
lunation
make time
mark time
meantime
mean time
medieval
menology
meridian
meteoric
midnight
momently
natal day
New Style
next week
noontide
noontime
not often
November
nowadays
obsolete
occasion
ofttimes
old times
on the dot
our times
Passover
pass time
postdate
postpone

previous
promptly
punctual
recently
right now
ringtime
Saturday
seasonal
seedtime
semester
solar day
solstice
some time
Space Age
sporadic
Steel Age
Stone Age
suddenly
take time
temporal
this week
Thursday
timeless
time-worn
tomorrow
too early
twilight
ultimate
until now
untimely
up-to-date
weeklong
whenever
year-book
yearlong
years ago

yoretime
Yuletide
adulthood
afternoon
after that
after time
all at once
antiquity
Atomic Age
at present
bimonthly
Boxing Day
Bronze Age
Candlemas
canicular
centenary
childhood
Christmas
chronicle
civil time
civil year
clepsydra
continual
crepuscle
days of old
dayspring
decennary
decennial
decennium
due season
earliness
early bird
ember days
Empire Day
ephemeral
ephemeris

epochally
erstwhile
ever since
every hour
far future
first time
foregoing
forthwith
fortnight
from now on
gnomonics
Golden Age
great year
Gregorian
Hallowe'en
Hallowmas
happy days
hereafter
honeymoon
hourglass
immediacy
immediate
in a second
in due time
instanter
instantly
interlude
in the past
Julian day
Lammas day
later date
latter day
light year
local time
longevity
long-lived

long|since
long|spell
long|while
lunar|year
many|a|time
many|times
Mardi|Gras
Martinmas
mature|age
matutinal
meanwhile
mediaeval
menstrual
metronome
midday|sun
middle|age
midsummer
midwinter
mistiming
momentary
monthlong
nevermore
nightfall
nightlong
nighttide
night|time
nocturnal
octennial
oftentime
opportune
out|of|date
overnight
Pentecost
perennial
permanent
postcenal
preceding
precisely
premature
presently
quarterly
quarter|to
quotidian
recurrent
regularly
remote|age
right|time
Saint's|day
salad|days
sandglass
semestral
September
short|term
short|time
solar|time
solar|year
sometimes
space|time
spare|time
spend|time
stop|watch
Swiss|plan
temporary
temporize
therewith
till|death
time|being
time|check
time|clock
time|flies
time|limit
time|of|day
timepiece
times|past
timetable
to|this|day
transient
triennial
twinkling
two|shakes
upon|which
vicennial
waste|time
Wednesday
well-timed
wherefore
whereunto
whereupon
wrong|time
yesterday
afterwards
after|which
alarm|clock
Allhallows
all|the|time
anno|Domini
at|all|times
at|that|time
at|this|time
beforehand
before|long
beforetime
behindhand
behind|time
better|days
break|of|day
bygone|days
by|the|clock

centennial
childermas
chronogram
chronology
close of day
common time
consequent
constantly
continuous
cosmic time
crepuscule
days gone by
days of yore
Eastertide
Easter time
evanescent
eventually
Father's day
Father Time
fiscal year
fleetingly
frequently
futuristic
generation
Good Friday
half a jiffy
half an hour
half a shake
hardly ever
hebdomadal
Hebrew year
henceforth
here and now
heretofore
historical
immemorial
incidental
in good time
invariably
isochronon
Julian year
just in time
Lammastide
last chance
last minute
Lententide
lunar month
Methuselah
Michaelmas
middle-aged
Middle Ages
midmorning
millennium
moratorium
Mother's day
near future
nick of time
now or never
occasional
of the clock
olden times
one fine day
on occasion
on the eve of
Palm Sunday
posthumous
prehistory
present day
previously
proper time
repeatedly
retrospect
ripe old age
Sabbath day
seasonable
semiweekly
septennial
sextennial
short spell
small hours
soon enough
springtide
springtime
subsequent
summertide
summertime
thereafter
this minute
time-keeper
timeliness
time signal
time to come
time to kill
transitory
tricennial
triple time
ultimately
very seldom
vespertime
water clock
wedding day
whensoever
Whitmonday
Whitsunday
wintertide
wintertime
with the sun
wristwatch

years on end
yesteryear
adjournment
adolescence
after-dinner
against time
ahead of time
All Fools day
All Souls day
anachronism
anniversary
at intervals
bicentenary
bygone times
ceaselessly
chronograph
chronometer
chronoscope
coincidence
concurrence
continually
crack of dawn
crepuscular
cuckoo clock
day after day
day and night
day in day out
dead of night
endless time
ever and a day
ever and anon
everlasting
every moment
fin de siècle
flower of age
for evermore
former times
fortnightly
Gay Nineties
golden hours
good old days
halcyon days
half a second
hebdomadary
hereinafter
ides of March
immediately
in an instant
incessantly
in due course
inopportune
interregnum
Judgment day
lapse of time
leisure time
little while
livelong day
long-lasting
long overdue
march of time
microsecond
middle years
millisecond
modern times
momentarily
morningtide
morning time
never-ending
New Year's day
New Year's eve
night and day
once or twice
on the morrow
opportunely
opportunity
out of season
Passion week
penultimate
perennially
perfect year
perpetually
play for time
point of time
present time
prime of life
promptitude
punctuality
quadrennial
quarter past
sands of time
semi-monthly
shining hour
short notice
some time ago
split second
straightway
synchronism
synchronize
tempus fugit
thenceforth
the other day
this morning
this very day
time and tide
time drags by
time machine
time to spare
turret clock

twelvemonth
ultramodern
waiting|time
Whitsuntide
with|the|lark
Year|of|Grace
all|of|a|sudden
All|Saints|day
a|long|time|ago
ancient|times
Annunciation
antediluvian
antemeridian
ante|meridiem
Armistice|day
Ascension|day
Ash|Wednesday
auld|lang|syne
bide|one's|time
calendar|year
Christmas|day
Christmas|eve
consequently
contemporary
course|of|time
decisive|hour
decline|of|day
donkey's|years
eleventh|hour
Feast|of|Weeks
following|day
fourth|of|July
from|that|time
Greek|calends
Holy|Thursday
in|days|of|yore
Indian|summer
Innocents|day
in|olden|times
intermission
late|in|the|day
long,standing
many|a|long|day
metachronism
nychthemeron
occasionally
old,fashioned
once|in|a|while
on|the|instant
parachronism
periodically
postdiluvian
postmeridian
post|meridiem
postponement
postprandial
Quadrigesima
quinquennial
quinquennium
rare|occasion
red|letter|day
sempiternity
sidereal|time
sidereal|year
simultaneous
stall|for|time
standard|time
still|of|night
stitch|in|time
tercentenary
the|dawn|of|day
then|and|there

the year round
time and again
time-honoured
timelessness
time will tell
turning point
Twelfth night
twelve o'clock
unseasonable
witching hour
without delay
again and again
All Hallow's eve
April fool's day
Ascensiontide
at short notice
broad daylight
calendar month
Christmas-tide
Christmas-time
chronographer
chronological
days of the week
every few hours
every few years
every other day
financial year
for the present
from the outset
from the word go
generation gap
getting on a bit
golden jubilee
golden wedding
Greenwich time
Michaelmas day
old as the hills
once upon a time
Passion Sunday
quincentenary
Quinquagesima
retrospective
right up to date
round the clock
Shrove Tuesday
silver jubilee
silver wedding
some of the time
some other time
sooner or later
speaking clock
St Crispin's day
St Luke's summer
St Swithin's day
summer holiday
synchronology
the time is ripe
time after time
time marches on
time of arrival
time out of mind
tomorrow night
Trinity Sunday
tropical month
turn of the year
up-to-the-minute
up with the lark
vernal equinox
week in, week out
year in, year out
advancing years
before and after

TIME

behind schedule
breathing space
chronometrical
day in and day out
daylight saving
declining years
diamond jubilee
diamond wedding
during the night
Easter holidays
for ever and a day
for ever and ever
for the duration
from time to time
fullness of time
geological time
in ancient times
in course of time
interval of time
in the afternoon
in the beginning
in the meanwhile
Julian calendar
keep early hours
Maundy Thursday
midsummer night
month of Sundays
Pancake Tuesday
past and present
Remembrance Day
Rogation Sunday
sabbatical year
septuagenarian
Walpurgis night
witches Sabbath
against the clock
ahead of schedule
chronologically
contemporaneity
contemporaneous
continental time
continuation day
dominical letter
equinoctial year
every now and then
for a year and a day
fourth dimension
how goes the enemy
in the nick of time
month after month
months and months
months of the year
Mothering Sunday
night after night
once in a blue moon
once in a lifetime
put back the clock
put the clock back
quatercentenary
retrospectively
spur of the moment
St Valentine's day
Thanksgiving day
the morning after
this year of grace
tomorrow evening
tomorrow morning
world without end

Tools

awl
axe
bit
cow
die
dig
hod
hoe
jig
saw
adze
file
fork
hose
jack
mole
pick
pump
rake
tool
auger
brace
burin
delve
drill
gouge
jemmy
jimmy
knife

lever
mower
plane
punch
scoop
spade
tongs
wedge
bob|saw
bodkin
chaser
chisel
dibble
digger
eolith
gadget
gimlet
grater
hammer
harrow
jigsaw
mallet
muller
oil|gun
pliers
plough
ramrod
riddle
rip|saw

roller
scythe
shaver
shears
shovel
sickle
spigot
stylus
tedder
trowel
wrench
bandsaw
bradawl
buzz|saw
cadrans
chopper
cleaver
cold|saw
crowbar
forceps
fretsaw
gripper
hacksaw
handsaw
hatchet
hayfork
hayrake
mattock
pickaxe

pincers
riffler
rotator
scalpel
scraper
shuttle
spanner
spatula
sprayer
stapler
toolbox
woodsaw
air|drill
billhook
calipers
cant|hook
chainsaw
clippers
cross|bit
dividers
Dutch|hoe
edge|tool
flash|gun
flat|iron
handtool
penknife
polisher
power|saw
saw|knife

TOOLS

scissors
spray|gun
tommy|bar
tweezers
air|hammer
arc|welder
belt|punch
blow|torch
can|opener
cement|gun
corkscrew
die|sinker
drop|drill
eidograph
excavator
fly|cutter
grease|gun
hair|drier
hand|drill
handspike
implement
jackknife
lawn|mower
pitchfork
plumb|line
road|drill
rock|drill
secateurs
steam|iron
telescope
tin|opener
tyre|lever
bowie|knife
box|spanner
claw|hammer
coal|shovel
cold|chisel
compass|saw
cultivator
drop|hammer
edging|tool
garden|fork
garden|hose
goat|sallow
hole|cutter
keyhole|saw
pantograph
paper|knife
peen|hammer
pipe|wrench
powder|mill
twist|drill
whirl|drill
brace|and|bit
butcher's|saw
circular|saw
dovetail|saw
drilling|rig
electric|saw
electron|gun
garden|spade
glass|cutter
machine|tool
pillar|drill
ploughshare
pocketknife
power|shovel
pruning|bill
pruning|hook
ring|spanner
rotary|drill
safety|razor

11/15 LETTERS

sanding disc
screwdriver
steam hammer
steam shovel
surgeon's saw
tamping iron
watering can
wheelbarrow
battering ram
carving knife
electric iron
garden roller
garden shears
garden trowel
hedge trimmer
hydraulic ram
marlinespike
masonry drill
palette knife
pruning knife
ratchet drill
sledgehammer
soldering gun
two-handed saw
pick and shovel
precision tool
hammer and tongs
pneumatic drill
hammer and sickle

Trade

CA	due	pro	bank	chip	dues
co	dun	put	bear	coin	dump
HP	EEC	rig	body	co-op	dust
rd	fee	sag	bond	corn	duty
bag	IOU	SET	boom	cost	earn
bar	job	sum	buck	crop	EFTA
bid	lot	tag	bulk	curb	fair
bob	Ltd	tax	bull	deal	fees
BOT	net	tin	bury	dear	file
buy	oof	tip	call	debt	fine
cap	owe	VAT	cant	desk	fire
COD	par	wad	cash	dibs	firm
con	pay	agio	cess	dole	fisc
dot	pit	back	char	drug	free

fund
gain
game
gift
gild
gilt
giro
glut
gold
good
haul
hawk
heap
hire
hive
hold
hype
idle
IOUs
item
lend
levy
line
list
loan
long
loss
make
mart
meed
milk
mill
mint
nail
note
paid
pawn
PAYE
peag
perk
pool
post
rags
raid
rate
reap
rent
risk
roll
roup
ruin
sack
safe
sale
salt
save
scab
sell
shop
sink
slug
sold
stag
swap
tare
task
tick
till
tout
vend
visa
wage
ware
work
agent
amass
angel
assay
asset
at|par
audit
baron
batch
beans
bears
bid|up
block
blunt
board
bogus
bones
bonus
boost
booth
brand
brass
broke
bucks
bulls
bunce
buyer
buy|up
by,bid
cadge
cargo
cheap
check
chink
chips
chore
clear
clerk
costs
craft
crash
cycle
debit
depot
Dives
dough
dowry
draft
entry
Ernie
exact
files
float
forge
funds
gilts
gnome
goods
gross
guild
hoard
house
index
ingot
issue
lease
lucre
maker
means
Midas
miser
money
ochre
offer
order
owing
panic
paper
piece
pitch
plant
pound
price
prize
purse
queer
quota
quote
rails
rally
rebuy
remit
repay
rhino
rocks
salve
scalp
scoop
score
scrip
set|up
share
shark
shift
short
skill

slash
slump
smash
smith
snide
spend
spiel
spots
stake
stall
stand
stint
stock
store
strop
tally
taxes
terms
tithe
token
trade
treat
trend
truck
trust
usury
utter
value
venal
wages
wares
welsh
works
worth
yield
abacus
accept
accrue
admass
afford
agency
agenda
amount
appeal
arrear
assets
at|cost
avails
backer
banker
barker
barter
bazaar
bearer
boodle
borrow
bought
bounce
bounty
bourse
branch
broker
budget
bureau
bursar
button
buying
buy|out
cambio
career
cartel
cash|in
change
charge
cheque
client
coffer
consol
copper
corner
costly
coupon
cowrie
credit
crisis
custom
dealer
deal|in
debtee
debtor
defray
demand
dicker
drawer
dunner
emptio
enrich
equity
errand
estate
excise
expend
export
figure
fiscal
fold|up
freeze
future
garage
gazump
godown
go-slow
gratis
grease
growth
guinea
haggle
hammer
hard|up
hawker
import
impose
impost
in|bulk
in|cash
income
in|debt
in-tray
jobber
job|lot
labour
leader
ledger
lender
liable
living
luxury
mammon
merger
minute
moneys
monger
monies
notice
nugget
octroi
odd|job
odd|lot
office
on|call
oncost
on|tick
option
outbid
outcry
outlay
outlet
output
packet
parity
patron
pauper
pay|day
pay|for
paying
pay-off
payola
pay|out
peddle
pedlar
picket
pirate
pledge
plunge
Plutus
pocket
policy
profit
public
purvey

TRADE

racket
raffle
rating
ration
realty
rebate
recoup
redeem
refund
reject
remedy
render
rental
resale
resell
resign
retail
retire
return
reward
rialto
riches
ruined
salary
save|up
saving
sell|up
settle
shares
shorts
silver
simony
smithy
specie
spiral
sponge

spread
stable
staker
stocks
strike
sundry
supply
surtax
swings
tariff
taxman
teller
tender
tenths
ticker
ticket
towage
trader
treaty
tycoon
unload
unpaid
usurer
valuta
vendor
vendue
wallet
wampum
wealth
worker
wright
abscond
account
actuary
allonge
annuity

arrears
article
atelier
auction
auditor
automat
average
backing
bad|debt
balance
ballast
banking
bargain
berries
bidding
bonanza
bondage
boycott
bullets
bullion
bursary
buy|back
cabbage
calling
cambist
capital
cash|box
cashier
ceiling
chapman
charity
chinker
clinker
coinage
coining
company

concern
consols
contact
convert
coppers
corn|pit
cottons
counter
Croesus
cumshaw
Customs
customs
cut|rate
damages
daybook
dealing
declare
default
deficit
deflate
deposit
deviser
dockage
draw|out
due|bill
dumping
economy
effects
embargo
emption
endorse
engross
entrust
expense
exploit
exports

7 LETTERS

factory
failure
fall due
finance
flutter
foot lot
foreman
forgery
for sale
fortune
foundry
freebie
freight
full lot
futures
gabelle
gift box
go broke
good buy
good sum
go under
guerdon
half-day
harvest
haulage
head tax
holding
imports
inflate
in funds
intrust
invoice
ironmen
jingler
jobbers
jobbing

jobless
journal
killing
land tax
leading
lending
lettuce
limited
lockout
Lombard
long-run
lottery
lump sum
manager
man-made
mintage
mission
moneyed
nest egg
net gain
notions
nummary
oddment
on offer
on terms
on trust
opening
opulent
out-tray
package
parlour
parvenu
payable
pay cash
payment
pay rise

payroll
payslip
peddlar
pending
pension
pet bank
plunger
poll tax
poorman
portage
pre-empt
premium
prepaid
pricing
produce
profits
promote
pro rata
prosper
provide
pursuit
pyramid
realize
realtor
receipt
refusal
regrate
reissue
release
requite
reserve
retiral
returns
revenue
richman
rigging

rollers
roomman
rouleau
royalty
sacking
salable
salt tax
salvage
savings
seconds
selling
sell out
service
shekels
shopman
shopper
skilled
smelter
solvent
sponger
squeeze
stipend
storage
striker
subsidy
surplus
swindle
takings
taxable
tax-free
terrier
the city
tidy sum
trade in
trading
traffic

tranche
trustee
utility
vacancy
vending
venture
voucher
walkout
war|bond
warrant
wealthy
welfare
well|off
welsher
wildcat
workday
above|par
accredit
affluent
after|tax
agiotage
agronomy
amortize
appraise
at|a|price
auditing
automate
badly|off
bad|money
ballyhoo
bankbook
bank|loan
bank|note
bank|roll
bankrupt
base|coin
basic|pay
bear|pool
bear|raid
beat|down
below|par
blackleg
blue|chip
board|lot
boardman
bondager
boom|town
borrower
boutique
breakage
brochure
bull|pool
bull|raid
business
buying|in
campaign
carriage
cashbook
cash|down
cash|sale
circular
clientry
close|out
cold|cash
commands
commerce
consumer
contango
contract
converts
counting
creditor
credit|to
currency
customer
cut|price
day|shift
dealings
defrayal
director
disburse
discount
disposal
dividend
dry|goods
earnings
embezzle
employee
employer
emporium
entrepot
estimate
evaluate
exchange
expended
expenses
exporter
face|ruin
finances
fire|sale
flat|rate
floorman
for|a|song
free|gift
free|port
function
gasworks
gazetted
gazumper
gift|shop
gilt|edge
giveaway
gold|mine
gold|rush
good|will
gratuity
grow|rich
hallmark
hard|cash
hard|sell
hardware
hoarding
homework
hot|money
huckster
importer
in|arrear
increase
indebted
industry
in|pocket
interest
in|the|red
investor
issuance
issue|par
jeweller
junkshop
keep|shop
kitemark
knitwork
labourer
lame|duck
largesse

8 LETTERS

large sum
legation
levanter
lifework
live high
live well
long side
low price
low water
make a bid
make good
manifest
man power
mark down
material
maturity
merchant
mint drop
monetary
moneybag
moneybox
monopoly
mortgage
net price
net worth
no charge
notation
notecase
oddments
off price
on credit
on demand
on strike
operator
opulence
ordinary
overhaul
overhead
overseer
overtime
par value
passbook
pawn shop
pay talks
pin money
pipeline
pittance
position
post paid
poundage
practice
premises
price cut
price war
proceeds
producer
property
prospect
purchase
put price
quit rent
rack rent
rag trade
rainy day
receipts
reckoner
recorder
recovery
refinery
register
regrater
rent-free
rent roll
requital
reserves
retailer
retainer
richesse
richling
round lot
round sum
rush hour
salaried
saleroom
salesman
salt down
sanction
scalping
scarcity
schedule
security
self-made
shipment
shipyard
shopping
short-run
showcase
showroom
sideline
sinecure
small sum
soft cell
solatium
solidity
solvency
spending
spot cash
spot sale

square up
sterling
sundries
supertax
supplies
swapping
takeover
tallyman
taxation
tax dodge
taxpayer
time bill
tolbooth
tool shop
toolwork
top price
trade gap
trade off
treasure
Treasury
turnover
underbid
undercut
usufruct
valorize
valuable
venality
vendible
vocation
wash sale
watchdog
well-to-do
wharfage
workaday
work late
workroom

workshop
write off
absconder
ad valorem
affiliate
affluence
aggregate
allowance
amount due
appraisal
arbitrage
arrearage
avocation
back shift
bad cheque
bank clerk
bank stock
barrow boy
bartering
bear panic
blind pool
board room
bond issue
bon marché
bonus bond
borrowing
box office
brand name
breadline
brokerage
bucketing
bull panic
buy in bulk
by auction
by-bidding
by-product

cable code
cable rate
call price
cash grain
catalogue
cellarage
cheapjack
check rate
clearance
clientage
clientele
co-emption
coin money
commodity
costerman
cost price
craftsman
death duty
debenture
deduction
defaulter
deflation
depositor
dime store
directors
direct tax
dirt cheap
discharge
dishonour
dismissal
dollar gap
draw wages
drug store
easy money
easy terms
economics

economies
economise
emolument
establish
exchequer
exciseman
excise tax
executive
expansion
expensive
exploiter
export tax
extortion
face value
fair price
fair trade
fat profit
fiat money
financial
financier
firm offer
firm price
flash note
flat broke
flotation
free trade
full purse
gilt-edged
going rate
gold piece
good price
greenback
guarantee
guarantor
half-price
handiwork

hard goods
hard money
head buyer
heavy cost
high price
high value
holy stone
hot market
hush money
import tax
in arrears
incentive
income tax
in deficit
indemnity
inflation
insolvent
insurance
in the city
invention
inventory
job of work
joint bank
keep books
knock down
late shift
legal bond
liability
life's work
liquidate
list price
long purse
lossmaker
low-priced
luxury tax
mail order

make a sale
market day
marketing
means test
middleman
moneybags
money belt
mortgagee
mortgager
neat price
negotiate
net income
night safe
officiate
off market
on account
on the nail
operative
order book
outgoings
out of debt
out of work
outworker
overdraft
overdrawn
overheads
overspend
patronage
patronize
pay dearly
pay in kind
paymaster
pecuniary
pecunious
penniless
penny wise

petty|cash
piecework
piggy|bank
plutocrat
poorly|off
portfolio
pound|note
pourboire
practical
priceless
price|list
price|ring
price|rise
prime|cost
principal
profiteer
promotion
purchaser
qualified
quittance
quotation
ratepayer
ready|cash
real|wages
recession
reckoning
reduction
redundant
reference
refinance
reflation
registrar
reimburse
repayment
resources
restraint

sacrifice
sale|block
salesgirl
sales|talk
secretary
sell|short
shift|work
shop|floor
short|sale
short|side
sight|bill
single|tax
situation
soft|goods
sole|agent
soundness
speculate
spendings
spot|grain
spot|price
stability
stamp|duty
statement
stock|list
stockpile
stock|rate
strike|pay
strongbox
subsidize
substance
sumptuary
surcharge
sweatshop
sweet|shop
syndicate
synthetic

take|stock
tax|return
technical
the|actual
the|market
the|street
tie-in|sale
timocracy
tollbooth
trade|fair
trademark
trade|name
trade|sale
tradesman
traffic|in
treadmill
treasurer
undersell
union|card
unit|trust
unsalable
unskilled
up|for|sale
utilities
utterance
valuation
vendition
wage|claim
wage|scale
warehouse
wash|sales
wealth|tax
well-lined
whitewash
wholesale
work|force

workhouse
work|study
World|Bank
acceptance
accountant
accounting
accumulate
adjustment
advertiser
appreciate
apprentice
assessment
assignment
at|a|bargain
at|a|premium
at|the|spear
auctioneer
auction|off
automation
average|out
bank|credit
bankruptcy
bearer|bond
bear|market
best|seller
bill|broker
bill|of|sale
blood|money
bondholder
bonus|stock
bookkeeper
bucket|shop
bulk|buying
buy|and|sell
buy|futures
calculator
capitalism
capitalist
capitalize
chain|banks
chain|store
chancellor
chargeable
chargehand
cheapening
cheap|skate
cheque|book
chrematist
chrysology
closed|shop
closing|bid
collateral
colporteur
commercial
commission
compensate
conference
consortium
contraband
cost|centre
coupon|bond
credit|card
credit|slip
curb|broker
curb|market
daily|bread
dead|market
deep|in|debt
defalcator
defrayment
del|credere
demand|bill
department
depository
depreciate
depression
direct|cost
dirty|money
dividend|on
dollar|bill
dummy|share
Dutch|treat
easy|market
economizer
efficiency
employment
encumbered
end|product
enterprise
estate|duty
Eurodollar
evaluation
ex|dividend
exorbitant
exposition
false|money
fancy|goods
fancy|price
fancy|stock
filthy|rich
first|offer
fiscal|year
fixed|price
fixed|trust
flat|market
floor|price
forced|sale
free|gratis

free market
free sample
free trader
freightage
full stocks
funded debt
give credit
gold nugget
go on strike
go shopping
government
green pound
grindstone
half stocks
handicraft
hand market
have in hand
head office
heavy purse
high-priced
hold office
honorarium
import duty
imposition
in business
income bond
incumbered
incur a debt
industrial
insolvency
instalment
in the black
in the money
investment
job-hunting
joint bonds
joint-stock
jumble sale
laboratory
lighterage
liquidator
livelihood
living wage
loan market
long market
long seller
loss leader
management
man of means
marked down
marketable
market hall
mass market
meal ticket
member bank
mercantile
merchantry
Midas touch
monetarism
monetarist
moneyed man
money order
monopolist
monopolise
moratorium
negotiable
never never
nightshift
nominal fee
nominal par
nonpayment
note of hand
numismatic
obligation
occupation
off licence
oil of palms
on the block
on the cheap
on the rocks
on the shelf
opening bid
open market
out of funds
overcharge
paper money
pawnbroker
peppercorn
percentage
picket duty
pig in a poke
pilot plant
plutocracy
pocketbook
power plant
pre-emption
preference
prepayment
price index
price level
printworks
Prix unique
production
profession
profitable
prospector
prospectus
prosperity

provide|for
purchasing
pure|profit
put|and|call
ration|book
ready|money
real|estate
recompense
recoupment
redeemable
redundancy
remittance
remunerate
repair|shop
reparation
repository
repurchase
retail|shop
retirement
rock|bottom
round|trade
run|up|a|bill
salability
sales|force
saving|bank
saving|game
scrip|issue
second,hand
securities
serial|bond
settlement
settle|with
share|index
shoestring
shopkeeper
shop|window
short|bonds
sick|market
skilled|man
slave|trade
slow|market
smart|money
soft|market
sole|agency
speciality
speculator
split|shift
spondulies
statistics
steelworks
steep|price
stock|issue
stockpiles
stony|broke
straitened
stronghold
strongroom
sum|of|money
swap|horses
take|a|flier
taskmaster
tax|evation
technician
technocrat
the|needful
thin|margin
Third|World
ticker|tape
tour|of|duty
trade|board
trade|cycle
trade|guild
trade|price
trade|route
trade|union
treaty|port
typewriter
typing|pool
underwrite
unemployed
upset|price
wad|of|notes
wage|freeze
wage|policy
walk|of|life
Wall|Street
waterworks
wealthy|man
well|afford
well,heeled
wholesaler
window,shop
working|day
work|to|rule
written|off
accountancy
account|book
acquittance
advertising
agriculture
antique|shop
appointment
asking|price
association
at|face|value
auction|ring
bank|account
bank|balance

TRADE

bank|holiday
bank|manager
bank|of|issue
Barclaycard
bargain|sale
bear|account
bear|the|cost
betting|shop
big|business
billionaire
bill|of|costs
black|market
blank|cheque
bonus|scheme
book,keeping
bottom|price
bread|winner
brisk|market
budget|price
bull|account
businessman
capital|gain
carbon|paper
cash|account
catallactic
caught|short
central|bank
certificate
chamberlain
chancellery
chemist|shop
chrysocracy
circulation
closing|down
come|to|terms
commodities
common|stock
company|rule
competition
competitive
comptometer
consumption
cool|million
co,operative
co,operative
copperworks
corn|in|Egypt
corporation
cost,benefit
counterfeit
cover|charge
cum|dividend
custom|house
customs|duty
danger|money
defence|bond
delinquence
demand|curve
demarcation
deposit|slip
devaluation
display|case
distributor
dividend|off
double|entry
down|payment
drive|a|trade
earn|a|living
economic|law
economic|man
economy|size
embarrassed
endorsement
established
estate|agent
expenditure
fabrication
fetch|a|price
filthy|lucre
fixed|assets
fixed|income
floor|broker
floor|trader
fluctuation
foot|the|bill
foreclosure
free|harbour
future|grain
future|price
gingerbread
gross|income
hard|bargain
high|finance
horse|market
hypermarket
impecunious
indirect|tax
industrials
inexpensive
institution
intercourse
ironmongery
joint|return
key|industry
king's|ransom
lap|of|luxury
legal|tender
liberty|bond

life savings
line of goods
liquidation
local branch
local office
long account
long service
loose change
machine-made
machine shop
made of money
manufactory
manufacture
market place
market price
mass-produce
merchandise
millionaire
minimum wage
mint of money
money broker
money dealer
moneylender
money's-worth
money to burn
negotiation
nest factory
net interest
net receipts
nuisance tax
numismatics
on easy terms
on good terms
on the market
open account
open-end bond
out of pocket
outstanding
overpayment
package deal
paper credit
partnership
pay cash down
pay on demand
pay spot cash
pay the piper
piece of work
pilot scheme
place of work
pocket money
polytechnic
possessions
postal order
pots of money
poverty line
poverty trap
premium bond
pretty penny
price-fixing
price freeze
price spiral
price ticket
property tax
proposition
provided for
purchase tax
put-up market
Queer Street
quoted price
raw material
reserve bank
resignation
restriction
retiring age
risk capital
rummage sale
run into debt
safe deposit
sales ledger
sales person
savings bank
self-service
sell at a loss
sell forward
sell futures
sharebroker
shareholder
share ledger
shopping bag
short change
short seller
single entry
sinking fund
slot machine
small change
small trader
sole emption
speculation
sponsorship
stagflation
stockbroker
stock dealer
stockholder
stockjobber
stock ledger
stock market
stockpiling
stocktaking

storekeeper
subsistence
supermarket
take|home|pay
take|over|bid
Tattersall's
tax|assessor
tax|gatherer
technocracy
the|have|nots
tight|budget
tight|market
time|bargain
tired|market
to|the|tune|of
trade|school
trading|post
transaction
travel|agent
truck|system
undercharge
underwriter
vendibility
wherewithal
working|life
workmanlike
workmanship
works|outing
world|market
active|market
ad|valorem|tax
amalgamation
amortization
amortizement
arithmometer
assembly|line
auction|stand
balance|sheet
bank|examiner
bargain|offer
bargain|price
barter|system
be|in|business
bill|of|lading
board|meeting
Board|of|Trade
bond|to|bearer
bottom|dollar
bottomry|bond
branch|office
broker's|agent
brokers|board
business|deal
business|life
businesslike
buyer's|market
buying|public
callable|bond
capital|gains
capital|goods
capital|stock
cash|and|carry
cash|register
casual|labour
catallactics
circular|note
clearing|bank
closing|price
common|market
compensation
consumer|good
cook|the|books
costermonger
cost|of|living
counting|room
credit|rating
critical|path
currency|note
current|price
customs|union
denomination
depreciation
direct|labour
disbursement
discount|rate
distribution
dollar|crisis
durable|goods
Dutch|auction
early|closing
earned|income
econometrics
economy|drive
entrepreneur
exchange|rate
exhaust|price
extend|credit
extravagance
fair|exchange
fill|an|office
first|refusal
fiscal|policy
fixed|capital
floating|debt
folding|money
foreign|trade
gate|receipts
general|store

get|rich|quick
going|concern
gold|standard
goods|for|sale
great|expense
haberdashery
hard|currency
high,pressure
hire|purchase
hungry|market
impulse|buyer
in|conference
indebtedness
interest|rate
internal|bond
in|the|gazette
joint|account
keep|accounts
labour|of|love
laissez,faire
leather|goods
line|of|credit
live|in|clover
lively|market
long|interest
make|a|bargain
make|a|fortune
make|delivery
make|one's|pile
manipulation
manufacturer
marginal|cost
mass,produced
mercantilism
monetization
money|changer
money|matters
mortgage|bond
national|bank
nearest|offer
nine|till|five
nominal|price
nominal|value
nouveau|riche
odd,lot|dealer
offered|price
offer|for|sale
office|junior
open,end|trust
opening|price
organization
packing|house
pay|as|you|earn
pay|in|advance
pegged|market
peg|the|market
ply|one's|trade
porte,monnaie
pressure|belt
price|ceiling
price|control
price|current
price|of|money
price|rigging
productivity
professional
profiteering
profit|margin
profit|motive
purse|strings
rags|to|riches
rate|of|growth
redeployment
regional|bank
remuneration
remunerative
reserve|price
retaining|fee
retrenchment
rigged|market
rig|the|market
rising|prices
rolling|stock
rubber|cheque
sale|by|outcry
sale|or|return
sales|gimmick
sales|manager
salesmanship
satisfaction
sell|on|credit
severance|pay
share|company
shareholding
short|account
show|business
slender|means
sliding|scale
state|lottery
steady|market
sterling|area
stock|company
stock|dealing
stockholding
stock|in|trade
stockjobbery
street|market
strike|action

strike it rich
strong market
superannuate
sustain a loss
tax collector
tax exemption
ten cent store
the long green
ticker market
trade balance
trade mission
trading stamp
travel agency
treasury bill
treasury note
trial balance
trustee stock
unemployment
variety store
watered stock
Welfare State
without a bean
working class
working order
advertisement
asset stripper
bank messenger
Bank of England
bank overdraft
bank statement
budget account
budget surplus
bulls and bears
burial society
business hours
cash dispenser
cash in advance
cash on the nail
clearance sale
clearing house
commercialism
commercialist
company report
concessionary
confetti money
confidence man
consumer goods
copartnership
cost effective
counting house
credit account
credit balance
credit company
credit squeeze
crossed cheque
current assets
depressed area
discount house
discount store
excess profits
eye to business
falling prices
filing cabinet
financial year
fire insurance
free trade area
fringe benefit
going for a song
impulse buying
incorporation
industrialism
in Queer Street

life assurance
life insurance
Lombard Street
man of business
millionairess
modernisation
money no object
multinational
multiple store
Parkinson's Law
payment in kind
payment in lieu
penalty clause
petticoat lane
price increase
private income
private sector
profitability
profit and loss
profit sharing
protectionism
protectionist
public company
purchase price
raise the money
rate for the job
rates and taxes
regular income
sellers market
service charge
small business
small investor
spending spree
stock exchange
strike breaker
subcontractor
tax-deductible
trade discount
trade unionism
trade unionist
trading estate
value added tax
white elephant
wild-cat strike
accident policy
asset stripping
balance of trade
bargain counter
bill discounter
capitalisation
cash on delivery
certain annuity
clearance house
company meeting
concessionaire
consumer demand
corporation tax
cost accountant
cost accounting
cost efficiency
current account
deposit account
direct-debiting
discount broker
distressed area
expense account
eye for business
family business
finance company
free enterprise
free of interest
full employment

gnomes of Zurich
holding company
imprest account
inertia selling
letter of credit
lighting-up time
limited company
Lloyd's register
market research
mass production
merchant banker
monthly payment
national income
national wealth
ordinary shares
overproduction
over the counter
penny-in-the-slot
peppercorn rent
Peter principle
private company
production line
pyramid selling
quality control
rate of exchange
rate of interest
second-hand shop
shopping centre
simple interest
superannuation
surrender value
tariff reformer
three-mile limit
under the hammer
unearned income
vending machine
vested interest
visible exports
window shopping
working capital
American Express
bargain basement
building society
business as usual
business circles
business contact
business manager
business studies
business venture
capital gains tax
carriage forward
cash transaction
closing-down sale
commission agent
company director
company promoter
complete annuity
cottage industry
deferred annuity
deferred payment
department store
development area
distress warrant
dividend warrant
do a roaring trade
electricity bill
endowment policy
entrepreneurial
exchange control
family allowance
floating capital
foreign exchange

15 LETTERS

franking machine
friendly society
golden handshake
income tax demand
income tax rebate
income tax relief
income tax return
insurance broker
insurance policy
investment trust
invisible import
labour intensive
lightning strike
marine insurance
money for old rope
national savings
no claim discount
non profit making
preference stock
public ownership
purchasing power
registration fee
regular customer
reserve currency
rock bottom price
service industry
settle an account
sleeping partner
supply and demand
suspense account
under the counter
unemployment pay
world of commerce

Transport and Communications

A1	cab	guy	leg	rut	UFO
AA	cam	HMS	log	sea	van
go	car	hop	map	ski	via
GT	cat	hoy	MOT	SOS	way
M1	cog	hub	mph	STD	yaw
ABC	cox	jet	oar	sub	ahoy
ace	fan	jib	oil	tar	A one
aft	fin	jog	ply	ton	auto
air	fly	key	ram	top	axle
ark	gad	lag	rev	tow	back
bay	gas	lap	rig	tub	bail
bus	gig	lee	run	tug	bank

bark
beak
beam
bend
biga
bike
bitt
blip
boat
boom
boot
brig
bunk
buoy
buss
cart
case
code
cork
crew
curb
dash
deck
dhow
dial
dive
dock
dory
drag
draw
dray
duck
fare
fast
flee
flit
flow
ford
fore
fork
gaff
gait
gear
gyro
hack
haul
head
heel
helm
hike
hold
hood
horn
hove
hulk
hull
idle
jack
jeep
junk
keel
kerb
kite
knot
land
lane
lift
line
list
lock
loop
lost
luff
Mach
mail
mast
mini
moke
mole
moor
navy
nose
oars
pace
park
pass
path
pier
poop
port
post
pram
prop
prow
pull
punt
push
quay
raft
rail
reef
ride
ring
road
roam
roll
rove
saic
sail
salt
scow
ship
sink
skid
skip
skis
sled
span
spar
spin
stay
stem
step
tack
tail
tank
taxi
tide
toll
tour
tram
trap
trek
trim
trip
trot
tube
tyre
vang
veer
vent
wain
wake
walk
warp
wash
wire
yard
yawl
zoom
abaft
afoot
afoul
alley
aloft
amble
araba
avion
awash
balsa
barge
beach
below
berth
bilge
blimp
board
bosun
brail
brake
buggy
byway
cabby
cabin
cable
canal
canoe
cargo
choke
chute
cleat
climb
coach
coast
coble
coupe
craft
crank
crash
crate
cycle
dandy
davit
ditch
dodge
dolly
drift
drive
drome
E-boat
embus
facia
fanal
ferry
flare
fleet
flier
float
flota
fluke
foist
forth
glide
going
guard
guide

haste
hatch
hawse
hiker
hobby
hoist
horse
hurry
jaunt
jetty
jolly
jumbo
kayak
kedge
ketch
lay|by
leech
lie|to
light
liner
loran
lorry
march
morse
motor
mount
naval
nomad
on|tow
orbit
pedal
pilot
pitch
plane
praam
prang
pylon
Q|boat
racer
radar
radio
rally
range
reach
relay
rev|up
rider
ropes
rotor
route
royal
sally
screw
sedan
shaft
sheer
sheet
shell
shift
shunt
sidle
skiff
skirt
skull
slips
sloop
smack
smash
spars
speed
spill
sprit
stage
stall
stamp
start
steam
stern
stray
strip
strut
stunt
sweep
Telex
thole
ton|up
track
trail
train
tramp
tread
trike
truck
trunk
U|boat
umiak
U|turn
valve
visit
way|in
wharf
wheel
xebec
yacht
Z|bend
aboard
abroad
access
adrift
afloat
airbus
airing
air|log
airman
air|ram
airway
alight
anchor
argosy
armada
arrive
artery
ascent
astern
avenue
aweigh
back|up
banger
bargee
barque
barrow
basket
bateau
beacon
berlin
big|end
bireme
boatel
bomber
bonnet
bowser
braces
bridge
bucket
bumper
busman
by|lane
by|pass
bypath
byroad
caique
calash
call|up
camber
canard
canter
canvas
careen
career
carfax
carina
chaise
clutch
coaler
cobble
cockle
conner
con|rod
convoy
copter
course
cruise
cut|out
cutter
decked
de|icer
depart
detour
dinghy
divert

diving
dogger
driver
dry|run
dugout
earing
egress
elevon
embark
engine
escape
exodus
fender
fiacre
flight
flying
fo'c'sle
funnel
galiot
galley
gallop
garage
gas|jet
gasket
glider
gocart
gunnel
hangar
hansom
haul|to
hawser
hearse
hooker
hot|rod
hove|to
hubcap

hurtle
hustle
idling
impact
intake
in|trim
island
jalopy
jet|lag
jetsam
jet|set
jib|guy
jigger
jostle
junket
kit|bag
klaxon
landau
lascar
lateen
launch
leeway
letter
litter
lock|up
lorcha
lugger
mahout
marina
marker
mayday
mirror
mizzen
mobile
module
motion

nip|off
nose|up
octane
on|deck
one|way
on|foot
onward
outing
outset
oxcart
packet
paddle
petrol
pharos
pickup
pile|up
piston
porter
propel
pursue
radial
ramble
ram|jet
randem
rating
ratlin
reefer
return
rigged
rigger
ring|up
rocket
rudder
runner
runway
sailor

saloon
sampan
sculls
seaman
seaway
sender
set|out
sheets
shoran
shroud
siding
signal
skates
skyway
sledge
sleigh
smoker
sortie
sparks
spiral
splice
spring
stocks
stoker
strake
street
stride
stroll
subway
surrey
swerve
tackle
tandem
tanker
tannoy
tartan

tender
ticker
ticket
tiller
timber
tin|can
toddle
toggle
torque
totter
towbar
travel
troika
trudge
tunnel
turret
unmoor
valise
vessel
volant
voyage
waggon
wander
way|out
whaler
wherry
whisky
address
aerobus
aground
aileron
air|base
airboat
air|crew
airdrop
air|flow
airfoil
air|jump
air|lane
air|legs
airlift
airline
air|miss
airpark
airport
airship
airsick
air|taxi
ambages
arrival
autobus
autocar
autovac
aviator
aviette
baby,jib
baggage
bail|out
ballast
balloon
banking
barge|in
battery
bay,line
beeline
bicycle
biplane
birdman
blister
boating
boatman
bobstay
bollard
bomb|bay
booking
booster
bow|fast
bowline
boxhaul
box,kite
boxseat
britzka
bulwark
busline
bus|stop
buzzing
buzz|off
caboose
call|box
capsize
capstan
capsule
captain
caravan
caravel
cariole
carpark
carport
carrack
carrier
catboat
cat,head
cat's,eye
catwalk
channel
chariot
charter
chassis
chopper
chutist
circuit
clipper
coaster
cockpit
collide
collier
commute
compass
contact
co,pilot
coracle
courier
crack,up
crewman
crock,up
cruiser
cyclist
day|trip
descent
detrain
dodgems
dogcart
draught
drayman
dredger
drifter
drive,in
droshky
dry|dock
dry|land
ejector
emplane
engaged
en|route

entrain
exhaust
explore
express
fairing
fairway
felucca
fetch|up
flattop
flivver
flyboat
flyover
fly|past
foretop
formula
founder
four-oar
freeway
frigate
frogman
futtock
galleon
galleys
gangway
gearbox
getaway
get|lost
gliding
go|ahead
go|below
go|by|air
go-devil
gondola
grapnel
growler
guichet
gunboat
gun|deck
guy-rope
gyro-car
hackney
halyard
hammock
handbag
harbour
hardtop
harness
haywain
head|for
head|off
headset
headway
heave|to
helibus
helipad
highway
holdall
hot|line
hurry|up
iceboat
impetus
impulse
ingress
Jack|Tar
jaw|rope
jet|pipe
jib|boom
jibstay
journey
joy|ride
keelson
keep|off
killick
killock
landing
lanyard
L|driver
learner
lee|helm
lee|tack
leeward
leewide
lift-off
lighter
logbook
L|plates
luggage
lugsail
lymphad
Mae|West
magneto
mail|van
maintop
make|for
make|off
man-o|war
mariner
marline
Martian
matelot
meander
migrant
milk|run
minibus
minicab
minicar
minisub
mission
monitor
mooring
mud|hook
nacelle
no|entry
oarsman
odyssey
offside
old|salt
omnibus
on|board
ongoing
on|the|go
opening
orbital
outride
painter
parking
parting
passage
pathway
payload
phaeton
pig|boat
pillion
pinnace
piragua
pirogue
polacca
polacre
pontoon
postage
postman
precede
proceed
Pullman

pullout
pushcar
railway
ratline
rebound
reentry
retrace
retreat
reverse
rideout
rigging
ringoff
ripcord
roadhog
roadmap
roadtax
rolling
ropetow
ropeway
rowboat
rowlock
runaway
runinto
runners
sailing
satchel
saunter
scamper
scooter
scupper
scuttle
sealane
sealegs
seasick
seaward
sendoff
setsail
shallop
shipway
shuttle
sidecar
skidpan
skipper
skysail
sleeper
slipway
smashup
spanker
sputnik
starter
startup
station
steamer
steward
stopway
surface
sweeper
swifter
tackler
tailend
tailfin
takeoff
tartane
taxicab
taxiing
taxiway
telpher
Telstar
termini
testhop
tilbury
tohorse
tonneau
topdeck
topmast
topsail
topside
torsion
tourist
towards
towboat
towpath
towrope
tractor
traffic
trailer
traipse
tramcar
tramway
transit
travels
trawler
tripper
trireme
trolley
trundle
trysail
tugboat
tumbrel
tumbril
turning
twinjet
vagrant
vehicle
viaduct
visavis
visitor
voiture
volante
voyager
wanigan
warship
waybill
wayfare
wayworn
welcome
winging
wingtip
wrecker
yardarm
zooming
aerodyne
aerofoil
aerogram
aeronaut
aerostat
airborne
airbrake
aircoach
aircraft
airfield
airframe
airliner
airroute
airscout
airscrew
airspace
airspeed
airstrip
airwoman
allatsea
alleyway
altitude
approach

TRANSPORT AND COMMUNICATIONS

area|code
arterial
at|anchor
autobahn
autogyro
aviation
aviatrix
backfire
back|seat
backstay
backwash
bargeman
barnacle
barouche
beam|ends
bearings
becalmed
bilander
binnacle
black|box
boat|deck
boat|hook
boat|line
bodywork
bolt|rope
bowsprit
Bradshaw
brancard
broach|to
brougham
bulkhead
bulwarks
cabin|boy
cable|car
cableway
camshaft
caracole
carriage
cast|away
catapult
cat's|eyes
causeway
clarence
clearway
coachbox
coachman
coachway
coasting
cockboat
commuter
Concorde
converge
corridor
corvette
coxswain
crabbing
crescent
crossing
crossply
cruising
cul-de-sac
curricle
cylinder
dahabeah
deck|hand
derelict
dipstick
dismount
ditty|bag
downhaul
dragoman
dragster
drag|wire
driftway
drive|off
driveway
dust|cart
eight-oar
elevator
emigrant
emigrate
entrance
envelope
equipage
Europort
evacuate
even|keel
exchange
excursus
fall|back
farewell
fast|line
ferryman
fireboat
flagging
flagship
flatboat
flat|spin
flat|tyre
floating
flotilla
flywheel
fogbound
footfall
footpath
footslog
footstep
forefoot
fore|jack
fore|lift
foremast
foresail
foreship
forestay
foretack
foreyard
forkroad
fuel|ship
full|load
fuselage
gad|about
galleass
garboard
gasoline
get|ahead
go|aboard
go|ashore
go|astray
go|before
go|by|rail
Godspeed
gradient
grounded
half|deck
handcart
hang|back
hatchway
hawse|bag
head|fast
head|into
heel|over
heliport
helmsman
highroad

8 LETTERS

high|seas
homeward
horse|box
horseman
icebound
ice|yacht
ignition
in|flight
in|motion
inner|jib
intercom
ironclad
jackstay
jerrican
jet|pilot
jet|plane
jet|power
jettison
journeys
joy|rider
joystick
jumbo|jet
junction
jurymast
jury|sail
kamikaze
keel|over
kickback
knapsack
land|ahoy
landfall
larboard
lateener
launcher
leeboard
lee|sheet

level|off
life|belt
lifeboat
life|buoy
life|line
life|raft
lift|wire
log|canoe
longbeat
longeron
long|haul
loose|box
mail|boat
main|deck
main|lift
mainline
mainmast
main|road
mainstay
main|yard
manifold
man|of|war
maritime
masthead
mine|ship
momentum
monorail
moon|base
moonsail
moon|ship
moonshot
moonwalk
moorings
motorbus
motorcar
motoring

motorist
motorway
muleteer
multi|jet
navarchy
nearside
nose|cone
nosedive
nose|down
nose|into
oil|gauge
old|crock
oleo|gear
oncoming
one|horse
on|the|run
open|road
operator
ordinary
outboard
outer|jib
overhaul
overland
overpass
overseas
overtake
overturn
passer|by
passover
passport
pavement
periplus
pilotage
platform
Plimsoll
poop|deck

porthole
portside
port|tack
post|boat
postcard
postcode
progress
pulsejet
puncture
pushcart
put|to|sea
quadriga
radiator
railroad
receiver
red|light
reef|band
reef|knot
rickshaw
ring|road
road|sign
roadster
rockaway
roof|rack
ropeband
ropework
rucksack
runabout
run|ahead
rush|hour
sailboat
sail|free
sail|loft
schedule
schooner
scout|car

seafarer
seagoing
seaplane
sea|route
set|forth
shanghai
sheerˌleg
sheer|off
ship|ahoy
shipmate
ship|oars
shipping
short|hop
shoulder
show|a|leg
showboat
side|road
sideslip
side|step
sidewalk
silencer
skidding
skid|mark
slip|road
slow|down
slow|lane
snap|roll
sociable
spaceman
spar|deck
speeding
squad|car
staff|car
stanhope
start|off
start|out
staysail
steerage
steering
sternway
stock|car
stopover
stowaway
straggle
straying
stunt|man
suitcase
tackling
tag|along
tail|boom
tailpipe
tail|skid
tail|spin
taxi|rank
telegram
teletype
terminal
terminus
tholeˌpin
throttle
toboggan
tollgate
tramline
traverse
tricycle
trimaran
trim|sail
trim|ship
turbojet
turn|away
turn|over
turnpike
under|way
unicycle
velocity
victoria
volatile
volplane
wagonˌlit
wardroom
warplane
water|bus
waterway
wayfarer
wayˌtrain
wear|ship
wheelies
wind|cone
wind|drag
wind|sock
windward
wing|over
wireless
withdraw
yachting
Zeppelin
zero|hour
aboutˌship
addressee
aerodrome
aeromotor
aeroplane
after|deck
air|bridge
air|pocket
air|sleeve
airworthy
all|aboard

9 LETTERS

altimeter
ambulance
amidships
amphibian
anchorage
applecart
astrodome
astronaut
atom|liner
autopilot
autopista
backropes
back|water
bandwagon
bargepole
basic|load
Bath|chair
below|deck
bilge|keel
bilge|pump
black|gang
blockship
blue|peter
boathouse
boatswain
boat|train
bobsleigh
bon|voyage
boulevard
bowl|along
box|waggon
broadside
bubble|car
bulldozer
bus|driver
cab|driver
cablegram
cabriolet
canalboat
cargo|boat
carpet|bag
cartwheel
catamaran
charabanc
chauffeur
chief|mate
clearance
clew|lines
coach|road
coachwork
collision
combat|car
concourse
conductor
cosmonaut
couchette
countdown
crankcase
crash|boat
crash|land
crocodile
crossjack
cross|road
crosstree
crowd|sail
crow's|nest
curbstone
cut|and|run
dashboard
Davy|Jones
day|letter
day|return
deceleron
departure
depot|ship
destroyer
diesel|oil
diligence
dining|car
dip|switch
direction
dirigible
dirt|track
disembark
diversion
dodgem|car
drag|force
drift|wire
drive|away
drop|a|line
duffel|bag
Early|Bird
earphones
empennage
escalator
esplanade
estate|car
excursion
extension
false|keel
family|car
fare|stage
ferryboat
first|mate
first|rate
flying|jib
footropes
forebrace

foreroyal
foresheet
freeboard
free|wheel
freighter
French|lug
front|seat
fuel|gauge
funicular
gain|speed
gallivant
gangplank
gather|way
gear|lever
ghost|ship
give|a|ring
globe-trot
go|aground
gondolier
goose|step
grand|tour
grapevine
gross|lift
groundhog
guard|ship
guard's|van
guess|warp
guest-rope
gyropilot
gyroplane
handbrake
hansom|cab
hatchback
haversack
hawse|hook
hawsepipe
headphone
helidrome
hit-and-run
hitch|hike
hoist|sail
hook|a|ride
horseback
houseboat
hump|speed
hydrofoil
ice|skates
immigrant
immigrate
inch|along
indicator
itinerant
itinerary
jaunty|car
jaywalker
jet|bomber
jollyboat
kerb|drill
kerbstone
kick|start
lag|behind
landaulet
landplane
land|rover
launching
launch|pad
leave|home
letter|box
leviathan
lightship
limousine
lose|speed
lower|boom
lower|deck
lunar|base
Mach|meter
mail|coach
mainbrace
mainroyal
mainsheet
major|road
make|haste
manoeuvre
mass|media
milestone
milkfloat
milometer
mine|layer
miss|stays
mizzentop
monoplane
moonraker
morse|code
motorbike
motorboat
motorcade
mule|train
multi-prop
navigable
navigator
newsflash
nosewheel
ocean|lane
ocean|trip
on|the|move
on|the|wing
orientate
orlop|deck

9 LETTERS

outrigger
overboard
overdrive
overshoot
pack|horse
palanquin
pancaking
parachute
party|line
passenger
patrol|car
periscope
phone|book
phone|call
pillar|box
pilot|boat
point|duty
police|car
police|van
portfolio
post|haste
postilion
powerboat
power|dive
pressgang
privateer
prize|crew
promenade
propeller
racing|car
radar|nose
radio|beam
radiogram
ram|rocket
reach|land
reef|point
river|boat
road|block
road|sense
roadstead
road|works
rocket|car
rocket|man
rotor|ship
round|trip
royal|mast
royal|road
royal|sail
rudder|bar
saddlebag
sailplane
sally|port
saloon|car
sand|yacht
satellite
saucerman
sea|anchor
seafaring
sea|gasket
seaworthy
semaphore
set|on|foot
sharp|bend
sheer|hulk
shipboard
ship|of|war
ship|plane
ship|route
ship's|crew
shipshape
shipwreck
sidelight
sidetrack
sight|land
sightseer
signal|box
signalman
single|jet
skyriding
slowcoach
slow|train
small|boat
snowshoes
sonic|boom
sonic|wall
space|crew
spacedock
spaceport
spaceship
space|suit
spacewalk
spare|part
speedboat
speedster
spinnaker
sports|car
spritsail
stage|boat
stanchion
starboard
stateroom
steal|away
steamboat
steam|line
steamship
steersman
step|aside
stern|fast

sternpost
stevedore
stokehold
storeship
storm|boat
stratojet
streetcar
stretcher
strike|out
stringers
sub,chaser
submarine
surfacing
surfboard
switch|off
tailboard
tail,light
tailplane
tail|rotor
tail|shaft
take|leave
taximeter
taxiplane
tea|waggon
telegraph
telemotor
telepathy
telephone
telephony
telephoto
test|pilot
third|mate
timenoguy
timetable
touch|down
traipsing
tramlines
transport
traveller
triptyque
troopship
trunk|call
trunk|line
trunk|road
turboprop
turbopump
turn|aside
turn|round
turret|top
twin,screw
two,seater
ufologist
underpass
under|sail
upper|deck
vehicular
war|galley
water|line
whaleback
whaleboat
wheel|base
wheel|spin
white|line
wirephoto
yachtsman
able|seaman
aboard|ship
access|road
adventurer
aerobatics
aeronautic
a|head|start
air|control
air|cruiser
air|hostess
air|service
air|steward
air|support
A1|at|Lloyd's
amber|light
ambulation
ambulatory
anchor|deck
antifreeze
automobile
ballooning
balloonist
ball|turret
barkentine
barrel,roll
batten|down
battleship
bear|down|on
Bermuda|rig
Black|Maria
blind|alley
boneshaker
branch|line
breakwater
bridge|deck
bridle|path
brigantine
bubble|hood
bucket|seat
bus|service
bus|station
cabin|plane
camouflage

cantilever
cargo plane
cast anchor
catch a crab
catch a ride
chapel cart
clear house
clew-garnet
coach horse
cockleboat
column gear
command car
congestion
connection
contraflow
control rod
conveyance
cosmodrome
country bus
covered way
cow catcher
crankshaft
crossroads
dandy horse
dawn rocket
day tripper
decampment
delta wings
dickey seat
disemplane
dive bomber
diving-bell
double bend
double-prop
double-reef
downstream
drift along
drift angle
drop anchor
dusk rocket
emigration
evacuation
expedition
expressway
fall behind
feed system
fire engine
first class
flight deck
flight path
flight plan
flight time
floatplane
fly-by-night
flying boat
flying wing
footbridge
fore and aft
forecastle
forerunner
foresheets
forge ahead
four-in-hand
four-master
gain ground
gather head
gear change
glass coach
go in the van
goods train
green light
ground crew
ground loop
hackney cab
hawsepiece
headlights
heatshield
heave round
heave short
helicopter
High street
hitch-hiker
hit the deck
home and dry
homecoming
hovercraft
hydroplane
icebreaker
inflatable
inter-urban
invalid car
jaywalking
jet fatigue
jet fighter
jigger mast
Jolly Roger
Joyce stick
juggernaut
jury rigged
jury rudder
knockabout
landing run
landlubber
lateen sail
lead the way
lettergram
lie athwart
life jacket

lighthouse
locomotion
luggage van
main artery
make tracks
manipulate
manoeuvres
marker buoy
martingale
middle deck
midshipman
mizzenmast
mizzen sail
mizzen stay
monkey deck
monkey rail
motorcoach
motorcycle
motor truck
naval cadet
navigation
nose turret
ocean-going
ocean liner
on a bowline
on the march
on the rocks
open waggon
outer space
overbridge
packet boat
packet line
packet ship
paddle boat
parcel post
pathfinder
patrol boat
pedestrian
Penny Black
petrol pump
petrol tank
picketboat
pilgrimage
pilothouse
pilot plane
pipe aboard
port anchor
port of call
post chaise
Post Office
propellant
propulsion
public walk
quadrireme
quadruplex
radial tyre
rear mirror
reduce sail
rendezvous
repair ship
rescue boat
rev counter
ride and tie
ride a storm
right of way
road safety
roadworthy
robot plane
rocket boat
rocket ship
rope bridge
roundabout
round-house
roustabout
rowing boat
safety belt
safety wire
sail teaser
sally forth
seamanship
second mate
sedan chair
sens unique
servo-pilot
set the pace
sheepshank
shipmaster
sidesaddle
side street
single-prop
skyscraper
sky writing
slipstream
sloop of war
smoking car
solo flight
spacecraft
spare wheel
speed limit
square away
square sail
stagecoach
stand first
state barge
static tube
step-rocket
stewardess
streamline

submariner
sun|compass
supercargo
supersonic
supply|ship
suspension
switchback
tachometer
tanker|ship
target|boat
tea|clipper
telegraphy
telepathic
television
telewriter
telpherage
test|flight
test|rocket
thumb|a|lift
ticker|tape
tip|up|lorry
toll|bridge
topgallant
touring|car
tracklayer
traffic|jam
train|ferry
trajectory
travelling
travel|sick
travel|worn
triaconter
triphibian
trolley|bus
true|course
turret|ship
two|wheeler
undershoot
under|steam
useful|lift
vanity|case
velocipede
veteran|car
V|formation
vintage|car
volitation
volplaning
wanderings
wanderlust
watercraft
water|plane
watertight
way|station
way|traffic
wheel|chair
wheelhouse
whirlybird
windjammer
windscreen
wing|mirror
abandon|ship
accelerator
aeronautics
afterburner
after|shroud
air|controls
airsickness
air|terminal
air|umbrella
anchor|fluke
armoured|car
articulated
assault|boat
attack|plane
balloon|sail
battleplane
beaten|track
belaying|pin
bid|farewell
blind|corner
blind|flying
break|ground
built|up|area
bullock|cart
carburetter
card|compass
carriageway
carrick|bend
catch|a|train
caterpillar
cat's|whisker
centreboard
close|hauled
club|topsail
coach|driver
cockleshell
combat|plane
come|forward
compartment
contraprops
convertible
country|road
cover|ground
crash|helmet
crash|waggon
crowd|of|sail
delivery|van
destination

distributor
double march
dreadnought
driving test
ejector seat
engaged line
engine gauge
entrainment
escape hatch
escape route
exhaust pipe
fares please
find one's way
fishing boat
fishing dory
fishtailing
fleet of foot
flight strip
flying kites
flying speed
flying visit
forced march
fore-topsail
forward deck
galley slave
gather speed
get under way
go alongside
goods waggon
go overboard
Gran Turismo
ground speed
gyrocompass
hawse timber
head for home
highway code
hit the trail
horse litter
hug the shore
ignition key
immigration
interceptor
in the saddle
in the wake of
jaunting car
journeyings
journey's end
kedge anchor
keep station
kite balloon
laminar flow
landing deck
landing skis
lazy painter
leading edge
leave-taking
limber board
line engaged
loop the loop
lorry driver
lose one's way
luggage rack
lunar module
magic carpet
main skysail
main topsail
make headway
make sea room
make strides
man from Mars
merchantman
mess steward
minesweeper
mizzen-royal
montgolfier
moon landing
moon station
mooring buoy
mooring mast
morse signal
Moses basket
motor launch
motor vessel
mystery tour
naval rating
naval vessel
near the wind
night letter
orientation
ornithopter
out-of-the-way
outside loop
package tour
paddle wheel
parachutist
paratrooper
penteconter
peregrinate
peripatetic
petrol gauge
phone number
pick up speed
pillion seat
pony and trap
portmanteau
private line
push bicycle
put into port

quarter deck
quarterjack
quinquereme
racing shell
radio beacon
radio mirror
request stop
rescue plane
reservation
retroaction
retro-rocket
reverse turn
road haulage
road licence
road traffic
rocket motor
rocket plane
rocket power
rotorblades
running knot
sailing boat
sailing ship
scuttlebutt
search plane
seasickness
second class
self starter
send packing
set in motion
Shanks's mare
Shanks's pony
sheet anchor
shelter deck
ship the oars
shroud lines
shuttle trip
sightseeing
sinking ship
skysail mast
sleeping bag
sleeping car
soft landing
solar rocket
space centre
space flight
space island
space patrol
space rocket
space travel
spanker boom
spanker gaff
speedometer
stagger wire
standing lug
steal a march
steam engine
steam launch
step rockets
stern anchor
stern sheets
straphanger
string along
stunt flying
submersible
subsonic jet
switchboard
synchromesh
tailless jet
take the lead
tandem plane
telecontrol
teleprinter
telpher line
testing area
three-in-hand
three-master
ticking over
torpedo boat
trafficator
transmitter
transporter
travel agent
true heading
trysail gaff
tube station
under canvas
underground
vapour train
waggon trail
waggon wheel
waiting-room
walking tour
weather deck
weather side
weigh anchor
wheelbarrow
wing loading
wrong number
aircraftsman
airfreighter
air-sea rescue
all systems go
approach road
arrester hook
arterial road
autorotation
baby carriage
Bailey bridge

beaching|gear
beacon|lights
bearing|plate
belly|landing
between,decks
blind|landing
cabin|cruiser
cable|railway
caulking|iron
centre|anchor
change|course
channel|patch
chart|a|course
citizen's|band
clear|the|land
coach,and,four
coach,and,pair
coachbuilder
companionway
conning|tower
control|stick
control|tower
counter|march
crash|barrier
crash|landing
cylinder|head
desobligeant
dialling|code
dialling|tone
dispatch|boat
double,decker
draught|horse
dual|controls
East|Indiaman
ejection|seat
end|of|the|line
entrance|lock
escape|rocket
fighter|pilot
fishing|fleet
fishing|smack
flight|tester
flying|circus
flying|saucer
flying|tanker
forestaysail
forward|march
free,wheeling
freight|train
fuel|injector
Gladstone|bag
glide|landing
globetrotter
go|by|the|board
ground|tester
hackney|coach
happy|landing
harbour|light
heavy|cruiser
hedgehopping
hospital|ship
inclinometer
in|the|train|of
inverted|spin
Jacob's|ladder
jet|propelled
king's|highway
landing|craft
landing|field
landing|light
landing|speed
landing|stage
landing|strip
launching|pad
level|landing
light|cruiser
long|distance
longshoreman
lost|and|found
luggage|label
luggage|train
maiden|flight
maiden|voyage
main|staysail
make|good|time
make|progress
manned|rocket
man|overboard
merchant|ship
monkey,rigged
motor|scooter
night|fighter
off|like|a|shot
overnight|bag
pantechnicon
parking|light
parking|meter
parking|orbit
passing|place
perambulator
petty|officer
pilot|balloon
plain|sailing
platform|deck
pleasure|boat
pleasure|trip
Plimsoll|line
Plimsoll|mark

postage stamp
pressure suit
puddle jumper
pursuit plane
quarterlight
radar scanner
radar station
radio compass
radio monitor
radio station
raise the dead
return ticket
ride at anchor
ride bareback
road junction
rocket assist
rocket engine
rocket glider
roller skates
rolling stock
rolling stone
rough passage
running board
running light
sailing barge
sailing canoe
sailing yacht
season ticket
shape a course
shipping line
shoot ballast
single-decker
slacken speed
sonic barrier
sound barrier
space capsule
space station
spanker sheet
sparking plug
speed of sound
square-rigged
square-rigger
stall landing
steer clear of
steering gear
stream anchor
streamlining
Sunday driver
sunshine roof
survival suit
take bearings
take-off strip
tallyho coach
tearing hurry
tender rocket
the bitter end
thoroughfare
three-wheeler
through train
ticket office
touch the wind
tourist class
traffic light
train service
transmission
travel agency
trolley track
tubeless tyre
upset the boat
utility plane
VIP transport
walk the plank

Wandering Jew
weatherboard
weather sheet
windward side
aerial railway
armoured train
begging letter
Belisha beacon
booking office
breakdown gang
bridge of sighs
bush telegraph
carriage drive
Channel tunnel
coach building
command module
communication
conducted tour
conductor rail
container port
container ship
corridor train
distant signal
driving lesson
driving mirror
driving school
electric train
excess luggage
express letter
flying machine
foot passenger
forced landing
globe trotting
ground control
homeward bound
horse and buggy
jet propulsion
landing ground
left hand drive
level crossing
number engaged
paddle steamer
panda crossing
penny farthing
peregrination
peripatetical
petrol station
pontoon bridge
postal address
postal service
poste restante
power steering
press campaign
press cuttings
pressure cabin
printing press
promenade deck
public address
public highway
Queen's highway
radiotelegram
railway engine
railway system
railway tunnel
restaurant car
return journey
road transport
roller coaster
roll on roll off
rule of the road
sailing orders
scenic railway

shock absorber
shooting brake
space platform
speed merchant
station master
steering wheel
stepping stone
strato-cruiser
telegraph pole
telegraph wire
telephone book
telephone call
telephone line
through ticket
traffic island
traffic lights
transportable
transport cafe
transport ship
transshipping
trunk dialling
turning circle
turn the corner
unadopted road
undercarriage
zebra crossing
automatic pilot
breakdown truck
catenary system
coaling station
dead man's handle
diesel-electric
disembarkation
excursion train
filling station
first class mail
first class post
flight recorder
floating bridge
full steam ahead
inland waterway
luggage carrier
no thoroughfare
observation car
package holiday
passenger train
personal column
person to person
platform ticket
quarantine flag
radiotelegraph
radiotelephone
rear-view mirror
registered mail
registered post
reversing light
road traffic act
running repairs
service station
shuttle service
space traveller
steering column
telegraph cable
telephone kiosk
telephotograph
three-point turn
three-speed gear
through traffic
traction engine
traffic manager
traffic signals
transportation

trustee|account
wild|goose|chase
carriage|and|pair
double|white|line
dual|carriageway
excursion|ticket
express|delivery
Grand|Union|canal
hackney|carriage
invalid|carriage
marshalling|yard
message|received
motorway|madness
mountain|railway
moving|staircase
pelican|crossing
picture|postcard
pleasure|steamer
point|of|no|return
prairie-schooner
press|conference
public|transport
radiotelegraphy
railway|carriage
railway|crossing
refreshment|room
road|fund|licence
second|class|mail
second|class|post
special|delivery
stamping|machine
telephone|number
temperance|hotel
ticket|collector
ticket|inspector
vertical|take-off
victualling|ship
windscreen|wiper

Trees

ash	sal	coca	sorb	alder	briar
bay	sap	coco	teak	algum	brier
ben	yew	cone	tree	almug	broom
box	akee	cork	twig	arbor	brush
elm	bark	dhak	upas	aspen	cacao
fig	bass	dita	whin	balsa	carob
fir	bast	ilex	wood	beech	cedar
gum	bole	palm	abele	birch	copse
log	bosk	pine	abies	bough	cubeb
oak	bush	root	acorn	brake	ebony

5/7 LETTERS

elder
frith
furze
glade
gorse
grove
hedge
henna
holly
hurst
jarul
kokra
kokum
larch
lilac
maple
myrrh
palay
pipal
plane
ramus
roble
roots
rowan
sapan
shrub
sumac
thorn
tilia
trunk
zamia
abroma
acajou
antiar
arbute
arolla

banyan
baobab
bog oak
bo tree
bransh
carapa
cassia
catkin
caudex
cornel
daphne
deodar
forest
gingko
jarool
jarrah
jujube
jungle
kalmia
kittul
laurel
lignum
linden
loquat
manuka
myrtle
papaya
pinery
platan
poplar
privet
prunus
queach
rattan
red bud
red fir

sallow
sapota
sappan
souari
spruce
sumach
sylvan
timber
walnut
wattle
willow
ailanto
ambatch
arbutus
babussu
bebeeru
blue gum
boscage
boxwood
bullace
cajuput
catalpa
chamise
chamiso
conifer
coppice
coquito
cork oak
cow tree
cypress
dagwood
dogwood
duramen
durmast
fig leaf
fir cone

foliage
foliose
genipap
gum tree
hickory
holm oak
hop tree
juniper
leafage
leaflet
lentisk
logwood
madrona
margosa
oakling
palmyra
pinetum
platane
pollard
pruning
rampick
rampike
red pine
redwood
sapling
sapwood
sequoia
service
spinney
sundari
syringa
taproot
tea tree
thicket
wax tree
wych elm

TREES

Yule log
ailantus
alburnum
allspice
arboreal
ash plant
barberry
basswood
beam tree
beefwood
caatinga
calamite
carnauba
chestnut
cinchona
cinnamon
clearing
coco tree
coco wood
cork tree
date palm
date tree
deadwood
dendroid
forestry
Greek fir
guaiacum
hardwood
hawthorn
hemp palm
hemp tree
holly oak
hornbeam
iron bark
ironwood
jack tree
kingwood
laburnum
lavender
magnolia
mahogany
mangrove
manna ash
mesquite
milk tree
milkwood
oleander
palmetto
palm tree
pear tree
piassava
pinaster
pine cone
pine tree
quandong
rain tree
rambutan
red cedar
red maple
rosemary
rosewood
royal oak
sago palm
sapindus
shadbush
sloetree
softwood
sweet bay
sweetsop
sycamine
sycamore
tamarack
tamarind
viburnum
witch elm
woodland
wood pulp
adansonia
albespyne
algarroba
aloes wood
alpine fir
andromeda
arboretum
balsam fir
balsa wood
brier bush
brushwood
buckthorn
bully tree
bussu palm
butternut
casuarina
chaparral
chincapin
cocoa wood
crowberry
deçiduous
dwarf tree
evergreen
forsythia
grape tree
greenwood
ground ash
heartwood
hydrangea
in blossom
ivory palm

9/11 LETTERS

ivory tree
Judas tree
lancewood
lilac tree
maple leaf
outer bark
paulownia
peach palm
petty whin
pitch pine
plane tree
poison oak
pyracanth
quebracho
rose apple
rowan tree
royal palm
sagebrush
sapodilla
sassafras
satinwood
Scotch elm
Scotch fir
Scots pine
shade tree
shrubbery
silver fir
sloethorn
snowberry
soapberry
star anise
stone pine
thorn tree
tulip tree
underwood
wax myrtle
whitebeam
widow wail
wych hazel
almond tree
annual ring
blackbully
blackthorn
bladder nut
bottle tree
brazilwood
bullet tree
butter tree
button bush
buttonwood
calamander
chinquapin
coniferous
coral berry
cowrie pine
crown graft
dead finish
dendrology
Diana's tree
Douglas fir
dragon tree
Durmast oak
eucalyptus
fiddlewood
goat's thorn
greasewood
greenheart
hackmatack
laurustine
manna larch
nothofagus
olive grove
orange wood
palm branch
paper birch
pine needle
plantation
prickly ash
quercitron
raffia palm
rain forest
red sanders
rose laurel
sandalwood
silver bell
silver tree
spring wood
sugar maple
tallow tree
tree of life
tree tomato
turpentine
underbrush
white cedar
white thorn
witch hazel
yellow wood
African teak
amboyna wood
American elm
burning bush
cabbage palm
cabbage tree
cajuput tree
camel's thorn
coconut palm
copper beech
cotoneaster

honey locust
hound's berry
Japan laurel
juniper tree
laurustinus
lignum vitae
mammoth tree
mountain ash
olive branch
palm cabbage
poison sumac
prickly pear
purpleheart
pussy willow
shittah tree
silver birch
slippery elm
spindle tree
sweet-willow
undergrowth
varnish tree
white poplar
wintersweet
xanthoxylum
balsam of Peru
balsam of Tolu
bougainvilia
calabash tree
Canada balsam
checkerberry
chestnut tree
Christ's thorn
cucumber tree
decorticated
dragon's blood
frankincense
massaranduba
monkey puzzle
Norway spruce
Philadelphus
piassava palm
plantain tree
poison laurel
quaking aspen
ramification
rhododendron
sea-buckthorn
snowdrop tree
Spanish broom
spurge laurel
tree of heaven
umbrella-tree
virgin forest
wellingtonia
afforestation
almond blossom
amygdalaceous
arboriculture
bird's-eye maple
Christmas tree
cranberry tree
deforestation
dendrological
horse chestnut
savanna forest
weeping willow
arboricultural
cedar of Lebanon
flowering shrub
Lombardy poplar
maidenhair tree
mistletoe bough

15 LETTERS

arboriculturist
Dutch|elm|disease
Spanish|chestnut
tree|of|knowledge

Vegetables

cos
pea
pod
rue
sot
bean
beet
cole
dill
herb
kale
leek
mace
mint
okra
peas
root
sage
sium
slaw
spud
basil
caper
chard
chive
cibol
clove
cress
cubeb
kraut
onion
patch
pease
roots
salad
savoy
swede
thyme
tuber
borage
carrot
celery
chilli
cow|pea
endive
fennel
floret
garden
garlic
ginger
greens
growth
legume
marrow
murphy
pea|pod
pepper
potato
radish
runner
savory
sprout
tomato
turnip
bay|leaf
blewits
cabbage
caraway
cardoon
chervil
chicory
collard
gherkin
haricot
lettuce
olitory
oregano
parsley
parsnip
potherb
produce
pumpkin
salsify
seakale
seed|pod
shallot
skirret
soybean
spinach
sprouts
succory
weed|out
beetroot
borecole
brassica
broccoli
camomile
capsicum
celeriac
chick|pea
coleslaw
cole|wort
crucifer
cucumber
dillseed
egg|apple
egg|fruit
egg|plant

VEGETABLES

escarole
greenery
green pea
kohlrabi
Lima bean
mad apple
main crop
marjoram
peasecod
plantain
potherbs
root crop
rosemary
rutabaga
scallion
soy beans
split pea
tuberose
turmeric
zucchini
artichoke
asparagus
aubergine
beet sugar
carob bean
chick-peas
cold frame
cole-garth
colocynth
coriander
crucifera
dried peas
garden pea
green bean
green peas
Lima beans
love-apple
navy beans
new potato
pinto bean
red pepper
snap beans
soya beans
sugar beet
sword-bean
tree-onion
vegetable
alexanders
broad beans
butter bean
coffee bean
cos lettuce
cotton tree
cotton wood
cruciferae
French bean
garden peas
green beans
jardiniere
kidney bean
potato peel
red cabbage
runner bean
salad plant
sauerkraut
Scotch kale
sea-cabbage
string bean
vanilla pod
water cress
Welsh onion
wolf's peach

butter beans
cauliflower
celery stick
French beans
green pepper
horseradish
runner beans
scarlet bean
sea colewort
spring onion
string beans
sweet potato
winter cress
asparagus tip
cabbage patch
chilli pepper
corn on the cob
Covent Garden
haricot beans
lamb's lettuce
mangel wurzel
market garden
marrowfat pea
marrow squash
Spanish onion
spring greens
St John's bread
water parsnip
kitchen garden
mangold wurzel
root vegetable
cabbage lettuce
green vegetable
Brussels sprouts
globe artichokes
vegetable garden
vegetable marrow

Virtues

hope
love
faith
charity
justice
prudence
fortitude
temperance

Visual Arts

ART
cut
dye
gum
hue
lac
oil
pen
pot
sit
urn
arty
boss
bust
calk
cast
clay
copy
daub
dope
draw
etch
film
fire
flat
flux
form
gild
gilt
glue
head
kiln
lake
lens
limn
line
mark
mask
nude
oils
oven
pose
roll
seal
shot
show
snap
soup
tile
tint
tone
tool
turn
turn
vase
view
wash
work
batik
block
brush
burin
cameo
carve
chalk
chase
china
craft
crock
curio
delft
drawn
dryer
easel
fired
frame
genre
glass
glaze
gloss
glyph
grave
hatch
image
inlay
Japan
lines
model
motif
mould
mural
op-art
paint
photo
piece
pin-up
plate
point
prime
print
prism
pupil
rough
scape
scene
sculp
shade
shape
slide
smear
Spode
spool
stain
stamp
still
stone
study
style
throw
tinct
tinge
trace
turps
virtu
wheel
artist
azo-dye
bedaub
bisque
bite-in
blazon
blow-up
bronze
calque
camera
canvas
carved
carver
chased
chaser
chisel
chroma
colour
crayon
crible

6/7 LETTERS

cubism
cubist
dauber
déjà vu
depict
design
doodle
drawer
dyeing
eat out
effigy
enamel
engild
etcher
figure
filter
firing
fresco
glazed
graven
graver
incise
limner
madder
magilp
mallet
marble
master
medium
megilp
mobile
mock up
mosaic
museum
opaque
parget
pastel
pencil
plaque
pop art
poster
potter
primer
relief
rococo
school
screen
sculpt
shadow
sketch
statue
studio
symbol
talent
tripod
viewer
acid dye
acushla
aniline
art deco
art form
art work
atelier
baroque
biscuit
camaieu
cartoon
carving
ceramic
chasing
classic
close by
coating
collage
colours
copyist
Dadaism
dash off
develop
diorama
draught
drawing
ebauche
ecorche
enchase
engrave
enlarge
etching
faience
fast dye
Fauvism
furnace
gallery
gilding
glyphic
glyptic
gouache
graphic
graving
gravure
high art
imagism
incised
lacquer
linocut
montage
moulded
moulder
off tone
outline
painter
palette
pattern
picture
pigment
plaster
portray
pottery
preview
primary
profile
realism
relievo
scenist
scratch
shading
shutter
spatula
stencil
stipple
tableau
tachism
tempera
tessera
the arts
thinner
tinting
tintype
tooling
touch up
tracery
tracing
varnish
woodcut

abstract
acid|kiln
aesthete
airscape
anaglyph
aquatint
art|autre
art|class
artcraft
artefact
artifact
artiness
artistic
artistry
art|paper
autotype
autotypy
Barbizon
basic|dye
burinist
calotype
ceramics
charcoal
chromism
ciselure
clayware
colorama
creation
curlicue
dark|room
demitint
depicter
designer
dry|paint
dry|plate
dyestuff
eclectic
eggshell
emblazon
emulsion
enchased
engraved
engraver
enlarger
exposure
exterior
fair|copy
figurine
fine|arts
fire|clay
fixative
freehand
frescoes
fretwork
futurism
glyptics
graffiti
graffito
graphics
Greek|urn
grouping
half|tint
half|tone
hatching
in|relief
inscribe
intaglio
interior
intimism
lapidary
likeness
limekiln
majolica
mandorla
modelled
modeller
monument
movement
negative
original
paint|box
paintbox
painting
panorama
pargeter
pastiche
pastille
pastoral
photomap
picturer
plein|air
portrait
positive
potsherd
printing
repousse
sculptor
seapiece
seascape
sketcher
skiagram
skyscape
slapdash
snapshot
spectrum
staining
statuary
stop|bath

symbolic
tachisme
tapestry
tessella
the brush
tinction
tincture
turn a pot
vignette
virtuoso
zoom lens
aesthetic
anastasis
anastatic
aquarelle
art critic
art lesson
art-minded
art school
bas-relief
beaux-arts
blackware
blueprint
box camera
bric-a-brac
brick kiln
brushwork
cameo ware
cameraman
cartridge
cerograph
champleve
china clay
chinaware
chiseller
chromatic
cityscape
clean line
cloisonné
collodion
collotype
colorific
colourful
colouring
colourist
crayonist
cyanotype
cyclorama
decorator
delftware
designing
developer
distemper
enameller
encaustic
enchasing
engraving
ferrotype
flash bulb
flash tube
glassware
goldsmith
Gothicism
grisaille
grotesque
headpiece
heliotype
heliotypy
inscriber
kalamkari
landscape
lay-figure
lithotint
lithotype
low relief
manual art
medallion
mezzotint
microcopy
microfilm
miniature
modelling
modern art
modernism
objet d'art
off-colour
oil paints
old master
oleograph
paintress
paper clip
pargeting
parge-work
pasticcio
pen-and-ink
photocopy
photogram
photostat
pictorial
porcelain
portrayal
portrayer
prefigure
prismatic
projector
reflector
represent
rice paper

rotograph
rough|copy
scrimshaw
sculpture
secondary
sgraffito
sketching
sketch|pad
skiagraph
statuette
still-life
stippling
stoneware
symbolism
symbology
tablature
tailpiece
talbotype
technique
telephoto
tenebrist
throw|a|pot
townscape
treatment
triquetra
undercoat
vitascope
vorticism
wax|figure
whiteware
whitewash
wirephoto
wood|block
woodcraft
woodprint
work|of|art

xylograph
zinc|plate
acid|colour
aesthetics
anaglyphic
aniline|dye
art|gallery
art|nouveau
arty-crafty
automatism
avant|garde
background
beaten|work
Berlin|ware
bibliofilm
block|print
cameo|glass
caricature
carmagnole
cartoonist
cement|kiln
ceramicist
cerography
china|stone
chiselling
chromatics
chromatism
chromogram
chromotype
cinecamera
classicism
cloudscape
coloration
colour|film
colourless
comic|strip

crosshatch
crouch|ware
Crown|Derby
dead-colour
decoration
delineator
draughting
drawing|pin
emblazonry
embossment
enamel|kiln
enamelling
enamellist
enamelware
exhibition
figuration
figurehead
flashlight
foreground
full|colour
functional
futuristic
glazed|ware
grand|stone
graphic|art
Grecian|urn
half|relief
handicraft
heliograph
high|colour
high|relief
illuminate
illustrate
impression
jasper|ware
kinetic|art

light meter
linography
linseed oil
lithograph
luminarist
lustreware
masterwork
metalcraft
micrograph
microprint
monochrome
monumental
mordant dye
natural dye
naturalism
neoclassic
oil colours
oil painter
ornamental
paintbrush
pastellist
pedal wheel
photoflash
photoflood
photogenic
photograph
photometer
photomural
photoprint
phylactery
picaresque
pigmentary
plasticine
polychrome
port-crayon
power wheel
proportion
pure colour
queen's ware
Raphaelite
repoussage
rich colour
riverscape
Rockingham
scenograph
sculptress
sculptural
sculptured
sculpturer
Sèvres ware
shadowgram
show of work
silhouette
sketchbook
sling paint
statuesque
steel plate
stereotype
stonecraft
stovehouse
surrealism
surrealist
terra cotta
tessallate
turpentine
view finder
warm colour
water glass
waterscape
wax etching
wax process
wood carver
zincograph
zylography
abstract art
abstraction
achromatism
alto-relievo
anaglyptics
brush stroke
cavo-relievo
ceramic ware
cerographer
ceroplastic
charcoalist
chef d'oeuvre
chiaroscuro
Chinese clay
cloisonnage
coat of paint
colorimeter
colouration
colour-blind
colour cycle
colour gamut
colour print
composition
connoisseur
copperplate
delineation
dichromatic
discoloured
draughtsman
earthenware
eclecticism
electrotype
engravement
enlargement

etching ball
flash camera
French chalk
gild the lily
glass blower
glyphograph
graphic arts
heliochrome
ichnography
illuminator
illustrator
in low relief
insculpture
landscapist
life drawing
Limoges ware
linographer
lithography
living image
local colour
madder bloom
masterpiece
Meissen ware
miniaturist
museum piece
object of art
objet trouvé
oil painting
ornamentist
papier-mâché
perspective
photography
photorelief
picturesque
pinacotheca
plein-airist
pointillism
pointillist
portraiture
potter's clay
press camera
primitivism
proportions
psychedelic
range finder
romanticism
rotogravure
rough sketch
Satsuma ware
scenewright
scenography
sculpturing
shadowgraph
silversmith
snap shooter
snapshotter
solid colour
still camera
tile painter
tissue paper
water colour
wood carving
xylographer
zincography
aestheticism
architecture
artist's model
artist's proof
basso-relievo
brass-rubbing
bright colour
camera lucida
candid camera
caricaturist
cave painting
ceramography
ceroplastics
chaleography
chiaro-oscuro
Chinese paper
chromaticity
colour circle
colour-filter
cottage china
design centre
drawing-board
drawing paper
Dresden china
Elgin marbles
etching point
fashion plate
genre painter
glyphography
heliogravure
hollow relief
illumination
illustration
in high relief
kaleidoscope
lantern slide
lignographer
line engraver
lithographer
lithographic
lithogravure
magic lantern
metallograph
mezzo-relievo

old Worcester
opaque colour
paint the lily
palette knife
panchromatic
photoengrave
photoetching
photographer
photographic
photogravure
photomontage
picture frame
pointelliste
pointillisme
portrait bust
poster colour
potter's earth
potter's wheel
reflex camera
reproduction
riot of colour
rough draught
rough outline
scene painter
sculptograph
self-portrait
shadow figure
sneak preview
spectrograph
stained glass
stereo camera
street artist
technicolour
time exposure
tracing paper
tripod camera
wall painting
water colours
wax engraving
wax modelling
Wedgwood ware
well-composed
white pottery
zincographer
action painter
art exhibition
black and white
calligraphist
cross-hatching
daguerreotype
expressionism
expressionist
Flemish school
glass printing
impressionism
impressionist
pre-Raphaelite
primary colour
willow pattern
action painting
art for art's sake
foreshortening
pavement artist
picture gallery
vanishing point
abstract painter
charcoal drawing
draughtsmanship
picture restorer
portrait gallery
portrait painter

Warfare

AB	van	dart	impi	rout	arrow
GI	vet	D-day	jack	rush	at bay
GI	war	dike	jamb	shot	at war
MP	ally	dirk	jeep	slug	baton
RA	ammo	dove	Jock	spit	beset
RE	Ares	duck	keep	spur	blade
RN	arms	duel	kill	stab	blank
arm	army	dump	kris	stab	blast
axe	A-war	duty	levy	tank	blitz
bow	AWOL	epee	load	tuck	Boche
cap	ball	exon	lock	unit	bolas
cut	band	feud	mail	WAAF	brave
dud	barb	file	Mars	WACS	broch
foe	bard	fire	mere	wage	Buffs
gat	bill	fish	mine	wall	burst
gun	bird	flak	MIRV	ward	cadre
Hun	bola	foil	moat	WAVE	chute
NCO	bolt	fort	mole	wing	clash
POW	bomb	fray	navy	WRNS	corps
RAF	bone	guns	Odin	yomp	cover
ram	bout	hate	peel	zone	ditch
rat	Bren	hawk	peon	Zulu	draft
rod	butt	helm	pike	AA-gun	drive
row	camp	hero	post	A-bomb	enemy
sap	club	hilt	rack	aegis	feint
spy	cock	hold	rank	arena	fence
sub	coif	host	rath	armed	field
TNT	Colt	H-war	riot	armet	fight
Tyr	cosh	ICBM	rock	array	flail

flank
fleet
foray
fosse
front
fusee
fusil
grape
guard
harry
H|bomb
H|hour
jerid
Jerry
jihad
jingo
knife
kukri
lager
lance
leave
Luger
melee
mound
onset
orgue
parry
pavis
plate
poilu
posse
power
Provo
rally
range
ranks
rebel
recce
redan
repel
rifle
rowel
sally
salvo
scarp
scene
scout
sepoy
serve
shaft
shako
shell
shoot
siege
skean
sling
snake
sowar
spahi
spear
spike
spray
spurs
squad
staff
steel
stick
stone
storm
sword
targe
tasse
tommy
tommy
train
troop
truce
U|boat
uhlan
visor
WAACS
WAAFS
waddy
Woden
wound
WRACS
Wrens
abatis
ack|ack
action
air|arm
air|gun
alpeen
Amazon
ambush
animus
Anzacs
archer
Archie
argosy
armada
armour
askari
assail
attack
barbel
barrel
batman
battle
beaver
bellum
big|gun
billet
bomber
breech
bugler
bullet
bunker
camail
cannon
casque
castle
casual
charge
cohort
column
combat
convoy
cordon
corium
creese
cudgel
cuisse
curfew
curtal
dagger
defeat
defend
detail
donjon
dry|run
duello
dugout
dumdum
enlist
ensign
escarp
escort
Exocet
fewter
flight
foeman
forage
forces
gabion
galoot
glacis
glaive
gorget
greave
gunner
gun|shy
Gurkha
gusset
hagbut
hammer
hanger
hanjar
harass
heaume
helmet
hot|war
hussar
impact
impale
in|arms
inroad
jereed
jingal
laager

labrys
lancer
legion
lorica
mailed
maquis
marine
Mauser
merlon
minnie
morion
mortar
musket
muster
muzzle
oilcan
outfit
panzer
parade
parole
patrol
pavise
pellet
pepper
petard
picket
pierce
pistol
pogrom
pompom
powder
pow-pow
quiver
rafale
Rajput
ramrod

rapier
rappel
ray gun
razzia
rebuff
reduit
report
revolt
rioter
rocket
rookie
salade
sallet
salute
sangar
sapper
sconce
scutum
sentry
set gun
shield
slogan
sniper
sortie
sparth
spying
strafe
strike
swivel
talion
target
tenail
thrust
to arms
tocsin
Toledo

tom-tom
trench
troops
tulwar
turret
vallum
valour
Vandal
victor
volley
war cry
war dog
war god
weapon
womera
yeoman
Zouave
abattis
advance
air raid
amnesty
archery
armoury
arsenal
assault
assegai
atom gun
atom war
baldric
barrack
barrage
barrier
bar shot
basinet
bastion
battery

bayonet
bazooka
beat off
Bellona
big guns
big shot
blowgun
Boer War
bombard
bombing
booster
bravado
Bren gun
bricole
brigade
buckler
bulldog
bulwark
caisson
caitiff
calibre
caliver
caltrop
cap-a-pie
carbine
carcass
carrier
cashier
cavalry
chamade
chamber
charger
chicken
citadel
cold war
command

7 LETTERS

company
conchie
conquer
cordite
corslet
cossack
coupure
courage
courser
crusade
cudgels
cuirass
curtain
curtana
cutlass
dastard
defence
disband
distaff
dragoon
draught
dry fire
dudgeon
dueller
dungeon
echelon
enomoty
fall out
fend off
fighter
firearm
fortify
fortlet
foxhole
gallant
gallery
gas bomb
gas mask
germ war
gisarme
go to war
grapnel
grenade
gunboat
gundeck
gunfire
gunlock
gunnage
gunnery
gunning
gun park
gunplay
gun port
gunroom
gunshot
hackbut
halberd
handjar
harness
hatchet
hauberk
heroism
Hessian
heyduck
hold off
holster
holy war
hostage
invader
jackman
jambeau
jankers
javelin
jollies
jump jet
knifing
kremlin
lambast
lamboys
longbow
Long Tom
lookout
lunette
lyddite
machete
make war
maniple
mantlet
marines
martial
matross
megaton
militia
missile
mission
morrion
neutral
offence
on guard
open war
outpost
outwork
paladin
panoply
parados
parapet
patriot
pedrero
petrary
phalanx
pikeman
pillbox
platoon
poleaxe
poniard
private
quarrel
rampage
rampart
ravelin
recruit
red army
redcoat
redoubt
regular
repulse
retreat
riposte
Sabaoth
sabaton
salient
samurai
sandbag
Seabees
section
self bow
service
shoot at
shooter
shotgun
soldier
Spartan
sparthe
spinner

WARFARE

sten|gun
supremo
tactics
tear|gas
tenable
testudo
theatre
the|fray
torpedo
traitor
trigger
trooper
tumbril
uniform
veteran
victory
wage|war
war|club
ward|off
war|drum
warfare
war|game
warhead
warlike
warlord
warpath
warring
warrior
warship
war|song
weapons
wind|gun
woomera
wounded
yatagan
yomping
aceldama
activate
air|force
air|rifle
air-to-air
all-clear
alliance
ammo|dump
anabasis
anti-mine
arbalest
armament
armature
armoured
arms|race
arquebus
art|of|war
atom|bomb
attacker
aventail
ballista
banderol
barbette
barbican
barracks
bartisan
baselard
battalia
battling
bear|arms
besieger
betrayer
blockade
blowpipe
bludgeon
bomb|rack
bomb|site
brattice
brickbat
broadaxe
Browning
buckshot
buttress
buzzbomb
campaign
cannonry
casemate
catapult
cavalier
chaffron
chamfron
champion
chasseur
chivalry
civil|war
claymore
cold|feet
commando
conflict
corselet
crossbow
cry|havoc
culverin
cylinder
defender
demilune
deserter
destrier
division
doughboy
drum|call
drumfire
drumhead
duellist
dynamite
embattle
enfilade
enlistee
entrench
envelope
errantry
escalade
exercise
falchion
falconet
fasthold
fastness
fencible
field|gun
fighting
file|fire
fireball
fire|bomb
firelock
fire|upon
flotilla
fortress
fugleman
furlough
fusilier
gambeson
garrison
gauntlet
Great|War
guerilla
gunflint
gunmetal
gunpoint

8 LETTERS

gunsmith
gunstick
gunstock
hang fire
heavy gun
hedgehog
herisson
hill fort
hireling
hornwork
howitzer
infantry
informer
invading
invasion
invasive
ironclad
janizary
jazerant
jingoism
jump area
killadar
knuckles
lancegay
land army
land mine
langrage
last post
launcher
Leon mine
Lewis gun
loophole
magazine
mailclad
man of war
mantelet
marksman
martello
massacre
Maxim gun
melinite
militant
military
mobilize
muniment
munition
mushroom
musketry
nerve gas
open fire
ordnance
orillion
outguard
overkill
pacifist
palisade
palstaff
palstave
partisan
password
pauldron
petronel
pikehead
poltroon
puncheon
quisling
quo vadis
recreant
regiment
renegade
repulsor
reserves
reveille
revolver
ricochet
rifleman
risalder
runagate
safehold
scabbard
scimitar
sentinel
shrapnel
side arms
siege cap
skean dhu
skirmish
soldiery
solleret
space gun
spadroon
spearman
spontoon
squadron
stabbing
stalwart
Star Wars
stave off
stiletto
stockade
strafing
strategy
struggle
surprise
surround
take arms
tenaille
the front

the|sword
time|bomb
tomahawk
Tommy|gun
total|war
transfix
trenches
turnback
turncoat
turntail
up|in|arms
uprising
vambrace
vamplate
vanguard
vanquish
vendetta
war|cloud
warcraft
war|dance
warfarer
war|horse
war|hound
war|paint
war|whoop
Waterloo
wayfarer
weaponry
world|war
yeomanry
zero|hour
accoutred
aggressor
air,to,ship
ambuscade
arch|enemy
army|corps
army|issue
army|lists
arrowhead
artillery
assailant
atomic|gun
atomic|war
attacking
attrition
automatic
auto,rifle
backplate
ballistic
banderole
bandolier
bastinado
battalion
battleaxe
battlecry
beachhead
beefeater
beleaguer
bellicism
bellicose
Big|Bertha
blackjack
bloodshed
bomb,happy
bombs|away
bombshell
bombsight
booby|trap
boomerang
broadside
Brown|Bess
brown|bill
camouflet
cannonade
cannoneer
caparison
carronade
carry|arms
cartouche
cartridge
casemated
castellan
cease|fire
chain|mail
chain|shot
challenge
chamfrain
chassepot
cold|steel
combatant
combative
conquerer
conscript
crackshot
cross|fire
defensive
derringer
desert|rat
deterrent
detonator
discharge
doodlebug
double|sap
drop|a|bomb
earthwork
embattled
encompass

enemy camp
enemy fire
escopette
espionage
explosive
face guard
fence wall
field army
fieldwork
fire a shot
firepower
fireworks
first line
flintlock
flying sap
fortalice
fortified
fourth arm
free-lance
front line
fulgurite
fusillade
gas attack
gelignite
gladiator
grapeshot
grenadier
guardsman
guerrilla
gun battle
guncotton
gunpowder
gun turret
habergeon
harquebus
headpiece
heavy fire
heroic act
Home Guard
hostility
hydrobomb
incursion
incursive
in defence
ironbound
irregular
irruption
janissary
jesserant
katabasis
keep guard
keep vigil
lance-jack
langridge
last ditch
legionary
levy war on
lie in wait
lionheart
logistics
long-range
Luftwaffe
make war on
man-at-arms
manoeuvre
march past
matchlock
mercenary
militancy
minefield
minuteman
monomachy
munitions
musketeer
musketoon
needle gun
nose guard
nosepiece
offensive
onslaught
open order
operation
other side
overthrow
panoplied
parachute
peel-house
peel-tower
pikestaff
prick-spur
projector
protector
pugnacity
pyroxylin
ram rocket
rearguard
rebel call
rebellion
rerebrace
ressaldar
rifle ball
rocket gun
rocket man
roundhead
round shot
rowel spur
Royal Navy
sally port

saltpetre
sea battle
seat of war
sentry box
shellfire
signalman
single sap
ski troops
skyrocket
sky troops
slaughter
slingshot
slung shot
small arms
small bore
small-shot
smoke bomb
soldierly
soldier on
sonic mine
son of a gun
spearhead
spring gun
stand fire
stink bomb
strategic
subaltern
submarine
super bomb
surprisal
surrender
swivel gun
sword-play
take sides
tank corps
target day
task force
tit for tat
torpedoed
torpedoer
trainband
trench gun
troopship
truncheon
under arms
under fire
vigilante
volunteer
warmonger
War Office
war rocket
watchword
white flag
woomerang
zumbooruk
activation
active army
active duty
active list
adventurer
aerial bomb
aerial mine
aggression
aggressive
Air Command
air service
ambushment
ammunition
antagonism
Armageddon
armed force
armed guard
armed truce
armigerous
armipotent
arm's length
atomic bomb
atomic pile
atom-rocket
ballistics
barbed-wire
battle flag
battle hymn
battle line
battlement
battleship
blitzkrieg
blockhouse
bold stroke
bombardier
bowie knife
box barrage
breastwork
bridgehead
brigandine
broadsword
bugle corps
call to arms
camel corps
camouflage
campaigner
cannon ball
cannon shot
cantonment
carabineer
carry on war
cavalryman
coastguard

10 LETTERS

coat of mail
combat area
combat team
commandant
contingent
cross staff
cuirassier
declare war
defendable
defensible
demobilize
detachment
direct fire
dragonnade
dragoonade
drawbridge
drummer boy
embankment
encampment
engarrison
eprouvette
escalation
expedition
faint heart
fieldpiece
field train
fiery cross
fire trench
firing area
flying bomb
flying tank
Foot Guards
foot rifles
Gatling gun
ground fire
ground mine
ground zero
halberdier
heavy armed
impalement
incendiary
investment
jingoistic
knighthood
knobkerrie
kriegspiel
lambrequin
lay siege to
Life Guards
light armed
line of fire
loaded cane
long knives
lookout man
machine gun
martiality
militarism
militarize
militiaman
missile man
mob tactics
mount guard
mural crown
musket shot
mustard gas
napalm bomb
no man's land
nuclear war
obsidional
occupation
old soldier
on the march
operations
other ranks
over the top
oyster mine
paratroops
percussion
petrol bomb
picket duty
point blank
portcullis
private war
projectile
raking fire
rally round
raw recruit
Resistance
revolution
rifle range
rocket bomb
rocket fire
rules of war
run through
second line
sentry duty
serviceman
shellshock
shillelagh
short range
siegecraft
siege train
six shooter
slit trench
smallsword
smooth bore
spill blood
stand guard

state of war
strategist
stronghold
submachine
sure as a gun
sword fight
swordstick
sworn enemy
take to arms
tenderfoot
ten-pounder
test rocket
touch paper
trajectile
trajectory
under siege
vanquisher
volunteers
war goddess
Winchester
air-to-ground
anti-missile
anti-tank gun
area bombing
armed combat
armed forces
armoured car
auxiliaries
barnstormer
battle array
battledress
battlefield
battle order
battle plane
battle royal
beach master
bersaglieri
besiegement
blockbuster
bloody shirt
blunderbuss
bombardment
bomber pilot
bomb-release
bow and arrow
breastplate
British Army
British Navy
buck private
bulletproof
buoyant mine
bushwhacker
cameraderie
castellated
castle guard
caterpillar
change sides
combat train
contentious
countermine
crack troops
declaration
demibastion
depth charge
dive-bombing
emplacement
enemy action
engine of war
enlisted man
envelopment
fighting man
fire a volley
fire tactics
firing party
firing squad
firing table
first strike
fission bomb
flare rocket
flying corps
footed arrow
footslogger
foot soldier
forced march
force of arms
friend or foe
full harness
full of fight
gang warfare
generalship
germ warfare
giant powder
ground-to-air
guerrillero
guncarriage
hair trigger
hand grenade
heavy armour
heavy bomber
high dudgeon
hill station
Horse Guards
horse pistol
hostilities
infantryman
Irish Guards
iron rations
land warfare

light bomber
lionhearted
Lochaber axe
loggerheads
look daggers
magazine gun
Maginot line
Marine Corps
might of arms
military man
mine thrower
moral defeat
mountain gun
naval bomber
naval forces
nitre powder
nitrocotton
nuclear bomb
open warfare
pattern bomb
peace treaty
picket guard
plate armour
platoon fire
postern gate
powder grain
Provisional
put to flight
rallying cry
rank and file
rebel action
reconnoitre
recruitment
regular army
retro-rocket
rolling fire
safe-conduct
safety catch
Scots Guards
service call
ship-to-shore
shock troops
shooting war
shoot to kill
shuttle raid
Signal Corps
smell powder
smoke rocket
smoke screen
sneak attack
soldatesque
soldierlike
soldiership
spent bullet
stand at ease
stand of arms
step rockets
stormtroops
stray bullet
subdivision
Swiss Guards
sword in hand
take by storm
thin red line
Tommy Atkins
torpedo boat
trench knife
trigger talk
true colours
trusty sword
under attack
Underground
up and at them
warlikeness
war of nerves
warriorlike
war to end war
water cannon
wooden horse
wooden walls
acoustic mine
anti-aircraft
appeal to arms
armour-plated
army reserves
artilleryman
atomic cannon
awkward squad
banzai charge
battering ram
battleground
beat a retreat
belligerence
breakthrough
breechloader
buccaneering
bushfighting
cannon fodder
cannon's mouth
civil defence
council of war
countermarch
court martial
cut-and-thrust
daggers drawn
deadly weapon
demi-culverin
dumdum bullet

WARFARE

Dutch courage
electron bomb
encirclement
engines of war
entrenchment
escaramouche
false colours
field of blood
flame-thrower
floating mine
flying column
forward march
fowling piece
gladiatorial
go over the top
grand tactics
ground forces
guerrilla war
guided weapon
heavy dragoon
home reserves
homing rocket
horse and foot
horse marines
hydrogen bomb
lady from hell
launching pad
leathernecks
Light Brigade
light dragoon
line of action
line of battle
machicolated
magnetic mine
march against
marching song
Medical Corps
medium bomber
military zone
mine detector
mobilization
moral courage
moral support
moral victory
muzzle-loader
naval militia
naval reserve
naval warfare
on the warpath
Parthian shot
Pearl Harbour
picked troops
pioneer corps
plunging fire
powder charge
pyrotechnics
quarterstaff
reactivation
religious war
rifled cannon
rifle grenade
rocket attack
second strike
sharpshooter
shock tactics
shoulder a gun
shoulder arms
siege warfare
signal rocket
single combat
standing army
stormtrooper

stouthearted
sudden attack
supply troops
sword bayonet
tactical unit
take the field
theatre of war
tooth and nail
trench mortar
trigger happy
under the flag
vertical fire
virus warfare
warmongering
white feather
who goes there
yellow streak
active service
Andrew Ferrara
armaments race
armed conflict
arms and the man
army exercises
articles of war
assault course
baptism of fire
battle cruiser
battle honours
battle-scarred
bayonet charge
beleaguerment
bomber command
breechloading
British Legion
cartridge-belt
cavalry charge
cheval-de-frise
Churchill tank
cobelligerent
combat fatigue
comrade in arms
counter-attack
desert warfare
disengagement
dispatch-rider
drill sergeant
evasive action
Exocet missile
field hospital
field of battle
fighter patrol
first world war
Flammenwerfer
flying colours
flying officer
force de frappe
foreign legion
fortification
generalissimo
guard of honour
guided missile
gunnery school
high-explosive
lance-corporal
light infantry
line of defence
listening post
machine gunner
Messerschmitt
Military Cross
Military Medal
mine detection

mini-submarine
muzzle loading
non-resistance
nuclear weapon
order of battle
order of the day
passage of arms
Peninsular War
pitched battle
prisoner of war
put to the sword
quarter-gunner
quartermaster
reinforcement
royal air force
running battle
sabre-rattling
scorched earth
senior service
sergeant-major
Siegfried line
staff-sergeant
striking force
sublieutenant
sub-machine gun
trench warfare
two-edged sword
unarmed combat
Victoria Cross
war department
war to the death
wing commander
yeoman service
action stations
airborne forces
airborne troops
aircraftswoman
Air Vice-Marshal
ammunition dump
army cadet force
army manoeuvres
barrage balloon
battle stations
blank-cartridge
blockade runner
captain-general
cavalry officer
chevaux-de-frise
cloak-and-dagger
coastal battery
coastal command
colonel-in-chief
colour-sergeant
comrades in arms
conquering hero
demobilisation
field ambulance
field artillery
fifth columnist
fighter command
fight to a finish
flag-lieutenant
freedom fighter
guerrilla chief
guerrilla force
heavy artillery
horse artillery
incendiary bomb
liaison officer
light artillery
marching orders
militarisation

military police
military tattoo
muzzle velocity
non-operational
nuclear warfare
nuclear warhead
operations room
orderly officer
ordinary seaman
pincer movement
powder magazine
Pyrrhic victory
reconnaissance
regimental band
Royal Artillery
Royal Engineers
Royal Fusiliers
Royal Tank Corps
squadron-leader
street fighting
supreme command
unknown soldier
unknown warrior
urban guerrilla
warrant officer
Wars of the Roses
winter quarters
adjutant general
air chief marshal
aircraft carrier
Anderson shelter
armed to the teeth
armoured cruiser
Brigade of Guards
chemical warfare
displaced person
first lieutenant
gentleman-at-arms
Grenadier Guards
light machine-gun
military mission
military service
Molotov cocktail
Morrison shelter
Mulberry harbour
national defence
national service
naval engagement
naval operations
non-commissioned
observation post
officer of the day
on active service
orderly corporal
orderly sergeant
parachute troops
rearguard action
recruiting drive
regimental march
second-in-command
spoils of victory
sword-and-buckler
telescopic sight
territorial army
up guards and at 'em

Weight

lb
oz
cwt
ton
dram
gram
kilo
mass
carat
gerah
grain
libra
livre
minim
pound
scale
stone
tonne
uncia
denier
dirhem
drachm
gramme
netton
shekel
longton
quintal
scuple
tonneau
assay|ton
decagram
decigram
gram|atom
gross|ton
kilogram
short|ton
centigram
hectogram
metric|ton
milligram
myriagram
ounce|troy
troy|ounce
carat|grain
troy|weight
avoirdupois
centigramme
gram|molecule
hundredweight
imperial|weight

Wonders of the World

Colossus,|The
Pyramids,|The
Palace|of|Cyrus
Temple|of|Diana
Hanging|Gardens
Tomb|of|Mausolus
Statue|of|Zeus,|The

Works of Literature and Music

Job
Kim
She
Aida
Emma
Lulu
Maud
Brand
Comus
Faust
Fetes
Kipps
La Mer
Manon
Medea
Norma
Scoop
Tosca
Alcina
Amelia
Becket
Ben Hur
Carmen
En Saga
Ghosts
Hassan
Helena
Iberia
Jenufa
Lolita
Martha
Mignon
Nuages
Oberon
Otello
Rienzi
Rob Roy
Rokeby
Salome
Semele
Sylvia
Trilby
Utopia
Walden
Adonais
Aladdin
Amadeus
Babbitt
Beowulf
Camilla
Candida
Candide
Don Juan
Dracula
Electra
Erewhon
Euphues
Fidelio
Giselle
Ivanhoe
Lord Jim
Lycidas
Macbeth
Manfred
Marmion
Ma Vlast
Mazeppa
Messiah
Nabucco
Othello
Rebecca
Ring, The
Shirley
Sirenes
Ulysses
Volpone
Werther
Wozzeck
Adam Bede
Adam Zero
Alcestis
Anabasis
Antigone
Arabella
Bells, The
Born Free
Carnaval
Carnival
Catriona
Cenci, The
Coppelia
Cranford
Endymion
Everyman
Falstaff
Gloriana
Hay Fever
Hiawatha
Hudibras
Hyperion
Idiot, The
Idomeneo
Iliad, The
In the Wet
Iolanthe
Jane Eyre
King Lear
La Boheme
L'Allegro
Lavengro
Les Noces
Lucky Jim
Moby Dick
Parsifal
Patience
Peer Gynt

WORKS OF LITERATURE AND MUSIC

Pericles
Rasselas
Sea Drift
Swan Lake
Tom Jones
Turandot
Villette
Waves, The
Aeneid, The
Agamemnon
Beau Geste
Billy Budd
Brigg Fair
Capriccio
Cavalcade
Checkmate
Choephori
Coningsby
Cox and Box
Critic, The
Cymbeline
Dandy Dick
Don Carlos
Dr Zhivago
Dubliners
East Lynne
Egoist, The
Eumenides
Euryanthe
Hard Times
Hobbit, The
I, Claudius
I Puritani
Kidnapped
Kubla Khan
Les Biches

Lohengrin
Mein Kampf
Men at Arms
Mikado, The
No Highway
On Liberty
Papillons
Prince, The
Pygmalion
Rigoletto
Rivals, The
Ruddigore
Saint Joan
Siegfried
Tom Sawyer
Venusberg
Vice Versa
Warden, The
All for Love
Animal Farm
Appalachia
Bleak House
Borough, The
Cannery Row
Casabianca
Cinderella
Citadel, The
Coriolanus
Das Kapital
Die Walkure
Don Quixote
Dunciad, The
Dynasts, The
Howards End
Il Seraglio
Inferno, The

In Memoriam
Intermezzo
I Pagliacci
Jamaica Inn
John Gilpin
Kenilworth
Kingdom, The
La Gioconda
La Traviata
Les Troyens
Lorna Doone
Lysistrata
My Fair Lady
My Son, My Son
Nelson Mass
Odyssey, The
Oedipus Rex
Only Way, The
On the Beach
Our Village
Pantagruel
Persuasion
Petroushka
Planets, The
Prelude, The
Prince Igor
Relapse, The
Rural Rides
Seagull, The
Seasons, The
Semiramide
Tannhauser
Tempest, The
Tono Bungay
Trojans, The
Uncle Remus

10/12 LETTERS

Uncle Vanya
Vanity Fair
Vile Bodies
War Requiem
Water Music
Westward Ho!
American, The
Apostles, The
As You Like It
Big Sleep, The
Black Beauty
Blue Bird, The
Boule de Suif
Cakes and Ale
Creation, The
Cruel Sea, The
Doll's House, A
Don Giovanni
Don Pasquale
Firebird, The
Georgics, The
Greenmantle
Harp Quartet
Hedda Gabler
High Windows
HMS Pinafore
Hymn of Jesus
I Like it Here
Il Penseroso
Il Trovatore
Jack and Jill
Journey's End
Judith Paris
Little Eyolf
Little Women
Loved One, The
Love for Love
Luisa Miller
Mary Poppins
Middlemarch
Minute Waltz
Mrs Dalloway
Mr Standfast
Newcomes, The
Now We Are Six
Noye's Fludde
Ode to Autumn
Oliver Twist
Peter Grimes
Peter Simple
Pippa Passes
Princess Ida
Princess, The
Puss in Boots
Redgauntlet
Rosmersholm
Salut d'Amour
Sea Symphony
Silas Marner
Sorcerer, The
South Riding
Stalky and Co
Stenka Razin
Tale of a Tub, A
Talisman, The
Tam o'Shanter
Trial by Jury
What Katy Did
Wild Duck, The
William Tell
Women in Love
Wrong Box, The
Alchemist, The
Anna Karenina
Antiquary, The
Apple Cart, The
Archduke Trio
Areopagitica
Ash Wednesday
Barnaby Rudge
Blithe Spirit
Brighton Rock
Buddenbrooks
Caretaker, The
Charley's Aunt
Childe Harold
Cosi fan Tutte
Danse Macabre
Decameron, The
Dogs of War, The
Dombey and Son
Epithalamion
Eugene Onegin
Excursion, The
Four Quartets
Frankenstein
Golden Ass, The
Grand Duke, The
Guy Mannering
Handley Cross
Julius Caesar
Karelia Suite
Khovanschina
Kinderscenen
Kreisleriana
La Sonnambula
Le Pere Goriot
Les Huguenots

Les Sylphides
Linz Symphony
Little Dorrit
Locksley Hall
Lost Chord, The
Madame Bovary
Major Barbara
Manon Lescaut
Moll Flanders
Moonstone, The
Old Mortality
Owen Wingrave
Paradise Lost
Piers Plowman
Porgy and Bess
Precious Bane
Private Lives
Prothalamion
Rheingold, Das
Rip Van Winkle
Rogue Herries
Romany Rye, The
Sardanapalus
Spring Sonata
Trout Quintet
Twelfth Night
Valkyries, The
Whisky Galore
Albert Herring
Almayer's Folly
Andrea Chenier
Angel Pavement
Arms and the Man
Art of Fugue, The
Bab Ballads, The
Black Arrow, The
Black Mischief
Blue Danube, The
Boris Godounov
Brave New World
Cancer Ward, The
Carmina Burana
Chanson de Nuit
Clock Symphony
Crown Imperial
Death in Venice
Der Freischutz
Dido and Aeneas
Doctor Faustus
Doctor Zhivago
Fame is the Spur
Finnegans Wake
Ghost Train, The
Gondoliers, The
Harold in Italy
Hatter's Castle
Jungle Book, The
Just So Stories
La Cenerentola
L'Elisir d'Amore
Mabinogion, The
Magic Flute, The
Magistrate, The
Mansfield Park
Metamorphosen
Nutcracker, The
Odessa File, The
Orb and Sceptre
Path to Rome, The
Peg Woffington
Private Angelo
Religio Medici

Schindler's Ark
Sketches by Boz
Songs of Travel
Sons and Lovers
Stamboul Train
Tarka the Otter
Timon of Athens
Under Milk Wood
Utopia Limited
Virginians, The
White Devil, The
Winnie the Pooh
Winslow Boy, The
Zuleika Dobson
Ambassadors, The
Andrea del Sarto
Battle Symphony
Bees Wedding, The
Book of Snobs, The
Brief Encounter
Chanson de Matin
Choral Symphony
Cider with Rosie
Claudius the God
Coral Island, The
Country Wife, The
Crotchet Castle
Darkness at Noon
Decline and Fall
Deep Blue Sea, The
Die Zauberflote
Ein Heldenleben
Emperor Quartet
Entertainer, The
Eroica Symphony
Forsyte Saga, The
Four Just Men, The
Gay Lord Quex, The
Golden Bough, The
Goodbye Mr Chips
Great Gatsby, The
Handful of Dust, A
Horse's Mouth, The
Jude the Obscure
Kreutzer Sonata
Le Morte d'Arthur
London Symphony
Loom of Youth, The
Lord of the Flies
Lord of the Rings
Lost Horizon, The
Lyrical Ballads
Madam Butterfly
Man and Superman
Masterman Ready
National Velvet
Nightmare Abbey
Nine Tailors, The
Of Human Bondage
Our Man in Havana
Pickwick Papers
Plain Dealer, The
Prague Symphony
Quentin Durward
Rhapsody in Blue
Rights of Man, The
Robinson Crusoe
Roderick Random
Romeo and Juliet
Separate Tables
Shropshire Lad, A
Siegfried Idyll

Sinister Street
Sins of my Old Age
Slavonic Dances
Spring Symphony
Stones of Venice
Time Machine, The
Town Like Alice, A
Tragic Symphony
Treasure Island
Tristram Shandy
Uncle Tom's Cabin
Venus and Adonis
Vicar of Bray, The
Voices of Spring
Water Babies, The
Widowers Houses
Winter's Tale, The
Woodlanders, The
African Queen, The
Allan Quatermain
Ariadne auf Naxos
Bartholomew Fair
Beggar's Opera, The
Child of our Time, A
Christmas Carol, A
Clarissa Harlowe
Dangerous Corner
Daphnis and Chloe
Divine Comedy, The
Emperor Concerto
Emperor Waltz, The
Essays of Elia, The
Faerie Queene, The
Fanny by Gaslight
Farewell to Arms, A
Frenchman's Creek
From the New World
Golden Legend, The
Gone with the Wind
Goodbye to Berlin
Gotterdammerung
Haffner Symphony
Hansel and Gretel
Heartbreak House
Huckleberry Finn
Iceman Cometh, The
Invisible Man, The
Italian Symphony
Jupiter Symphony
Le Nozze di Figaro
Letters of Junius
Life for the Tsar, A
Look Back in Anger
Moonlight Sonata
Northanger Abbey
Old Wives Tale, The
Our Mutual Friend
Passage to India, A
Pearl Fishers, The
Peregrine Pickle
Peter and the Wolf
Puck of Pook's Hill
Put out More Flags
Raindrop Prelude
Rite of Spring, The
Rupert of Hentzau
Samson Agonistes
Samson and Dalila
Scholar Gipsy, The
Serenáde to Music
Simon Boccanegra
Soldier's Tale, The

15 LETTERS

Tanglewood Tales
Three Men in a Boat
Titus Andronicus
To the Lighthouse
Waiting for Godot
Waldstein Sonata
Weir of Hermiston
Woman in White, The
Yarrow Revisited
You Never Can Tell

Writers

Fry	Hume	West	Freud	Moore
Hay	Hunt	Wren	Gogol	Noyes
Kyd	Kant	Zola	Gorki	Orczy
Lee	Knox	Aesop	Grimm	Ouida
Poe	Lamb	Auden	Hardy	Paine
Amis	Lang	Bacon	Heine	Pater
Baum	Lear	Bates	Henry	Pepys
Bell	Livy	Behan	Henty	Plato
Bolt	Loos	Blake	Homer	Pliny
Buck	Lyly	Burke	Ibsen	Pound
Cary	Mann	Burns	Innes	Reade
Dane	Marx	Byron	James	Rilke
Dell	Mill	Camus	Jeans	Scott
Elia	More	Capek	Jones	Shute
Eyre	Muir	Clare	Joyce	Smart
Ford	Nash	Dante	Kafka	Smith
Gide	Ovid	Defoe	Keats	Spark
Glyn	Owen	Donne	Lewis	Stein
Gray	Pope	Doyle	Locke	Stern
Hall	Saki	Dumas	Lodge	Stowe
Home	Sand	Eliot	Lorca	Swift
Hood	Shaw	Ellis	Lucan	Synge
Hope	Snow	Evans	Mason	Tasso
Hugo	Webb	Frayn	Milne	Twain

WRITERS

Verne
Waugh
Wells
Wilde
Woolf
Yeats
Young
Zweig
Anstey
Archer
Arnold
Asimov
Austen
Bailey
Balzac
Barham
Barrie
Belloc
Benson
Binyon
Borrow
Brecht
Bridie
Bronte
Brooke
Browne
Bryant
Buchan
Bunyan
Burney
Butler
Caesar
Chekov
Cicero
Clough
Conrad
Cooper
Coward
Crabbe
Cronin
Daudet
Davies
Dekker
Dryden
Empson
Evelyn
Farnol
France
Frazer
Gibbon
Goethe
Gordon
Graham
Graves
Greene
Hawkes
Hemans
Henley
Hesiod
Hobbes
Holmes
Holtby
Horace
Howard
Hughes
Huxley
Jerome
Jonson
Landor
Larkin
London
Lytton
Mailer
Malory
Miller
Milton
Morgan
Morris
Musset
Newman
O'Neill
Orwell
Parker
Pascal
Pindar
Pinero
Pinter
Proust
Racine
Ruskin
Sappho
Sartre
Sayers
Seneca
Sidney
Squire
Steele
Sterne
Tagore
Thomas
Villon
Virgil
Waller
Walton
Wesker
Wilcox
Wilson
Addison
Anouilh
Aquinas
Beckett
Bennett
Blunden
Boswell
Bridges
Campion
Carlyle
Carroll
Chaucer
Chekhov
Cobbett
Cocteau
Colette
Collins
Corelli
Dickens
Dodgson
Douglas
Drayton
Dunsany
Durrell
Emerson
Erasmus
Flecker
Forster
Gallico
Gaskell
Gilbert
Golding
Haggard
Harnett
Hartley
Hazlitt
Herbert

7/9 LETTERS

Herrick
Hopkins
Housman
Ionesco
Johnson
Juvenal
Kipling
Leacock
Lehmann
Lessing
Malraux
Marlowe
Marryat
Martial
Marvell
Maugham
Mauriac
Maurois
Merimee
Moliere
Murdoch
Nabokov
Newbolt
Nichols
Osborne
Patmore
Peacock
Pushkin
Rimbaud
Russell
Saroyan
Sassoon
Shelley
Simenon
Sitwell
Southey
Spencer
Spender
Spenser
Spinoza
Surtees
Tacitus
Terence
Thomson
Thoreau
Thurber
Tolkien
Tolstoy
Ustinov
Wallace
Walpole
Webster
Whitman
Andersen
Apuleius
Beaumont
Beerbohm
Berkeley
Betjeman
Browning
Campbell
Catullus
Christie
Congreve
Day Lewis
De la Mare
Disraeli
Faulkner
Fielding
Fletcher
Forester
Kingsley
Koestler
Lawrence
Lovelace
Macaulay
MacNeice
Mallarme
Melville
Meredith
Merriman
Mirabeau
Mortimer
Petrarch
Plutarch
Rabelais
Rattigan
Rossetti
Rousseau
Schiller
Sheridan
Sinclair
Smollett
Stendhal
Stoppard
Strachey
Suckling
Tennyson
Thompson
Tibullus
Trollope
Turgenev
Vanburgh
Verlaine
Voltaire
Whittier
Xenephon
Aeschylus

WRITERS

Aristotle
Blackmore
Boccaccio
Cervantes
Churchill
Coleridge
Corneille
De la Roche
De Quincey
Descartes
Du Maurier
Euripides
Goldsmith
Hemingway
Herodotus
Isherwood
Linklater
Lucretius
Mackenzie
Masefield
Middleton
Mitchison
Montaigne
Nietzsche
Pasternak
Priestley
Sophocles
Steinbeck
Stevenson
Suetonius
Swinburne
Thackeray
Trevelyan
Wodehouse

Wycherley
Ayckbourne
Ballantyne
Baudelaire
Chatterton
Chesterton
Conan Doyle
Drinkwater
Fitzgerald
Galsworthy
La Fontaine
Longfellow
Maupassant
Pirandello
Propertius
Quintilian
Richardson
Strindberg
Thucydides
Wordsworth
Dostoievsky
Maeterlinck
Omar Khayyam
Shakespeare
Yevtushenko
Aristophanes
Beaumarchais
Macchiavelli
Quiller-Couch
Rider Haggard
Solzhenitsin
Wittgenstein
Sackville-West
Marcus Aurelius

Signs of the Zodiac

Leo	Cancer	Scorpio
Aries	Gemini	Aquarius
Libra	Pisces	Capricorn
Virgo	Taurus	Sagittarius

NOTES

NOTES

NOTES

NOTES

NOTES

NOTES

NOTES

NOTES

NOTES

NOTES

NOTES

INDEX

Aeroplanes: TRANSPORT
Algebra: MATHEMATICS
Alloys: MINERALS
Area: LENGTH
Arithmetic: MATHEMATICS
Armour: WARFARE or HERALDRY

Ballet (terms): MUSIC
(titles): WORKS OF MUSIC
Banking: TRADE
Botany: BIOLOGICAL SCIENCES
Bridges: ARCHITECTURE
Building Materials: ARCHITECTURE
Burial Places: ARCHITECTURE
Business: TRADE

Calendar: TIME
Card Games: PASTIMES
Chivalry: HERALDRY
Church Government: RELIGIONS
Climate: METEOROLOGY
Clocks: TIME
Coins: MONEY
Commerce: TRADE
Communications: TRANSPORT
Cooling: HOUSEHOLD ITEMS or FOOD
Cosmetics: CLOTHES
Craft: VISUAL ARTS
Crime: LAW
Crosses: HERALDRY
Currency: MONEY

Dance (ballet): MUSIC
(popular): PASTIMES
Defence: WARFARE
Dentistry: MEDICINE
Domestic: HOUSEHOLD ITEMS
Drama (terms): LITERATURE
(words): WORKS OF

LITERATURE
Drugs: MEDICINE

Ecclesiastical: RELIGIONS
Employment: TRADE
Engineering:
MACHINERY or
PHYSICAL SCIENCES
Entertainment: CINEMA
or THEATRE
Examinations:
EDUCATION

Fabrics: CLOTHES
Fashion: CLOTHES
Festivals: RELIGIONS
Figures of Speech:
LITERATURE
Finance: MONEY or
TRADE
Flags: HERALDRY
Footwear: CLOTHES

Games: SPORTS
Geology: GEOGRAPHY
Geometry:
MATHEMATICS
Grammar: LITERATURE

Headgear: CLOTHES
Herbs: VEGETABLES
History: LITERATURE
Hobbies: PASTIMES
Hospitals: MEDICINE

Illnesses: MEDICINE
Instruments: MUSIC

Journalism:
LITERATURE

Kitchen: HOUSEHOLD
ITEMS

Land Formations:
GEOGRAPHY
Language: LITERATURE
Legal Terms: LAW

Maps: GEOGRAPHY
Market Terms: TRADE
Metals: MINERALS
Monuments:
ARCHITECTURE
Motoring: TRANSPORT

Nautical: MARINE or
TRANSPORT
Numbers:
MATHEMATICS

Operas: WORKS OF
MUSIC

Operatic Characters: LITERARY CHARACTERS

Pastimes: SPORTS
People: OCCUPATIONS
Philosophy: EDUCATION
Photography: VISUAL ARTS
Poets: WRITERS
Pottery: VISUAL ARTS
Printing: LITERATURE
Professions: OCCUPATIONS
Psychiatric Terms: MEDICINE
Punctuation: LITERATURE

Radio: CINEMA AND TV
Railways: TRANSPORT
Reptiles: INSECTS
Roads: TRANSPORT
Rocks: MINERALS
Rooms: FURNITURE

Sculptors: ARTISTS
Seas: OCEANS
Seasons: TIME
Ships: MARINE or TRANSPORT
Shrubs: TREES
Signals: TRANSPORT
Speed: LENGTH
Stars: ASTRONOMY

Teaching materials: EDUCATION
Television: CINEMA
Towns: CITIES
Travel: TRANSPORT
Trigonometry: MATHEMATICS

Vehicles: TRANSPORT
Volume: LENGTH

Weapons: WARFARE
Weather: METEOROLOGY
Writing Materials: EDUCATION

Zoology: ANIMALS or BIOLOGICAL SCIENCES